The person charging this material is responsible for its return to the library from which it was withdrawn on or before the **Latest Date** stamped below.

Computers in Public Administration:
An International Perspective

OTHER TITLES OF INTEREST

GEORGE, F. H. Introduction to Computer Programming

HYNDMAN, D. E. Analog and Hybrid Computing

KORNFELD, N. R. Introduction to Computers

WASS, C. A. A. & GARNER, K. C. Introduction to Electronic
Analogue Computers, 2nd edition

DREYFUS, B. (ed.) Proceedings of the 4th International
CODATA Conference on Generation, Compilation, Evaluation
and Dissemination of Data for Science and Technology

COMPUTERS & EDUCATION

An International Journal

Editor: Professor Andrew A. Pouring, Aerospace Engineering
Department, US Naval Academy

The aim of this journal is to establish a forum for communication
in the use of digital, analog and hybrid computers in all aspects of
higher education. The principal emphasis will be on college undergraduate and graduate use, but papers on unusual developments are
also accepted.

For free specimen copy and subscription details please write to your
nearest Pergamon Press office.

Computers in Public Administration:
An International Perspective

A Reader

Samuel J. Bernstein

Department of Public Administration, Baruch College,
The City University of New York

PERGAMON PRESS INC.

New York · Toronto · Oxford · Sydney · Frankfurt

U.K.	Pergamon Press Ltd., Headington Hill Hall, Oxford OX3 0BW, England
U.S.A.	Pergamon Press Inc., Maxwell House, Fairview Park, Elmsford, New York 10523, U.S.A.
CANADA	Pergamon of Canada Ltd., P.O. Box 9600, Don Mills M3C 2T9, Ontario, Canada
AUSTRALIA	Pergamon Press (Aust.) Pty. Ltd., 19a Boundary Street, Rushcutters Bay, N.S.W. 2011, Australia
FRANCE	Pergamon Press SARL, 24 rue des Ecoles, 75240 Paris, Cedex 05, France
WEST GERMANY	Pergamon Press GmbH, 6242, Kronberg-Taunus, Pferdstrasse 1, Frankfurt-am-Main, West Germany

Copyright © 1976, Pergamon Press Inc.

Library of Congress Cataloging in Publication Data

Bernstein, Samuel J   comp.
    Computers in public administration.
    Includes bibliographies.
    1. Electronic data processing--Public administration
--Addresses, essays, lectures. I. Title.
JF1525.A8B47   1975   350'.00028'54   74-22430
ISBN 0-08-017869-3

For my late father

JOSEPH BERNSTEIN ל"ז

to whom social service was the

paramount value

Printed in Great Britain by A. Wheaton & Co, Exeter

Contents

*Criminal Justice and Police Administration
and Public Safety*

Sanitation and Waste Management

Education

Traffic Management

Housing

Welfare

The Editor

Samuel J. Bernstein (Ph.D., The University of Pennsylvania) is associate
professor and chairman of the Graduate Department of Public Administration, Baruch College of the City University of New York. His primary
professional interests are quantitative methods and computer-based models and their utilization in the analysis of public policies, programs and
administration. He has served as consultant to the Executive Office of the
President, Washington, D.C., The Comptroller's Office of the City of New
York among other public agencies. At present he is also associate editor of
the *Journal of Computers and Urban Society* which is devoted to
improving the use of computer and computer related techniques in the
solving of urban problems. Professor Bernstein's publications are in
various planning, public administration and political science journals. He is
co-editor and co-author of *Readings in Urban Policy Analysis: Quantitative Approaches* as well as co-author of *Urban Policy Analysis: A Model
Simulation Approach.*

Foreword

I have compiled this book on *Computers in Public Administration: An International Perspective* for both students and practitioners in the public service who are searching for basic educational materials that would enhance their understanding of the role of computers in government. In this regard I consider the need to be in the form of a single book which addresses the needs of the consumer of computer systems and applications: the public executives and managers as well as students of public administration.

Given this need I have taken a novel approach in regard to educating public administrators as to the potential of the computer improving the public service. Rather than proceeding from a technical approach to answer the question of how computers work, a descriptive approach is proposed that catalogues different computer-based systems and applications. This accounts for the book's form of readings which is partitioned into a structure emphasizing four major components: Management Information Systems, Management Administrative Areas, Functions of Management, and Learning the Utilization of the Computer. The question of how computers work, thus, is derivatively answered by understanding what computers do. The descriptive approach used here is in juxtaposition to an entire genre of books with titles like *What is the Computer?*, *The Computer and the Manager, Statistical Data Processing.* As such, the technical requirements for understanding the material presented here is minimal. A general knowledge of computers and of simple statistics, however, is assumed for understanding the details of the various computer-based models described herein.

In order to enrich the presentation I have tried to collect together in one place, from various published and unpublished sources, reports of systems and applications in the public sector. My sources of information have included a spate of computer and computer-related journals, conference proceedings, symposium reports, as well as government documents and new reports. Furthermore, in order to enrich the scope of material and to provide for universality of experience, I have tried to draw on documents reporting recent European computer applications as well. This, it is hoped, will provide the reader with a comparative and development administration perspective for the overall state of the art in public computer systems and applications. Similarly, I have appended a selected but extensive bibliography for each major topic heading discussed.

At this point it would be remiss of me not to acknowledge the assistance of the persons who helped make this effort see the light of day. First and foremost my thanks are to the authors who cooperated with me in presenting the materials between the covers of this book. To Mrs. Arline Landow who was indispensable in collecting the articles and maintaining rapport with the various authors involved, I say it would have been impossible without her. In this regard my graduate assistant, Mr. Lazar Ledereich, and Mr. A. Isaac Bernstein greatly aided in the reviewing and cataloging of the works presented here and in preparing the extensive bibliography. My thanks are in order to Gerald Deegan, Vice-President of Pergamon Press, for his continuous encouragement in light of many other conflicting demands. Last and not least I am grateful to my wife, Deena, for her patience during the late nights which were required to bring this and other works to fruition.

Preface

Management—private or public—is largely a process of handling information: that is, selecting it, comparing it, and then acting upon it. The selecting information function involves managers' choice of which data to give his attention to first. The comparison function is more subtle and complex; it involves the manager relating new data which he is continuously selecting and integrating it with the old which he already possesses. The comparison function is at the essence of decision making—it touches setting goals (where we want to be, compared to where we are), establishing programs (which of several programs offers comparative advantage), evaluating progress (how we are doing in comparison to our plans). Each of these kinds of decisions requires the public administrator to compare information about how things were to how they should or are likely to be. Acting upon these comparisons is that part of the decision process which involves the personal touch of the administrator which no machine can ever undertake.

Computers, as information handling machines, can clearly play an increasingly important role in the managerial functions of information selection and comparison. This book shows how computers are presently being utilized and how they may be utilized to improve these management processes in public administration. Four focal points are emphasized: management information systems, managerial administrative areas, functional administrative areas, and learning and utilizing the computer.

In the managerial administrative area the discussions focus on concerns internal to the administration of agency units. These discussions begin with the principles and problems in designing public information systems.

Two overall management systems for the public sector are then reported. There follows a description of two essential administrative applications within public agencies, finance and personnel. Our discussion concludes with analysis of efficiency of computers in the public sector.

Within the functional administrative areas our concern is with the relationship of the public agency to its clientele and external environment. The specific applications which give dimension to this relationship extend from criminal justice to recreation and beyond. Nine sample function applications are thus discussed here. In each application emphasis is on showing how services to the public are improved through the computer.

In learning and utilizing the computer, the emphasis is on showing how the public executive may be more effectively educated to the potential usages of the computer in the public sector. Further, the use of simulation as a tool for improved public policy making is discussed.

The final section concern is reserved for an evaluation of the job undone. From the above we may conclude that the computer and its technology has made major inroads in many aspects of public administration in the United States as well as other parts of the industrial world. An evaluation of impact would reveal, however, that we may have successfully learned to inventory streets, traffic, pollution rates, land use, police records, tax statements, etc.; however, we have not adequately "humanized" or "socialized" the computer to the human element in the service relationship between governmental agencies and the people they serve. It is on this note of circumspect that we conclude but with hints for possible solutions.

List of Contributors

The biographical sketches of the authors who have contributed to this book are appended here. They are listed in order of the contributions to the text.

Bastiaan K. Brussaard has been Director of the Municipal Data Processing Center of Rotterdam since 1961. In this capacity he has been active in the organization of National Information Systems for the public sector. Also, Mr. Brussaard is Adjunct Professor of Applied Informatics at the Technical University, Delft, The Netherlands. Previously, his work involved extensive engagements in Indonesia which utilized his electrical and industrial engineering skills. In 1957 he joined the Computer group of Royal Dutch/Shell Petroleum serving as project leader and consultant in the computer field for the operating companies of Royal Dutch.

Mr. Brussaard received his Master's Degree in Business Economics from the Rotterdam School of Economics.

Samuel J. Bernstein is Chairman and Associate Professor of Public Administration at the Baruch College of the City of New York. Previously, Dr. Bernstein was consultant to the Executive Office of the President, Washington, D.C.; the Controller's Office of the City of New York; and the Department of Transportation Planning and Engineering of the Polytechnic Institute of New York. He was a visiting faculty member of the Executive Seminar Center; the United States Civil Service Commission in the New York Region. Dr. Bernstein's publications appear in various journals including *Traffic Quarterly, The Twentieth Annual Volume of TIMS, The Journal of Socio-Economic Planning Sciences, Policy Sciences.*

The author received his Ph.D. degree at the University of Pennsylvania in May, 1969.

S. Duus Østergaard has been the IBM representative to the Danish local authorities since 1970. In the same year (1970) he was awarded the Danish Zeuthen-prize for a thesis on investment models, which was published in the *Swedish Journal of Economics* in 1971.

The author is graduated from the University of Copenhagen, 1970, with a Master's Degree in Economics, with special interests in computer science, operations research, and statistical applications.

Dr. Steven Savas is presently Professor of Public Systems Management in the Graduate School of Business of Columbia University. His research and teaching is in the area of productivity in local government, encompassing technological, managerial, and institutional factors.

Previously, he was Deputy City Administrator for New York City where he directed the Management Science Unit: the first such group in any city government of the United States. Before this Dr. Savas was manager of urban systems at IBM applying advanced data processing and management science methods to urban problems.

Dr. Savas holds a Ph.D. degree from Columbia University and B.A. and B.S. degrees from the University of Chicago.

Robert Amsterdam is presently employed by the Bureau of the Budget of the city of New York. His primary concerns are with the design of computer systems to manage and identify the property of New York City. Presently, this involves the development of a city owned real estate information system. He helped in the design and implementation of GIST (Geographic Information System) which is now used by many New York City agencies to coordinate information concerning land and buildings.

Prior to joining the New York City government, he designed computer systems for private industry and lectured on urban information systems at Columbia University and New York University.

Mr. Amsterdam holds an M.A. degree in Systems Analysis from Rutgers University.

Cecil Marks is presently Assistant Secretary of the Civil Service Department, London, England. He is also the head of the Statistics 2 Division responsible for personnel information systems, in particular PRISM.

Mr. Marks began his computer career in 1955 when he joined a team at the National Physical Laboratory, Teddington, England, working on the application of computers to Government office work. From 1957–1960 he managed the first United Kingdom Government ADP installation (HEC 4). Following this, he continued in Government as a computer consultant. He was a founding member of the British Computer Society of which he became a Fellow in 1968, and is currently serving on its governing Council.

Charles B. Woodward is presently project manager in Engineering Sciences and Systems and Programming with the Service Bureau Corporation in Inglewood, California. His expertise is in the mathematical modeling of dynamic systems and linear programming. Previously, Mr. Woodward was with the Systems Dynamics Unit of the Rocketdyne Division of North American Aviation. The author received his M.S. degree in Chemical Engineering from the Oklahoma State University in 1962.

J. A. Tiffin transferred from the Ministry of Defence (Navy) to computer work at the Treasury Department in 1961 and was closely involved in a number of important United Kingdom government EDP projects. He became head of the branch for government civil EDP projects in 1965. He later took charge of EDP policy and planning work in the Civil

Service Department and was Vice-Chairman of the Intergovernmental Council for EDP. He transferred to the Department of Trade and Industry in 1970 as Assistant Secretary in charge of Management Services at the Business Statistics Office.

Dilip R. Limaye has extensive experience in the application of operations research and computer science techniques in the field of regional and urban planning. As Vice-President of Management Sciences for Decision Sciences Corporation, Mr. Limaye is responsible for directing quantitative analyses involving the application of advanced techniques of systems analysis, information technology, and risk analysis.

Mr. Limaye previously worked as Senior Economic Analyst for the Sun Oil Company, where he was responsible for development of a management information system and a corporate planning model for top management, and as Manager of Operations Research at the Vertol Division of the Boeing Company, which involved the application of aerospace technology for the solution of urban transportation problems.

He has authored or coauthored several technical papers on the application of the operations research and management sciences techniques to urban and regional planning and has an M.S. degree in Operations Research from Cornell University.

Donald F. Blumberg is President of Decision Sciences Corporation of Jenkintown, Pennsylvania. His experience includes the direction of major projects in urban and community planning and in the development of simulation models for regional and urban analysis. He has been a consultant to the Office of Economic Opportunity (OEO), the Institute for Defense Analysis (IDA), the Advanced Research Projects Agency (ARPA), the city of Toronto, the province of Ontario, and The Canadian Manpower Development Commission.

Mr. Blumberg received his M.S. degree in Industrial Management and Operations Research from the University of Pennsylvania. His recent activities include the development of the PROMUS system for Toronto and the NUCOMS system for HUD.

Melvin Bockelman has been the Manager of the Computer Systems Division of the Kansas City Missouri Police Department since 1966. His mission was to design a modern police computer system which improved criminal intelligence and thereby assisted in reversing the rising crime indices in Kansas City.

Prior to joining the Police Department, Mr. Bockelman was a member of the United States Air Force Air Defense Command in Colorado Springs, Colorado.

Mr. Bockelman took his postgraduate-training courses at the University of Hawaii and the University of California. He is a graduate of the Advanced System Design Course at IBM and the Systems Design Course at the University of California.

Professor Henry F. Soehngen is Chairman of the Department of Civil Engineering at the Polytechnic Institute of New York. His major fields of interest include Photogrammetry, Computer Science and Applications, Surveying and Land Use Planning. His publications appear in *Civil Engineering Series* of the University of Illinois, *Photogrammetria, The Journal of Socio-Economic Planning Science,* and *The Journal of Water Pollution Control Federation.*

Professor Soehngen received his M.C.E. degree at the Polytechnic Institute of Brooklyn in 1947 and pursued further advanced training in Photogrammetria Engineering at the International Training Center in Delft, The Netherlands.

Professor Paul R. DeCicco is presently technical director of the Center for Urban and Environmental Studies of the Polytechnic Institute of New York and Professor of Civil Engineering. Professor DeCicco holds a professional engineering certificate with a variety of consulting assignments in the area of environmental and sanitary engineering utilizing computer applications. He has worked on National Science Foundation (1961), Atomic Energy Commission (1963), and Public Health Service (1964) grants in the area of computer applications. His recent publications appear in McGraw-Hill's *Encyclopedia of Science and Technology*. The *Journal of* Water Pollution Control Federation and Publications of the ACM.

Martin Stankard is presently a member of the staff of Arthur D. Little, Inc. Cambridge, Massachusetts. His primary concerns are with marketing and financial planning problems in private industry—especially in the quantitative analysis of strategic decisions. Prior to joining Arthur D. Little, he was a Research Analyst at the Management Sciences Center of the University of Pennsylvania where his concerns were with improving public sector systems. His work involved program planning and budgeting in school systems, multi-objective decision problems, and scheduling computer-based instruction systems.

Dr. Stankard received his Ph.D. degree in Management Sciences from the University of Pennsylvania.

Dr. Roger L. Sisson is the Associate Director of Government Studies and Systems, Inc. which specializes in the design and use of planning and budgeting systems for public institutions, development and application of planning methods, and managing research programs.

Before joining Government Studies and Systems, Dr. Sisson was an Associate Professor of Operations Research in the Wharton School of the University of Pennsylvania where in addition to teaching operations research and data processing, he did applied research on methods of allocating resources in school districts and basic research on conflict phenomena.

Dr. Sisson's consulting positions include IBM, General Electric, Baltimore and Ohio Railroad, and more recently, for the School District of Philadelphia, the U.S. Office of Education, Western Interstate Commission for Higher Education and others.

The author's publications appear in the *Educational Technology, the Journal of Socio-Economic Planning Sciences, ERIC*, and include many research reports.

Professor Edmund J. Cantilli is Associate Professor of Transportation Planning and Engineering at the Polytechnic Institute of New York. His expertise is in the areas of Traffic Safety, Transportation Safety, Urban Planning, and Urban Geography.

He was formerly affiliated with the Port of New York Authority as Engineer of Traffic Safety. His studies and research including developing an automated system for traffic accident recording and analysis; traffic improvements at airports, tunnels, bridges, and terminals resulting in significant accident reductions. His present research concerns transportation plans, mass transportation and community values, oversaturated street networks, traffic and transportation needs of the aging and the handicapped.

Dr. Cantilli is a professional engineer and received his Ph.D. degree in Transportation Planning and Traffic Engineering from the Polytechnic Institute of Brooklyn.

Robert B. Dial is Chief of the New Systems Requirements Analysis Branch of the Urban Mass Transportation Administration, U.S. Department of Transportation. Prior to his entry into Federal Government service in 1971, he spent two years with the Puget Sound Regional Transportation Study and six years with Alan M. Vorhees Associates, where he designed and implemented computer software systems for application in land use and transportation planning. He has received a Bachelor's degree in Mathematics, a Master's degree in Civil Engineering, and a Ph.D. degree in Transportation Planning from the University of Washington. He has served on committees of the Highway Research Board, the American Institute of Planners, the Association for Computing Machinery, and the Organization for Economic Cooperation and Development.

Edward N. Dodson is Director of the Economics Department of General Research Corporation, Santa Barbara, California. He received a Bachelor degree from Yale University and a Ph.D. degree from Stanford. He has worked for the Raytheon Company and Stanford Research Institute prior to joining General Research Corporation. Dr. Dodson's research interests and publications include urban transportation, regional economics, resource analysis of R & D programs, and the interactions of technology with economics.

Jon R. David is President of Systems RDI Corporation of New Jersey which specializes in computer advisory services for public and private organizations. His particular expertise is in feasibility studies and systems applications utilizing minicomputers. Prior to his affiliation with Systems RDI, Mr. David held senior positions with ITT World Communications, The Goddard Space Flight Center, and RCA.

Mr. David holds an M.S. degree in Statistics from Columbia University.

Norbert Dee is a Senior Environmental and Land Use Planner in the Social and Systems Sciences Department of Battelle's Columbus Laboratories in Columbus, Ohio. He received his Ph.D. degree in Geography and Environmental Engineering from the Johns Hopkins University. Dr. Dee's principal research efforts are in the development and application of methodologies to solve environmental and land use problems. He has initiated the development and application of Environmental Evaluation Systems for the Bureau of Reclamation, the Corps of Engineers, and the Environmental Protection Agency. He was also involved in developing a computer model for evaluating environmental and economic trade-offs in the state of Arizona. He is a member of the American Geophysical Union, the American Water Resources Association, the American Society of Civil Engineers, among other professional organizations.

Jon C. Liebman is Professor of Environmental Engineering in the Department of Civil Engineering of the University of Illinois at Urbana-Champaign. He received his Ph.D. degree from Cornell University in Sanitary Engineering. Before assuming his present position he served on the faculty of the Department of Geography and Environmental Engineering of the Johns Hopkins University. Dr. Liebman's principal research interest is in the application of operations research methods to urban and environmental engineering problems. He has published extensively in the field of water resources and is currently engaged in research on techniques for the routing of solid waste collection vehicles. He is a member of the American Society of Civil Engineers, The Institute of Management Sciences, the American Association of University Professors, among other professional organizations.

Herman E. Koenig received all of his Engineering degrees at the University of Illinois, the B.S. in 1947, the M.S. in 1949, and the Ph.D. in 1953. With the exception of one year after the

B.S. as a project engineer for the Delco Products Division of General Motors and periods of consulting with Reliance Electric and Engineering Company, all of his career has been spent in engineering education at the Massachusetts Institute of Technology, the University of Illinois, and at Michigan State University. He came to Michigan State University in 1955 as an assistant professor of electrical engineering and has risen through the ranks until attaining his present position as Chairman of the Department of Electrical Engineering and Systems Science. He has authored some 30 technical publications and two textbooks in his short term at Michigan State. While serving as department chairman, he has also served as director of a National Science Foundation grant on *Ecosystem Design and Management* involving scientists from some ten academic departments. In 1968 he received the Distinguished Faculty Award at Michigan State University for his outstanding contributions to teaching and research. He is a Fellow member of IEEE.

Dean L. Haynes received his Ph.D. from Michigan State University in 1960 in the field of Entomology. From 1960 to 1965 he worked as a Forest Ecologist for the Canadian Department of Forestry in a project directed at control of the spruce budworm in New Brunswick, Canada. His area of the program was to develop a model of invertebrate predation of the pest species. From 1965 to 1967 he worked in insect ecology at North Dakota State University at Fargo, North Dakota. In 1967 he joined the staff at Michigan State University to teach ecology and conduct research on the population dynamics of the cereal leaf beetle, an insect attacking small grains in Michigan. He is a research associate of the U.S.D.A. and member of the Entomological Society of America, the Entomological Society of Canada, and the British Ecological Society.

P. David Fisher received his B.S. degree at the University of Pittsburgh in 1963 and his Ph.D. degree from the Johns Hopkins University in 1967. Both degrees were in Electrical Engineering. From 1967 to 1969 he was a senior engineer at Westinghouse Electric Corporation's Aerospace Division in Baltimore, Maryland, where he participated in research and development activities related to microwave and optical communication systems. He joined the faculty at Michigan State University in 1969 and is currently an associate professor of electrical engineering and systems science. His current research interests relate to the development and implementation of suitable monitoring, data management, and communication systems required for the on-line control of ecological communities. He is a member of both the IEEE and the American Physical Society.

Isaac L. Auerbach is President and Founder of the Auerbach Corporations which provides consulting services to management in business, industry, and government in all aspects of computer operations in Europe and the United States and publishes the authoritative Auerbach Computer Technology Reports which are recognized worldwide as the standard encyclopedia reference service for the data processing industry.

Mr. Auerbach is the founder and first president of the International Federation for Information Processing (IFIP): a multinational federation of professional technical societies in 34 nations, the official organization of the world's computer community. He has published extensively in technical journals and holds numerous patents in the electronic computer field.

Mr. Auerbach holds an M.S. degree in Applied Physics obtained from Harvard University in 1947.

Robert W. Blanning is Assistant Professor of Management at the Wharton School of Finance and Commerce, University of Pennsylvania. He received his B.S. degree in Physics from the Pennsylvania State University, and an M.S. degree in Operations Research from the Case Institute of Technology, and a Ph.D. degree from the University of Pennsylvania specializing in operations research and management information systems. He was formerly Assistant Professor of Management in the College of Business and Public Administration at New York University. He is coauthor (with William F. Hamilton and Terrill A. Mast) of *Linear Programming for Management*, published by Entelek, Inc.

Arie Y. Lewin is Associate Professor of Management and Behavioral Science at the Graduate School of Business Administration, New York University. His book, *Behavioral Aspects of Accounting*, was published by Prentice-Hall in 1974. Professor Lewin holds a Ph.D. degree from the Graduate School of Industrial Administration of the Carnegie Mellon University.

Myron Uretsky is Professor of Computer Applications and Information Systems at the Graduate School of Business Administration of the New York University. His technical expertise has been focused in the areas bearing on accounting and management. He is coauthor with N. Churchill and J. Kempster of *Computer-Based Information Systems for Management: A Survey*, published by the National Association of Accountants.
  Professor Uretsky holds M.B.A. and Ph.D. degrees from the Ohio State University.

Abe Gottlieb is presently a Senior Planning Analyst with the Pennsylvania Office of State Planning and Development where he is engaged in the study and research of economic, population and fiscal trends of the State and its regional areas. Prior to this position, Mr. Gottlieb was Senior Economist with the Delaware Valley Regional Planning Commission where he directed a series of planning research studies dealing with current and projected economic and demographic developments for the Philadelphia metropolitan area.
  He has taught urban and regional planning and urban sociology as an Adjunct Professor at the Pennsylvania State University and Fairleigh Dickinson University. Mr. Gottlieb's publications include articles on economic analyses, planning and computer impacts and have appeared in *Commentary*, the *Journal of the American Institute of Planners*, and *Computers and Automation*.

Joseph Weizenbaum is Professor of Computer Science in the Department of Electrical Engineering at the Massachusetts Institute of Technology. He completed his formal education (in mathematics) at Wayne State University in 1951 and began his career in the computer field. Before joining MIT he was a Fellow at the Center for Advanced Study in Behavioral Sciences, Stanford, California. He also participated in the development of ERMA, the first computer system designed for the banking industry. His main contributions to the computer art consist of SLIP, a list processing language extension to algebraic languages such as FORTRAN and ALGOL, and ELIZA, a program for natural language comhunication between man and machine. Professor Weizenbaum's current research is on the social impact of computers and computation.

CHAPTER I

An Overall Computer Development and Management Information Policy

Among the reasons commonly cited for a government's failure to fully avail itself of the benefits of computers and electronic data processing (EDP) are the lack of competent personnel, lack of central control, lack of funds, lack of understanding, unwillingness to share, and organizational resistance to change. Underlying these reasons is a basic lack of commitment to the coordinated development of automated information systems. Central control and the consolidation of EDP activities at any level of government are necessary to assure such development and this in turn requires the creation of a strong technically competent central EDP authority.

Two reasons may be said to account for governments not readily moving in the direction of EDP authorities. First, while the savings of efficient computer centers may run as high as several million dollars annually, the amount of money involved represents only a very small portion of a government's total budget. Recognizing this, and faced with seemingly more pressing problems, some officials feel that the dollar savings alone simply cannot justify the political costs of consolidating EDP activities. Some of these political costs may include greater auditing potential to expose government activities to public view and a greater need for technically competent personnel, thereby diminishing the potential for straight political appointments. Second, a past history of incompetent EDP management has made some officials skeptical about the successful implementation of any but the most routine computer applications. The classic syndrome in this regard may be described as follows: A government allocates millions of dollars for the development of a relatively simple accounts payable system. After 12 months have elapsed and after having spent a good portion of the initial allocation, the system is not ready. Announcements and retractions on the final implementation follow in the second year. The system is still not completely operational until the end of the fourth or the beginning of the fifth year. Given the widespread nature of these occurrences, officials—elected and administrative—cannot be blamed for thinking that a request for funds to establish a central EDP authority is not more than a call to throw away good money after bad.

Nevertheless, various research efforts on computer applications and systems during the decade of the sixties concluded a greater need for broader information system capability for governments. Such efforts included work at the University of Southern California, The University of Connecticut, the Travelers Research, and the IBM–New Haven project. The major proposals from these efforts may be summarized in terms of simultaneous improvements in:

- Integrating information technology and decision processes.
- Realigning organization structure.
- Modifying role perception and developing personnel skills for the new synergistic technologies of computer and computer-related systems.
- Expanding the stock of knowledge about information systems.
- Altering the social millieu in which information systems are built.*

Based on the above research, the Urban System Interagency Committee (USAC) in the United States government was formed to help implement centralized management information systems (MIS). The first reading in this chapter abstracts that part of the USAC report that focuses on the planning, development, and administration of integrated municipal management information systems. Juxtaposed to this is the article of Mr. Brussaard of the Municipal Data-processing Center of the Netherlands which relates the Dutch experience with centralized data management, also at the municipal level. In the article which follows, Messrs. Bernstein and Hoxie address the growing importance of the interface between teleprocessing and computers in public administration.

The underutilization of computer and computer-related technologies to date in the public sector is the basic assumption of the articles and the

---

*From: Kenneth L. Kraemer *et al. Integrated Municipal Information Systems: The Use of the Computer in Local Government,* New York: Praeger, 1974.

organizational requisites for planning and implementing new systems where systems are broadly defined is the focal point. Emphasis is on the need to develop *comprehensive administrative policies* for the planning and management of computer systems in the public sector. How to effectively improve public services delivery is the goal set by USAC.

1

IMIS Planning, Development, and Administration*

KENNETH L. KRAEMER,† WILLIAM H. MITCHEL,‡
MYRON E. WEINER,§ AND O. E. DIAL**

INTRODUCTION

Given an understanding of the need for an integrated municipal system the question naturally arises: "How does one go about constructing IMIS?" This chapter looks at the processes by which computer-based information and decision systems are conceived and carried out. Basically, those processes are three:

- Systems planning, including preplanning and formal systems planning.
- Systems development, including detailed system design, application programming, procedure and data conversion, and system implementation.
- Systems administration of the foregoing activities and related orientation and training, monitoring and evaluation, and organization-building activities.

---

*From: Kenneth L. Kraemer *et al. Integrated Municipal Information Systems: The Use of the Computer in Local Government*, New York: Praeger, 1974.
†Associate Professor, Graduate School of Administration, University of California at Irvine.
‡Adjunct Professor, Claremont Men's College, Claremont, California.
§Associate Professor, Institute of Public Service.
**Visiting Professor, Long Island University.

This threefold process is essentially similar to the nine-step process described in RFP-H-2-70 although expressed somewhat differently here. Minor changes have been made here to adapt the USAC research and development process to the typical city's needs and to present the material in a more integrated and less technical manner[1].

This article presents an overview of the systems planning, development, and administration processes rather than a detailed discussion. It emphasizes those things that political and administrative leaders must understand, support, and provide for if they are to achieve acceptable levels of, and benefits from, computer utilization. The discussion herein applies to any IMIS project whether broad or narrow in scope, that is, whether a system, subsystem, or component-oriented project. A particular city may pursue the activities outlined here in a different order. Some cities may overlook certain activities because they are already at a more advanced stage of development. However, the activities discussed will be or will have been carried out at some point in time.

The three IMIS building processes that constitute the major subject of this article are preceded by three additional subjects: factors contributing to successful IMIS projects; general approaches to IMIS; and size of city and cost.

FACTORS IN IMIS SUCCESS

Successful completion of an IMIS project depends upon many technical and nontechnical factors. However, experience has demonstrated that certain factors (those listed in Fig. 1) appear to be more critical than others.

Assuming the municipality has or can secure the necessary technical

Fig. 1 Critical factors in an IMIS project.

capability in electronic data processing, successful completion of the IMIS project substantially rests upon support, participation, and involvement in the project by operating department administrators, the municipal chief executive, and the legislative body.

Success also requires the cooperative working together of information systems specialists and municipal functional administrators and specialists. It is impractical for a functional administrator to devote his full time to operations while the system that is to become part of these operations in the future is being designed and implemented. The reasons why the user as well as the computer expert should participate in systems planning are several:

- The administrator has a better understanding of the function that the computer is to support.
- The administrator will have to use and operate through the new system. It is unlikely that anyone who has not participated closely in the design of the new system will be inclined to use it, feel that the system meets his operational needs, or trust its performance.

Success also requires that the IMIS project and the information systems activity be regarded like any other important municipal activity with respect to relating its structure and performance to municipal objectives. That is, the activity must have the status, resources, and support of the other major activities of municipal government such as police or finance.

GENERAL APPROACHES TO IMIS

Where to Start?

Every municipal government has some kind of information system in existence. Usually it is manual and highly decentralized. For example, from the perspective of an information specialist, the tax collector's information system includes: routine daily data collection activities; daily storage and retrieval actions; data storage in the form of files, reports, maps, forms, and records; people processing data; and making decisions. These and similar activities pervade the municipal organization and are more or less organized into a set of small, independent systems that work reasonably well in many instances.

What is it, then, that triggers a felt need for improving these systems?

One city manager offers the following explanations:

> Usually the move [to EDP] is manifested by some malfunctioning such as sloppy, inaccurate or delayed results from processing of some routine paper work such as utility bills or payroll records. Sometimes it is just out of concern for the expense of keeping certain records current. Occasionally, it is just inquisitiveness or the recognition of a common data processing application [2].

A former city manager expressed it as follows:

> In exercising administrative responsibilities for the city . . . , the management team adheres to two basic beliefs. We believe that good service produces the best possible public relations, and we believe that facts, properly applied, are more powerful than special interests and more dependable than political expediency. . . .
>   We have found that the need for information to support operations . . . activities has intensified our need for electronic data processing equipment. . . . In continuing management analyses, the computer helps to chart the fight against crime, reports on equipment efficiency, helps to control spending, evaluates garbage collection routes, and performs other valuable functions [3].

When computer technology is introduced into the municipality's existing information system, many information and decision processes will remain unaffected. The reason for this is that many forms of information in municipal government are impossible or uneconomic to computerize. Included here are such things as systems designed to handle telephone calls, notes written on margins of reports and memoranda, looks on a citizen's face at a public hearing, knowledge of which municipal personnel work together well, articles in the local newspapers, and many others.

The traditional image of the areas where the computer can be utilized in municipalities is for the accounting type activities that have large processing volumes, are routinely and frequently performed, and are well defined and understood. However, this traditional image of computer usage and trends in the actual use of data processing are changing as the relationship of municipal activities and information processing becomes better understood. Appropriate uses of the computer have been extended to include:

1. Operational support, where the computer is used to aid in the actual conduct of government operations for activities such as work and facility scheduling, dispatching, inventory control, purchasing, licensing, customer service, and library circulation control. Here the computer is used instead of people to execute operating procedures, keep operating records, provide for file inquiry, and signal for specific action.
2. Inquiry and information retrieval, where the computer's record-

keeping capability is used to support such activities as police and fire investigations, library bibliographic search, field search of criminal records, and management or planning information searches.

3. Scientific and analytical computing, where the computer is used to perform complex or repetitive calculations for such activities as engineering design and utility operations analysis; or where the computer is used for special calculation or simulation of some specific area of government operations to obtain better insight into a problem and to permit evaluation of alternative courses of action.

4. Process control, where the computer is used to control some physical process or operation such as traffic signal control or utility system operations.

Thus, the use of computer-based technology has been extended into many operations of municipal government. In fact, most experts agree that the computer is used for its greatest potential only when it is used directly in support of municipal operations.

The question for many cities, then, is how to start improving municipal government activities through the use of modern, computer-based information and decision technology rather than how to tackle a program for the installation of hardware and development of traditional accounting type applications. The time lag for initiation of the newer approach may be longer, but the benefits to be derived from the technology may be more than correspondingly greater.

Approaches to Developing an IMIS

In order to begin developing an IMIS, the municipality must have an EDP capability. Ultimately, this capability consists of people, computer hardware and related software, and procedures related in a systems pattern to accomplish the objectives of IMIS. There are essentially three classes of approaches to obtain or develop this capability:

1. In-house, with the city developing its own resources.
2. Out-of-house, through city reliance on and purchase of outside organizational services.
3. A combination of in-house development and use of outside resources.

There is general agreement that ultimately some in-house capability is required for evolving an adequate data-processing activity. But the diversity of cities and their varying states of EDP development require considerable openness about the appropriateness of any of the various approaches. No one approach has yet been established as the "best" way and probably will not be. Each city may safely explore each of the main approaches and their combinations to determine that which best suits it. Therefore, each approach is discussed. A summary comparison of in-house and out-of-house approaches is provided in Fig. 2.

It should be pointed out, however, that if a city lacks any existing EDP capability, a first step is to hire someone with both the technical and managerial skill to build or direct a team that can pursue IMIS whether developing the system in-house or using outside resources or both. Often, this step may be preceded by obtaining advice from outside individuals or consultant organizations regarding whether to pursue IMIS at all. In this regard, it should be noted that there is no easy, inexpensive way of acquiring an IMIS. Some conservatism appears warranted when a municipality is tendered a cheap, quick, or painless opportunity to acquire an IMIS. The studies made by USAC strongly suggest that quick and inexpensive approaches seldom produce a satisfactory or economic use of EDP.

In-House Development

This approach often works best where the city already has some EDP capability and considerable experience with computers and information systems. The development of IMIS then becomes a special, planned effort of an ongoing data-processing activity.

However, few cities have either the basic capability or experience required to build an IMIS. Many cities operate only tabulating equipment or operate computers as though these were tabulators because their people lack the necessary concepts, skills, financial, or organizational resources to do better. Therefore the city that chooses to develop an IMIS in-house needs to understand that it will be a major administrative undertaking. IMIS development requires that a substantial mixture of skills and resources be committed by the municipality. In most cases, a systematic upgrading of EDP staff and computing facilities must be planned and achieved. Municipal non-EDP personnel also must be trained and organized to be part of the development effort.

The major advantage of in-house development is that it results in the establishment of a capacity within the municipality for continually

	IN-HOUSE	OUT-OF-HOUSE

Advantages

IN-HOUSE

Most likely to meet municipal needs over the long run.

Increases opportunity for management and operating personnel participation and involvement in systems planning and design.

Information systems activities may be used as a change mechanism within municipal government aimed at general improvement.

Cost is less in the long run, especially if cooperative arrangements are used.

Systems more responsive to municipal needs.

Permits development of requisite EDP staff who are also knowledgeable about municipal policies and problems.

OUT-OF-HOUSE

Specialized skills available.

Range of experience available.

Off-the-shelf computer applications packages may be available.

Can supplement in-house effort during peak periods or for large processing demands.

Can be used to provide for transition to eventual in-house effort.

Can be used to test new applications without interference with in-house operations.

Greater computing capacity sometimes available for large or specialized analytical jobs.

Competitive market conditions may reduce costs for limited applications.

Specific achievements may occur faster.

Disadvantages

IN-HOUSE

May require long period of time to develop capability in-house and to see results.

Probably too costly for the smaller cities unless done under cooperative arrangements.

Initial or "start up" costs may discourage council approval.

OUT-OF-HOUSE

Communications breakdown or delay.

Accessibility to outside source may be limited or inconvenient.

Outside source may be unable to adjust to municipal schedule of needs and priorities.

Special jobs may cost more.

Tends to postpone unduly the development of an in-house capability.

City becomes overly dependent upon outside organization for information services.

City fails to develop its own personnel skills.

Costs include billing, but also delay, liaison, monitoring and control.

Outside source may be inflexible in adapting to city problems or unaware of them.

Fig. 2 Some advantages and disadvantages of in-house and out-of-house approaches to developing an information systems capability.

evolving the IMIS to meet changing conditions and needs. That capacity resides in the data processing activity created and, equally importantly, in the municipal personnel who use the system and who participated in its development. It is these operational users who will be the prime movers in the continuous expansion, improvement, and use of the system and who will demand and support its evaluation. Other advantages of this approach are shown in Fig. 2.

Use of Outside Resources

This approach works best where the city lacks any existing data processing capability. There are essentially two routes that can be taken: (1) contract procurement for the entire spectrum of information services, and (2) contract procurement of system planning and development work. Before discussing these, however, two major disadvantages of using outside resources must be stated. First, most consulting or service organizations are of limited help where an integrated system is desired because they too have been trained in the individual applications approach. Second, use of these outside organizations frequently results in only minimal capability within municipal government for continued evolution of the system.

The first route involves relying entirely on an outside organization to provide the municipality with the necessary services. This is done through a service contract in which the city purchases information services much the same as it does garbage collection, emergency ambulance, health code enforcement, tax assessment and collection, engineering design and calculation, and similar services. To the extent that the city has technically competent people to prepare, monitor, and evaluate performance under such contracts and to the extent that sufficient service organizations exist to truly compete for the service contract, this is a feasible approach in the short run.

In the long term, however, the competitive price advantage may be lost for the municipality eventually may be forced to buy the service from one supplier. That is, the municipalities' operations and the information systems to support those operations are so closely interrelated that rarely is it possible to change over to another supplier after a large portion of the municipality's operations have been automated. Further, present experience with this approach is limited. Few cities use it or have used it for a sufficient length of time to discover what the long-term negative effects are.

The second route is using outside consultants or organizations for

systems planning and development. This takes the form of a contract with a
service bureau or systems organization to plan and develop an IMIS for the
municipality. Included in the contract are provisions for the education
and training of municipal technical and nontechnical personnel so that the
new system can be operated and maintained by the municipality.

This route is advantageous when the outside organization already has
developed a system or subsystem for another municipality. The transfer of
that system to a second municipality then can be accomplished at a cost
below that for which the second municipality could develop the system on
its own. The problem of course is to find organizations with such
experience—probably less than two dozen exist.

In-House Development With Outside Assistance

This approach is used most often by cities regardless of size, experience, or existing EDP capability. For most cities this is probably the best
intermediate approach in that the municipality evolves its own capability
but retains the flexibility of using outside organizations whenever appropriate. For example, the city that lacks any capability can initially contract
with an outside organization to develop a portion of IMIS and simultaneously train municipal personnel to operate and maintain the new system
and to develop additional new systems. These systems also can be
operated on an outside organization's equipment until such time as the
municipality has developed a sufficient work load to justify in-house
hardware and obtains its own. Finally, when the municipality has its own
people, hardware and related software, and systems procedures, it may
still contract for outside assistance in specialized areas or as supplemental
staff. The critical factor in utilizing this approach is to have a well-
developed set of specifications against which the outside agency will
contribute and its performance will be judged.

The Consortium Approach

The USAC research and development program is probably the most
formal illustration of combined in-house development and utilization of
outside resources. Although the context is that of research and development, the USAC model is useful to comtemplate for an IMIS development in which research is not involved.

On the assumption that few municipalities possessed a sufficiently
broad range of talents and experience to develop IMIS, the USAC
Request for Proposals ("RFP-H-2-70") recommended that each respond-

ing municipality form a consortium normally to be made up of three types of organizations:

1. The municipal government.
2. A systems/software firm.
3. A university or research organization.

This recommendation was also included to ensure that a broad base of competence would be developed for subsequent availability when other cities engaged in their development of an IMIS.

The award municipalities are the prime contractors to the federal government for execution of the research and development projects. Associated with each municipality, as subcontractors, are a private systems/software organization and a university or research center. The objective of these three-party consortiums is to develop working information system products that are immediately useful but that also can be transferred for use in other municipalities with a minimum of revision and conversion.

The municipality's particular role in each consortium is to provide overall project management, financial and human resource support, hardware support, and the specific working data generated by operations, all of which are needed for developing and operating the information system. The systems/software subcontractor supplies technical management and information systems specialists to work jointly with municipal personnel in performing the research and development tasks. The university provides governmental specialists and behavioral scientists for monitoring project impacts, educating and training municipal personnel, and evaluating project results.

The IMIS project staff, therefore, is a composite of people from these three primary resources. It is essentially a dynamic matrix organization in that the particular composition of people and their relationships changes as the tasks to be accomplished change. Each project staff is tied to the local operating government by responsibility to the municipality's chief executive, by a policy committee of government officials, and by one or more user committees composed of people in the units affected by the project. Generally, the IMIS project staff also establishes coordinative or working relationships with citizens, other local governments in the area including counties, and the state government.

The combination of these three agencies appears to be working well in evolving the USAC prototype systems. There is substantial evidence to suggest that such an approach is within the capability of many cities and when properly evolved can enhance materially a city's chance of success. It is also probable that the benefits to the local university or college and to the software firm will be significant.

Size of City and Cost

Computers and information systems may not be suitable for every municipality. This limitation is not technological, however. It is a matter of a city's willingness to commit substantial human and financial resources, accept change in traditional ways of operating, and provide vigorous leadership and political support.

Approximately 70% and more of the U.S. cities above 50,000 population presently are using computers in some fashion as illustrated by Fig. 3. No city possesses a comprehensive and integrated municipalwide information system. A few cities are making great strides toward developing parts or components of such a system. Generally, however, most cities now using computers have yet to begin using them in a fashion that exploits the potential benefits of EDP. Both the recent USAC-sponsored "state of the art" study of 79 cities and the ICMA 1970 survey of 868 cities over 25,000 population support this generalization[4].

IMIS, whether partial or complete, is costly. The "state of the art" study revealed that the most sophisticated cities, that is, those in the top 25% with regard to experience and achievements, spend about 1% of their

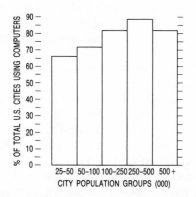

Fig. 3 U.S. cities using computers by city population groups. (Source: Constructed from data contained in Malchus Waltington, ADP in municipal government, *Management Information Service Reports*, Vol. 2, No. 10 (Washington, D.C.: International City Management Association [ICMA], 1970); and ICMA, *Municipal Yearbook* (Washington, D.C., 1968).)

annual operating budgets for electronic data processing. The top ten cities spend 2–3% for EDP. It is the view of USAC that a 2.5–3% factor is required to reach "critical mass."

Figure 4 shows the maximum, mean, and minimum annual EDP expenditures of cities in five population groups as reported in the USAC and ICMA surveys. These numbers are illustrative of the absolute dollar amounts spent by cities for EDP. Although less useful as a planning guide than the USAC standard of 2.5–3% of annual operating expenditures, the absolute expenditure variability illustrates current investment patterns among cities. And investment appears highly related to achievement. Generally, the cities with high experience and achievement levels in the USAC study were also those with substantial investment.

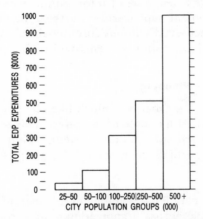

Fig. 4   Average total EDP expenditures by city population groups.

SYSTEMS PLANNING

Need for Planning

Given the investment required, it seems reasonable to expect that cities would plan their IMIS projects on a long-range basis—that the same forethought would be given to the plan of projects as is given to any one component project. In fact, the evidence suggests just the opposite. Cities have settled unthinkingly into EDP on a piecemeal, incremental basis. Experience has also demonstrated that without substantial systems planning, municipalities develop isolated islands of mechanization that

ᴀve little possibility for future integration and little room for a continued
and expanding pattern of EDP. Such isolated and independent applications are unnecessary and unjustifiable economically.

An IMIS cannot be developed all at once. It can be acquired only on an
incremental basis beginning with those components that have a high
precedence ordering and/or cost-effectiveness. IMIS, as USAC now sees
it, is really a federation of parts of components of municipal operating
functions. The justification for implementing the parts of IMIS, therefore,
relates to cost-effectiveness considerations of the operating functions and
to system requirements that one function precede another in a predetermined pattern of development. The way in which a city ideally prepared
for EDP is through systems planning. Planning is necessary because the
magnitude, complexity, and cost of information systems are too great to
permit their development haphazardly. Further, the objective of integration rarely can be achieved without forethought about how the various
components of the information systems will be interrelated.

Functions of Systems Planning

Systems planning as a process is much like planning in other contexts.
It is an attempt to chart a course of action to achieve the most effective
use of computer-based information systems. Thus, systems planning
performs several important functions in IMIS projects. Among these are
the following:

1. Avoidance of parallel development of major elements that are
   widely applicable across organizational lines, for example, personnel and payroll, purchasing, inventory control, etc.
2. Establishment of a uniform base in terms of which it is possible to
   determine the sequence of development of the major system elements in terms of their payoff potential, natural precedence, probability of success, and relative needs of the various operating
   departments.
3. Minimization of the cost of achieving an integration of related
   data-processing applications.
4. Reduction or elimination of small, isolated applications that must be
   developed, maintained, and operated.
5. Provision for adaptability or expansion of the system to community
   growth and government change without requiring periodic, major
   costly redesign.

6. Provision of guidelines for and direction to continuing systems development studies and projects.
7. Provision of a basis for anticipating both short and long-term costs and benefits.

Objective for Effective Use of Computers by Municipalities

The particular objectives sought by an IMIS project are to some extent peculiar to the municipality served and must be developed in each instance out of local circumstances by the people involved. At a general level, however, several objectives will be characteristic of all these IMIS projects. These were among those embodied in "RFP-H-2-70." Within the goal of an integrated approach to municipal use of computers, the functions of computer-based systems are to:

- Support or perform directly the operational activities of municipal governments and facilitate the management of those operations.
- Increase the productivity of the municipal government's staff so that improved or increased services can be delivered within the resources available.
- Produce sufficient economic benefits so as to make its incremental implementation feasible and justifiable.
- Operate in a manner to assure the continuous support and involvement of clerical and operational employees, department managers, and city officials.
- Protect the individual citizen's privacy from unreasonable or unjustifiable intrusion.
- Adapt readily to change as conditions in the community and municipal government require.

Systems Planning Activities

Unless a city already has a plan and is embarked on developing its IMIS, the first phase of work to be instituted by the city will be systems planning. Such planning is also to be considered a continuous effort throughout the life of IMIS. That is, since both the community and municipal government will change over time, so will the IMIS that supports and is an inherent part of government change to satisfy evolving community problems and needs. The task of systems planning is to create a basis for initiating action (capital, people, hardware, etc.) leading to a viable EDP operation and also to provide for the continual adaptation of

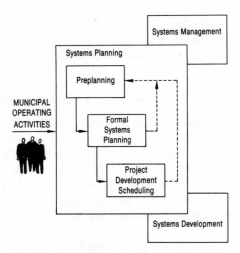

Fig. 5   Planning the development of IMIS.

IMIS as it evolves. The focus here is on preplanning and formal systems planning as shown in Fig. 5.

Preplanning

A major preplanning effort is necessary most often where the municipality lacks any basic capability for undertaking an IMIS, or, having capability, lacks an organized effort. The preplanning task is similar in many respects to the conduct of a feasibility study wherein determinations are made about:

- How to develop sufficient interest among professionals, managers, and political leaders to pursue IMIS.
- How the municipality will organize to conduct the work.
- The scope and magnitude of IMIS development, that is, whether a "total" system or subsystems.
- The specific objectives of IMIS.
- Manpower and financial resources.
- Orientation, education, and training required to begin work with the context of the specific municipality.

In addition, however, preplanning for IMIS will also include exploration of:

- What is IMIS?
- Why does the city need an IMIS? What will it permit the city to do

that cannot be done now? Or, what things that the city does not will it permit to do better?
- What benefits will accrue to the city from IMIS?
- How much will it cost? And are the benefits commensurate with the costs?
- What will its impact be on the city's personnel?
- What established guidelines, prototypes, and other material now exists that can reduce substantially the design and implementation costs?
- How do city (and contract) personnel become familiar with "the state of the art" in IMIS?

These questions must be explored individually for each city by that city. If the city lacks the required professional and technical expertise to do so or desires an independent review of an internally developed position, consideration should be given to hiring outside consultants or a consultant organization.

In addition to outside advice, city officials should budget for and make site visitations to other government jurisdictions where demonstrated successes have been achieved. Such visits have educational value and also provide assurance that computer technology may be used in a very sophisticated manner. Finally, they provide an opportunity for both the policy and the managerial people to discover how their contemporaries react to the system and how the system changes established patterns of operation.

The outcome of preplanning should be a major increase in understanding what IMIS is, a proposal for more detailed exploration, and a commitment to such exploration by top administrators and officials. If these do not eventuate, the probability is great that the city is not yet ready for IMIS.

Formal Systems Planning

The task of formal systems planning consists of development of a step-by-step prescription for achieving specified IMIS objectives. It includes three interrelated tasks: systems analysis; systems conceptualization; and project development scheduling.

Systems Analysis

Systems analysis is concerned with a detailed examination and documentation of the existing information processing and decision processes of the municipality. This work also must examine present and emerging perceptions of urban governments and how municipalities in particular can better meet their roles with the aid of information technology.

Since the primary objective of IMIS is to utilize fully information technology for a wide range of municipal government processes, the basic approach of systems analysis should include a comprehensive analysis of the municipal government and the environment in which it operates. The aim of this analysis is to delineate those areas of the municipality's operations, planning, and management that can be improved and strengthened by computer-based information and decision technology. Because systems analysis involves great detail and a systematic evalua- tion of all municipal operations, several additional comments are in order. First, in most instances the insights developed about the city and about opportunities for improvement apart from EDP justifies the effort. Second, the systems analysis work should involve the members of the city's staff as well as members of the systems group (whether in-house or consultant). Because the USAC/IMIS involves automation of routine operations, those affected by it should understand how the current system operates (or does not) as well as how it could operate (systems concep- tualization). Involvement of the city's staff at this first phase undoubtedly helps create the receptive atmosphere required for subsequent implemen- tation.

Systems Conceptualization

Systems conceptualization is concerned with development of a framework for IMIS taking the existing system into consideration but going considerably beyond it. The purpose of conceptualization is to identify the components or parts of the IMIS and how they are to be interrelated. The end product of this phase is not only a conceptualized IMIS but also a plan of projects for implementation based upon prece- dence ordering and development priorities.

From management's standpoint, system conceptualization is the crucial function in the development of an EDP system intended to support and be part of government operations. IMIS, by its very nature, must be developed and implemented incrementally, one activity or application at a time. These, in turn, eventually result in a more or less comprehensive computer-based system. In order to succeed in the construction of such a complex structure, each application must fit into some overall framework. This framework is the conceptual design or master plan for IMIS.

Project Development Scheduling

In deciding where to start the systems development effort, municipalities frequently choose those areas about which the most is known and where the benefit can be obtained for the least system effort. This is an appropriate strategy provided that such a decision is made within the framework of the conceptualized design or master plan and provided that precedence relationships of functions being automated are recognized and followed in subsequent implementation steps.

The notion of precedence relationships is important in project programming. It generally refers to the time sequence in which related operational activities take place. It also may refer to the fact that from a systems perspective one or more applications must be developed and operationalized before others can be initiated. For example, priorities in public finance applications from a systems standpoint are shown in Fig. 6.

In attempting project programming, the following questions are useful for managers to ask:

- In what area would improvement contribute the most to our citizens' welfare and satisfaction with their government?

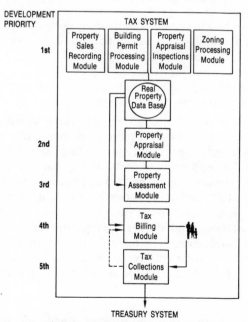

Fig. 6 Precedence relationship in tax system modules.

- What are our most important areas of concern?
- What functions are performing below par?
- Where do we have the least amount of control?
- What are the most important decisions we make? How could they be improved with better information?

In asking these types of questions, management will tend to select the highest payoff areas for their computer applications rather than the easiest and most obvious. Although clerical displacement cost savings can be measured with ease and accuracy, the greatest benefits of using a computer in government frequently lie elsewhere. They lie in the areas of improved operations where the benefits often appear intangible and are difficult to measure in advance. The following areas of municipal government are illustrative of those that yield the greatest benefits when successfully automated:

- Planning and control of emergency services such as police, fire, rescue, and ambulance.
- Customer services such as permits, licenses, and utilities.
- Traffic engineering and control.
- Inventory control and procurement.
- Construction and maintenance planning, scheduling, and operations of physical facilities such as public buildings, streets, utilities, and parks and recreation facilities.
- Health and hospital services.
- Tax assessment and collection, treasury management and control of revenues, investments, and debt service.

These and similar payoff areas should receive attention and primary emphasis when computer-based systems are being planned and specific projects programmed. Generally, accounting and financial reporting should be viewed as subordinate parts of the main system development thrust. Municipal subsystems in the area of process control, such as traffic signal control or utility operations control, can be implemented in parallel with other operational subsystems since the stress with such systems will be on instrumentation, and different computer equipment, as well as different system implementation talent, will be utilized. However, such systems obviously must be related to the operations activities of which they are a part. They should not be developed in isolation.

Comment

Analysis, conceptualization, and project scheduling generally are carried out sequentially for the full scope of the municipal system. These systems planning tasks result in a complete analysis of information processing activities of the municipal government, a conceptual design or master plan for IMIS, and a plan of projects and project plans for the phased development of IMIS.

SYSTEMS DEVELOPMENT

The task of systems development is aimed at translating the conceptualized system into an operable computer-driven system. It involves detailed systems design, applications programming, procedures and data conversion, and systems implementation. (See Fig. 7.)

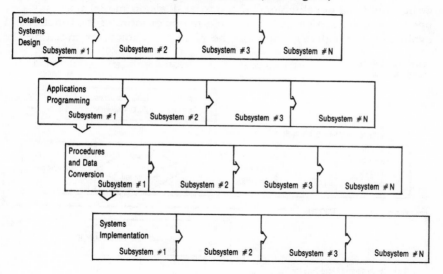

Fig. 7 The elements of systems development.

Detailed Systems Design

Detailed systems design involves specification of information input, processing, and output requirements and the relations among these for each activity to be automated. It requires an understanding not only of how each activity is presently conducted, but also how each should be conducted and how various activities relate to one another.

The notion of decision and decision models is important to detailed systems design. From an information processing standpoint, municipal activities can be viewed as a sequence of "microdecisions," which when modeled are susceptible to complete automation. A model is a representation of a decision or a sequence of decisions. It is a formalization of the relationships that are asserted to exist among data.

In their most complete form, decision models specify the stimuli needed to trigger a decision, the data relevant to predefined choices, the rules for selection among the choices, and the action implications of various choices.

The task in detailed systems design, therefore, is the development of such decision models for each activity to be automated. Figure 8 illustrates two related microdecisions in the tax appraisal area.

Where complete decision models cannot be specified, detailed systems design involves development of a partial decision model that may rely upon a human decision maker to perform one or more of the functions of evaluating alternatives, applying the rules for choice, or initiating the

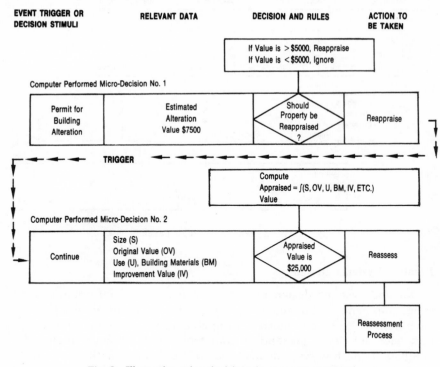

Fig. 8   Illustrative microdecisions in property appraisal.

action implied by the choice. Such partial decision making should be thought of as a man-machine interface. Further, in some cases, it may be impossible to develop even partial decision models. Then the most that can be done is to supply the information deemed relevant or implied by the human decision makers, or to supply a general capability to interact with a data base from which the decision makers might determine which information seems relevant.

The result of detailed system design generally will be a set of documents that contains the following:

1. Definition of the information outputs to be produced. In an automated sequence of decisions, the output from one decision will be the trigger for another. In partially automated decisions, the output definition will include examples of the reports or action notices to be produced and examples of the way in which inquiries will be answered.
2. Definition of the required processing presented in the form of detailed flow charts. These charts will show which data must enter the process, where the data comes from, what is to be done with the data, and how the outputs are to be produced. It will also show what data files are required and how they are to be kept current and used. Finally, it will show what facilities and equipment will be used.

Applications Programming

The way in which a detailed design for a segment of a subsystem is readied for performance on the computer is through the preparation of computer software. Although several different types of software are used in an information system, that of immediate concern to the users is the applications programming. An applications program consists of a set of "computer" instructions and related documentation on how to perform a particular municipal activity. In the terms used in the discussion of detailed systems design, a program is a model of the information processing required to perform the activity. Workable and efficient programs must be prepared before the information system design can be installed and operated. The development of such programs can be and usually is a highly specialized and technical activity, but there are several matters of more general interest to be considered:

1. The programming effort should be coordinated with the detailed design work. Further, programming itself should be integrated. The

past tendency has been to break up the programming staff into different types of programmers working on different applications. The result has been little overall integration and little chance for cooperative accumulation of experience to occur.

2. The particular software developed or used should be within the capability of municipal data-processing personnel to maintain and modify.
3. Programming should be developed on a modular basis to provide for the interchangeability of programs among applications.
4. Uniform standards and procedures for programming are mandatory, and emphasis should be placed on thorough documentation of all programs developed.

Procedures and Data Conversion

Preparation for implementation of the new systems will require the conversion of organizational and manual procedures to conform to the new data-processing system. These procedures relate not only to the details of how data are to be recorded but also when, where, and by whom such recording is to occur. Implementation preparation will also require conversion of the data that is input to the system into machine-readable form. To facilitate this task, techniques of source data automation are often introduced. They include such things as paper tape produced as a by-product of a cash receipting machine, optical scanning devices, data recorders, and portable paper or magnetic tape recorders for meter readings.

Systems Implementation

Systems implementation involves using the information system in actual operations. It is extremely unlikely that a complete system can ever be installed and operated at one time. The organizational impacts would be too great, and the benefits of experience from incremental installation would be lost. Therefore, operational implementation usually is phased on a subsystem component, or module basis. In this context, it is likely that operation of some components will parallel the detailed design and systems development of others.

The various implemented components should be operated for a reasonable period of time during which the full capabilities of the new system are used. Emphasis should be placed on having the potentialities of the system utilized repeatedly by the relevent municipal employees, that is, the users of the system.

The new system must be operated for a time in parallel with the old system. This is done to prevent serious disruption to ongoing operations in the event problems develop with the new system and to provide for comparison of the old and new systems. However, after the new system has been evaluated as successful, care must be taken to insure that the old system is discontinued.

SYSTEMS ADMINISTRATION

Parallel with the systems planning and development tasks are several administrative tasks that occur throughout the IMIS project. These are orientation and training, monitoring and evaluation, and organization and management.

Orientation and Training

Computer-based information systems, whatever their scope, are new to most people in municipal government. Further, municipal EDP personnel require continuous training and development to keep up with the current state of the art of information technology. If outside experts in information systems are involved, they frequently require greater understanding of municipal government and its activities. Potential users require training not only for operation of particular parts of the system developed, but also for understanding sufficient to permit their contribution to the system's adaptation and evolution. The IMIS project, therefore, involves political and executive level orientation, orientation for those within the system environment, training for project personnel and system users, and community education.

Political and Executive Level Orientation
The municipality will need to provide orientation for organizations and key policy-making officials, both inside and outside the municipal jurisdiction, whose cooperation and support are essential to the success of the IMIS project. Within the municipality, these include the legislative body, other elected officials, the chief executive, and key department heads. Support may also be required from similar groups in other local governments and from citizen groups. Thus project orientation will need to address such things as: the objectives and nature of the project; plans for

the conduct of the project; and the various roles, responsibilities, commitments, and actions required.

Orientation for Those Within the System Environment

Orientation also will need to be provided for personnel and organizations directly involved in the project and its resulting system. These people include those municipal employees responsible for operation and maintenance of the developed system, those who will be providing inputs to the system, and those who will be users of the system's products and services.

Such orientations or training sessions are the mechanism by which employees and organizations will be prepared to cope with the impact resulting from implementation of IMIS. It is vitally important that personnel and organizations be ready to accept the changes and to fill their various roles as each increment of the system is implemented. The training or orientation should be so designed as to avoid the disruptive effect of change when it falls too heavily on staff or others who have not been prepared to handle it. A series of courses about computers and information systems might be provided as an integrated part of the orientation effort for different categories of personnel in the municipal organization, for example, clerical, technical, professional, managerial, and others, as appropriate.

Training for Project and System Personnel

Several types of training will have to be provided for technical personnel of the project team and for municipal personnel who will operate and maintain the developed system. Among these are:

- Technical training in systems analysis, decision analysis, system design, programming, equipment operation.
- Use of new procedures, forms, and reports.
- Use of information: retrieval techniques, graphic display, interpretation of data.
- Impact of information system development: strategies of change, and changes affecting personnel, organizations, and functions.
- Use of analytic methods: mathematics, statistics, simulation modeling, operation research, economic analysis, and cost-benefit analysis.

Community Education

A special type of education and information program may be desirable for the community. Such a program may elicit interest and support for the project and establishes a communication vehicle in the event problems develop during implementation. Further, since the citizens are to be the prime ultimate beneficiaries of the new system, they should be continually informed of its objectives and progress.

Monitoring and Evaluation

Monitoring of progress necessarily is required throughout the duration of the IMIS project. It is required for management control and for early detection of problems that retard, or unanticipated successes that advance task completion targets. The tools for monitoring include such things as PERT/CPM, milestone schedules, work performance charts, and cost charts.

Monitoring of organizational and behavioral impacts may also be desirable. This may be formalized through the use of periodic surveys and interviews with municipal personnel, or informal through normal project personnel and training officer contacts with municipal employees. Such monitoring is required to insure that the incidence of change does not fall too heavily on staff and other personnel who are ill-prepared to handle it. Careful observation and small experimentation can be utilized to determine the appropriate rate of change and strategies for introducing change. Acceptance of the project by municipal personnel and citizens is essential to the introduction of the new system into the municipality.

The municipality also will need to undertake self-evaluation of IMIS project objectives, processes, arrangements, progress, and results. Much of this evaluation occurs as a part of ongoing project monitoring. However, formal technical evaluation is also required, preferably by a group outside the IMIS project staff. Technical evaluation involves comparison of planned IMIS capabilities with those actually achieved. It also involves comparison of operations of the new system with the old. The objective here is to test the extent to which planned achievements have been met and to measure the increases in service efficiency and/or effectiveness brought about by the system.

Organization and Management

All of the foregoing activities involved in achieving a satisfactory IMIS require an EDP organizational and managerial capacity within the municipality. As suggested in the earlier discussion on approaches to developing an EDP capacity, the managerial capacity may range from a few individuals who monitor private contracts to a complex consortium of municipal, private, and other public agencies. Further, IMIS projects usually are developed within an existing data processing context that must be considered regardless of the approach taken. This section therefore discusses several organizational and managerial relationships important to IMIS projects: organizational location and status of the IMIS project staff, internal organization of information systems activities in municipal government, IMIS project team, and relationships with other operating municipal units.

Organizational Location and Status of IMIS Project Staff

Traditionally, the data-processing function in municipal government has been located at the third or fourth organizational level. As shown in Fig. 9, a typical organization chart would show the mayor or city manager, finance officer, and manager of data processing. In some instances data processing would be at an even lower level.

This particular location pattern emerged during the days of punched-card tabulating when most of the work was accounting oriented. When computers replaced tabulating equipment, data processing tended to remain under finance even though other departments began using data-

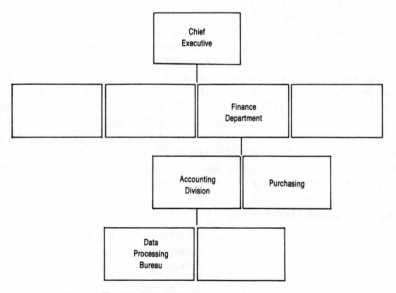

Fig. 9 Traditional location of data-processing activity.

processing services because accounting-type services were considered primary and the major potential use for the technology.

Several problems have resulted from this location pattern:

1. Data processing has been dominated by the functional area in which it is located, usually finance, but also other activities when located elsewhere than finance.
2. Services to functions other than finance have received second place and have been slow to develop.
3. Managers of data processing have had difficulty discussing extension of services with other department heads because proposed extensions must go through the particular parent organization.
4. Data-processing managers have been unable to perform their educational role for other departments because access to other department heads has been limited. These departments, in turn, have been slow to demand service because of their limited knowledge of the technology's potential.

As departmental and top managements have begun to recognize the municipalwide applicability of EDP, it has moved up to the second organizational level. As shown in Fig. 10, the emergent patterns are either departmental status with a director of information systems or staff status directly under the chief executive. The main advantage of these arrangements in addition to facilitating municipalwide service is that data-processing plans can be developed without a particular functional bias and can be coordinated better with other municipal plans.

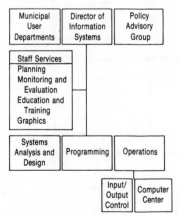

Fig. 10 Internal organization of data-processing activity.

IMIS project teams also appear best located at the level of top management or on a par with other departments. In fact, if the municipality has an existing data-processing organization, the IMIS project should be related to that unit but also maintain some independence. This is to prevent dominance of data-processing operations over the IMIS development activity.

Internal Organization of Data-processing Activities

As shown in Fig. 11, data-processing departments are usually organized on a functional basis and include the following:

- A systems function responsible for analysis and design.
- A programming function.
- An operations function including the computer center and related clerical processing associated with input and output of the computer.
- A management function concerned with management and planning for IMIS, for specific projects, for monitoring and evaluation of project implementation, for education and training, and for outside relations.

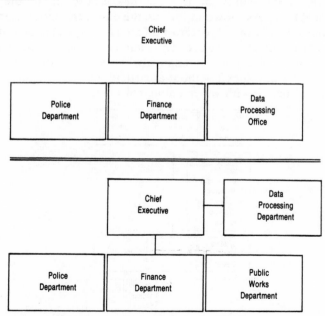

Fig. 11 Newer locations of data-processing activity.

In addition, the data-processing activity must be related to the general government through a committee structure that performs:

- A policy function for guiding IMIS development, obtaining support, and providing outside advice.
- A user function for providing inputs to systems planning and design and for evaluating system effectiveness from the departmental users' standpoint.

The IMIS Project Team

Given a data-processing activity of the scope outlined above, the IMIS project team will be drawn primarily from people within the systems and programming function plus people from the operating departments for whom the system is being designed. These people may be assisted by the municipal training function and by outside consultants, whether individuals or an outside organization.

The IMIS project manager ideally should be a person with broad knowledge of the municipal government, experience in municipal government, and technical knowledge of computers and information systems. This man should be the first hired. He should then be given the task of developing an IMIS and the organizational and administrative capacity required.

Relations with Municipal Operating Units

The operating units of the municipality are the clients of the IMIS project staff. As with other municipal enterprises, however, it is insufficient for the staff to conceive new system projects and then attempt to sell them to the operating units. Such behavior tends to elicit distrust, concern that the new system design will be mediocre, or concern that the system will fail to operate properly when installed.

Experience has shown that project implementation proceeds best when the clientele or users actively participate in system planning and development. In fact, it is likely that IMIS cannot be designed or implemented without participation by professional and high-level people from the operating units. Although the ways in which the clientele may participate are many, three are especially important. The first is as active members of the IMIS project planning. The second is as users, operators, and evaluators during the conversion and testing phases of implementation. The third is as overseers of the project. This role should be performed by the top managers and their assistants in the various city departments.

These people may constitute a technical management advisory committee, or they may constitute a policy board along with other managers, the chief executive, political leaders, and knowledgeable citizens. The primary purpose of this policy and advisory participation is to promulgate understanding of the project, to secure substantive and technical inputs from the operating units, and to insure the system meets operational requirements.

SUMMARY

It should be clear from the discussion in this article that unless IMIS results in real improvements in the management and performance of municipal operating activities, both its development and continued operation will be unjustifiable. Little has been said thus far about the benefits of IMIS. The reason for this is that the subject is so basic to the justification for IMIS that the anticipated benefits of IMIS merit separate discussion.

REFERENCES AND NOTES

1. Readers interested in greater technical discussion are referred to RFP-H-2-70 *Municipal Information Systems*, Washington, D.C.: Department of Housing and Urban Development (July 30, 1969 as amended), and to the books listed in the bibliography.
2. Cornett, William F., Jr. *A Paper on Electronic Data Processing for Cities*, Fullerton, Calif.: City Administrator's Office, (undated), p. 2.
3. Brownlee, Jerry L. and Cooley, Errol H. A city manager looks at the management sciences, *Using Advanced Management Techniques*, Washington, D.C.: Arthur D. Little, Inc. (1968), pp. 4–5.
4. Dial, O. E., Kraemer, Kenneth L., Mitchel, William H. and Weiner, Myron E. *Municipal Information Systems: The State of the Art in 1970*, Washington, D.C.: Department of Housing and Urban Development (1971); Urban Data Service, Malchus Watlington, *ADP in Municipal Government* Washington, D.C.: International City Management Association, Vol. 2, No. 10 (1970).

2

The Need for an Overall Policy for Information Systems and Computer Services in the Public Sector*

B. K. BRUSSAARD

Municipal Computer Center, Rotterdam, Netherlands

1. THE PROBLEM AND ITS CAUSES

Most countries do not have an *overall policy* † for the development and operation of *information systems* ‡ and *computer services* § in the public sector.

The main causes that such an official policy does not exist may be summed up as follows:

Firstly, the different levels and entities of a government structure (central-state/regional-local) have higher or lower degrees of autonomy in a number of aspects. This goes for an even higher extent for (semi) public

---

*Reprinted from the *Proceedings of the World Conference on Informatics in Government*, The IBI–ICC, Florence, Italy, October 1972, pp. 135–140.

†Under an *overall policy* is understood some kind of explicit long-term and short-term planning. The purpose is to avoid duplication in the development of systems and the procurement of information, to provide computer services under optimal economies of scale and above all to supply the information required to coordinate and integrate the public activities in a country.

‡Under *information systems* is understood the whole of information collection, processing, distribution and usage with a more or less permanent and routine character in a given organizational structure. The operation of information systems includes both the technical and the economic management of the systems.

§Under *computer services* is understood the provision of manpower, hardware and software, to develop, implement, operate and maintain information systems. Computer services also include the use of these facilities for purposes of an incidental character in an organizationally indifferent environment (e.g., scientific and technical calculations).

organizations which have a more or less independent status outside the strictly governmental sphere.

Examples are: academic and other educational institutions, postal services, public utilities (energy, transport, etc.).

Even if strong central directives exist, for example, in the fields of personnel and financing, these directives generally do not exist so far in the field of information systems and computer services. If it is tried to provide some guidance in the field of automation this is vehemently opposed with an appeal to exactly this autonomy, however small it may be in general or however irrelevant it may be with respect to information processing.

Secondly and partly as a result of the autonomy complex, there is insufficient knowledge and apprehension of the similarities and connection of information requirements and computer applications in the public sector as a whole. The problems and possibilities are not being investigated because existing organizational units are not interested in looking over their own walls. If they do so, they feel that it might endanger their own freedom of action. Normally there also are no special organizational units which have as a formal task to improve information systems and computer services in the public sector.

Thirdly, organizations controlled by elected politicians have a tendency to be more interested in small but spectacular results at short notice than in long-term goals of a mediate nature and corresponding high investments. As the development and implication of information systems take time and cost a lot of money even to an extent not exactly known beforehand, automation projects tend to rank low on the priority lists of public institutions.

Fourthly and lastly, hardware manufacturers and software suppliers have no interest in national cooperation and coordination in the field of public data processing. From their point of view this might only result in tougher negotiations, higher requirements on the part of their customers in some cases, and in the short run even in lower sales.

2. THE REASONS FOR SOLVING THE PROBLEM

Despite these strong and lasting causes of the lack of an overall policy there are growing and even compelling reasons to come to some form of data-processing policy in the public sector.

These reasons may be summarized as follows:

1. There is an increasing need for coordination and integration of public activities and of management of public activities at all levels and in all sections. This need is growing because the relative and absolute size of the public sector in comparison with the private sector is increasing in almost all countries. Moreover, the diversity and complexity of public activities is increasing at the same time.

   The first prerequisite to cope with these problems is the qualitative improvement of the information, not only to manage existing public agencies and services internally, but above all to tune them in to each other, to the demands of the public, and to the activities of the private sector. Only on the basis of consistent and timely information (statistics, analyses, and prognostics) will it be possible to design feasible policies and to modify them properly according to new developments and requirements.

2. At the same time, and this is often overlooked, a comprehensive information policy would make it possible to maintain and consolidate the in itself desirable autonomy of government levels and organizational entities in spite of the growing complexity and interdependancy of public and private activities. An appropriate measure of decentralization of their responsibilities and powers increases efficiency and flexibility by well known organizational and psychological processes. The decentralization can only be granted without loss of coordination and integration, however, if it can be made sure that the activities at all levels and in all sections of public activity rest on the same basic information. Actually, the deficiency of the information or even the ignorance with respect to the question of which information is required, has in the past often been the reason to centralize the control of activities or the activities themselves. Information systems which fill these needs will strengthen the case of local autonomy and organizational decentralization.

3. The integrated information systems crossing organizational and political borders will improve the service to the general public by faster and simultaneous dealing with matters presently handled at organizationally and geographically dispersed locations. The establishment of "public services centers" where the power-supply company can be dealt with, tax payments can be discussed, the police or social services, etc. may be contacted, are only feasible with the help of information systems which cut across existing organizational walls. Each step in this direction is worthwhile but

can only be taken within the context of an overall long-term outline of a possible future set-up.

4. The coordination of computer services will minimize the cost of data processing itself, at a given level of information quality.

   More important is that at a given cost-level the coordination of computer services will enable maximization of the quality of the information. The improvement of the information quality has its effects not only on the public sector as a whole but also on the internal management of public organizational units. In this last respect there is hardly any difference between public and private organizations. Better information is a way to improve the cost-effectiveness at all operational levels.

The problems are similar in different countries but they are so only in principle. When studying publications on data processing and when investigating automation in the public sector in different countries, it appears to be difficult to compare situations and exchange experiences. It is almost impossible to draw general conclusions from these comparative studies other than the very common ones given above. It is certainly not possible to transfer specific solutions for specific problems, for example, information systems for land-registry. It may be of interest to give some hypotheses on possible causes of this unpleasant situation:

1. The differences in national, economic, and other objective circumstances (size, density, and dispersion of population, employment, etc.) also determine the technical and economic characteristics of information systems.

   Over and above this, the differences in political organization and the diversion in the division of tasks, responsibility and competences (by law and by custom) between and within the public and private sectors determine to a large extent the organizational set-up of computer services and the scope of information systems.

2. There are a lot of difficulties in defining and understanding a common terminology (even when using one natural language, for example, English). Public administration is much more specific and history-bound than industry and business administration. These last ones are relatively new and homogeneous all over the world. Moreover, the international multifunctional companies which bring about a lot of practical dissemination of knowledge and experience in their fields, have no counterpart in the public sectors.

Whatever the exact reasons are of the lack of similarity, we shall have to live and to work with the idea that to a large extent we shall have to find new solutions for our own problems in each of our own countries. Perhaps we may take some comfort, however, from the thought that also in the private sector even within one country, the actual exchange of systems and computer programs did not take a high flight either, despite the fact that the solutions applied are similar to a great extent.

3. DIFFERENT TYPES OF INFORMATION SYSTEMS

When trying to give a certain pattern to a discussion on information requirements in the public sector from the point of view of the users, it is necessary to distinguish different types of information systems.

The first distinction that can be made is between "administrative" information systems and "operational" information systems.

Under administrative information system is understood an information system which is policy oriented.

Under operational information system is understood an information system which is management oriented.

Take for instance information systems which have as their information objects the population or pieces of land or vehicles. If a system is policy oriented there will generally be no interest in identified or identifiable objects. These systems could also be characterized as statistical systems. The information is used for general investigations, for planning purposes, or for the preparation of legislation.

If the system has an operational character, that is, if it is management oriented, there will generally be interest in identified or identifiable objects. These systems could also be characterized as registrational systems. The information is used by operational agencies for the execution or, if necessary, the enforcement of the law, or for rendering services, or supplying products to individual persons and social or economic entities.

The important point is that in the two cases the technical and organizational set-up of the (sub) systems is very different. A lot of controversy in the field of public information systems is the result of insufficiently clear concepts concerning these points. The whole matter is complicated by the fact that one and the same physical collection of information may serve for both purposes. This connection may not only be attractive from an economic point of view but it may also strengthen the quality of the information (correctness and consistency) and the protection of the information (privacy and confidentiality) provided the appropriate organizational and technical measures are taken. This is not the place to analyse the point of protection of the information, see however Ref. 1.

A further subdivision of operational information systems is possible when a distinction is made between systems for:

1. Mainly clerical tasks, for example, tax departments and postal clearing services.
2. Mainly personal services, for example, in education and public health.
3. Mainly operational management, for example, postal services and utilities.

This subdivision can be made much more detailed, eventually ending in a simple enumeration of computer applications related in one or more, rather arbitrarily chosen aspects. The function of such a subdivision is only that sometimes organizations and officials are willing to admit some measure of similarity of information systems in related fields of activity on the basis of such an analysis. A gradual exposition of this similarity, also in organizations which at first sight are rather different, may lead to the conclusion that it could be worthwhile to cooperate and integrate.

More fundamental is the distinction between dedicated or goal-oriented systems (e.g., for hospitals or schools or electricity companies) and means-oriented or general application systems (e.g., personnel or material systems or more general work order and budget systems). The distinction is more fundamental because at some phase each information policy has to take the decision to what extent general goal- or means-oriented systems are going to be developed for certain groups of agencies. The choice cannot be made on the basis of technical and economic considerations only. Organizational and psychological considerations may make it desirable to accept some degree of duplication. It is certainly not so that for the whole of an organizational unit either the goal- or the means-oriented structure has to be chosen. A certain mix may be optimal, for example, the information set-up in hospitals or schools may be means-oriented for personnel (especially payments) and goal-oriented for patient care and pupil administration. In these same examples the goal-oriented systems, can be connected again with an integrated population system. Means-oriented systems have a wider application field than the goal-oriented systems, as the latter can only be used in the same type of organizations. Goal-oriented systems for different types of organization may on the other hand at least partly deal with the same information on the same information objects (e.g., individuals). Means-oriented systems may be generally applicable but the information need not be the same and they need not be related in the objects. For both types of systems use can often be made of the same hardware, hard software, and specialized personnel.

An information policy should therefore comprise at least the following aspects: hardware, hard software, and personnel; information systems themselves (designs, programs, working instructions, and so on); and the information itself. Each foregoing step may be to some extent a prerequisite for the next one.

From the point of view of the system-designer, entirely different distinctions are relevant but these are not discussed here any further. These technical distinctions are closely related to technical subjects such as data-base management and equipment configurations and directly derived from response-time requirements, the geographical dispersion of information sources and user locations, and above all from quantitative descriptions of data files and their use.

4. SOME HINTS FOR SOLVING THE PROBLEMS

Some practical starting points for the formulation and the execution of a policy for information systems and computer services can be indicated as follows:

1. A long-term plan for the structure of information systems and computer services (organizationally, technically, and financially) should be developed gradually. It could start with a simple non-detailed but comprehensive enumeration of existing plans which is often lacking now. It could end in at least a consistent overall picture of a possible future structure against which new decisions can be checked.

2. A gradual development should keep an even pace with the possibilities to maintain the plan both with regard to the description of the actual situation at a certain moment, and with regard to the development and modification of existing plans. Apart from a very general and rough overall picture, it is better to leave some sectors of public activity out of the consolidation of plans and the formulation of policies than to lose contact with reality.

3. Agencies developing isolated activities on their own should be stimulated to cooperate. They should be coordinated by all possible budgetary means and by conditional subsidies or by legislation and other directives including the modification of existing ones, wherever applicable. It is not wise to rely on one way of bending a situation in a desired direction, for example, by legislation only. All permitted means should be used simultaneously, for example, penetration of courses of lectures or other internal or external schemes for training or refreshing personnel of public institutions. Also the conscious use of rotation schemes and career plans to get informed and capable persons on important and crucial points in the organization can advance integration considerably.

4. All standard organizational criteria for deciding on the decentralization problem in the field of computers should be applied (Ref. 2). Economies of scale could be optimal in large centralized existing entities such as universities and transport or port authorities.

   In those cases it should be considered to leave them out of overall policy plans but even in these cases proper attention should also be given to: the agreement of their basic policy data with other public activities; the optimalization of services to the general public including those of other agencies; and the avoidance of duplication of efforts as long as it does not interfere with the active participation of the organizations involved.

5. In theory and in practice the notion should be disseminated that the activities of public organizations can be connected, integrated, and coordinated by information. In the field of information processing this may affect the autonomy of an operational entity, but it is a prerequisite to maintain autonomy in other fields, and it promotes the ultimate goal of public activities as a whole. Therefore, and not for economical reasons only, the development and operation of information systems and computer services cannot be left solely within the competence of individual public organizational entities themselves.

Reference 1

Central government is not and should not be interested in information on individually identifiable persons. Agencies responsible for certain fields of activity should only have access to the information relevant for their work, etc. These and other requirements can be worked out and fulfilled. For a general analysis see:

Brussaard B. K., *Computer Management and the Protection of Privacy.* Conference book of Computer Management, 1972, Amsterdam (IFIP Administrative Data Processing Group), pp. 43–46.

Mindlin Albert, Confidentiality and local information systems, *Public Administration Review*, November/December 1968, pp. 509–517.

Reference 2

The problems connected with centralization of computer facilities are thoroughly discussed in:

Kordes F. G., Policy on automation in government departments—Centralization or decentralization of computers, *IAG Journal*, Vol. 3, No. 2 (1970), pp. 179–203.

Glaser George, The centralization versus decentralization issue: Arguments, alternatives and guidelines, *IAG Journal*, Vol. 4, No. 1 (1971), pp. 15–28.

3

Teleprocessing the Computer and Public Administration: The Search for Policy*

S. J. BERNSTEIN AND L. E. HOXIE

*Dept. of Public Administration, Baruch College Cuny,
The City University of New York, New York, N.Y.*

Litton Communications, Melville, Long Island, New York

I. INTRODUCTION

Effective computer utilization, in the formulation of economic and social policies, is an indispensible part ᴏ⌣ ⌐ional planning. Effective utilization has its impact upon the planning process in two dimensions: (1) information systems, and (2) analytical planning aids. These dimensions are interrelated in that the first speaks to the organization of data and the second provides the means of converting the data into improved intelligence for public policy making and services of delivery. This is accomplished by: increasing the scope of information available for planning purposes; increasing the flexibility in planning permitted by the greater interaction between planners and their data; increasing the utilization of analytical decision aids by enhancing the data-base accessibility necessary for planning, policy analysis, and evaluation.

This paper attempts to show a way of building a teleprocessing capability in an orderly and economically advantageous way to enhance public administration with full awareness of the potential differences between them.

---

*This article to a large measure is based on previous study: Computer communications and the developing nations: The search for policy, *Proceedings of the World Conference on Informatics in Government*, The IBI-ICI, Florence, Italy, October 1972, pp. 87–95.

44

Specific emphasis is on: reviewing the present experience and the state of the art with respect to fulfilling computer communications of governments; indicating the gap between present public policies toward this new synergistic technology of computer communications and actual conditions reflecting the degree of successful policy implementation; and outlining policy and organizational recommendations for achieving requisite levels of information transfer capabilities in the decades of the 70s and 80s while always keeping the cost-efficiency factor fully visible.

II. BACKGROUND CONDITIONS

The movement of information through airwave, cable and/or hybrid systems either via CRTS, data-phone, computer audible signals, etc. occupies an increasing portion of computer research and development budgets. The purpose of this added investment in recent years is geared to significantly increasing the effectiveness and credibility of automated equipment in aiding complex problem solving, decision making, data processing and information retrieval, and dissemination in both the private and public sectors. The derivative benefit may be said to be the improvement of business and governmental performance.

The very general nature of the above statements embraces a variety of particular activities involved with computer communications and conceals their highly interrelated technical, socio-economic, and even political ramifications for public policy-making purposes. Three basic issues, however, may be said to summarize the problems confronting governments with regard to developing and managing computer communications capability. In each, guidelines for the formulation of public policy is required.

1. Equipment capability, compatibility, and reliability.
2. Uncontrolled development of computer communications systems and programs, and the underutilization of available resources.
3. Communication needs of different entities—individual, industrial, and governmental—which cannot be satisfied.

One, dimensioning measures for teleprocessing capability, compatibility, and reliability are essential. Grading systems in terms of criteria representing each dimension in pre- and post-procurement phases, then become the information base for rating present and planning future computer and teleprocessing capacities.

Two, upon this base national plans may be formulated that emphasize the efficient utilization of resources in expanding present equipment and system capabilities. To accomplish this, different resource allocation models, utilizing the above criteria, are to be developed and utilized by the requisite governmental planning and regulatory agencies concerned with teleprocessing.

Three, the need here is for policy provisions which insure the fulfillment of private industrial, interindustrial, public agency, and interagency computer communications resources. This requires a governmental undertaking encompassing several tasks. The first task is the categorization of existing computer communications resources and capabilities. A second is the establishment of a related information mechanism whereby existing as well as future computer communication needs may be examined from the perspective of total present and projected future capacity. A third requires the determination of the "interoperability" of various computer communications systems and users such that common-user systems, based on common-carrier principles, may be considered feasible alternatives for maximizing the utilization of large-scale information transfer systems as well as their investment utility. Special relevance must be ascribed to this recommendation for state and local governments with limited development capital.

In addition to these policy requirements, there are organizational requisites that must be considered by governmental administrations if effective computer communications policies, described by the parameters above, are to be successfully implemented. This primarily involves the establishment of an institutional focal point within a national government for assessing, coordinating, planning, and effecting computer communication developments. The specific charges to this governmental commission or agency for accomplishing these objectives are:

1. Interfacing governmental and private institutional computer communications needs.
2. Establishing procedures for rating and categorizing computer communications uses for allocation of available resources.
3. Formulating investment policies for expanding information transfer capacity.
4. Designing a masterplan for future needs which also considers relevant tradeoffs over time.

At present there is a significant gap between the technological capabilities of teleprocessing and its utilization. The benefit to narrowing this gap stems from the fact that in large-scale organizations, teleprocessing is one of the basic models for improving communications and control. By improved use of telecommunications, therefore, it is possible to increase governments planning, management, and service delivery capacities.

To accomplish this, it is necessary to begin with the consideration of the integrated administrative requirements within government to be charged with promulgating a comprehensive national computer communications policy. To be realistic about organizational requirements first demands an awareness that government administrative capabilities, computer capacities (machine and manpower), and communication utilization vary. Teleprocessing policy, therefore, must be flexible, pragmatic, and functionally specific to the needs of individual governmental units. This is a most significant factor because there is a tendency in organizational analysis to ignore local technical, social, and economic needs and to imitate so-called "super computer and teleprocessing systems." These latter systems, although functional, may bring little appreciable benefits in computer communications capability above what simpler and less expensive communication transfer systems, more fitting to local needs and conditions, can provide although the pressure is always to copy the larger and more sophisticated "supersystems."

In the following pages a package plan for formulating and implementing telecommunications policy for national, state, and local governments is described predicated on the conditions and requisites indicated above.

III. THE POLICY PLAN

A. The Establishment of an Administrative Focal Point in Government

At present, there exists few organizational focal points within government to coordinate teleprocessing. Although multiagency responsibility does exist for government-wide management of automatic data processing and telecommunications respectively, there is little planning and regulation of the interface problems of computers and teleprocessing. For example, the Federal Communications Commission as well as the Office of Telecommunications Policy in the United States Government are primarily concerned with communications media and usage but not with the transmission of information. At the national level in the United States, this administrative gap is in part attenuated by private enterprise which has the financial power to undertake the research, development, and *implementation* of computer communications systems itself (e.g., data-net). However, because unbridled competition may lead to uneconomical results in terms of inferior installations it is essential to establish a Telecommunications Commission. The charge of this Commission is to plan and manage the national development of combined data processing and telecommunications capacities nationally, regionally, and locally.

The structure of the agency is to be tied to all other governmental agencies presently utilizing or planning to utilize computer and/or telepro-cessing capacity. This is to be accomplished by drawing up a planning board in the agency whose membership is constituted by representative directors of all these other units. Consistent across-the-board planning and implementation of supporting policy programs at all governmental levels is thereby achieved. Diagramatically this may be shown as follows:

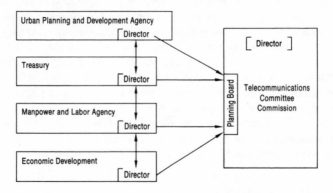

Fig. 1

The general powers of the planning board are to set, investigate, and define the policy parameters for the development of computer communi-cations systems.

B. The Policy Parameters

1. Identifying and satisfying government agency and interagency as well as private computer communication needs.
2. Assessing present government agency and private utilization of the government's overall computer communication systems.
3. Determining the value of the computer communication resources to different government, private and/or shared users.
4. Identifying, combining, and reconciling needs of similar computer communication usage programs.

5. Establishing a single cohesive direction for computer communication policy efforts by establishing the managerial framework for coordinating the various proposed computer communication policies of different users and promulgating an overall national computer communication policy.
6. Assuring the most economical and efficient design and mix of computer facilities, transmission media, switching capabilities, and other computer communication system components.
7. Integrating the procurement and utilization of computer communication systems and equipment and fostering the development of "common-carrier" type computer communications systems.

C. The Formation of Performance Data Bases

In order to effectively consider these parameters in formulating an enlightened teleprocessing policy, a correlated computer communications data base must be organized. The data base is to provide a series of consistent information points to determine:

1. What has been accomplished to date in terms of adding capacity?
2. What is presently being done?
3. What future decisions have to be made?
4. A detailed course of action to effect policy realizations must be developed.

The object than may be said to give the Teleprocessing Commission an ongoing profile of national computer communications resources, how they are evolving over time, and a means for management of future growth. Further, this over-time profile provides evaluation standards for performance of computer communications equipment and systems: that is, whether or not equipment and systems are meeting desired or specified needs and how experience on present performance vis-a-vis previously specified needs may be used to improve future definition of needs.

IV. AN INTEGRATED POLICY PROCESS

The administrative and policy components indicated above were described as part of the workings of an established governmental commission. In this last section we consider the necessary "start-up" phases. An initial comprehensive study is recommended at the outset focusing on: (1) the manpower and organizational requisities of the Telecommunications Commission and its locus within overall governmental administration, and (2) the policy making and implementing functions of this Commission in conjunction with the informational requisites for government teleprocessing activities.

The staffing for this project would come from various governmental computer and/or communications users, relevant university departments (like mathematics), computer and social sciences, and private industry. This grouping is to serve in a monitoring and joint research capacity with various outside computation and communication consulting groups and expert persons for analyzing the factors described above and establishing the importance and expected utility of the information base on these factors in building a particularly suited teleprocessing policy and activities for the nation in question.

The strategic reasons for the study as a first step are twofold: (1) defining information that may be considered indispensible for effective policy planning and administration of the Telecommunications Commission, and (2) the political ease of justifying and implementing the recommendations of a committee study encompassing the various vested interests in computer communications or teleprocessing.

Providing this useful base of information for policy definition and practical planning involves six stages.

Stage I   Definition of Current Status of Government Computer Communication Activities

This stage would be designed to determine the current nature and extent of computer communications usage within government. In other words, to find out exactly what the government's interests are. With the enormous range of government computer teleprocessing system possibilities, it is essential to begin with existing systems and the identification of policy-related problems currently being experienced. In this way, the strengths and weaknesses of currently operating computer communication systems can be identified so that policy formulation pertinent to subsequent technological and developmental efforts can be concentrated on areas where such policies will most likely be immediately productive. Such data would also be needed to determine the areas where certain communication computer specifications or standards may be required and to decide in what manner certain teleprocessing functions should be performed when designing future, or integrating with existing, communication computer systems.

Another aspect of this problem definition stage would be a review of existing and potential economic and social issues as they might impact upon the government's reliance on its teleprocessing resources. Also to be determined, would be the government's dependence upon non- or quasi-governmental common-carrier systems, as well as an assessment of the government's current utilization of its computer communication.

Stage II Definition of Future Status of Government's Computer Communication Activities

Stage II would be designed to gather information pertaining to existing potential government computer communication applications and the nature of their respective operating needs for unique, as opposed to shared, usage of teleprocessing systems. This phase would also assess information concerning how existing communication computer functions are being performed by government agencies and their ability to handle such functions in the future. Thus, the computer communication capabilities and support requirements of existing systems, as well as those needed in the future, should be obtained. Further, an assessment would be made of existing government agency organizational capabilities to support policy level decisions in the computer communications area. Study, during this stage, would also obtain information on any major constraints that might exist in the area of teleprocessing in terms of existing policy, systems, future systems, interagency/industrial coordination, and current economic and social issues.

Stage III Development of Computer Communications Policy Alternative Courses of Action

This stage would be designed to answer what and why something need and should be done. Alternative courses of action would be formulated and the rationale for each would be developed, based on the information obtained in Stages I and II. From this data, policy makers would be able to gain an understanding of the need and justification for specific policy actions in certain areas. Of particular interest in this stage of the study would be the analysis of any existing constraints (i.e., future satellite communication system usage) and their potential impact on the government's computer communication interests. This information would be most useful in determining official government positions on these various issues and justifying courses of action that would mitigate their impact on computer communications policy formulation efforts.

Stage IV   Development of Policy Supporting Managerial Responsibilities and Organizatorial Relationships Within Government

Stage IV would be designed to bring into focus the various managerial responsibilities, which must exist within government, to insure the support, consistency, and administration of formulated computer communications policy. Emphasis, in this stage, would be placed on the determination and analysis of the most viable organizational format for utilization of the computer communications resource, in terms of providing unique and/or common computer communication services to government users. From this analysis, policy supporting requirements and organizational relationships would then be structured in such a way as to meet government demands for computer communication systems and services and yet be consistent with the government's computer communications resource capabilities.

Stage V   Development of a Recommended Course of Action

Stage V would be designed to tie together all of the foregoing stages. A recommended course of action would be developed, in terms of selecting a direction and determining an approach through which the government's computer communications resource can be structured, allocated, and controlled so as to maximize its use and effectiveness. The recommended course of action effort would be based on the information gathered, an analysis of the most viable alternatives, and a listing of specific actions affecting future policy that must be taken now, including the formulation of key government position papers.

Stage VI   Documentation, Oral Presentation, Consultation

Stage VI would be designed to present the information gathered in the proposed study effort in such a way as to assist interested government officials in the formulation of viable, enlightened, and comprehensive computer communications policy. Emphasis in the report would be on:

1. Establishment of organization mechanisms through which inter-agency unanimity of purpose can be achieved.
2. The gathering of information on:
   a. Current and future computer communication needs.
   b. Regulatory implications for local, regional, and national systems.
   c. Equipment and systems trade-offs.
   d. Inventory of current computer communication operations, coun-

tries, and technological forecasts of equipment and service demand.
3. The analyzing of such information, in terms of improved governmental interrelationships with society.

V. CONCLUSION

The search for a national computer communications or teleprocessing policy is a fairly complex and complicated endeavor. First, because it involves massive governmental organizational elements. Second, because it impacts on almost every large-scale economic segment of the society. Third, because it involves relatively large scale investments over longer time ranges for the developing nations. The present paper is an attempt to conceptualize planning/implementing procedures for effectively coping with some of the organizational and policy problems in developing computer communication capacity for governments—national, state, and local. Our emphasis in this regard is general, aiming to sketch the guidelines leaving detailed and more in-depth discussion for individual governmental limits. These guidelines should be utilized to insure the orderly and economically advantageous use and growth of computer telecommunications use for improved public service.

We see some of the benefits from this approach as coming in the following areas:

1. An increased understanding of teleprocessing leads to more flexibility for policy makers in planning and monitoring public agency performance and thereby improved living conditions.
2. The present national, state, and local inventories in both hardware and software computer communications may be determined as leading to more sharing through teleprocessing grids and thereby leading to greater cost effectiveness in the utilization of computers.
3. A guide for the formulation of a comprehensive teleprocessing policy is shown which incorporates socio-economic and political conditions as well as direct technical conditions.
4. The need for matching equipment sophistication with actual and projected teleprocessing requirements is shown.
5. The ways to avoid the problems, pitfalls, setbacks, and resultant policy vacuums, which until the present have been characteristic of building computer and computer-related capabilities in government, are shown. A shorter time frame for effecting the benefits of teleprocessing capability thus may be expected.

REFERENCES

Friend, J. K. and Jessop, W. N., *Local Government and Strategic Choice*, Taverstock/Sage, London, 1969.

Hinrichs, H. H. and Taylor, Graeme M., *Programming Budgetting and Benefit-Cost Analysis*, Goodyear Publ. Co., Pacific Palisades, California, 1969.

Information for A Changing Society: Some Policy Considerations, OECD, Paris 1971, 48 pp.

Tinbergen, Jan, *Development Planning*, McGraw-Hill, New York, 1967, 256 pp.

MacBride, Robert O., *The Automated State*, Chilton Book Co., Philadelphia, 1967.

Thomas, U., *Computerized Data Banks in Public Administration*, OECD, Paris, 1971, 68 pp.

Implications and Questions

It would seem that proposing an overall computer development policy is a self-evident imperative. Experience, however, has shown few empirical referents that satisfy this condition. Reasons often cited for this failure include lack of funds, competent personnel, central control, and resistance to change. As indicated in the introduction, however, the underlying reason for all of this is the basic lack of commitment to coordinated development of computer systems. The first two readings in the present chapter attempted to show the organizational way for overcoming this basic difficulty. The latter of the two (Brussaard) reported on the already full operating computer system of the Dutch Municipalities: a format of which is being used by the Local Government's Data-Processing Authority of Israel and in part by the States of Pennsylvania and California. The last article (Bernstein and Hoxie) focuses on the role of teleprocessing—a relatively new synergistic technology, which interfaces with the computer, adding tremendous flexibility for management.

The rationale from the public policy perspective for this discussion is that a comprehensive cooperative approach to information systems is proposed which highlights the problems of meeting the varied technological as well as organizational concerns in building a sophisticated computer and related teleprocessing systems for public agencies. From these readings, a set of policy implications may be indicated for both the professional administrator as well as the student in regard to the development of information systems for public agencies.

(1) Any policy for the development of computer and computer-related management information systems in the public sector must account for the organizational and "background" differences that characterize public agencies. Although the problems in government *A* requiring computerization for improvement seem similar to the problems in government *B*, it is difficult to compare situations beyond their theoretical levels. Packaged solutions without modifications by and large, therefore, are not to be favored. The readings in this chapter, similarly, are pitched at the general level to emphasize effective *common approaches* to management information problems in public organizations rather than on *common solutions* that have been used effectively elsewhere. It is for the reader to consider these approaches as guidelines for developing policies appropriate to the specifications of his or her own management information systems problems.

(2) Organizational planning is an essential ingredient for the completion of public agency management information systems. Planning must contain the necessary flexibility for retooling the system without a complete overhaul for each contemplated technological as well as organizational change. Emphasis should be given to two factors: the expansion factor, which permits additions to the system in terms of new programs and new organizational subunits; and the cooperation factor, which encourages various agencies to cooperate in developing shared uses. For example, teleprocessing may be used in this regard as the conduit for sharing existent large-scale computer systems and for the formation of common data bases to be shared by different management groups, thereby minimizing costs stemming from present duplications.

(3) Successful planning organizationally, technically, and financially should proceed incrementally but should be based on a master plan that clearly describes present operations in each of the sections, departments, and/or agencies interfacing with a new information system.

An outline of planning technique for diagnosing and projecting information needs for management is provided below. It is called the Diagnostic Study/Planning Concept* and aims to provide management with a complete approach to systems development planning; that is, providing management with an effective basis for decision making and controllable implementation.

The approach is constituted by two major components: a *survey* having three subcomponents, and a *profile* being a two-part written report.

The *survey* is the initial phase of the Diagnostic Study during which data is collected, and after analysis, classified and arranged to establish, as equitably and accurately as possible, the basis for recommendations, suggested implementation, and management techniques.

The survey encourages and promotes participation so that all participants feel completely involved in the study as well as committed to the subsequent recommendations for implementation. The survey has three levels of participation (*presentation, group interviews*, and *individual interviews*) and allows for a detailed examination of the situation as it currently stands at the time of the study, coupled with an exploration and analysis of an agency's organizational and suborganizational future needs.

---

*This approach to Management Information Systems was originally developed by S. C. Naggar Associates, Management Consultants, New York City and the author is grateful to Mr. Serge Naggar, President, for permitting the utilization of these ideas.

The *presentation*, made to all participants, outlines the purpose of the study—to develop computer-based Management Information Systems—and describes the way the survey will be conducted. During the presentation and to reinforce it, an explanatory booklet is distributed. This written summary of the oral presentation provides each participant with dialogue forms which they are encouraged to fill out whenever they have a thought, problem, or opinion concerning the study. This initial presentation is the first exposure participants are given to the survey and it is important to their subsequent enthusiasm and participation.

Dialogues submitted as a result of the presentation tend to focus primarily on the everyday problems and irritants faced by the participants while performing their function. Besides providing a controlled outlet-channel for their problems and an excellent sample of the current situation, this level of the Survey promotes and sustains participation.

The *group interview* is a confidential interview with a group of up to 15 participants with similar functional interests. Group interviews considerably widen the scope and depth of our analysis due to the stimulation provided by the group in the discussion controlled by our consultant. After a group interview, its participants are given the opportunity to express themselves privately and on an individual basis during a short confidential interview with the interviewer.

The *individual interview* is a private and confidential in-depth interview with individual participants, generally, selected by management and an outside interviewer/consultant. Individual interviews provide a broadened scope and increased analytical understanding to systems problems. This stems from the private and confidential nature of the exchange between the politically uninvolved interviewer/consultant and the individual participant who is either in a management or decision-making position.

When it is impractical to interview all the participants, a representative sample is interviewed. In this case, the individuals selected for interview are usually among the decision-making groups and those who have shown a special interest, aptitude or imagination in their work, especially as it related to the objectives of the Diagnostic Study for new systems development.

All interviews follow a predetermined discussion format based upon the objectives of the study and the participants' job functions. To provide our consultant with some background-interview information, participants are asked to complete and return, prior to their interview, a confidential form describing their function.

The *profile* is the two-part written report of the Diagnostic Study. The first or summary part presents an overall synthesis of the situation and highlights the most important concepts of the study. The second part, presented as a series of decision modules, is devoted to a very detailed analysis of each subject examined during the survey.

Each decision module in the profile provides the reader with a complete and documented analysis of the subject, a clear-cut recommendation, and a thorough discussion of the likely implementation consequences. As a result, policy makers can independently evaluate the implications of each recommendation prior to making a decision and to committing any resources.

The structure of the profile is ideally suited to permit management to take overall as well as incremental (module-by-module) decisions with full knowledge of their consequences including the probable reactions of the participants and future users toward a proposed recommendation. It is also structured so that all levels of participants and future users become involved, on a selective basis, in some portions of the decision making (i.e., selected decision modules); as a result, changes important to specific participants can be made to certain modules without destroying the overall validity of the profile. This limited decision-making ability contributes largely to winning the approval and cooperation of the participants and future users in the subsequent implementation phase.

The key elements to our Diagnostic Study are our ability and experience to promote participation; interview effectively; analyze, synthesize, and present results in an objective, unbiased, pragmatic, controllable, and implementable manner while guaranteeing all participants full confidentiality, and the agency a maximum of analytical coverage to proceed intelligently with the introduction of MIS without disruption to present operations.

In conclusion, the student should be aware of three basic questions in systems development:

1. Is there a plan for developing Management Information Systems which adequately accounts for the specifications of the particular organizational context?
2. Will a new computer-based information system significantly help improve performance and productivity and where?
3. Are the projections and estimates for planned utilization realistic?

In the following chapters various computer information systems are reported which show how the computer may help in both the internal management and the administration of public agency functions.

Selected Bibliography

ARTICLES

Boettinger, Henry M. People and systems—The creative tension, *S.A.M. Advanced Management Journal* (Society for the Advancement of Management), Vol. 34, No. 1 (January 1969), 35–44.

Brodey, Warren M. and Lindgren, Nilo, Human enhancement: Beyond the machine age, *IEEE Spectrum* (Institute of Electrical and Electronics Engineers), Vol. 5, No. 2 (February 1968), 9–93.

Brown, J. R. The effect of automation on organization, *Air University Review* (July–August 1967), 64–67.

European computer conference, *European Review*, Vol. 20, (Spring 1970), pp. 15–16.

Haak, Harold H. The evolution of a metropolitan data system, *Urban Affairs Quarterly*, Vol. 3, No. 2 (December 1967), 3–13.

Parker, John K. Closing the intelligence gap, *Public Management*, Vol. 50, No. 7 (July 1968), 170–171.

BOOKS

Aa, H. J. van der, ed. *International Computer Bibliography: a Guide to Books on the Use, Application and Effect of Computers in Scientific, Commercial, Industrial, and Social Environments*, Amsterdam, Netherlands, Stichting het Nederlands studiecentrum voor informatica, 1971.

Apter, Michael, *Computer Simulation of Behavior*, New York, N.Y.: Harper and Row, 1971.

Beshers, James M. *Computer Methods in the Analysis of Large-Scale Social Systems*, Massachusetts Institute of Technology Joint Center for Urban Studies Services, MIT Press, 1968.

Boore, William F. and Murphy, G. *Computer Sampler Management Perspectives on the Computer*, New York, N. Y.: McGraw-Hill, 1968.

Bowen, Howard R. and Mangum, Garth L., eds. *Automation and Economic Progress*, Englewood Cliffs, N.J.: Prentice-Hall, 1966, 170 pp.

Braffort, P. and Hirschberg, D., eds. *Computer Programming and Formal Systems*, Amsterdam, Netherlands: North Holland Humanities Press, 1963.

Clarke, Robin, ed. *Computer Revolution*, New York, N.Y.: Dutton, 1973.

Computers in the Public Service: An Annotated Bibliography 1966–69, Chicago, Ill.: Public Automated Systems Service, 1969.

Cross, Hershner, *Computers and Management*, Boston: Harvard University Graduate School of Business Administration, 1967, 121 pp.

Dutton, J. M. and Starbuck, J. R. *Computer Simulation of Human Behavior*, New York, N.Y.: Wiley and Sons.

Emerick, Jr., Paul L. and Wilkinson, Joseph W. *Computer Programming for Business and Social Science*, Homewood, Ill.: Irwin, 1970.

Fry, T. F. *Computer Appreciation*, New York, N.Y.: Philosophical Lib., 1972.

Gould, I. H. *IFIP Guide to Concepts and Terms in Data Processing*, Montvale, N.J.: American Federation of Information Processing Systems Publications, 1971.

Harris, Roy D. and Maggard, Michael J. *Computer Models in Operations Management,* New York, N.Y.: Harper and Row, 1972.
Henley, J. P. *Computer-Based Library and Information Systems,* New York, N.Y.: American Elsevier, 1970.
Hollingdale, S. H. and Toothill, G. C. *Electronic Computers,* Baltimore, Md.: Penguin Books, 1970.
Hull, T. E. and Day, D. D. *Computers and Problem Solving,* Reading, Mass.: Addison-Wesley, 1969.
Kochenburger, Ralph J. *Computer Simulation of Dynamic Systems,* Englewood Cliffs, N.J.: Prentice-Hall, 1972.
Martin, Francis F. *Computer Modeling and Simulation,* New York, N.Y.: Wiley and Sons, 1968.
Martin, James T. and Norman, Adrian, R. *Computerized Society,* Englewood Cliff, N.J.: Prentice-Hall, 1970.
Morrill, Jr., Chester, *Computers and Data Processing Information Sources,* Detroit, Mich.: Gale Research Co., 1969.
Moy, Roland F. *Computer Simulation of Democratic Political Development:* A Test of the *Lipset and Moore Models,* Beverly Hills, Calif.: Sage, 1971.
Nikolaieff, George A. *Computers and Society,* Boston, Mass.: Wilson Hill Co., 1970.
Rose, Michael, *Computers, Managers and Society,* Baltimore, Md.: Penguin Books, 1970.
Rosenberg, Jerry M. *Computer Prophets,* New York, N.Y.: Macmillan, 1969.
Schumacher, Bill, G. *Computer Dynamics in Public Administration,* New York, N.Y.: Spartan, 1967.
Shaffer, William R., ed. *Computer Simulations of Voting Behavior,* New York, N.Y.: Oxford University Press, 1972.
Smith, John. *Computer Simulation Models,* New York, N.Y.: Hafner, 1968.
Snow, C. P. *Public Affairs,* New York, N.Y.: Scribner, 1971.

MONOGRAPHS

Council of State Governments, *Interstate Conference on Automatic Data Processing:* Its *Impact on Public Policy and Service,* RM-386. Lexington, Ky.: CSG, 1965, 168 pp.
National Commission on Technology, Automation, and Economic Progress. *Statements Relating to the Impact of Technological Change:* Appendix Volume VI, Washington, D.C.: Government Printing Office, 1966, 309 pp.

CHAPTER II

Managerial Administrative Areas

It is a frequently forgotten truism that from the perspective of management, information has value not for what it is but for what it improves the doing of: that is, the effectiveness and efficiency of management and organizational performance and productivity. The principal basis for developing computer applications in public administration is to increase the effectiveness, efficiency, and economy of government. In sum, improved public services delivery should flow from the increased effectiveness. This comes about by improving the two generic managerial functions: information gathering and selection; and information comparison.

Improvement in *information gathering and selection* in public management is achieved by the computer in the following four areas:

1. Lowering the costs of present information-handling in the public organization.
2. Improving the processing of available data and information.
3. Increasing decision makers' accessibility to information for better decision making.
4. Reducing the unavailability of required information.

The quality of information processing by computer similarly has improved dramatically through the increased speed, sureness, scope, simplicity, selectivity, sophistication, and even the security of data handling. Improved accessibility, notably, has come about through fast response terminals and on-line systems. Increased information needs, the high cost of data maintainance, and data security still, however, remain great challenges for the cost-effective introduction of computers in the support of management process and systems in the public sector.

Improvement in the *information comparison* function of public management through computerized operations is based on the contribution which EDP may make to:

1. Recognition of organizational problems or opportunities.
2. Planning, analysis, and problem solving.
3. Decision making.
4. Evaluation of agency performance on decisions.

In both the information selection and comparison functions of management it should be emphasized that the computer contributions flow from the expression *contribute to* rather than *perform*. Computerization alone does not execute any of the management processes. EDP provides the improved information base for acting. In this capacity it plays a supportive but crucial role.

The following articles contain examples of current computer applications relevant to the internal managerial processes of public agencies. Emphasis is on how organization performance is improved through information gathering and information comparison functions. Mr. Østergaard begins with a discussion of the improved local government performance resulting from a Management Information System for Aalborg, Denmark, a small city of 156,000 persons. The potential for improved functioning of large urban government—New York City—is then shown by Messrs. Savas and Amsterdam in the GIST Management System. These two are juxtaposed to show how computers may help in two dramatically different governmental contexts. A public Personnel and Financial System for public administration is then shown and lastly the question of how to gain organizational efficiency in large-scale public sector applications in the development stage is addressed by Mr. Tiffin.

4

Design of Public Information Systems: I. Principles and Implications*

S. DUUS ØSTERGAARD

IBM, Copenhagen, Denmark

1. INTRODUCTION

In the Scandinavian countries as well as in most industrialized Western countries the last 25 years have seen marked increases in that part of the gross national income which is being spent by the public sector. This fact is partly due to the increased demand for social and educational services as well as the need for construction of costly transportation facilities.

In Denmark this development and the trends up to 1985 have been investigated by a committee headed by the director of the treasury. According to this report, a conservative estimate indicates that in 1985, 50% of the labor force will be employed by the public, and about 60% of the national income will be used for public purposes. The report emphasizes, however, that these figures will be vastly underestimated unless an effort is being made to reduce the rate of increase in public spending.

The most significant conclusion is that an appropriate allocation of the resources depends on the provision of an effective tool of control. It is pointed out that one of the major reasons for the increase in public spending during the past decade has been the lack of a total overview and the need to reinforce national planning agencies.

To quote the report:

> The information that is available to the departments—and thus to government and parliament—is in many cases obviously incomplete and subject to excessive delays. In many cases even this information is not properly collected and analyzed in order to establish a suitable basis for the decisions that are being made.

*From Papers on the First World Conference on Informatics in Government, October 16–20, 1972, Florence, Italy; published by the International Computation Center, Rome, Italy.

These are critical comments and I shall not attempt to estimate to what extent they are applicable. I merely take them as a sign of serious interest in an indepth debate on public information processing.

In this section I shall outline the problems of primary concern, the basic requirements of future public information systems, and finally, I shall discuss some important economic implications.

First of all I want to distinguish between two types of requirements or demands that can be laid down for public information processing: political demands and operational requirements. The political demands include the definition of the limitation of the system and even the degree and nature of control and security measures. The operational requirements include all the specifications on which the performance and effectivity will depend. Even though these types of demands to a certain degree are overlapping, I shall concentrate on the operational requirements.

Another problem that calls for attention is that the objectives for public decision making are rarely so clearly defined as they generally are in the private sector. One reason for this is that the objectives set by politicians often comprise a great number of elements which are difficult to quantify, and another reason may be that politicians prefer not to be too specific because of a desire for flexibility later on. This might very well be a problem in the design phase of an information system. How is it possible to measure efficiency when you do not know what the intended results should look like?

To illustrate some of the problems mentioned, take for example a complex social problem that requires action from several agencies. This presents an obvious problem, since it might involve both national and local agencies, and since the national agencies are responsible to different ministries. The personal data are registered in various separate files, and in certain cases the result will be parallel processing and duplicate registration.

The scope of the objectives is partially limited by the legislation, but the possibilities of discretion allow the individual agencies some freedom of action without aiming at coordination of objectives or efforts.

The Danish Social Welfare Research Institute has investigated actual cases of this kind, and this has contributed to a change in the structure of the Danish social aid, aimed at amalgamation and coordination of the tasks of various agencies.

To overcome the difficulty of how to design an overall information system in the organizational surrounding we know today, the most simple way to start is to consider the social events that call for public action. This set of events can then be structured into a hierarchical organization of transactions, which is interrelated for technological, economic, or social reasons. In this case the information system as such becomes independent of the existing administrative structure.

The transaction types might be divided by level into the following categories:

1. Single events.
2. Activities.
3. Programs.
4. The total system.

The single events are the "smallest" events in the society that can trigger a reaction from a public agency. (For example, unemployment, crime etc.)

An activity will then be a group of events that are interrelated for technological, economic, social or other reasons. (For example, youth delinquency, air pollution etc.)

The corresponding program is a complex of activities that provide the basis for political or administrative objectives. (For example, social welfare, transportation etc.)

2. MAIN PROBLEMS

It has been a common practice for most data-processing applications in the public sector to solve the administrative problems for specific offices or agencies. I find this to be a philosophy of doubtful value in the future, and I hope to clarify my point of view in the following.

A characteristic to note about the administrative structure is that departments and directorates, as well as counties and municipalities, can maintain direct contact with the individual citizens.

Another characteristic is that all levels are involved in the planning of task, execution and, in turn, follow up on the performance. The information that is needed to carry out this different kind of task is mainly the same or closely interrelated.

In addition to this vertical structure one can consider the horizontal division of labor by professional fields. This division can cause problems when and where the professional fields interlock and maybe are in conflict with a major objective.

Thus, the main objectives of a public information system must be: to provide a better basis for decision making on all levels; to minimize the overall administrative costs related to collecting, storing, processing, and distribution of information; and to be independent of the actual organizational structure in order to avoid conflicts of interest and duplication of work.

The major design problems resulting from these objectives are:

1. Division of authority.
2. Communication between different agencies.
3. Registration problems.

The division of authority within the public sector is naturally greatly influenced by political objectives. The Scandinavian countries, for example, have a long tradition of geographic decentralization. Arguments against this philosophy are improved planning capabilities in a centralized structure, as effected in the defense sector and part of the taxation system. When there is a strong desire for decentralization, the information system must be so designed as to provide a means for national planning without diminishing the authority of local government.

The problem of providing an improved communication between different agencies is partly tied up with the division of authority, but concerns primarily the horizontal division of professional fields. The design of an information system must take into account the problems of overlapping authority.

The registration of necessary information is carried out by a great number of separate agencies. This means that some (or most?) of the information is collected and recorded by several authorities concurrently. This involves the risk that not all files are updated to the same level at the same time.

On each level we can further distinguish between performing, planning, and controlling functions.

A design like this can contribute considerably to a great reduction in the communication that I have mentioned and at the same time can reduce the redundancy problem of registration.

This enables us to make a modular design of an information system that can be implemented step-for-step without taking the existing administrative structure into account, and without the need for reorganization because of later changes in this administrative structure.

Following this approach it is not important whether we wish to centralize all public data processing in one large installation or scatter it between a number of installations—from a technical point of view both solutions are possible.

3. REQUIREMENTS OF PUBLIC INFORMATION SYSTEMS

The operational requirements of an information system fall within the areas of systems design and hardware requirements.

If we are interested in a decentralized network of installations, as is the case in most European countries, the problems of systems design include the distribution of partial data bases among the different installations. The hardware requirements must include the possibility of communication between the different installations. Let us have a closer look at these requirements.

The systems design should be primarily tailored to facilitate data collection and data control. Figure 1 may be used as a model to link the partial data bases in accordance with the division between single events, activities, program, and the total system. Here, primary information may be transferred to higher levels of the hierarchy in the shape of statistical information, references to the primary information, or in direct form.

A design like this serves several purposes—the most significant point being the possibility of making a modular design. Cost as well as work load will be high, and it is difficult to imagine how the entire system can be implemented overnight, once and for all. The modular design enables successive adaptation and easier implementation of the modules.

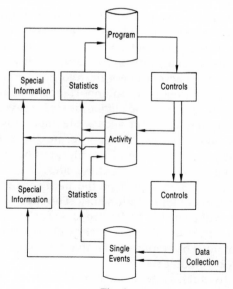

Fig. 1

A hierarchical design also has the advantage that, in a number of cases, it enables smooth transition from the present fragmentary design of public files to a still better integrated structure. To a great extent it will be capable of meeting the flexibility requirements, that is, the possibility of continuous adaptation of the system to changes in objectives, organization, and registration specifications.

We have to consider the security aspects, emergency procedures, and the problem of privacy. A reduction of the redundancy, present today in public files, increases the security of updated information when and where it is needed. When primary data is stored in one place, then it may be economically safe to spend a great deal of effort in creating check-routines to verify this data.

Emergency procedures to minimize the risk of a breakdown must be outlined in the design phase. Different levels of emergency procedures can be specified as: measures against a total breakdown; measures against breakdown of critical applications; data-base integrity; and sporadic, errors in the communications network.

The problem of privacy can be solved in numerous ways: nowadays it is almost a question of economy. How much is one prepared to pay to get the maximum protection of personnel integrity? It is indeed possible to protect an entire data base, partial files, and even segments of records against unauthorized use.

What are the hardware requirements in a public information system? An efficient and smoothly functioning data base/data communication system must be based on direct access storage media. In this type of system, tape solutions can probably be utilized only in connection with specific routine tasks, where it is not desired to provide inquiry facilities or where the response time is of no importance. One problem should be pointed out in this context. The difficulties of converting existing and planned sequential files to direct access files may postpone the data so that it becomes advantageous to incorporate these files into the full information system—not because of the files, but because of the application programs that are tied up with these files.

Another very interesting aspect of the hardware requirements is the need for a network of communication lines. The speed of transmission that is possible today will probably be far too slow for an integrated computer network. However, this problem may very well be solved before we know it, but a point that must be emphasized is that the computers in this network must be able to communicate.

The software for such systems must be capable of the following major functions:

1. Dynamic allocation of storage and peripherals to user tasks.
2. Supervision of transfer of data between data bases.
3. Supervision to prevent updating of a data field from coinciding with another update function for the same data field.
4. The data administration and access methods must be designed to make the user program independent of the physical location and representation of data.
5. In addition, the control programs must be capable of performing the normal functions known from existing operating systems.

We have every reason to believe that in a few years most of these requirements will be met, and also the solution to the problem of data independency for the user programs will be known.

An example of this is found in the hierarchical type of organization known as Data Language 1 (DL/1). The principle of this type of information is that the physical organization of a file in well-defined modules gives the user the possibility to create an arbitrary logical structure of the file. An example of this kind will be given below.

By this technique it is possible to optimize the physical storage method with regard to response times and storage efficiency in connection with the changing profile of the applications utilizing the data base. This optimization can be carried out completely independently of the user programs, which saves the cost of conversion. Also, new types of information may be added without interfering with existing programs, a solution that sharply reduces program maintenance costs.

4. REGISTRATION OF REAL ESTATE—AN EXAMPLE

To exemplify the application of the hierarchical data organization, I will consider a possible design of a real estate register. A real estate data base can serve a number of various purposes and several different agencies:

1. Real estate taxation.
2. Registration of deeds.
3. City planning.
4. Road construction.
5. Public utilities.
6. Mortgage credit statistics.
7. Statistics on dwellings and housing.

These tasks may be regarded as activities corresponding to the outline in Section 2.

Figure 2 shows the information for the real estate activity (or cadastral agency). It appears that portions of the information also concern other activities, such as information on real estate taxation and information on sewers and power supply.

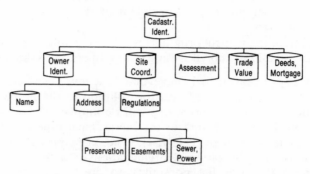

Fig. 2   Real estate register.

Figure 3 illustrates some of the information available for estate taxation. Using owner's identification as a key entry we gain access to information on assessment, deductions, tax, etc.

Figure 4 illustrates the basic information for a typical statistic: that is, the census of dwellings, normally performed once every ten years.

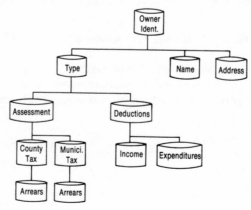

Fig. 3   Real estate taxation.

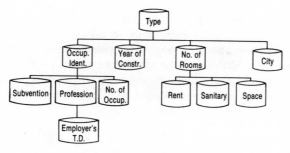

Fig. 4 Statistics on dwellings.

If all these problems should be solved by means of one single data base, this will contain the information indicated in Fig. 5 (plus, of course, a lot of other relevant information not mentioned here).

With the aid of the hierarchical organization any arbitrary item of information, such as a site coordinate, may be used to receive access to any other information. This makes it possible to specify a series of different data complexes, or so-called logical data bases.

By this procedure we obtain flexible response possibilities, better possibilities for adding supplementary information, and the possibility of making a stepwise implementation of the data base.

Another question remains to be answered: Where should the data base be placed? As the degree of utilization of detailed information is

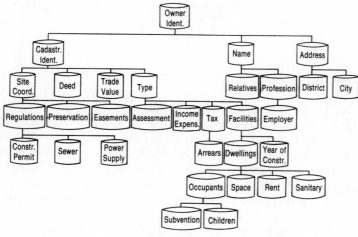

Fig. 5

concentrated geographically near the place where the data is collected, it would in this case be most expedient to create partial data bases for separate, larger, geographical areas and connect these regional centers to a central data base containing the central personnel register, the central address register, and perhaps a future central trades register.

Whether the partial data base should be placed centrally or in a regional center will depend on the following costs:

1. The use of the partial data base for centralized tasks: cost of transportation from region to center, corresponding costs of transportation from center to region, intraregional transportation costs.
2. Storage costs: the difference between actual storage costs in center and region.
3. Measures of security: costs of establishing emergency routines in case of breakdowns in center and region respectively, as well as politically determined costs of protecting individual privacy.
4. Waiting time: costs of waiting time in center versus costs of time at the ultimate terminal locations.
5. Network capacity: costs of creating a network oriented towards a central installation with regard to peak load versus costs of a network oriented towards regional centers, presumably with a lower peak load at each site.

As a conclusion to this example I hope to have demonstrated the possible benefits from creating a data base without being restricted by the organizational structure.

5. ECONOMIC IMPLICATIONS

The task of making a proper investment decision calls for serious consideration. It is a common practice, that a choice between alternative solutions to a particular data-processing problem is made on the basis of comparison of the costs of the individual alternatives. This is probably an acceptable way of doing this as long as we are only concerned with simple routine applications that are intended to replace well-known manual routines, but when it comes to the design of information systems, the entire problem is different. The scope of information systems is to provide a better basis for decision making as well as for routine functions, or—in other words—it is the overall efficiency of the administrative system that we are trying to maximize, not the best solution from a computer point of view.

Faced with the problem of how to make a proper economic evaluation of public information systems, we have to consider a lot of secondary benefits and so-called intangibles.

In many cases it seems impossible to find an economic expression for these intangibles. For instance: How are we to measure the improvement of the quality of the decision? How much is "better service" worth to the society?

It seems safe to say that most benefits require some form of transformation, while the costs generally are well-defined. It is indeed very tempting to suggest that the so-called Benefit-Cost analysis be applied to this area because it has proved to be an efficiency tool in many other areas of public decision making. I find it hard to believe that more secondary benefits call for evaluation when it comes to public information systems than is the case when the Benefit-Cost analysis is applied to city planning.

Further, the philosophy of the Benefit-Cost analysis is very similar to the technique of decentralization pointed out in Sections 2 and 3.

I shall not attempt to outline all possible elements of a Benefit-Cost analysis, but I should like to discuss some important economic implications in the light of the Benefit-Cost philosophy.

First of all I will distinguish between the long-run effects of establishing an integrated information system and the short-run effects that show up during the period of implementation and initial stages.

Now, let us have a look at some of the long-run effects.

Resource Allocation

One of the primary objectives must be to provide a basis for better utilization of all kinds of resources. The rate at which the public sector expends the share of the total supply of manpower can be reduced substantially, and it should be possible to make an economic evaluation of the impact on production and welfare.

As for capital expenditure, an improved knowledge of the basic economic figures as well as improved tools for planning and coordination will contribute to a safer management of short-term public intervention and long-term investments. Also private business will obtain better possibilities to schedule production and investments. It is admittedly more difficult to assign monetary values to these aspects, but a way out of this dilemma might be to simulate past history and try to evaluate the possible different results.

Increased Service

It is obvious that the individual citizen will be able to obtain improved service, for example, in the shape of information on all legislation and rules that are applicable to him in specific cases. Also, duplicate reporting could be avoided. Nowadays, employers submit a number of reports containing duplicated information to various authorities, and this kind of benefit can be expressed very well in terms of money.

But what is service when it boils down to facts? One of the most important aspects is a reduction of response time, and this kind of service might be of great economic importance.

Faster reporting would make the planning authorities more efficient; Fig. 6 shows an example of fluctuations in the balance of payments. An adverse change in the development will not be ascertained until some time

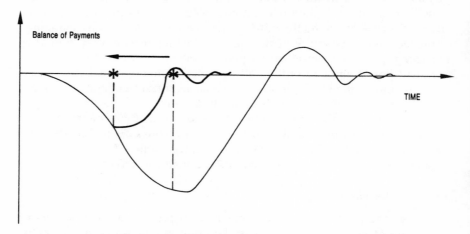

Fig. 6   Faster reporting: smaller fluctuations.

has passed, and in order to restore the balance, the severity of the measures taken must be increased accordingly. If the information could be provided sooner, the severity of the necessary steps could be reduced and economic fluctuations could be avoided to a greater extent. Most economists will have a word or two on the implications of this.

It is also possible to look at this problem in another way. The left section of Fig. 7 shows the value of a decision as a function of the quantity of information, that is available. Think of a surgeon needing information to save a patient's life. We assume that the value of the

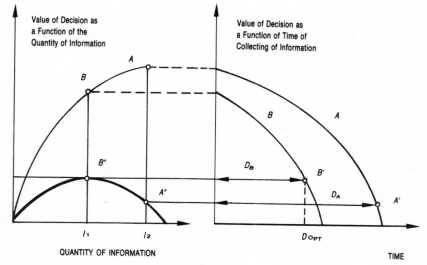

Fig. 7

decision, the patient's chance of survival, will increase in proportion with the quantity of information.

A decision made on the basis of the quantity of information I_2 will then have the value A if I_2 is available immediately. If it takes time to collect I_2, then the value of the decision will decrease accordingly, that is, our patient may die during the observations. This point is indicated in the right section of Fig. 7, curve A showing the decrease.

If the collection time is D_A, the actual of the decision will only be A'', as shown on the bold curve on the left. This curve has its optimum at a quantity of information $= I_1$.

From Fig. 8 we can see the importance of a reduction of the data collection time. We will now use more information, provide it faster, and thus increase the value of the decision made.

I think this reasoning is relevant, whether the patient is a human being or the national economy. This reasoning is due to Langefors (Sweden), who outlined this idea in his *Theoretical Analysis of Information Systems.*

Besides these two main areas of interest, resource allocation and improved service, several other implications on society will show up. I will not attempt to make a complete listing, but only mention such things as "quality of life," possible impact on the political life, etc.

In the long run we can expect to realize rather heavy costs in public

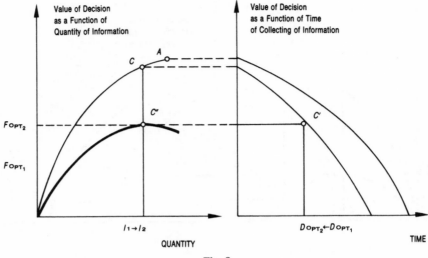

Fig. 8

information processing if we are not willing to make an attempt to coordinate the existing and planned applications.

The cost factors in the long run are mainly those we have already discussed: costs of collecting, storing, processing, and communicating information, costs of emergency procedures, security measures, and a most important factor: education and training for these advanced systems. The level of education is likely to set the limit for the speed at which the modules in the system can be established. Education, however, is not only a cost factor, because both public and private enterprises undoubtedly will benefit from this.

As regards the short-term effects, I will concentrate on the problems of structural reorganization, political aspects of the problem of decentralization, and the initial costs.

Reorganization

No matter what kind of administrative structure we are aiming at, it may not be realistic to imagine that this structure will be unaffected by the implementation of an information system. This will be true especially within the data-processing departments of the public sector.

Sudden changes in manpower requirements, education and retraining should be avoided if at all possible. Also, there is a problem that during the transition from one system to another we may encounter differences in the ways public authorities handle similar matters, unless the transition is made in a very short time. On the other hand, this involves the risk of insufficient testing of the new procedures. We must realize these aspects in connection with the establishment of the individual modules in the total system, so that the decision-making authorities as well as the citizens are able to make a realistic evaluation of the impacts.

Decentralization/Centralization

In the short run we have to await clarification of the political wishes concerning the division of authority. Technologically, both centralized and decentralized solutions are possible, but the advantages and disadvantages of the solution selected for a specific purpose may vary considerably.

Initial Costs

Even though manpower and levels of education are likely to be the decisive factors for the speed at which the system can be created, there are, of course, considerable financial factors as well. These apply especially to the establishment of a fast telecommunications network, to the programming effort, and possibly conversion costs for the existing solutions.

I have briefly referred to some of the aspects we must consider if we want to make a proper evaluation of the effects that the introduction of information systems will have on the community. An analysis should always be matched against the best alternative, because we must ask ourselves what can be substituted for the proposed solution and what differences are there between the existing possibilities?

6. CONCLUDING REMARKS

In this section I have outlined some of the major problems that must be considered before a successful attempt to design a public informations system can be carried out.

We have touched some of the major principles of design, among which the principle of modularity seems to be the most important. It is to be expected that an increasing number of people will become involved in the discussion of these problems during the next decade, but, in my opinion, this is no reason for postponing the construction of the first modules in a total system of integrated data bases. The criteria for which parts should be implemented first are short-term advantages, foreseeable modifications, and the long-run benefits.

So far, many projects have been implemented on the basis of the short-term benefits. The decision should better still be based on the advantages that can be obtained by integrating the partial project with already established applications. In my opinion, the long-run benefits are the decisive factors in this connection.

Consequently, there is a demand for a thorough analysis of the future requirements of public data processing. In the required analysis the emphasis should be on the long-run benefits of the individual projects. The final priority should be given by an authority that has the power to unite the wishes of involved parties.

II. A City Information System—A Case Study

1. SURVEY BACKGROUND

Public use of EDP has so far been dominated by isolated stand-alone systems on which certain problems or problem complexes have been solved with the use of EDP. On the whole this processing has been performed within the framework of the existing administrative organization and has not had appreciable interdepartmental effects.

However, as stressed in Section I of this paper, the development of the computer technology during the last few years has made it obvious that the greatest potential benefits of EDP in the municipal administration will be derived from problem solutions across the dividing lines of the existing organization, problem solutions in which information retrieval and communications are automated.

The main reasons are that the municipal administration is based primarily on files, and that file maintenance, file searches, and the resulting communication between departments are very time-consuming. Another reason is that a municipality's administrative service level and its possibilities of achieving optimum planning depend on the expedience and the speed at which information can be compiled and made available.

The data-processing developments that enable total and interdepartmental problem solutions have been achieved mainly in the fields of data bases and data communications. Nowadays, it is technically possible to establish a centralized municipal data base of suitably organized information that can be communicated via terminals to decentralized locations where it can be used for the processing of individual jobs as well as for planning and control purposes. However, the implementation of data-processing systems to meet these interdepartmental and total requirements necessitate comprehensive analyses of the requirements prior to the actual systems development.

The comprehensive interdepartmental and integrated designs of the systems required, make it necessary to implement the development in phases, according to a long-term schedule based on an analysis of the requirements. This is the only reasonably certain way of ensuring that investments in systems development and reorganization of the administrative work are made in an appropriate and coordinated way. It was on this background that the city of Aalborg (156,000 inhabitants), Kommunedata's Aalborg Center (formerly, the Jutland Municipalities Computer Center), and IBM agreed, in August/September 1971, to carry through an analysis of the requirements.

The survey was implemented in the following phases:

1. Data collection, including questions on the degree of automation, files in use, transactions, manpower consumption, all distributed on major tasks.
2. Analysis, including a total survey of files.
3. Outline of a municipal data base.
4. Preparation of an outline of the development of the municipal automation, including existing data-processing applications, new applications, priority scheduling, required resources, budget, and time schedule.

The survey was commenced about October 1, 1971, and was carried out by a task force and a control panel consisting of personnel from the city of Aalborg, Kommunedata's Aalborg Center, and IBM.

2. ANALYSIS

Phase 1, the data collection, was carried through in the fourth quarter of 1971. During this period, all departments of the city of Aalborg were visited and interviewed. The purposes were:

1. To list the contents and applications of all the files used for daily administration purposes.
2. To obtain a knowledge of the city's interdepartmental communication on the various transactions.
3. To record the tasks and procedures of the different departments.

All departments of the city contributed to this collection of facts. The information on processing times for transactions may be rather inaccurate, whereas the remaining facts appear to be very reliable.

The collected information was analyzed in the first quarter of 1972. Some of the most important results of the analysis are:

1. The administrative sectors in the city of Aalborg have 1349 manual files, and most of these concern the principal entities: persons, economy, and real property.
2. Each month, about one million file transactions are performed— about two-thirds of these are update transactions, the remainder file searches.
3. The communication between the departments of the city comprises about 350,000 messages each month.

Above figures do not include the data-processing center's files, on which there are about 7 million transactions each month. These figures show that to a great extent the city of Aalborg has automated—but not integrated— its administration.

The manual file maintenance and searches and the internal communication represent a considerable part of administrative personnel's total efforts. It was estimated that these tasks cover about one-third of personnel time, or all the work hours of 300 fulltime employees.

The size of the city and the geographic spread of its administration are important factors which affect the file organization and the scope of the communication. For example, the average number of registrations for each citizen in the city is 33, and most of the registers include information on addresses; this means that each of the roughly 40,000 address changes each year involves between 20 and 30 file updates.

The most significant result of the analysis is that it indicates that one of the greatest benefits that can be obtained through the use of electronic data processing in the future administration of the city is the resource economy that can be effected in the file handling and internal communication areas.

Independently of the collection of facts and the analysis of these, the municipal functions have been systematically reviewed in order to identify and map out the areas which comprise tasks that can be performed successfully by electronic data processing. This review resulted in the compilation of a list of those function areas where it is expected that EDP can be used to advantage within the next five to ten years.

These function areas comprise primarily tasks that are data base oriented, which means that they use files that can also be used for the performance of other tasks. Obviously, it would be an advantage to collect these files in a data base and thus avoid duplication of information. The list includes tasks which will not use the data base as well.

The various tasks were evaluated and scheduled by priority on a provisional basis with a view to convert them to EDP. The evaluation criteria used are, first, the estimated economic result of a conversion to EDP, with the emphasis on the release of resources, and second, the value that an EDP solution has to the municipality's service level and overall planning.

This has resulted in the compilation of a priority list comprising about 40 tasks or projects, for which the evaluation indicates that the use of EDP will be an advantage; these jobs should, therefore, be included in a long-term development plan for the city's use of electronic data processing.

3. A CITY DATA BASE

This review of the current municipal administration revealed certain characteristics of the methods used for the collection, storage, and distribution of information. The current information processing system is concentrated on the processing officer; this means that the officer responsible for the handling of a matter has a preferential claim on immediate access to the information required primarily by him. The data-processing file organization, which we know today, has been designed on this basis. Information is collected and stored for defined purposes, rather than for general use.

This system will work efficiently as long as the number of separate files is fairly small and as long as there is no demand for integrated information. If, however, a casual need for integrated information arises in such a system, it will often be a major job to compile the necessary information from the individual sources.

Integrated information is a basic requirement of the controlling and planning agencies of the municipal administration. While it was previously sufficient to make plans and budgets for one year at a time and to check compliance with them once every quarter, it has now become essential to regard planning and control as reciprocal efforts that must be performed continuously throughout the year.

The conventional information system is not designed to support continuous planning. The status of the projects in progress, for example, can be checked only as of the first day of the month, and even then it is impossible to check the causes of any deviations, since the system does not provide access to simultaneous information that can throw light on the deviations.

The following facts should be emphasized:

1. The existing information processing system is concentrated on the processing officer.
2. Therefore, the same information will be stored by several manual files.
3. This causes an updating problem when the information is modified.
4. It is difficult to provide reasonably fast answers to spontaneous questions involving several departments.
5. There are no means of direct communication to enable examination of a sequence of causes and associated interrelated information items.
6. Instead, there is much internal communication with the officers and clerks who have access to the files that contain parts of the required information.
7. Because of the many files that must be updated for each change, errors and discrepancies between files will occur and cause delays in the processing.
8. It is difficult to check the correctness of the file contents and to prevent unauthorized use of the information.

As an alternative to this type of information processing, today's electronic data processing provides data base solutions.

A data base is built around one centralized data file that contains all the information collected and stored in the municipality and required for more than one task, the principle being that information is stored in only one place. The information is cross-referenced, so that, for example, information on a land registry title number can be used as a starting point for the retrieval of information on the owner, his address, income, family, etc.

The benefits of the data base oriented information system include:

1. The system is designed to provide information on a general basis for the officer who processes individual matters as well as for control and planning purposes.
2. In principle, information is stored in only one place; this ensures faster and safer updating.
3. Interdepartmental questions can be answered.
4. The internal communication between processing officers, and the number of outside inquiries received by them, are reduced considerably, since all processing officers now have access not only to the information they used to have but also to other necessary information that they previously had to obtain from other departments. Thus, the data base principle virtually provides a complete file for each officer.

The data base system makes it possible to establish many different safeguards, which provide much better precaution against unauthorized use than the current manual systems do. These safeguards ensure, primarily, that only authorized officers can gain access to the information.

The computerized base is a common tool, utilized by all branches of the municipal administration. Its major advantages are that it minimizes the maintenance and compilation of information and makes the information generally available for case processing, planning, and control.

The entire report from the survey contains an outline of a municipal data base which it is proposed to establish stage by stage with the ultimate objective of including information for all sectors of the municipal administration.

4. PROPOSED DEVELOPMENT PLAN

The proposed development plan is to provide a long-term plan for the implementation of the 40 or so data-processing tasks or projects from which the city will derive the greatest benefits. According to the priority scheduling, these projects were analyzed in detail. Descriptions were prepared of the objectives, application areas, benefits, and activities necessary to implement each project. These descriptions have been used to evaluate the planning and programming resources required for each project.

The projects were incorporated in a long-term plan, covering seven or eight years and allowing for the scheduled priorities, the interdependence of the projects, and the desire to equalize the resource requirements over the time-span of the plan.

Typically, the data base oriented tasks require most resources and are most interdependent. It was planned to start the construction of the data base on a logically correct basis and in such a way that the data base can give the city major benefits from the start.

5. THE FIRST PROJECTS OF THE DEVELOPMENT PLAN

As appears from the outlined overall development plan, the following projects are scheduled for implementation before July 1, 1975.

Data base oriented projects:

1. Transactions involving personal data and income information.
2. Transactions involving social welfare information.
3. Accounting and associated reporting routines and retrieval possibilities.
4. Payment and collection system.
5. Data entry and data base maintenance.
6. Budgeting.
7. Transactions relative to personal tax assessment.
8. Transactions involving real property information.

Other projects:

9. Technical calculations.
10. Scheduling (for schools).
11. Education in EDP.
12. Traffic simulation.

These projects are described briefly in the following sections.

Transactions Involving Personal Data and Income Information

This project is designed to give the processing officers access to current personal data and income information so as to reduce the administration effort required to maintain the great number of manual files in which this information is contained today. The system provides access not only to such personal information as name, address, family, etc., but also to information on estimated income, latest final assessment data, and/or latest recorded income.

The project has been operating since June 1, 1973.

Transactions Involving Social Welfare Information

The objective is to give the social welfare processing officers access to an overview of the individual customer's contact with social welfare authorities, for example, information on pension payments, loans for accommodation deposit, welfare, domestic help, contact with the child and juvenile welfare, etc.

A common information system for all social welfare sectors would greatly facilitate the implementation of the so-called one-string system, which is based on the availability of such an overview.

The availability of this information is expected to save time, which can be used for the action processing activities, so that better service can be provided.

The project has been operating since April 1974.

Accounting and Associated Reporting Routines and Retrieval Possibilities

The accounting system is comprised of three parts: the recording system, the reporting system, and the inquiry system. The recording system involves a conversion of the chart of accounts and the introduction of planned economy accounting. These systems provide a better view of the municipality's financial situation and possibilities of faster action on indications of overexpenditure.

A new chart of accounts will primarily consider the needs of the planning functions as it will be possible to put cross-questions in order to carry through isolated analyses.

The reporting system aims at making it possible for the different departments to report transactions directly to the system in order to reduce the number of involved functions. This will, of course, necessitate automatic control procedures.

The inquiry system will give the officers, who process individual matters as well as the controlling and planning functions, direct access to relevant economic information. The system will be designed so as to provide automatic reporting of exceptions, for example, in the case of indications of overexpenditure.

The project is divided into three phases, the first of which has been operational since April 1974.

Payment and Collection System

This project is a superstructure of the accounting system. It deals with cash orders, control of payments, collection, recovery, and remittance.

The control with cash orders and the associated automatic set-off procedures aim at reducing the outstanding arrears of the city. The automatic remittance procedures will mean that contractor rebates can be turned to account efficiently and that respites and credit can be utilized better.

By combining the existing collection systems, the municipality will obtain the benefits of simpler accounting and reduction of the number of manual files for consumers and overdue accounts receivable.

The project is linked together with Phase 2 of the accounting system.

Data Entry and Data Base Maintenance

Updated information is a prerequisite for full utilization of the data base. The required updating necessitates direct reporting to the system from the processing officer or department responsible for the updating. This reporting is done via terminals designed to give the reporting officer access to the various control functions and to enable screen presentation of preprinted forms.

This project also offers another advantage, since the above method of reporting to a data-processing system is faster and safer than the conventional reporting via source document, keypunch section, mail, and preliminary handling, etc.

The same terminals can be used for both reporting and inquiries, for example, in connection with projects that concern transaction processing.

Budgeting

The budgeting of the municipal administration is a lengthy and often very circumstantial process.

One way in which this job can be made easier is to work with a clear, simple accounting system that makes it possible to allow for the interdependence of operations and constructions. At the same time, there is a great need for the possibility of preparing alternative budgets to clarify the choices.

Some of these problems can be solved by the budgeting project, which comprises automatic prognosis routines for preparation of budgets for two or more years with alternative action plans and for evaluation of the effects of different wage and price increases.

The budgeting system is also linked together with Phase 2 of the accounting system.

Transactions Relative to Personal Tax Assessment

This project, which is superimposed on the personal data and income information project, is designed to give the Taxation Department the information required for personal tax assessment. This information includes all taxation information for a three-year period, tax estimates, real property transactions, etc. Incidentally, the inquiry system can be extended to include various statistical control methods, so that a financial analysis can be concentrated on taxpayers whose income variations deviate considerably from the average. The project is also expected to release much of the manpower currently employed to handle the inquiries to the Taxation Department's manual files.

The project has been operating since April 1974.

Transactions Involving Real Property Information

The objective of this project is to permit inquiries on real property. This information includes data on owner, area, evaluation, and reported market value, etc.

This data is likely to be used particularly by the property taxation and property administration offices and the technical administration. In addition, the establishment of this part of the data base forms the basis of a collective detailed property registry for Aalborg and is expected to be used extensively in the future for city planning, preparation of area disposition plans, etc.

Technical Calculations

The purpose of implementing this project is to give the technical estimators access to a general data-processing tool which, via terminals, enables the execution of prepared standard programs (e.g., for sewage dimensioning) and provides programming facilities for the estimators. (Such terminal systems for technical calculations are currently operated by "Kommunedata".)

The project was started in January 1973.

Scheduling (for Schools)

Scheduling requires a major effort by the school administration officers.

If standard programs are made available, school timetables can be produced on the basis of information on limitations of rooms, teachers, etc. "Kommunedata" has today a scheduling system which is used by a number of schools.

Education in EDP

During the next few years there will be an increasing demand for basic data-processing education. "Kommunedata" can already offer the schools various terminal system solutions which give the students the opportunity to write and execute their own programs.

Traffic Simulation

In connection with the preparation of running traffic prognoses it will be a great help for the planners to have the opportunity to work with a stylized model of Aalborg's network of streets and to be able to test their assumptions concerning traffic density, changes in road plans, one-way traffic regulation, etc. This project necessitates the construction of such a model with the assistance of the Planning Secretariat.

6. ECONOMIC CONSEQUENCES

Immediately after the seven-year development plan was outlined, the very important phase of economic evaluation started off.

Because of the way the EDP projects were defined, very little interaction, and thus cross-effects, was to be expected between the projects. In this way, it was possible, on the whole, to concentrate on the consequences of each project per se.

The problems arose when we turned to the benefits. The benefits were divided into four parts:

1. Direct benefits resulting from administrative rationalization.
2. Secondary benefits resulting from alternative utilization of resources.
3. Benefits from better planning and control.
4. Derived benefits for the public (a higher level of service).

It very soon became obvious that the most accurate estimates were to be found in the first category.

Administrative Rationalization

Each EDP project was held up against the prevailing way of doing things. The file handling was described rather well in the data collection phase although the estimates on the labor requirements had to be reviewed and recompiled for each transaction type. Then the corresponding labor requirement for the alternative EDP project was estimated and generally 50% was added to this estimate to make it a conservative one. After this, the total labor requirement for each project was subtracted from the corresponding labor consumption of today's administration. For example, the result of the estimate for the project concerning transactions on personal taxation:

	Manhours/months		
	Today	Expected	Reduction
File inquiry	1704	1040	664
File update	3641	2296	1346
Communication between departments	4136	655	3481
Information processing etc.	7309	5960	1349
Total possible reduction (ca.)			6800

The heavy reduction in communication time is due to the fact that centralized filing of income information relieves the tax department from the burden to communicate this information to other departments, who now gain even faster access to this information than before by means of terminal.

Alternative Utilization of Resources

Because of the full employment situation that has existed in Denmark since 1963 and a number of new laws that has meant additional administrative burdens for local government, it has not been possible for the city administration to hire as many employees as needed to fulfill all the tasks they wished to. In other words: If it is possible to save, say, 10,000 man hours per month as a result of another way of doing things, then the direct benefit would be the cost of these 10,000 man hours. But, if it is possible to employ the labor force in another way, then the total benefit may exceed this figure.

Another example: The employees of the tax department in 1971 made assessment of 20% of the taxpayers. This resulted in additional taxes amounting to 6 million Danish crowns. It was estimated that a total assessment would have brought this figure up by at least another 6–10 million, had there been enough man hours available to make this possible.

Another example of the more traditional kind was found in the city inventories, especially the inventories administrated by the technical department, where a resource control system would make it possible to reduce the inventories and thus the invested capital.

Planning and Control

This category of benefits includes several remarkable examples. One of the most significant was that the net cash flow of the city showed enormous fluctuations—during one week the liquid asset varied from + 20 million Danish crowns to − 10 million.

By means of a tighter system of economic control, these fluctuations were estimated to be reduced by at least 10% on an average. In this way, it should be possible to reduce the interest paid on short-term loans and even invest the surplus money in a more profitable way.

Another example in this category of benefits stems from the planning of schools. When you plan for a new school, you need accurate demographic figures to tell you how many children you may expect to go to this new school.

Because the Danish school system prohibits more than 22 pupils per class, the number of classrooms planned for, traditionally, were very much on the safe side. In other words, if the population forecast can be refined, it is likely that one out of 20 classrooms need not be constructed, or approximately 5% of the construction sum can be avoided. For an ordinary Danish school this amounts to about 1.5 million Danish crowns.

In Aalborg, ten new schools are planned for during the 1970s.

Service to the Public

It is unquestionable that a more efficient administration will influence, in a positive way, the obtained level of service, but it might be difficult to estimate accurately the economic value of this improvement. In certain cases, however, it is possible to pinpoint some fairly acceptable figures.

The department that is responsible for the housing grants receives some 200 applications each month. To the citizen in question this normally means that he will have to spend some 45 minutes filling out forms on personal data, most of which is already registered in the tax department and in the population registration office. By means of a centralized data base system, the time the citizen will have to spend can be reduced to 15 minutes or a total reduction per month equal to 100 "public hours." This may not seem very impressive, but the corresponding figures are to be found in all transactions involving personal information.

After all the projects which were planned to be in operation before July 1975 had been evaluated along these lines, it was argued that as a basis for a political decision, the figures representing benefit categories 2, 3, and 4 might be too inaccurate to be trustworthy, although all parties agreed that the major benefits would arise here. It was then decided to concentrate on the direct benefits.

If a conservative estimate of direct benefits showed a substantial surplus over the estimated costs then the investment, in any case, would be considered desirable.

According to the report from the survey, the implementation of the listed projects was estimated to result in the following savings in man-hour consumption:

    1973   about   52,000 hours
    1974   about 296,000 hours
    1975   about 488,000 hours
    1976   about 580,000 hours.

For the purpose of preparing a financial estimate for the project, the value of one hour saved has been fixed at Dkr. 25,00 in the table below. (This figure does not include overhead costs, but is a normal average wage figure.) The report does not distinguish between the purposes for which the time saved is to be used:

1. Reduced headcount.
2. Improved service level (e.g., in the social welfare sector).
3. Solution of yet unsolved problems.

With this reservation, the economy of the project can be expressed as follows in millions of Dkr.:

	Debit	Credit	Net
1972		0.1	−0.1
1973	1.3	1.3	0.0
1974	7.4	1.8	5.6
1975	12.2	3.0	9.2
1976	14.5	3.1	11.4

These figures are rough estimates primarily compiled to illustrate proportions. This applies particularly to the debit figures. It is emphasized that
the table includes only projects proposed for implementation before July
1, 1975. Also, it was a prerequisite for the implementation of the project
that the city of Aalborg provided the manpower required for planning and
management of the training during the implementation phase. This
manpower requirement consisted of five officers, the expense of whom is
included in the table.

7. CONCLUSION

Project *Data Base* has been designed to clarify the requirements for
automation in the city of Aalborg and to outline the development of the
city's use of electronic data processing.

Correctly planned and introduced, the new data-processing applications can certainly become very significant factors in the city's organization as they can reduce headcounts, contribute to efficient administration,
planning and control, and improve the service level.

The establishment of a city data base will probably prove to be the most
significant improvement available to municipal administration today.
Moreover, in addition to the data base oriented tasks, there are many
other areas in which data processing can be used economically and
efficiently.

The derivative benefit of using new data-processing applications within
the municipality should be viewed, from an administrative point of view, in
terms of relating public activities and services to public revenues and/or
income. If increased spending for public activities and services beyond the
city's capacity is to be curbed it is only through up-to-date information
stemming from a computer system. This, in short, may be the best
argument in favor of extensive utilization of data processing.

The proposal described in the report comprises a stepwise establishment of a city data base and a successive development of problem
solutions, most of which are associated with the data base. The plan
consists of a long-term principles plan for 7–8 years and a firm short-term
plan for 2–2½ years. It is proposed to review these two plans regularly (e.g.,
twice a year), in the light of experiences and new developments.

This implies that the city's data-processing planning function should be
made permanent, and it should be stressed that efficient and continuous
planning and control are the major prerequisites for the success of the
data-processing projects.

Such planning and control, in conjunction with a step-by-step implementation, can ensure that the users will bring their influence to bear on the system and that the system will function as intended.

The size of the investments alone makes it significant to attain these objectives. In view of the tremendous potential benefits, which the municipality and the community can obtain from the system, it is very important to ensure optimum implementation through continuous planning and follow up and, particularly, through continued updating of the requirements analysis.

Appendix

Figures 9–12 represent the conceptual data base for the city of Aalborg information system.

The boxes represent segment types and include a number of datafields under the appropriate headings. The arrows represent pointers between the different entities.

Besides the entities shown, all relevant accounting information is represented by another entity, number 8. Whenever a segment type occurs under the heading "account," this represents information on transactions on the city's accounting system.

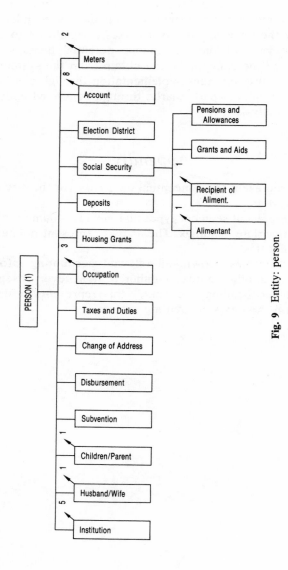

Fig. 9   Entity: person.

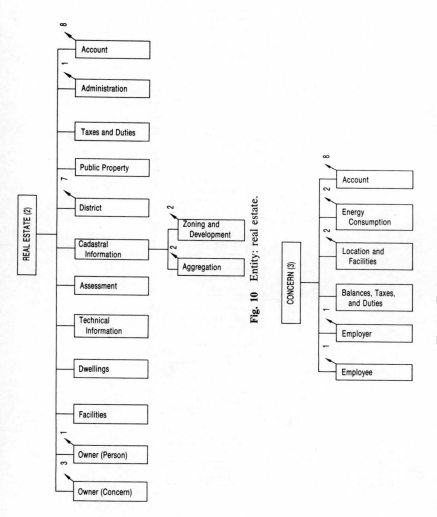

Fig. 10 Entity: real estate.

Fig. 11 Entity: concern.

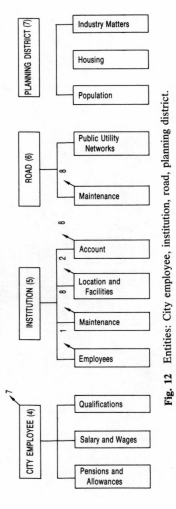

Fig. 12 Entities: City employee, institution, road, planning district.

5

Creation of a Geographic Information System (GIST)*

E. S. SAVAS, R. AMSTERDAM, AND E. BRODHEIM

Graduate School of Business Administration, Columbia University, New York
Office of the Mayor, City of New York, New York
PDA Systems, Inc., New York, N.Y.

I. INTRODUCTION

If one looks at a city in terms of blocks and blockfaces, it is readily apparent that many municipal departments are concerned, in one way or another, about some set of characteristics of these units. For example, one or more departments are interested in the following information: On what blockface or at what geographic coordinates is a particular parcel of property located? How many fires have been reported on a particular block? How many registered voters reside in a particular election district consisting of a number of blocks? Have any police calls originated from a certain block? and so forth.

There is a complementary group of questions concerning streets and their intersections. For example: What volume of traffic exists on it at different times of the day? Which sanitation route covers that street? How many and what kind of accidents occurred on that street segment?

Given this immense proliferation of interest in properties and streets, it is not surprising to find a very large number of files maintained by numerous city agencies, each one used for its particular parochial purpose. However, there is now a crying need on the one hand for data exchange between departments and on the other hand for more ready access to the stored information. A number of factors contribute to this need. First, there is a general recognition that urban problems are interrelated and that it is necessary to look at many facets of a problem

*Reprinted from the *Proceedings of the Urban Symposium,* of the Association of Computer Machinery, New York, 1970, pp. 99–118. The appendix to this chapter was prepared autonomously by Robert Amsterdam in November 1971 and modified for the presentation here.

and many factors in order to attack it. Second, the Model Cities program encourages and forces the cities to look at problems in this interrelated manner. Third, some cities, including New York, are moving in a substantial way in the direction of planning, programming, and budgeting systems which call for fundamental reappraisals and reexaminations of the activities of city departments and require an analytical examination of the costs and benefits of municipal programs. All of these factors require more frequent and more rapid access to data than was required in the past.

Typically, any new program demands data from many different departmental sources. In the case of New York, a major reorganization has been accomplished during the present administration, consolidating about 50 departments with mutual interests into a total of 10 superagencies (called Administrations), thereby encouraging more comprehensive planning and coordinated operation of related activities. The reorganization means that departments which perhaps were not communicating effectively with each other before are now forced to do so.

On March 9, 1969, Mayor John V. Lindsay announced that the city of New York was launching a computerized information system for the land and buildings in New York City. The objectives of the system, as stated by the Mayor, were to create new computer-accessible files that "will allow all city agencies to exchange—quickly and efficiently—data maintained in uncoordinated, cumbersome, and obsolete filing systems." A portion of this unified system, called GIST (Geographic Information System) had actually been under intensive study and development for some time. This effort is being undertaken by the City's Management Science unit in the Office of Administration, under the Deputy Mayor—City Administrator Timothy W. Costello, with the close cooperation and participation of the Department of City Planning, the Finance Administration, the Housing and Development Administration, and the Bureau of the Budget. In its initial phase, this system will make accessible to all city agencies that need it the geographically oriented data which is routinely gathered and maintained by an agency.

This paper broadly describes the requirements and concepts of the system and then the design and initial construction of the system.

II. GIST CONCEPTS

The three key features in the overall design philosophy of GIST are the following:

1. It will rely on agency-maintained satellite files rather than on a massive central repository of data.
2. It will employ a centralized, user oriented method of data interchange.
3. It will provide centralized tools for data analysis and display.

As examples of typical applications that may be envisioned for GIST, the Board of Elections may have data on the residence of registered voters, the Police Department may have data on the occurrence of requests for police help, the Board of Education may have data on the location of school-age children by age group, the Office of Civil Defense may have data on the location of fall-out shelters in the metropolitan area. The overall problem may be to determine the best district lines, the best assignment of children to schools or people to fall-out shelters, or to provide planners with a visual representation of the relative distribution of population or occurrences of events relative to facilities such as ambulance stations or major fall-out shelters.

Further, it is often desirable to merge this specific data with data of a more general nature. For example, in reviewing the relative situation of fall-out shelters to population, it will be desirable to merge census population data with fall-out shelter data. Similarly, in determining the percentage of people in an area who might be receiving public assistance, it is necessary to merge the files of welfare recipients with total population in that block or area.

The common denominator for the formation of districts or the presentation of data for visual analysis lies in attaching geographic coordinates to each data point. This has been the major emphasis to date—namely, the creation of the files and programs that will permit the assignment of a geographic coordinate to each data point. Auxiliary portions of the system include the capabilities of merging data, such as adding census data to specific population data, the capabilities for aggregating data by area, and the development of programs for data display.

Figure 1 is a functional flow chart of the system. An agency desiring to make use of GIST provides data it has gathered for a specific application. This data is first put into standardized format where required. The subsequent step is to attach geographic coordinates to each data point. Initially, this will be done by means of a standard merge program which can assess blockside information in one of the following three forms (see Fig. 2):

1. A block oriented file that orders blocks by their census tract and

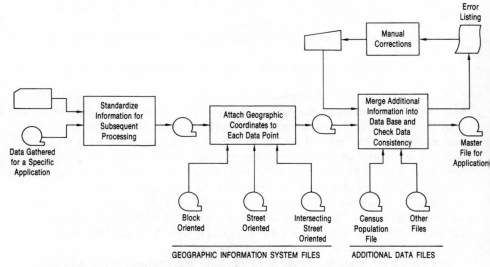

Fig. 1   Functional flow chart of a GIST application—preparation of master file.

- **BLOCK ORIENTED FILE**
  Census Tract (numerical sequence)
  Census Block (numerical sequence)
    Blockface (numerical sequence)
    Coordinates and other identifiers.
- **STREET ORIENTED FILE**
  Street Name (alpha-numeric sequence)
  Blockface (low house number sequence—
    alternating odd and even)
  Coordinates and other identifiers.

- **INTERSECTING STREET ORIENTED FILE**
  Street Name (alpha-numeric sequence)
    Intersecting street
  Reference coordinate and reference blockface.

Fig. 2   Organization of the three versions of the GIST file.

census block number and orders blocksides in clockwise order
around the block.
2. A street oriented file that orders streets in alpha-numeric sequence
   and orders blockfaces within the streets in ascending order of house
   numbers, normally alternating between odd and even numbers.

3. An intersecting-street oriented file that orders street names in alpha-numberic sequence and, within each street name, orders intersecting streets by the same sequence.

Depending upon the application, one or more of these files are utilized. For example, if the input data provided by the agency is by census designation, the block oriented version of the file would be utilized; if the input data is provided by house number, then the street oriented version of the file would be used; while if the data is given in terms of street intersections, the intersecting-street oriented version of the file would be utilized. Regardless of which version of the file is utilized, the output would consist of the input data with geographic coordinates attached.

The detailed blockside data approximates 80 million characters. Initially it is being stored on tapes in the three sequences just described. As usage of GIST grows, it is expected that storage on random access will become warranted. In that case, only a single file sequence will be needed.

The next step is to merge additional information such as census population data or information from other files available at the GIST data center. In this step, critical inconsistencies between the data sources could be detected and corresponding error listings generated. These error listings would be corrected by manual means either at a typewriter terminal which permits "text editing" of the errors, or by means of punched cards, which would be merged with the basic file. In either event, a master file for that particular application results. This ends the first part of the processing.

In the second part of the processing, the master file is the input to a number of standard software packages which can be sequenced in any desired order. For example, the master file could first be sorted into political divisions, and a districting procedure be applied to append election district designations within each of these divisions; then the final file could be processed through the plot tape program and a computer graphics device to give a visual representation of the election districts formed.

III. SYSTEM DESIGN

A. Source of Information

The GIST block file is a composite of information that is stored in three separate sources (see Fig. 3).

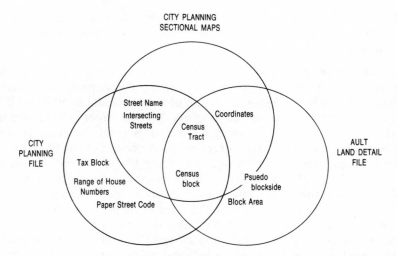

Fig. 3   Information structure of GIST sources.

1. The first is the City Planning Sectional Maps which are maintained by the New York Department of City Planning to reflect the existing and proposed legal street and block layout. These maps are regarded as the primary source of information for official streets. It should be pointed out, however, that there are many privately owned streets throughout the city from Riverdale in the Bronx to Breezy Point in Queens. Many of these are privately maintained and do not appear on the City Planning Maps.

2. A second source of information is the AULT Land Detail File, which was prepared from aerial photographs taken in 1962 by the Tri-State Transportation Commission. This file has the coordinates of each blockface in machine readable form. For those blockfaces where there is a significant curvature, the blockface is divided into pseudo-blocksides each of which is treated as a separate blockside record. This file also contains the computed area of each block. When the coordinate data from the AULT file is transformed into a graphic representation at the appropriate scale, the data can be visually compared with the coordinate data on the City Planning Sectional Maps. This is reflected by showing the coordinate data common to the City Planning Sectional Maps and the AULT file (see Fig. 3).

3. The third source of data is the City Planning Address Coding Guide.

This file contains the street name, intersecting street names, and range of house numbers for every blockface which either exists or is legally mapped. If a certain blockface is along a street that has a legal existence but which may not actually be developed for several years, the Coding Guide will indicate this by a "paper street" code.

One piece of information that is common to all three sources of data is the census tract and census block designation (see Fig. 3). The census blockside information is common to the City Planning file and the AULT file although there are numerous discrepancies in these designations as will be discussed below.

B. Choice of Approach

The basic problems in creating a comprehensive file from the three sources lies first in preprocessing the information such that a visual comparison of the data from the three sources can be made, and secondly, in providing for an efficient system to make the necessary modifications to correct inconsistencies and to verify these corrections.

The preprocessing consists of reformatting, listing, and providing plot tapes and necessary computer graphics to prepare the visual presentations from the data stored on magnetic tape. The editing and checking can either be done in a normal batch environment where corrections are first coded, a file update run is made, and further editing and corrections are performed. The alternative, which was the procedure chosen, is to perform the corrections on-line. This has the very significant advantage that the inconsistencies are detected, corrected, checked, and the final file created in a single operation. While this significantly increases computer cost, it permits a far more efficient utilization of personnel. A given area, usually a census tract, can be intensively studied and corrections made and verified while the area is fresh in the minds of the personnel involved. The alternative of first making an entry in a batch mode means that if subsequent problems develop, the personnel have to reacquaint themselves with the peculiarities of that area. Since the number of inconsistencies and "special" situations were quite numerous (initial estimates indicate that these run anywhere from 5% to 20% of all records, depending upon the area of the city), this appears to be the predominating factor.

The balance of the paper will discuss some of the problem areas that arose and the interactive technique that was developed for the creation of this file.

C. Generation of File

The AULT file is first transferred to a disk file and is plotted by census tract. A typical plot is shown in Fig. 4. This plot is to the same scale as, and is superimposed upon, the corresponding area of the City Planning Sectional Maps. The City Planning Sectional Maps are first preprocessed to assign highway sequence numbers to all highways.

These overlayed maps are used in conjunction with the listing prepared from the City Planning file, in a three-way checking procedure which is

TRACT 0153

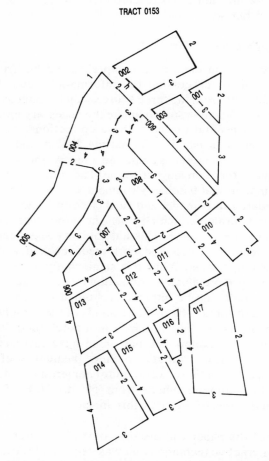

Fig. 4   Example of a census tract plot prepared from the AULT file.

the heart of the system being developed. The City Planning file listing identifies each blockface by census identification, the name of the street along which that blockface runs, and the names of the cross-streets (in clockwise order). This listing is verified against the overlayed map data. There are a large number of discrepancies that come to light in this process. Listed in the approximate order of their occurrence, these are as follows:

1. A blockface number is inconsistent between the City Planning file and the AULT file.
2. Disagreement between the shapes of blocks or identification of blocks between the City Planning Sectional Maps and the AULT file.
3. Disagreement on the street name between the City Planning Sectional and the City Planning file.
4. Blocks are omitted from one or more of the three sources of information.

Such discrepancies are marked on the map by means of colored stickers and are similarly indicated on the City Planning file listings. Unless unusual situations are present, the City Planning Sectionals are regarded as a primary data source and any discrepancies are corrected to be consistent with the City Planning Sectional Maps. However, in such cases where the City Planning Sectional Map does not indicate the block indicated on one of the other sources or another unusual situation, the Department of City Planning is asked to review such discrepancies and indicate the desired course of action.

Once this step has been accomplished, the corrections indicated on the maps and listings are performed by means of a system consisting of a Benson–Lehner digitizer and a typewriter terminal. The maps indicating the corrections and additions needed are placed on the digitizer which has previously been correctly scaled and adjusted so that it reads directly the coordinates of any point to which the cross-hairs are set. New or revised coordinates, as read from the digital voltmeter displays on the digitizer, are entered on an IBM 2741 terminal together with the actions indicated from the listings. The on-line program operates both on the AULT file and the City Planning files to correct the files until the operator is satisfied that they are consistent. At this time, he merges the files to create the GIST file.

The interactive system has numerous provisions for checking the precise records that are being operated on, for backspacing the records, and for displaying intermediate or final results. There is also provision for generating printer plots of new or modified blocks. The entire system is set up so that in one task the file is updated, merged, and checked.

In order to facilitate this critical operation, 29 special macro-instructions were written, each instruction fulfilling a unique function. A listing of the instructions with their meaning is shown in Fig. 5. This listing, as shown in the figure, is stored as part of the program that is available to the programmer at any time if he needs to refer to it. The instructions are written both in BAL and FORTRAN IV. The program is run on an IBM 360/67 operating under CMS (Cambridge Monitor System).

OPCODE	MEANING
STAR	PRINT STARTING RECORD
RDCP N	READ N CP RECORDS
RDAU N	READ N AULT RECORDS
MERG N	MERGE N RECORDS
BKCP N	BACKSPACE N CP RECORDS
BKAU N	BACKSPACE N AULT RECORDS
BKOT N	BACKSPACE N MERGE FILE RECORDS
PRCP	PRINT CP RECORDS
	OPERAND = 150, PRINT ALL RECORDS
	OPERAND = N, PRINT NTH RECORD
	OPERAND = M, N, PRINT MTH TO NTH RECORD
PRAU	SAME AS PRCP, EXCEPT AULT RECORDS
PROT	SAME AS PRCP EXCEPT MERGE FILE RECORDS
PRPT	PRINTER PLOT, OPERANDS TO BE EXPLAINED
CCPN	CHANGE CP NUMBERING
ADCP	ADD CP RECORD
CAUN	CHANGE AULT NUMBERING
CAUC	CHANGE AULT COORDINATES
ADAU	ADD AULT RECORD
END	INITIATE END ROUTINE
NEXC N	INCREMENT CP WORK RECORD BY N
NEXA N	SAME AS NEXC, EXCEPT AULT RECORD
LOCC	LOCATE CP RECORD
LOCA	LOCATE AULT RECORD
DELC N	DELETE NTH CP RECORD
DELA N	DELETE NTH AULT RECORD
CENT	INSERT CENTROID COORDINATES
TIME	GET CPU TIME (SECS.)
MERO N	MERGE N CP RECORDS WITH BLANK AULT RECORDS
FLAG	SET UP TO 5 FLAGS PER MERGED RECORD
POSC	GET CP RECORD NUMBER CURRENTLY BEING WORKED ON
POSA	SAME AS POSC, EXCEPT AULT RECORD

NOTE: IF N IS OMITTED IN ANY ONE ARGUMENT OPCODE, 1 IS ASSUMED

Fig. 5 Listing of instructions for GIST file creation.

Using the instructions of Fig. 5, the various discrepancies noted above, as well as others that occur with less frequency, can be rapidly and reliably corrected. A section of the printout resulting from typical operation of the system is shown in Fig. 6. It should be noted that this listing provides a very detailed account of all of the operations performed in the creation of the GIST file and serves as a valuable historical record giving the origin of this file if any section of it should be questioned at some future time.

```
posa

WORKING ON RECORD NO. 32 OF THIS AULT SET

READY
prau 32, 33
```

TRACT	BLOCK	SIDE	PSEUDO-SD	X COORD	Y COORD
49	8	4	0	500405	496841
49	8	5	0	500396	496879

```
READY

merg 2

READY

merg 10

READY

posc

WORKING ON RECORD NO. 44 OF THIS CP SET

READY

posa

WORKING ON RECORD NO. 44 OF THIS AULT SET
```

Fig. 6   Example of a typical sequence in the GIST file creation system.

The concept of the operation of the system can be described with reference to Fig. 6. The first instruction (indicated by lower case letters) is a request from the operator asking for his current position on the AULT file. This instruction is used if the operator is uncertain as to which record he is currently operating on. The computer responds by typing back (in upper case letters) the information that he is currently working on record number 32, and indicates on the next line that it is ready for the next instruction.

The next instruction from the operator is to print record number 32 and 33 from the AULT file. The computer prints an abbreviated version of these records as indicated and then indicates that it is ready for the next instruction. The operator can then check that the records are in a suitable condition to be merged and gives the instruction to merge the next two records (i.e., records 32 and 33 from the AULT file with the corresponding records from the City Planning file).

The computer indicates that it has accomplished this by typing back the word "READY."

Assuming that at this point the operator knows precisely where he is on both files and there are no problems on the next ten records, he simply gives the instruction "merg 10." This simply merges the next ten records from both files. The computer indicates that it has accomplished this by giving the response "READY."

In the last two operator inputs, the operator is requesting the position first on the City Planning file and then on the AULT file. The computer responds in both cases that he is currently working on record number 44.

This completes the description of the operations illustrated in Fig. 6. When new records must be created, an interactive scheme is utilized, illustrated in Fig. 7. The operator indicates that he wishes to add a City

```
adcp
ENTER: TRACT,TRACT SUF,BLOCK,BLOCK SUF,BLOCKSIDE,NO. OF BLOCKSIDES,  ?49, ,8,  ,4,5,
ENTER: STREET NAME,END,SUFFIX,   ?avenue of the americas,
ENTER: LOW INTERSECT STREET NAME,END,SUFFIX,   ?spring,st,
ENTER: HIGH INTERSECT STREET NAME,END,SUFFIX,   ?macdougal,st,
ENTER: BOROUGH CODE,CITY SECTIONAL MAP NUMBER,   ?0,12,
HIGHWAY, 'Y' OR 'N' .... ?n

READY
```

Fig. 7   Interactive creation of new records.

Planning record. The system then prompts him to enter, in turn, the various information required for this record. The computer prompting ends with a question mark, after which the operator enters the required information in the indicated format. If necessary, the operator can ask for a printout of the record to verify that it has, in fact, been properly entered.

D. Future Plans

The system being designed for the GIST blockside file will include a maintenance procedure. Also, the records include a number of flags that indicate the update status of the record as well as a number of special problem situations.

Future plans for the GIST blockside file includes the addition of information concerning the adjacent blockfaces to each blockface in the file.

Finally, the GIST information system calls for the addition of a lot file, which will give additional information concerning each tax lot on a blockface. Once completed, this will provide a very powerful tool for providing information to numerous city agencies and for performing a wide range of studies in an expeditious and relatively inexpensive manner.

*Appendix I**

A. SAMPLE APPLICATIONS

Since its implementation, the GIST system has been utilized in various New York City contexts. The applications tend to show how a common data base may be used by numerous agencies operating in different situations, thereby, fostering a more effective interchange and utilization of available data in public administration. The effectiveness in this regard stems from the reduction in duplicated information files, inconsistent information files, and incompatible information files. A sampling of the application by the various agencies is shown below. Following this are illustrations of computer-drawn maps of New York City based on GIST.

Office for the Aging

A file of 525,000 senior citizens, who have been issued half-fare transit passes, has been address-matched against the GIST GBF. Ninety-three percent of the records were successfully matched and health area, census tract and block, zip code and block center coordinate numbers were added to these records. The resulting file is being used in an origin-

---

*Prepared by Robert Amsterdam.

destination study of the need for a dial-a-ride service to drive elderly people to health clinics and hospitals. The file will also be used in conjunction with 1970 census data to evaluate the reach of Office for the Aging programs.

Department of Air Resources

A series of contour maps were generated showing the distribution of various polluting substances throughout New York City. Average measurements obtained from 27 monitoring stations were used as input data for the SYMAP program.

Real Property Assessment Department

In cooperation with the assessors, a tape file is being developed with a record for each building in the City and a full street address for each record. There are approximately 820,000 records in the current version of this file.

For a study of assessment procedures, a random sample of 10,000 properties was selected and classified. Block center coordinates were identified for each parcel. These were used to print maps pinpointing each parcel for the purpose of more detailed study.

Department of Buildings

To assist the City Council and the Department of Buildings in drafting new fire regulations covering fully airconditioned buildings, a listing of all office buildings over nine stories was printed from the current GIST building file.

Preliminary work has begun to capture Buildings Department data on new buildings and demolitions in order to maintain the GIST buildings file on a current basis.

Department of City Planning

The GIST GBF, which was developed in cooperation with the City Planning Department, was used to address-match a file of business establishments and identify each record by tax block, census block, and CPD (community planning district). The resulting file has been used in several small area studies by the Planning Department to determine the affects of new developments on existing business activity.

A Census Bureau file of 70,000 retail establishments was address-matched under Census Bureau supervision to add census tract and block number to each matched record. The overall match rate was 88%. The resulting file will be used by City Planning in a variety of small area studies.

Office of Civil Defense

The Community Shelter Plan being constructed for New York City requires the allocation of surveyed shelter spaces to neighboring residential and nonresidential populations. Shelter addresses were address-matched to the GIST GBF to determine the census block and tax block numbers for each shelter.

The GIST building file is being used to estimate the population of each structure for use in making specific building allocations.

Board of Education

The file of welfare recipients for July 1970 was address-matched to identify the census tract and block for each case. The resulting file was used by the Board to identify the number of school-aged children receiving public assistance in each school district. This was used in allocating federal funds to each community school board. A follow-up run is being made with the September 1971 recipients file.

Board of Elections

A pilot study was made, using approximately 100 city blocks, in which addresses of registered voters were located at their approximate positions on each block. This was used to re-draw voting precincts so that the number of voters at each polling booth would be more uniform.

Environmental Protection Administration

A system is under development to estimate the power needs (electric, oil, gas, telephone) and refuse build-up for each block in the city. It is planned that GIST building data will be used as a basic component of this system.

Department of Finance

The GIST staff has produced a program to develop a building address for each property from data contained in two different record types in the property assessors' punched card file. This program has been used by the Finance Department in providing addresses for tax lots involved in court proceedings.

The Tax Collector's file of retail cigarette vendors was address-matched to reformat and standardize the address of each dealer. The resulting file was used by the Finance Department to reorganize routes of cigarette tax collectors.

For a study of the real estate market, a Geospace plotter map was prepared showing every tax block in Manhattan. Selected blocks were density-shaded to show the distribution and amount of high-valued property that had changed ownership during the prior year. The map was used as an indicator of market interest and a clue to changing neighborhood values.

Health Services Administration

A system is being developed to address-match birth and death records weekly to indicate health area, health district, census tract, and census block. This will be used in compiling Department of Health reports, which are presently summarized by health area and health district. The addition of the census identifiers will permit other agencies to make greater use of these vital statistics data. A saving in clerical effort is anticipated when the new system is installed.

The Department of Mental Health is conducting a study of the travel routes and utilization by patients at the City's 500 mental health clinics. They used a printed listing of the GIST GBF to determine coordinate locations of each clinic.

To improve the dispersal and response times of ambulances, samples of ambulance calls have been address-matched to obtain the coordinates for each call address. The resulting data were used in simulations that justified establishing satellite ambulance stations, which are providing improved service at no additional cost.

A map of Bronx health areas was generated for Montefiore Hospital showing distribution of their outpatients by health area. This was used in an analysis of hospital facilities and planning techniques.

Housing and Development Administration

To assist the start-up of a new rent stabilization program, HDA's file of 150,000 apartment buildings was address-matched to identify the tax block for each building. This file is being used to obtain property tax data from financial records that are maintained by tax block number.

The Mayor's Complaint Office

A system is being installed to address-match all complaints for services received by the Mayor's office and code them to community planning districts. This will assist in following up on complaints that have been referred to operating departments for action.

Chief Medical Examiner

A series of maps are being prepared to pinpoint locations of certain categories of unnatural deaths over the last 12 months. These will include a map of addresses of drug-related deaths and a map of locations of murder victims. These maps are expected to assist law enforcement activities.

Police Department

A comprehensive review is being made of the Police Department's street code numbers to determine how these numbers can best be added to the GIST GBF. Through this effort GIST will be able to transmit data to the Police SPRINT system on new street openings.

Department of Social Services

The welfare recipients file for August 1971 was address-matched to identify health area and census tract for each record. Out of 428,000 records, 95% were successfully matched. The resulting file was used in creating summary reports for use in departmental operations.

A map was produced for the Social Services Department showing distribution of cases by health area. This was used in determining the location of a new field office.

B. ILLUSTRATIVE MAPS

In the computer drawn maps, which are shown for New York City, city land is shown in white against surrounded shaded areas. Each map shows the locations of 1000 randomly selected buildings of a particular category which are being examined in a study of property tax policy. These illustrate the diversity of the map types that can be prepared via GIST.

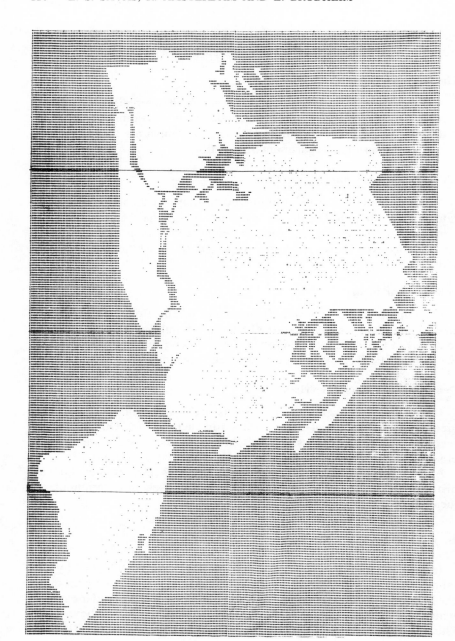

Fig. 8   One family dwellings.

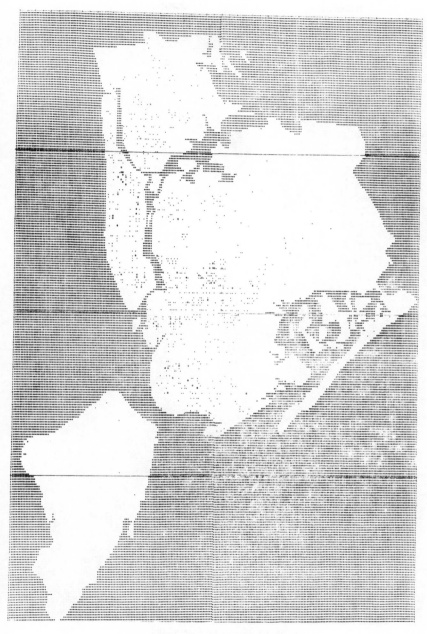

Fig. 9 Walk-up apartment buildings.

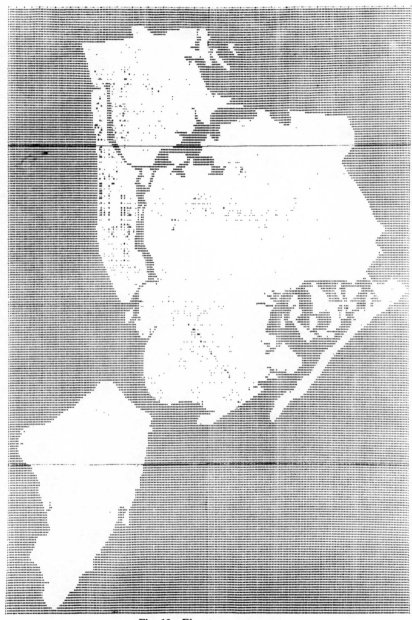

Fig. 10 Elevator apartments.

One Family Dwellings

This map shows private homes scattered broadly through the outer boroughs. Concentrations are highest in central and eastern Queens, southern Brooklyn, north-central Bronx, and northern Richmond.

Walk-up Apartments

This map shows tenement buildings more heavily concentrated in the older neighborhoods of the City. Densities are high throughout Manhattan, particularly in the lower East Side and Harlem. Densities are also high in central and eastern Brooklyn and in southern Bronx.

Elevator Apartments

The newer apartment buildings are shown lining the principal thoroughfares. In Manhattan, heavy lines are shown on the major east side and west side avenues. In the Bronx, the concentration is in the Jerome Avenue–Grand Concourse area. In Queens, apartment buildings are concentrated along Queens Boulevard. In Brooklyn the density is shown heaviest along Ocean Avenue.

6

Computer-based Personnel Information Systems*

C. P. H. MARKS

Civil Service Department, London, England

"Personnel" in the heading of this article comprises the 500,000 people employed in the United Kingdom Civil Service in a non-industrial capacity. That is to say, it includes everyone in central government from permanent heads of Ministries down to typists and clerks, but excludes people working, for example, as machine-tool operators or foundrymen in such places as dockyards and ordnance factories. It does not include people employed in local government, the nationalized industries, Post Office, the health service, police, transport or education.

The use of a computer for keeping personnel records is, of course, nothing new, and indeed one of its predecessors, the "Powers" punched-card "accounting machine" was used to analyse the annual Civil Service census records as far back as 1929. Subsequently, a continuously up-dated individual personnel record, kept centrally for all Civil Servants on "Hollerith" punched-cards, was instituted in 1947, and this was transferred to a computer in 1968. It is known as the Civil Service Central Staff Record (CSCSR).

The calculation of salaries for Civil Servants was first done by computer in 1957—and not just the progression from gross pay to net pay, but the revision of gross pay by applying the logic of salary determination rules to the personal data recorded. This included pay revision, for instance, on birthdays or anniversaries of appointment as appropriate, as well as the application of new pay scales and percentage cost of living increases. A considerable amount of personnel information useful to personnel managers and manpower planners is accordingly recorded on

---

*This article is British Crown copyright and is reproduced by permission of the Controller of Her Britannic Majesty's Stationary Office.

the various Ministry pay computers, but up to now it has not been harnessed for use in this way. All information for central statistical and manpower planning purposes has had to be obtained from the CSCSR.

SHORTCOMINGS OF EXISTING PERSONNEL RECORD SYSTEMS

In a very large organization the flow of information about what is happening to people, their recruitment, retirement, promotion, and so on, tends to be slow (except for the "fast lane" through to the pay system). It rises from level to level (see Fig. 1) with varying rates of progress and different degrees of accuracy. The keeping of personnel records tends to

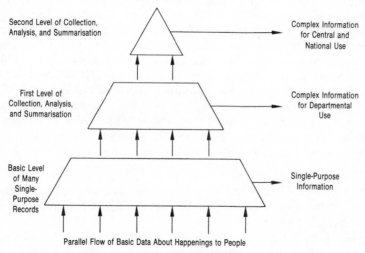

Fig. 1   Orthodox personnel information service flow.

be a low priority task which gets left undone when work thought to be more important comes along. This applies both to the manual and mechanical processes, but with the former especially, the work is tedious; low grade staff may be employed and errors are manifold. The CSCSR, having existed for over 25 years, presents a constant problem in how to keep it tolerably accurate and up to date. Its main defects are:

1. Inaccuracies developed progressively through its long life.
2. Difficulty in getting Ministries to provide prompt up-dating data.

3. Difficulty in obtaining historical information from the files, particularly in relation to "flows" through the manpower system showing, for instance, the promotion or wastage patterns.
4. The lack of a positive feed-back checking system for data.
5. The lack of a powerful information retrieval system.

NEW PERSONNEL INFORMATION SYSTEMS (I)—CMSR

Following the report in 1968 of the review of the Civil Service by Lord Fulton's Committee,* a new personnel record was set up to help improve personnel management particularly of the most senior level staff who now comprise an "open-structure." This has three levels, Permanent Secretary, Deputy Secretary, and Under Secretary, and all senior staff, irrespective of their old type grading or specialism, are eligible for these posts on merit and ability. To provide essential personnel information, particularly for specialists for whom no central record had previously been held, a new Central Management Staff Record (CMSR) was set up in 1970. This now covers some 11,000 people, and besides top level staff includes whole categories of staff, for example, statisticians and economists, who are largely managed centrally rather than by the individual Ministries.

The most important features of the CMSR record relate to job experience and educational/professional qualifications, a multiaxis system being used for both. Job experience is coded under five axes:

1. *Level*: as indicated by maximum of the salary range.
2. *Occupation*: The field with which a man is concerned, for example, Electronic Engineering, Quantity Surveying. (Up to three codes may be selected to describe a job.)
3. *Function*: Specifies how the individual fits into the surrounding organization, for example, Manager—Research and Development. (Up to two codes may be selected as some jobs may have more than a single aspect.)
4. *Type of Organization*: Describes the character of the employing organization, for example, Home Civil Service, Judiciary.
5. *Activity of Organization*: Describes the main activity or function of the employing organization, for example, Communications. This item only applies when specifying a job held outside the Home Civil Service.

*The Civil Service: Report of the Fulton Committee, Her Majesty's Stationary Office, London, June 1968.

Qualifications are recorded by level (with gradations for Class of Degree), and by subject grouping.

A powerful retrieval language SPECOL*—Special Customer Oriented Language—is used to get information from CMSR via remote terminal. This enables complex questions to be composed as a logical (Boolean) chain in a comparatively simple way. There is no restriction on the type of question which can be asked within the confines of the data, but broadly speaking the process is confined to selection and retrieval, and there are no mathematical operations apart from simple counts.

A typical question might be:

> Give the complete record of all people with at least three years service in Levels 21 or 31, aged between 30 and 40, not currently serving in either Treasury or Inland Revenue, who have either a degree subject Economics or any current or previous job experience of Economics, fluent in French or German.

Fuller descriptions of the CMSR system are to be found in papers by Bridle and Gregersen[1, 2]. Interesting comparisons can be made with the U.S. Government's "Executive Inventory" system and with the Canadian Government's "Datastream."

NEW PERSONNEL INFORMATION SYSTEMS (II)—PRISM

Whilst CMSR met some of the needs for personnel information stemming from the Fulton report, a much broader information base was needed to meet more fully the requirements of the rapidly developing personnel management and manpower planning services. In other words, it had to be a replacement system for the obsolete CSCSR, but it had not just to meet the information needs of the centre, that is, the Civil Service Department and the Treasury, but also the personnel management requirements of the individual Ministries. The new system, which came to be known as PRISM (Personnel Record Information System for Management), has these key features:

1. It is an integrated pay and personnel record system.
2. It operates as a two-level data base system serving both levels of management, central and departmental.
3. The central record is maintained as a collection of 500,000 individual

---

*Smith, Bernard, *A Computer Enquiry Language for the General User*, Civil Service Department, Her Majesty's Stationary Office, London, 1970.

personal records, and no attempt is made to hold any form of summary records.

4. It is maintained on true data base principles, that is, single notification of occurrences, data base recording (not functional file recording), and multiple outputs.

A schematic diagram of the two-level data base (or data bank) system is given in Fig. 2, which shows the central data base being fed with information automatically from the ring of peripheral computers. There will be nine or ten such peripheral machines maintaining an integrated pay and personnel record system for the various Ministries (Departments); some will serve a single Ministry, others will operate on an agency basis, with one serving up to 50 different Departments. There is a central computer which will have as its main task the maintenance of a central data base of personnel information on all non-industrial staff, kept up to date with information from the peripheral Departmental computers; this data base will be the source of personnel information to meet central users' needs. The central computer can be considered as the nerve centre of the information system and is located near London at the CSD Computer Centre at Chessington, Surrey. There is in fact a "twin"

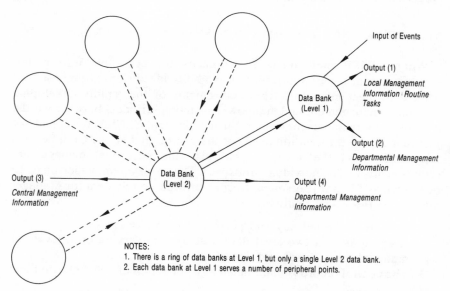

Input of Events

Output (1)

Local Management Information · Routine Tasks

Data Bank (Level 1)

Output (2)

Departmental Management Information

Output (3)

Central Management Information

Data Bank (Level 2)

Output (4)

Departmental Management Information

NOTES:
1. There is a ring of data banks at Level 1, but only a single Level 2 data bank.
2. Each data bank at Level 1 serves a number of peripheral points.

Fig. 2   Civil Service personnel information system: Schematic diagram of information flow for network system.

installation at this location, the other computer providing an agency service for about 100,000–125,000 people as indicated above. Both computers are models ICL 1904S manufactured by International Computers Limited.

Implementation of PRISM is planned in phases: by the end of the first phase, the target date for which is the end of 1974, the aim is to have all 500,000 non-industrial staff on computer payrolls, with an integrated, "non-pay," personnel record for each person. A subset of this combined record called the Central Personal Record (CPR) will be siphoned from the peripheral computers to the central data base. The contents of the CPR are listed in Appendix A. When the system is proven, the existing CSCSR will be superseded and it should be possible to dispense with many manual returns from Departments. An important task in the first phase will be concerned with enhancing payroll systems—so that as much work as possible is done automatically—and standardising them as far as practicable to avoid duplication of systems work and programming among Departments. In addition, the CMSR system already described will be dovetailed into, and become part of, PRISM, but it will still only cover the same limited number of high level and other centrally managed staff.

Developments beyond Phase I are currently (1973) being reviewed so that approval to proceed can be sought in time to ensure continuity of planning. In the main these developments, if approved, are likely to be aimed at improving the information systems within Departments rather than bringing more information to the centre. (Indeed, in some Departments developments of this kind are being introduced in conjunction with the mandatory Phase I records.) In general, the intention is for the basic personnel record to be extended to make it fully comprehensive, but further records may be developed, for example, one recording the qualifications and characteristics required for each post. Developments are also expected in the area of special programs for processing data to provide a more efficient service to management. The ultimate objective is for manual records and returns to be virtually eliminated—although personal files containing basic certificates and documents such as confidential reports will remain. The aim will be to keep printed output to the minimum and confine it as far as possible to precise information required to meet specific management needs.

PRISM—Information Storage and Retrieval

The basic PRISM philosophy is to be able to answer any question automatically and quickly within the logical derivations of the data recorded. The intention is that a user will sit at a remote terminal—a Visual Display Unit (VDU)—and, by having an interactive dialogue with the computer, progressively obtain from the huge mass of stored data the relatively small piece of useful information he requires. This process will be directly analogous to the way a man at present uses a terminal linked to a computer to work his way through an intricate mathematical or numerical problem: with PRISM he will work his way through an information selection problem, sometimes with the addition of a mathematical manipulation on the selected data.

If the aim is to answer *any* question which may arise, and recognizing that the variety of possible questions is almost infinite, it follows that data cannot be stored advantageously in any particular order, or in summary or digest form. It follows further that questions would normally necessitate running through the whole data base ($500,000 \times 75$ data elements) and, since many questions may be coming simultaneously through the various terminals, the problems of queuing and delays might appear daunting in the extreme. The PRISM solution to these problems is to completely "invert" the main file (held in conventional serial fashion), so as to create a "header" for every value of each record element, behind which are held the identities of the people who satisfy that value. A simplified example of part of a main file and an inverted record is shown in Fig. 3, from which it will be seen that "London" is a value in the element "location," and "Principal" a value in the element "grade." By simple Boolean operations on the comparatively short inverted lists, the selection process rapidly converges and enables answers to complicated questions to be obtained in acceptable response times at the terminals. Taking Fig. 3 for example, and using the Boolean (logical) operation "and" on the "Principal" list and the "Reading" list, the answer to the question "Who are the Principals working in Reading?" leads only to Mr. Smith (via identity 11). Further details of Mr. Smith can then be obtained, if required, from the main file using his identity "11" directly as the index. (This main serial file is called PRISMASTER.)

The PRISM inverted file is called "Countflow," and in addition to its main characteristic it is date sensitive, in that losses and gains to the various "headers" are recorded month by month in parallel lists. This provides four very great benefits:

1. The "current state" of the record is very much more accurate than can otherwise be achieved by the device of taking a threshold date just far enough back to eliminate the effect of reporting delays. This is because the record is based on the effective dates when events

KEY	SURNAME	GRADE	YEAR OF BIRTH	LOCATION
11	Smith	Principal	1930	Reading
12	Jackson	Executive Officer	1935	London
13	Smithers	Executive Officer	1930	London
14	Jarvis	Executive Officer	1935	Reading
15	Janion	Assistant Secretary	1930	London

THE SAME INFORMATION INVERTED—(COUNTFLOW)

Key

Principal	11		
Executive Officer	12	13	14
Assistant Secretary	15		
1930	11	13	15
1935	12	14	
Reading	11	14	
London	12	13	15

Fig. 3 Simple example of a serial file (PRISMASTER).

happened, rather than on the spectrum of events which happened to be reported by a particular date.

2. There is no necessity to keep separate historical or "snapshot" files.
3. It is as easy to obtain directly "flow" information (e.g., about wastage), as it is to get "stock" information (e.g., about numbers in post). This is particularly important for modern techniques of manpower modelling.
4. It is as easy to obtain information about past situations as it is about the present.

"Countflow" is described in more detail in a paper by Bellerby[3].

PRISM—On-line Access

As mentioned, the main access to the central PRISM data base will be by terminals, using VDUs in an interactive mode, but there will, of course, also be facilities both for fast bulk printing and for copying the page display from a VDU. Since up to 40 VDUs are planned for the first phase of PRISM development, and questions will range from the extremely simple (Give the record of a named person) to the quite complex (Produce a matrix nesting in several layers giving an age and seniority distribution of a particular grade), several problems have to be solved:

1. There must be an immediate response to the user for all "housekeeping" dialogue.
2. Long and intricate questions must not delay the answers being given to short and simple ones.
3. The answers to all questions must be within acceptable response times at terminals.
4. The expected traffic must not swamp the system.
5. There must be a hand-holding dialogue for the lay-user (e.g., a new personnel manager) with more sophisticated and direct methods available for the expert (e.g., a statistician familiar with the data).
6. Adequate privacy and security safeguards must be built into the system.

Our approach to problems 1–4 is to regard questions as if they were transactions, and to deal with them basically as "multi-transaction processing." International Computers Limited (ICL) have developed a system called "DRIVER" for their ICL 1900 Series machines which enables transactions to be regarded as threads carrying beads, each of which is processed individually with the threads being subsequently re-created after all beads are available. This has been modified to meet specific PRISM requirements into a piece of software called PDS (Prism Driver System) which is the main key to fast interaction and to questions "overtaking" each other.

Considerable use of mathematical models has been made to model the system at the systems design stage, prior to programming, so as to ascertain response times and see at what point traffic is likely to swamp the system. An unexpected bonus from this work was that in some areas it led directly to a more efficient programming approach than might otherwise have been adopted.

In order for the user, and particularly the inexperienced user, to be able to exploit the full power of the system, it was found necessary to create a special retrieval language. This, called PIRL (Prism Information Retrieval Language), enables the user both to describe the nature of what he wants done in a general sense (e.g., create a table) and to specify the required information in his own terms without a detailed knowledge of the data or how it is stored.

Security and Privacy

Although, as will be been from Appendix A, the Central Personal Record does not at this stage contain any particularly sensitive items, great care is taken to ensure that unauthorised users do not gain access to information. No computer system can be *absolutely* secure, and even the "last few places of decimals" of security can be immensely costly. The steps taken in PRISM are the equivalent of the care taken in the U.K. Civil Service for all confidential staff documents. All terminals have physical locks, and in addition each user has his own code key which he can (and should) change from time to time. If anyone attempts to break the code by trial and error, the system locks up after three tries and it is necessary to establish an entirely new connection from the terminal. Any such irregular attempt to tap the system is logged by the computer for immediate investigation.

Particular data areas receive special protection. Whereas some users (e.g., the appropriate personnel managers) are entitled to full information such as a man's complete history, others like statisticians will be barred, but will of course be free to use the basic data in a depersonalized sense.

These considerations are of particular importance to the Staff Associations or Trade Unions, which represent the individual Civil Servant. Throughout the development of all aspects of the PRISM system there has been close and genuine co-operation between Management and Unions and the latter are content with all that is planned, including the security/privacy aspects.

It is also regarded as important by both sides that the individual shall receive a regular print-out of his record. This has been done for CMSR from its inception and will continue with PRISM. Quite apart from its importance to the individual, it is an extremely useful method for checking the accuracy of the record.

PRISM—Current State

At the time of writing, the second half of 1973, computer programs were being tested and sample records being set up. During 1974, the central data base will be built up, ministry by ministry, so as to be completed by the end of that year. As far as is known, PRISM is unique in several respects, with its use of a totally inverted, date-sensitive file and its concept of interactive, reiterative terminal working to retrieve information from a massive data base. If these ideas work out well in practice they may well be applied to completely different information areas.

PRISM has been chosen by OECD (Organization for Economic Co-operation and Development) as one of eight personnel/manpower information systems in six European countries which have been the subject of case studies in depth. The report[4] has been published.

PRISM and Manpower Planning

By way of conclusion, it needs to be stressed that PRISM is not an end in itself; it is a tool to be used by managers and planners to enable them to do their work better. Manpower planning and personnel management are often considered to be two entirely different functions, but they really are not. They interlock very tightly indeed. Development of manpower models with the object of providing practical assistance to the personnel manager is progressing rapidly in the U.K. Civil Service, but this is not the place to begin to describe it. (Interested readers are referred to Smith[5], Bartholomew and Smith[6], and Hopes[7].) But the new approaches which are starting to be developed towards making the most effective use of the most precious resource in the Service, people, depend utterly on being able to get accurate and immediate information out of a vast mass of data. This is what PRISM is all about.

REFERENCES

1. Bridle, J. W. and Gregersen, R. J. The central management staff record—A personnel information retrieval system, *OSM Bulletin*, Vol. 26, No. 2 (May 1971), Her Majesty's Stationary Office, London.
2. Bridle, J. W. and Gregersen, R. J. CMSR—A personnel information system, *The Computer Journal*, Vol. 14, No. 4 (November 1971), British Computer Society, London.
3. Bellerby, P. A. (Group Capt. R.A.F.) PRISM—Countflow—A date sensitive inverted file. Paper presented at *Datafair 1973*, Civil Service Department, London, 1973.
4. *The Development of EDP in Manpower Areas.* (A comparative study of personnel information systems and their implications in six European countries.) Bayhylle, J. E. and Hersleb, A. eds., Organisation for Economic Co-operation and Development (OECD), Paris, 1973/74.
5. Smith, A. R., ed. *Models of Manpower Systems*, The English Universities Press Ltd., London, 1970.

6. Bartholomew, D. J. and Smith, A. R. *Manpower and Management Science*, The English Universities Press Ltd., London, 1970.
7. Hopes, R. F. A. Some statistical aspects of manpower planning in the Civil Service, *Omega*, the International Journal of Management Sciences, Vol. 1, No. 2 (1973). Pergamon Press, Oxford and New York.

APPENDIX A

PRISM PHASE I

Central Personal Record—Content

PRISM Standard Element No.	Element Name
	Basic Details
100	National Insurance number/Civil Service identity number
101	Surname—recorded date
102	Surname
103	Initials—recorded date
104	Initials
105	Date of birth
106	Sex
107	Marital status—recorded date
108	Marital status
112	Hours of work (part-time staff)—date
113	Hours of work (part-time staff)
114	Registered disabled
115	Employment status or type of appointment—date
116	Employment status or type of appointment
	Civil Service Career
200	Civil Service—date of entry
201	Civil Service—grade on entry
202	Civil Service—method of entry
203	Civil Service—source of entry
204	Department—date of entry
205	Department
206	Department—method of entry
207	Grade—date of entry
208	Grade
209	Grade—method of entry

PRISM Standard Element No.	Element Name
210	Grade—seniority date
211	Professional/scientific discipline—date of entry
212	Professional/scientific discipline
213	Occupational group or class—method of entry
214	Temporary promotion—date
215	Temporary promotion—grade
216	Responsibility allowance—date
217	Responsibility allowance—amount
	Academic and Professional Qualifications
300	Qualification—type
301	Qualification—awarding institution
302	Qualification—level of attainment—overall
303	Qualification—subject
304	Qualification—year of award, or year of cessation/reinstatement of membership of a professional institution
	Type of Office/Location
402	Type of office—date of entry
403	Type of office
404	Location area—date of entry
405	Location area
	Borrowed/Loaned
500	Borrowed staff—date of return
501	Borrowed staff—parent department
502	Temporary absence from Civil Service—date started
503	Temporary absence from Civil Service—date of return
504	Temporary absence from Civil Service—category
505	Temporary absence from Civil Service—type of outside employment or occupation
	Pay
600	Pay (national rate)—date of effect
601	Pay—national rate
605	Estains option
	Superannuation/Gratuity
700	Superannuation/gratuity scheme—date of entry
701	Superannuation/gratuity scheme

PRISM Standard Element No.	Element Name
702	Re-employed Civil Servant—date
703	Re-employed Civil Servant
704	Superannuation/gratuity emoluments—date
705	Total emoluments reckonable for superannuation or gratuity
706	Notional date of entry to service reckonable for superannuation or gratuity

Superannuation/Gratuity

707	Balance of unestablished service prior to 14 July 1949 not reckonable for superannuation purposes
708	Reckonable unestablished service prior to 14 July 1949—date
709	Date of entry to service reckonable for superannuation or gratuity
710	Established service—grade on entry
711	Established service—method of entry
712	Widow's pension—recorded date
713	Widow's pension option and the rate of contribution
714	Pension for an adult dependant—recorded date
715	Pension for an adult dependant—option
718	Invalidity pension—recorded date
719	Invalidity pension—option
720	Purchase of added years for superannuation purposes—recorded date
721	Purchase of added years for superannuation purposes—number
722	Purchase of added years for superannuation purposes—method

Leaving

900	Leaving—date
901	Leaving—cause
902	Leaving—nature of award
903	Leaving—type of new employment or occupation.

FINANCIAL ADMINISTRATION

7

Optimization of Long-range Municipal Multiple-resource Fiscal Policies*

CHARLES B. WOODWARD

The Service Bureau Corp., 5151 West Imperial Highway, Inglewood, California 90304

Abstract—The Metropolitan Water District of Southern California (MWD) levies taxes, sells water, and issues bonds to finance the cost of distributing water to member cities. A linear programming model was developed to assist MWD in determining the cost to the citizen of various fiscal policies. A matrix generator was prepared to produce the LP matrix using raw fiscal data as input. The LP output was translated by another program into budget reports to the Board of Directors. These tools permitted analyses which were practically impossible manually, permitting a savings of approximately $25 million.

MODERN municipal financial operations are large in scope and are growing larger. Local taxation is a major source of revenue. As taxpayers and municipal governing bodies become more concerned over the increasing tax burdens, techniques which have been proven in other areas are being applied to municipal problems. Frequently, scientific computers are used in the implementation of these techniques. This paper discusses the methods used by The Service Bureau Corporation, Los Angeles Scientific Computer Center, for the Controller's Office, Metropolitan Water District of Southern California, to analyze the effects of alternative fiscal policies.

The Metropolitan Water District of Southern California (MWD) was established by the California Legislature as a central agency to wholesale water to participating member municipalities. Policies of the District are

---

*Reprinted from the *Journal of Socio-Economic Planning Sciences*, Vol. 1, 1968, pp. 273–282.

established by the Board of Directors who represent the municipalities. MWD is beginning a long period of construction to permit the District to meet the increasing demands for water. The significant construction costs may be met by combinations of revenues generated through the District's authority to levy taxes, through sale of water to members, or through issuance of bonds authorized by elections. MWD annually collects and disburses revenues from property taxes and water sales in excess of $60 million. A recent election approved an $850 million bond issue (1966 Construction Bonds) to finance part of the cost of new construction over the next 25 years.

There are three major elements which contribute to the annual fiscal policies of the District:

1. Total tax rate.
2. Rate for each class of water.
3. Period and amount of bond issues and period of retirement.

In addition to these three major elements, there are numerous other factors which must be considered to permit the budget to be established. Some of these are:

1. Any obligation of the District may be met from the appropriate operating fund or from the General Fund. How should each of the nine major obligations of the District be met each year?
2. Five of the eight operating funds may receive tax monies. How should the annual tax revenues be apportioned among these five funds?
3. Should a bond issue consist of 1966 Construction Bonds or Water Bonds (authorized in a previous election) or some combination of both?

Manual determination of fiscal policies which yield minimum cost to the citizen in the form of low tax rates and low prices for water is made prohibitively complex by the multiplicity of alternatives. The Controller's Office, responsible for preparing the budget and making policy recommendations to the Board of Directors, desired an economical way to determine minimum-cost policies. A linear programming model was developed which permitted the study of many alternatives and indicated the comparative cost to the citizen of each particular fiscal policy considered.

THE MODEL

The mathematical model was comprised of cash flow equations representing the annual operation of the various funds for the 24 year period of the study. There were generally at least two equations for each fund—a cash balance equation and a reserves equation. The reserves equations were necessitated by the legal requirement that certain minimums be maintained in each fund.

Additional coupling equations were used to assure that expenditures from the appropriate operating fund and the General Fund were equal to the particular obligation being satisfied. Coupling equations existed for state contract payments, government charges, 1931 Bond I & R, 1966 Bond I & R, and construction. To further indicate the complexity of the model still other equations controlled the maximum tax rate, the maximum water rates, the maximum rate of increase in the price of water, and the total of 1966 Construction Bonds and Water Bonds issued. Two separate objective functions were implemented:

1. Minimization of cost to the citizen (expressed as total tax and water sales revenues).
2. Minimization of total bond interest cost.

Tax revenues were determined by multiplying the variable tax rate by the projected assessed property valuation. Similarly, water revenues were the product of rates and predicted water usage. The items of receipts and expenditures for each fund are shown in Table 1.

THE MATRIX GENERATOR

The similarity of the equations for each fund and the repetition for each of the 24 periods of the model suggested the use of a matrix generator. Two types of input data were required.

1. *Monetary data—Current tax rates and fund reserves projected fixed receipts and expenditures, maximum tax and water rates, bond interest rates, interest rates earned on investments, etc.* Monetary data were read in, manipulated as required, and stored for later use. The stored data became Right-Hand-Side (RHS) values and matrix coefficients in the LP model. Only those coefficients which varied with time had to be stored; nonvarying coefficients were incorporated in the model data.

2. *Model data—Number of periods, row names, vector names, and fixed coefficients.* Model data permitted generation of the LP matrix in

Table 1 Fund receipts and expenditures.

Fund	General	State Contract	Replacement Reserve	1931 Bond I & R	Special Tax	1966 Bond Construction	1966 Bond I & R
Receipts							
Taxes	X	X		X			X
Water sales	X						
Interest on investment	X	X	X	X	X	X	X
Bond sales						X	
Annexation charges	X*				X		
Expenditures							
Operation and maintenance	X						
Long-term purchases	X						
W Bond I & R	X				X		
1931 Bond I & R	X			X			
1966 Bond I & R	X						X
New construction	X					X	
Replacements	X		X				
State contract	X	X				X†	
Government charges	X						

*Only the annexation charges in excess of required reserves in the Special Tax Fund go to the General Fund.

†Bond Construction Fund monies may be used to satisfy the payments to the state, provided that the amount does not exceed that required for the additional charge for excess capacity.

Share Standard format, which consists of the three sections ROW ID, MATRIX, and Right-Hand-Side values. The ROW ID was generated from row name model data. MATRIX data came from vector name and row name model data; fixed coefficients came from model data; variable coefficients came from the stored monetary data. Fixed RHS values were contained in row name model data; variable values came from the stored monetary data. The repetitive nature of the model permitted generation of rows and vectors for the 24 periods of the study from just one set of row and vector names. Minor modifications to the matrix were made by additional logic in the matrix generator or by the use of the REVISE option in the LP code.

The matrix generator permitted the rapid preparation of input to the LP code. Once the generator logic was verified, only the relatively small input deck to the generator needed to be checked in detail for errors. Use of the generator greatly reduced the possibility of coding or keypunch errors in the model going undetected. Any errors should occur repetitively and become very noticeable.

The matrix generator was used each time there was a change in projected income and expenditures. So long as the mathematical model remained unchanged, the generator could easily provide a matrix containing revised coefficients or RHS values.

THE REPORT WRITER

Output from the SBC proprietary LP code, ALPAC, is sometimes difficult to interpret. Since results of the studies would be going to the Financial Committee and to the Board of Directors, a report writer was written which would translate the ALPAC output into formats similar to the customary MWD budget reports. Besides making the result meaningful to the Directors, the report writer was used to check results against input data to assure solution of the correct problem.

The identical monetary data, which was read into the matrix generator, were used by the report writer. Again, the data was manipulated and stored. Then the output from ALPAC, in the form of LIAISON data, which provide the optimum basis in BCD format, was read into the report writer. The code of the vector names was interpreted, and the values unscaled if necessary and stored for easy use by the output routines.

The first report presented the annual total cash flow. The activities of all funds were summed for each period to give the total operation for each of the sources of receipts and each of the expenditures. A sample page of the report is shown in Fig. 1.*

The second report showed the complete annual operation. For each period, the total cash flow was presented, followed by the operation for each of the funds. The report for fiscal 1966/67 is shown in Fig. 2. (All figures are from a report prepared during the second study.) At this point a check was made to assure that the sum of the individual fund operations matched the total figure; the total figure was obtained from the input

---

*To protect the District's sensitive data, tax and water revenues have been lumped together in these reports. Tax rates and water rates have been set to zero. The actual reports to the District showed tax and water rates and revenues as indicated.

$*.00/Year Water Rate increase to $**.00, Maximum Tax Rate = $0.**

TOTAL CASH FLOW

	1966/67	1967/68	1968/69	1969/70	1970/71	1971/72	1972/73	1973/74	1974/75	1975/76	1976/77	1977/78
Est. reserves 6/30	68178.	51766.	69274.	74058.	69514.	64366.	53176.	49517.	48295.	47860.	48844.	50051.
Est. receipts												
Taxes												
Water sales	62812.	70400.	77839.	81904.	94763.	102941.	111626.	120813.	129954.	139545.	149310.	154953.
Interest on inv.	2523.	1915.	2563.	2740.	2572.	2382.	1968.	1832.	1787.	1771.	1807.	1852.
Bond sales	35400.	153475.	149869.	146116.	124228.	41208.	20574.	8736.	0.	0.	0.	0.
Annexation chgs.	8922.	8916.	8916.	8916.	8916.	8916.	8916.	8916.	8916.	8916.	8916.	8481.
Total est. receipts	109656.	234707.	239187.	239677.	230479.	155446.	143083.	140297.	140657.	150232.	160034.	165286.
Estimated expen.												
Oper. + maint.	15131.	16319.	18651.	21126.	23772.	26048.	27148.	27901.	28559.	28562.	28594.	28648.
Long term purc.	850.	837.	823.	810.	797.	783.	770.	660.	567.	562.	557.	551.
MWD. bond I+R	17983.	17561.	17138.	16716.	13514.	9494.	9262.	9031.	8799.	8568.	8336.	7964.
1966 bond int	664.	4205.	9893.	15443.	20512.	23613.	24772.	25321.	25296.	24807.	24097.	23408.
1966 bond red	0.	0.	0.	0.	0.	0.	0.	0.	10086.	16013.	21832.	14946.
New construction	63195.	139080.	148242.	159189.	134060.	55274.	31617.	24877.	11841.	13318.	14189.	25847.
Replacements	287.	301.	316.	332.	348.	365.	384.	403.	424.	445.	467.	490.
State contract	24824.	35629.	36068.	27329.	39345.	47773.	49371.	49901.	52091.	53551.	57339.	59527.
Gov. charges	3134.	3267.	3272.	3276.	3281.	3285.	3419.	3424.	3429.	3422.	3416.	3538.
Total est. expen.	126068.	217199.	234403.	244221.	235629.	166635.	146743.	141518.	141092.	149247.	158827.	164918.
Tax rate on secured property	0.	0.	0.	0.	0.	0.	0.	0.	0.	0.	0.	0.
Untreated M and I water rate	0.	0.	0.	0.	0.	0.	0.	0.	0.	0.	0.	0.
Untreated A and R water rate	0.	0.	0.	0.	0.	0.	0.	0.	0.	0.	0.	0.

Fig. 1 Total cash flow report.

137

$*.00/Year Water Rate Increase to $**.00, Maximum Tax Rate = $0.**

SUMMARY OF FUND CASH FLOWS—1966/67

	Total All Funds	General Fund	State Contract Fund	Repl. Reserve Fund	1966 Bond Construction Fund	1966 Bond I+R Fund	Special Tax Fund	1931 Bond I+R Fund
Est. reserves 6/30	68178.	26000.	0.	16070.	0.	0.	3516.	22592.
Est. receipts								
Taxes								
Water sales	62812.	35860.	23609.	0.	0.	0.	0.	3343.
Interest on inv.	2523.	962.	0.	595.	0.	0.	130.	836.
Bond sales	35400.	0.	0.	0.	35400.	0.	0.	0.
Annexation chgs.	8922.	0.	0.	0.	0.	0.	8922.	0.
Total est. receipts	109656.	36822.	23609.	595.	35400.	0.	9052.	4178.
Estimated expen.								
Oper. + maint.	15131.	15131.	0.	0.	0.	0.	0.	0.
Long term purc.	850.	850.	0.	0.	0.	0.	0.	0.
MWD. bond I+R	17983.	0.	0.	0.	0.	0.	7275.	10708.
1966 bond int.	664.	664.	0.	0.	0.	0.	0.	0.
1966 bond red	0.							
New construction	63195.	34068.	0.	0.	29127.	0.	0.	0.
Replacements	287.	0.	0.	287.	0.	0.	0.	0.
State contract	24824.	0.	23609.	0.	1215.	0.	0.	0.
Gov. charges	3134.	3134.	0.	0.	0.	0.	0.	0.
Total est. expen.	126068.	53847.	23609.	287.	30342.	0.	7275.	10708.
Tax rate on secured property	0.	0.	0.	0.	0.	0.	0.	0.
Untreated M and I water rate	0.	0.	0.	0.	0.	0.	0.	0.
Untreated A and R water rate	0.	0.	0.	0.	0.	0.	0.	0.

Fig. 2 Annual cash flow report.

monetary data, where possible, or calculated from ALPAC results independently of the LP model. Further, total receipts and expenditures were calculated and the reserve balance checked. These checks proved to be invaluable in both debugging the report writer and in verifying the LP solution.

The third report presented the same results as the second, but in a different format. For each fund the receipts and expenditures were shown for each fiscal period. The operation of the General Fund for the first 12 periods is shown in Fig. 3.

The fourth report contained two parts. The first part showed the annual issues and retirements for bonds, interest and redemption (I & R) costs, and allocation of I & R costs between the General Fund and the 1966 Bond I & R Fund (Fig. 4). The second part, shown in Fig. 5, presented the 1966 Construction Bond Issue and Retirement Schedule. For each period of issue, the dollar amount of bonds is shown for the period in which they are to be retired.

STUDIES PERFORMED

Three separate studies were performed for MWD. The first two did not permit W-Bonds to be issued. Construction Bonds could be issued as required and retired whenever deemed appropriate by the LP solution. As may be noted from Fig. 5, the retirements were not uniform nor contiguous. There was some concern regarding the marketability of such retirement schedules. The schedule can be improved by manual manipulation of the computer results.

The first study was actually a feasibility solution to determine what problems would be encountered and to check the LP model, the matrix generator, and the report writer. The first study also permitted the Controller's Office to gain an appreciation for the information which could be obtained from the model, and permitted SBC to fully understand the policy and legal restrictions which governed operation of the funds.

Although the maximum tax rate was unacceptably high, the results obtained from minimizing total rax and water revenues were illuminating.

The original model was very tightly constrained. The matrix contained 434 rows and 687 vectors and was 0.97% dense with 243 equalities. The first feasible solution was obtained in about 45 minutes on an IBM 7094; the optimum came about 30 minutes later.

For the second study, total tax rates were made more realistic. Some 13

$*.00/Year Water Rate Increase to $**.00, Maximum Tax Rate = $0.**
GENERAL FUND

	1966/67	1967/68	1968/69	1969/70	1970/71	1971/72	1972/73	1973/74	1974/75	1975/76	1976/77	1977/78
Est. reserves 6/30	26000.	8976.	6882.	7331.	8885.	10819.	12022.	13209.	14465.	15724.	17047.	18405.
Est. receipts												
Taxes												
Water sales	35860.	38860.	44173.	46206.	57458.	64010.	71069.	78627.	86136.	94089.	102218.	106233.
Interest on inv.	962.	332.	255.	271.	329.	400.	445.	489.	535.	582.	631.	681.
Bond sales	0.	0.	0.	0.	0.	0.	0.	0.	0.	0.	0.	0.
Annexation chgs.	0.	0.	0.	8383.	9056.	8916.	8916.	8916.	8916.	8916.	8916.	8481.
Total est. receipts	36822.	39192.	44428.	54860.	66843.	73326.	80430.	88032.	95587.	103587.	111765.	115395.
Estimated expen.												
Oper. + maint.	15131.	16319.	18651.	21126.	23772.	26048.	27148.	27901.	28559.	28562.	28594.	28648.
Long term purc.	850.	837.	823.	810.	797.	783.	770.	660.	567.	562.	557.	551.
MWD. bond I+R	0.	0.	0.	0.	0.	0.	0.	0.	0.	0.	0.	0.
1966 Bond I+R	664.	4205.	9893.	15443.	20512.	23613.	24772.	25321.	35382.	40819.	45929.	38353.
New construction	34068.	3038.	0.	11931.	5793.	1957.	5933.	13584.	10311.	13070.	14152.	25842.
Replacements	0.	0.	0.	721.	0.	0.	0.	0.	0.	0.	0.	0.
State contract	0.	13620.	11340.	0.	10785.	16437.	17201.	15885.	16080.	15828.	17759.	17750.
Gov. charges	3134.	3267.	3272.	3276.	3281.	3285.	3419.	3424.	3429.	3422.	3416.	3538.
Total est. expen.	53847.	41286.	43979.	53306.	64939.	72124.	79243.	86776.	94327.	102264.	110407.	114682.
Tax rate on secured property	0.	0.	0.	0.	0.	0.	0.	0.	0.	0.	0.	0.
Untreated M and I water rate	0.	0.	0.	0.	0.	0.	0.	0.	0.	0.	0.	0.
Untreated A and R water rate	0.	0.	0.	0.	0.	0.	0.	0.	0.	0.	0.	0.

Fig. 3 Fund cash flow report.

140

$*.00/Year Water Rate Increase to $**.00, Maximum Tax Rate = $0.**

BOND TRANSACTION SUMMARY

(Dollar amount in 1000's)

	1966/67	1967/68	1968/69	1969/70	1970/71	1971/72	1972/73	1973/74	1974/75	1975/76	1976/77	1977/78
Bonds outstanding 6/30	0.	35400.	188875.	338744.	484860.	609089.	650297.	670870.	679606.	669520.	653507.	631676.
Bonds issued	35400.	153475.	149869.	146116.	124228.	41208.	20574.	8736.	0.	0.	0.	0.
Bonds redeemed	0.	0.	0.	0.	0.	0.	0.	0.	10086.	16013.	21832.	14946.
Bonds outstanding 7/1	35400.	188875.	338744.	484860.	609089.	650297.	670870.	679606.	669520.	653507.	631676.	616730.
Interest costs	664.	4205.	9893.	15443.	20512.	23613.	24772.	25321.	25296.	24807.	24097.	23408.
Redemption	0.	0.	0.	0.	0.	0.	0.	0.	10086.	16013.	21832.	14946.
Total I + R	664.	4205.	9893.	15443.	20512.	23613.	24772.	25321.	35382.	40819.	45929.	38353.
General fund I + R	664.	4205.	9893.	15443.	20512.	23613.	24772.	25321.	35382.	40819.	45929.	38353.
I + R fund I + R costs	0.	0.	0.	0.	0.	0.	0.	0.	0.	0.	0.	0.
Total I + R costs	664.	4205.	9893.	15443.	20512.	23613.	24772.	25321.	35382.	40819.	45929.	38353.

Notes:

1. 1966 Construction bonds may be issued during the first 23 years of the study. For the first 6 years of issue, redemption must be deferred 10 years—that is, bonds issued in 1966 may not be retired prior to 1976. Deferment of redemption after the first 6 years is optional.

2. Bond issue and redemption are assumed to occur on the first day of each fiscal year.

3. 1966 Construction bonds earn 3.750% per annum. Interest is paid semi-annually on 1/1 and 7/1 of the calendar year following the calendar year of issue.

4. All issues must be fully retired within the 24-year study period.

Fig. 4 Bond transaction summary.

141

$*.00/Year water rate increase to $**.00, maximum tax rate = $0.**

BOND ISSUE/REDEMPTION SCHEDULE
(Dollar amount in 1000's)

Year of retirment \ Year of Issue	1966/67	1967/68	1968/69	1969/70	1970/71	1971/72	1972/73	1973/74	1974/75	1975/76	1976/77	1977/78
1966/67												
1967/68												
1968/69												
1969/70												
1970/71												
1971/72												
1972/73												
1973/74							0.					
1974/75	18621.						1350.	0.				
1975/76							16013.	8736.				
1976/77		14946.					3211.	0.	0.			
1977/78	0.	0.	44243.				0.	0.	0.			
1978/79	0.	0.	10089.		30204.		0.	0.	0.	0.	0.	0.
1979/80	0.	0.	0.	0.	0.		0.	0.	0.	0.	0.	0.
1980/81	0.	0.	0.	0.	0.		0.	0.	0.	0.	0.	0.
1981/82	0.	0.	15811.	29515.	0.		0.	0.	0.	0.	0.	0.
1982/83	0.	35299.	0.	51187.	0.		0.	0.	0.	0.	0.	0.
1983/84	0.	0.	0.	0.	0.		0.	0.	0.	0.	0.	0.
1984/85	0.	56115.	0.	0.	0.		0.	0.	0.	0.	0.	0.
1985/86	0.	47115.	0.	0.	27573.		0.	0.	0.	0.	0.	0.
1986/87	0.	0.	79726.	0.	0.		0.	0.	0.	0.	0.	0.
1987/88	0.	0.	0.	19594.	66451.		0.	0.	0.	0.	0.	0.
1988/89	16779.	0.	0.	45820.	0.	41208.	0.	0.	0.	0.	0.	0.
1989/90	0.	0.	0.	0.	0.	0.	0.	0.	0.	0.	0.	0.

Fig. 5 1966 Bond issue and redemption schedule.

combinations of maximum tax rate and maximum rate of change in water prices were studied. The Government Charges Fund was eliminated; government charges were paid from the General Fund.

The optimum basis from the first study was used as a starting point for the second study. Approximately 20 minutes were required to get the first new optimum from the revised matrix. By trying the various combinations of tax and water rates in logical steps, each succeeding optimum was obtained by revising the previous solution, and required only 5–10 minutes to reach the new optimum solution.

For the third study, projected construction costs were revised significantly, causing revisions in operation, maintenance, and replacement costs. These changes to the matrix could have been implemented through the matrix generator. But other changes to the model were not compatible with the matrix generator. Some of these changes were:

1. The Government Charges Fund was eliminated.
2. The State Contract Fund and 1931 Bond I & R Fund were modeled separately. (Previously, these funds were combined.)
3. W-Bonds could be issued if all 1966 Bonds were outstanding.
4. Any 1966 Bond issue would have a 50-year series life, with the first redemption deferred until 10 years after issue.

Because of the major nature of the model revisions and anticipated continuing use of the revised model, a new matrix generator was developed. The results of the third study were to be presented to a Financial Committee meeting in five days, if possible. The matrix generator was rewritten and debugged in three and one-half days. One day later the results of six separate construction cost and water rate increase combinations were delivered to MWD. (Two of the combinations were unfeasible within the specified constraints.) The preliminary reports were reduced in content, giving only annual water and tax rates and bond issues and redemptions. The full reports, from a rewritten report generator, were ready about a week later.

The new matrix contained 604 rows and 908 vectors, and was 0.53% dense, with 281 equalities. The first optimum was reached in about an hour.

Without the use of a computer, it would have been impossible to determine the effects of the new construction costs in so short a time. Normally, new computer results can be obtained in one or two days, at a very reasonable cost. Even when the model was almost totally revised, the use of a computer permitted the new results to be obtained in a short time. Policy decisions have been made by the Board of Directors based on the results of the studies. One particular policy revision will save an estimated $25 million over the period of the study. The model will continue to be used as revisions are made to projected figures and as new policies are considered.

Acknowledgment—This study was performed for the Controller's Office of the Metropolitan Water District of Southern California. I am deeply indebted to Mr. George M. Carroll, Controller, for his encouragement in the preparation of this paper, and in particular for his permission to present portions of the results.

8

Gaining Efficiency in a Large Statistical Computing Unit*

J. A. TIFFIN

Business Statistic Office Management Service and ADP Branch, Newport, U.K.

1. INTRODUCTION

1.1 The Business Statistics Office (BSO) in the United Kingdom was set up on 1 January, 1969 to collect and process data obtained from industrial surveys and censuses, both long and short term, and to publish the results. The office was built up from the Board of Trade Census Office, and its aim was to centralize at least the collecting aspects of business statistics work, most of which has traditionally been decentralized in government departments, and to promote integration of the various inquiries by setting up a central register of business firms.

1.2 Some of the challenges facing the new office were:

1. In order to provide better industrial statistics, a new system with an emphasis upon short-period statistics was to be instituted, data being derived mostly from quarterly inquiries into product sales of firms and annual censuses into the structure of industry, rather than the very comprehensive censuses which have hitherto been conducted at intervals of roughly five years; a large data base combining information collected from the various kinds of survey was also envisaged.
2. The BSO was to be dispersed from London to South Wales (220 kilometres) to new accommodations.
3. The Office was to be doubled in size within five years to about 1100

---

*Reprinted from the *Proceedings of the World Conference on Informatics in Government*, The IBI-ICC, Florence, Italy, October 1972, pp. 704–711. British Crown Copyright. The Controller of Her Britannic Majesty's Stationary Office.

staff to cope with the envisaged workload, but most London staff, many of them experienced, would not transfer to Wales.

4. The BSO was to take delivery in Wales of a large computer—an ICL 1906A—of a different type from its London predecessor (ICL Leo III—installed 1963) and with an operating system of which little experience had been gained generally in the United Kingdom.

1.3   This paper describes the contribution the BSO's Management Services and ADP Branch (current size about 200 staff, 60 being systems analysts and programmers, 6 of these being under contract) has been making towards the solution of these challenges and the problems encountered. In the first place the differences needed in ADP organization, to move progressively from dealing with old-style statistics to the new system, are mentioned; then the introduction of computing and training standards; the changes in methods and computing facilities, and the efficiency of the computer itself; and finally, the costing and resource control measures being adopted in the Office in an attempt to ensure that the considerable clerical and other resources in this large paper factory are used to best advantage and that the possibilities of future computerization are kept in view.

2. ADP ORGANIZATION

Previous Situation

2.1   With longer term censuses, of the kind previously conducted by the Board of Trade Census Office, it was the practice to attach a separate computer team to each census project. Custom-built programmes were devised. The teams of ADP designers and programmers identified themselves closely with the statistical and clerical staff working on the projects, and they became expert in the special features of the censuses. Although collectively with the computer operations team they formed the ADP unit of the Census Office, they worked largely in isolation from each other. The main censuses were unrelated in nature and being spaced apart at such long intervals no great advantage was seen in concentrating upon common standards, techniques and systems which would probably be outmoded by changes in computer philosophy by the time the next censuses became due. Nevertheless, a limited number of general purpose housekeeping programmes were written to supplement the software provided by the manufacturer.

2.2 In fact, the staffing resources available to the teams were barely enough to handle the censuses themselves; their attempts to implement somewhat over-ambitious schemes for those early days in computing and consequent delays, which had repercussions on following censuses, led to some disillusionment in statistical sections and a partial reversion to clerical procedures.

New Situation

2.3 The new tasks facing the BSO called for changes in the ADP organization in that:

1. Experienced resources were still barely enough to cope with current census and survey work, and even those experienced resources were becoming depleted since many staff not going to Wales were losing interest.
2. Building a new team in Wales had to be approached gradually, the very small nucleus available being insufficiently strong to support a rapid increase and the engagement of computer expertise from outside being governed by Civil Service staff recruitment rules.
3. While it had been acceptable for five-year censuses to be serviced by separate ADP teams, the intention of creating an integrated system of industrial statistics meant, ipso facto, that a central approach to ADP considerations was required. At the least, common features of inquiries needed to be identified and handled by similar procedures.
4. Dealings with statistical users in other departments, as well as in the BSO, were growing fast.

2.4 It was decided to form a Management Services unit with four main elements:

1. A team of analysts and programmers to design and produce a first series of modules covering common procedures in the proposed new system of statistics and to concentrate initially on the whole suite of programmes for the new quarterly inquiries into product sales; in effect, an in-house software development team.
2. A second team to continue to deal with existing censuses and surveys, but with an eye to the use of common routines produced by the software development team, where possible.
3. An operating team, also with responsibility for hardware enhancements. Because of a shortage of suitable specialists, software and operating system matters were concentrated within team *a*. The

disadvantages of this measure were recognized, and the matter was to be kept under review.

4. A small Management Services and Planning team to act as a bridge to the statistical users, evaluate new jobs, coordinate plans, set up standards and operating procedures, give internal ADP training, and seek out new computer working methods.

2.5   Within a few months of being set up, the Branch recognized that users were experiencing difficulty in establishing precisely where the various ADP aspects of their tasks were being handled in the new organization; the Management Services and Planning team had insufficient staff to provide such a service to users and was also experiencing similar problems. It was decided, therefore, that the projects team handling existing censuses and surveys should be the point of contact with users whether they were dealing with an existing survey for which purpose-made programmes were being written, or whether the work was being processed through the new suite of programmes being developed by the in-house software team. This latter team would concentrate upon the future system rather than current matters.

2.6   But as the new system has progressed and become increasingly elaborate and suitable for current work, so the projects team has found itself less able to keep in touch with the working of the system—partially through lack of documentation mentioned later—and its longer term considerations. It has been necessary for the project officers to be supported by the development team when discussing detailed and even day-to-day matters. The users, too, have had to deal with the two teams and indeed with the operations team on inquiries which are working within the new system. Thus, a year after the last change, it is already evident that some re-organization must be contemplated. Consideration is now being given to replacing the project and development teams by teams reflecting the main functions of the new ADP system which is gathering impetus and displacing the present ad hoc arrangements for surveys and censuses. This move in itself could bring more communication problems for the statistical users, and in anticipation of this the planning and monitoring arrangements of the Management Services team will also require review. It is vital that any such change should be in a form acceptable to the users, if the various branches of the BSO are to be able to work closely together. Other minor re-arrangements are also needed to reduce tensions arising between the four teams mostly because of the rapid changes but also because of the somewhat unorthodox placing of operational software matters outside the operational team.

Subsequent Changes

2.7   It cannot be claimed that the MSADP organization is yet operating successfully in the eyes of the statistical users, both within and outside the BSO, and that jobs have generally been done to time, properly, and in a convenient way. Some users, perhaps no longer so conscious of past shortcomings, consider that they have less control over their projects than they would like in that their ADP commitment is only one of several being dealt with by the MSADP Branch. They feel that their work is unlikely to be given the resources and priority that they would deem essential, that too many resources are being committed to future systems, extended ADP training, and so on, and not enough to immediate problems. They can point to instances of development programmes being late, of operational work being spoiled, and of misunderstandings about what they wanted.

2.8   The view has been expressed that users could achieve considerable advantage if analysts and programmers were attached to each of the projects. However, such an arrangement militates against a central ADP approach which can help to promote and make easier the closer integration of the various statistical inquiries by developing similar file formats and up-dating, etc., procedures. Also, the introduction of common standards has not yet been consolidated and resources are currently too stretched to allow of purpose-built programmes. Nevertheless, the advantage to be gained could be worthwhile at a later date when a data-processing system properly taking account of standard procedures and techniques has been made to function satisfactorily.

2.9   MSADP Branch would say that its concepts are on the right lines; but it must be given time to settle down and develop; its staff resources have only recently been building up and are very raw; its computer and software system gave considerable initial trouble, and the pressure of events has been such that the situation could have been much worse than it is. Some of the problems currently being encountered could be avoided in the future by investment in forward planning now. Clearer networks and timely specifications could then be available and greater attention given to the allocation of resources.

2.10   The lesson learned is that while the individual units of computer staff ought to be left alone as much as possible when a new computer system is being built to enable those units to gain confidence, knowledge, and an understanding with their customers, a dynamic situation nevertheless exists. The miserable paradox which has to be faced is that frequent reappraisal of the organization is probably needed under the pressure of events and yet even if change is confined to higher levels of the organizational structure, this is certain to cause upset, insecurity, and new problems elsewhere. On the other hand, no change breeds efficiency unless remarkable foresight is shown in determining the initial organization.

3. COMPUTING AND TRAINING STANDARDS

3.1 It was realized at a very early stage that with only a few experienced staff likely to be available in Wales and with a need for an integrated approach to the various inquiries which had not existed previously, it was essential to introduce standard practices and training methods to avoid difficulties and incompatibilities at a later date. With a judicious mix of standards offered by the computer manufacturer, the National Computing Centre, the British Standards Institution, and other government establishments, a basic Standards Manual was produced for systems analysis and programming tasks. Very little original work was required on this aspect of standards, although a number of items of local interest such as data block sizes, or the need for a central forms design unit and standard formats, had to be pursued. More difficulty was encountered with operating standards because few appropriate parallels could be found elsewhere; also, the procedures needed under the George 3 computer operating system were very different from those used with smaller computers and had not been formalized. Eventually, a firm of computer consultants experienced in the use of the new operating system was engaged to devise and collate suitable operating standards.

3.2 While it can be said that the standards have been introduced, that the staff were keen to have them, and that they are being followed to a degree, it is evident that a further exercise is now wanted to ensure that their use is consolidated. Because of staff shortages and pressures of work, some documentation has been neglected; the use of a flowcharter, as a possible aid to documentation, was delayed until it could be handled by the new computer's operating system. Work control procedures have also not been entirely satisfactory and are being strengthened in that a series of progress reports extending from systems analysis work to the operational programme stage and catering for different management levels has been devised. This move is concurrent with an increased emphasis on central network planning which is being fostered by the Management Services and Planning team; it has been found that otherwise the user section has kept its own timetable of events and the ADP and other service sections their versions, with little interplay and some misunderstandings arising.

3.3 When the Standards and Procedures Manual was being planned, a nice balance had to be struck in promulgating mandatory and recommended practices; the latter are of much value to newcomers but if they are voluminous the obligatory sections can be overlooked. The BSO basic standards Manual was somewhat smaller, therefore, than its contemporaries. However, it is being found from experience that much more attention must be given to guidance on the way to approach ADP tasks in the statistics field, commending techniques, and evaluating software. A lot of virgin ground has still to be broken in this area, and significant gains in efficiency are believed to be possible. Guidance can be given during initial training of newcomers, but some experienced staff have not yet settled to the working environment that the new computer offers and could benefit from further training.

3.4 Special attention was given to training of staff in the knowledge that the new office was to be moved from London and a large computer installed at the new location. A lead-in computer, a smaller machine in ICL's 1900 range, was installed at the London office to take on fresh work and also tasks transferred progressively from the existing Leo 3 machine; at the same time the lead-in machine was to provide training facilities for staff moving to Wales and those recruited in Wales. A small team was appointed to study the operating system of the large computer which was relatively untried in service; arrangements were made for tasks to be run periodically under the operating system on the lead-in machine, although the system was not economically suitable for day-to-day working on this computer. The staff available familiarized themselves with the architecture of the new computer system and elementary attempts were made to write job descriptions for the operating system. An endeavour was made to keep the rest of the Branch informed of developments.

3.5 However, the mainspring of the BSO was still in London and although staff were gradually being recruited in Wales, the lack of a computer made training in depth difficult and unreal for them, especially as the urgency of the current workload was such that it was deemed unwise to entrust too much of it to the comparatively raw newcomers in Wales. When delivery of the large computer became imminent, the need for rapid transfer of responsibility from London came with surprising suddenness, many of the London staff finding other posts or losing interest. New staff had to be put on live work almost immediately after basic programming courses, instead of being given further formalized training, their supervisors, many of whom were already struggling with higher level duties in the absence of experienced staff, could not give them sufficient attention. Considerable problems were then being encountered with the operating system, despite the prior training, and further difficulty arose when modular programming with a test harness was introduced as a means of combating the rising workload. In both cases, the staff would have benefited from better training and assistance from the contractors directly responsible; expertise gained has now been marshalled into training lectures.

3.6 The ADP Training Officer could not readily keep in touch with new ADP staff, without interfering with line management, and concentrated on general ADP training for the rest of the Office. Now that the situation has settled down, the advantages are being explored of placing new programming staff in a training unit for 2–3 months; it is possible that greater efficiency could result from giving programmers, and even operators, longer in a formalized training environment with well designed exercises rather than job training soon after initial courses.

4. CHANGES IN METHODS AND COMPUTING FACILITIES

4.1 Such training would extend into the revised approach to statistical computing which has been adopted for the new system of inquiries. Instead of writing purpose-built programmes for each census or survey, even to cover functions which have basic similarities, the BSO is steadily building an in-house software system—Standard Industry Survey (SIS) suite of programmes. The aim is primarily to ensure that the various surveys are programmed to a common pattern, to aid integration of the new statistical system, but also to conserve the limited ADP resources available and in time to produce optimum methods of dealing with the various technical features of the inquiries. Up to the present, different registers of firms have been used for the various registers but many basically similar actions are then needed in selecting firms, sending them forms, reminding them, and receipting the forms returned. Similar actions are also needed for inspecting and processing the data received and presenting the results. Complications arise in dealing with the work in a functional, rather than inquiry-based manner, but a basic suite of programmes is now in use.

4.2 The original intention was to design a general purpose suite, not generalized to the extent that processing would be cumbersome and expensive and also capable of easy amendment and enhancement; thus, parameter-generated programmes would be formed from modules within the suite for the various kinds of inquiry. In the early stages, parts of SIS would be utilized for existing inquiries; for new types of inquiry some features would be written ad hoc until established SIS modules were available. In time, all inquiries would be handled within the SIS framework.

4.3 In practice, a working system is available and being heavily used although the introduction of some features was delayed until recently, notably, a pre-processor tabulation system prepared initially by a software house but now adapted to work within the BSO's computer operating system. Because of staff shortages, especially high quality and experienced people, short cuts had to be taken to meet time-scales, and some programmes were written monolithically, rather than in modules. These have been generalized to an unacceptable degree in that while it can be said that the processing for individual inquiries takes different routes through the programmes, there are sometimes unnecessary steps in the main programme; because of fire-brigade action, steps peculiar to particular inquiries have been grafted on to main programmes rather than written as independent modules or sub-routines. A reappraisal of SIS procedures is now taking place with the aim of restructuring and rewriting part of the suite by the end of 1973.

4.4 A major problem, still needing attention in the future, has been that the urgency of the task has led to the considerable amount of documentation on the SIS system getting into arrear because of the sheer volume of straightforward editing and printing considerations; this has caused inconvenience to the programming staff and statistical users alike.

4.5 Some improvement has been obtained in the development of computer programmes generally by the limited use within the BSO of teletype terminals to the computer. The benefits are still being evaluated, but apart from the fact that the turn-round of an hour or two is avoided by this method, the extra processing cost is also offset by the ease with which programmers can correct and improve their programmes. The programmers enjoy using this new tool, and their output is greater. After experiment, scope is also seen for the eventual use of visual display units when statistical files are being interrogated.

4.6 In addition to these developments, the moves towards integrated registers of firms and data files are emphasizing the need for more exchangeable discs rather than the magnetic tapes used for many years past in London. While the files are so large that a great number of them must still be held on tape, it would be quite impracticable to depend upon a tape system as such, handling hundreds of tapes in complicated processing sequences. A mixed configuration is accordingly being planned which will allow of about one-third of the files being on-line.

5. COMPUTER EFFICIENCY

5.1 During the whole of the changeover period, when work was being transferred to Wales, the operating system was being repeatedly modified and improved by the computer manufacturer; thus, routines, which had run successfully in London, could not always be processed immediately in Wales. This one factor accounted for much of the difficulty experienced over the first few months of operation and gave rise to some of the misgivings felt by statistical users, as mentioned earlier.

5.2 In the first place, the operating staff were almost entirely new and inexperienced and prone to make errors. They were blamed, and took the blame for difficulties that arose, until the cause could be identified; also in these early months, the hardware was giving trouble. Frequently, of course, failures that might have appeared to be attributable to hardware, software, or operator intervention, were simply the errors of programmers made to appear worse by the latter's own inexperience.

5.3 A result of these problems was that instead of being able to manage for some months, as initially envisaged, with one shift working and a modest array of peripherals until experience had been gained, overtime working was required almost immediately and a full second shift quickly thereafter to cope with the high incidence of investigatory work and additional resubmission of jobs. The configuration also proved inadequate, and further equipment was ordered.

5.4 It has been found that a very disciplined approach is needed with the George 3 operating system to a greater degree than was necessary previously with the earlier computer. Also, the ADP staff generally are not fully able to exploit this operating system which is, in any case, not yet completely developed. Optimum scheduling of work in the new environment is difficult to achieve. Commercial assistance has been used in an endeavour to improve efficiency, and although this has been of value, much remains to be done in consolidating job descriptions, taking account of experience, and sub-dividing programme suites. With 600 jobs a week already, most taking 15–20 minutes each but some taking 4–5 hours elapsed time, scheduling is clearly important; but suitable software is lacking at present. Continual improvements in the control and working procedures are being introduced in an effort to increase throughput and avoid errors and unnecessary rerunning.

5.5 In fact, the difficulty of evaluating the performance of the computer was soon realized and a commercial package, which is still being tailored to the needs of the installation, is being used to produce basic financial, costing, and management information about the throughput of the computer. Monitoring of the use of the individual hardware units could also be valuable in assessing the loadings of the various units in a developing situation.

5.6 One of the concepts of the George 3 operating system is that as part of its filestore it controls all directory files within the installation and the usage of magnetic media. This eliminates the need for manual recording in the more traditional installation but does require strict dumping and copying of the filestore for security purposes. It has proved necessary to experiment with these aspects in order to achieve a balance between operational efficiency and overheads.

6. COSTING AND RESOURCE ALLOCATION

6.1 Reference has been made to the costing package for computer operations which measures computer usages in financial terms. Although the rates used include an element for the computer room staff cost, this is miniscule compared with the total staff costs of the BSO, which is, in effect, a large paper factory. A costing system on factory costing lines was necessary to keep in proper touch with the setting up and grouping of the statistical and supporting sections of the BSO, all of which have been affected by the moves from London and the growth of the new statistical systems. The Management Services and Planning team has therefore introduced such a system which at present features simple, routine manpower utilization reports from every section of the office and, using average salary, etc., rates, expresses the result as "activity costs." The next stage is to link these financial data with section output details, with the immediate object of deriving unit costs for each processing stage and perhaps eventually leading to budgetary control on conventional industrial lines.

6.2 The accounting system should enable supervisory staff and senior management to exercise normal management options against an informed financial background, such as whether a particular job should be processed manually or by computer, and which processing aspects should be given priority for computerization in a period when ADP resources, particularly in practical experience, are insufficient.

6.3   In the final analysis, the statistical service stands or falls on its ability to deliver the goods on time. In this sense, cost considerations must take second place. What are needed by operations managers are flexible and yet effective measures of planning and control. Coupled with the costing system, therefore, has been an awareness that network analysis techniques must be fostered to make the best use of resources, and that an overall network for the BSO should be produced. At present, new major statistical projects are the subject of relatively simple network analysis, one or two of which have been computerized so far, but gradually the networks are being brought together. The task is urgent but difficult nevertheless.

7. CONCLUSION

The aim of the BSO management is to build an efficient organization and a level of cost-effectiveness which best reconciles the conflicting claims of product quality (i.e., accuracy of statistics), delivers dates (timeliness of presentation), and economical processing costs (efficient use of resources—both within the statistics service and the offices of the contributors). This cannot be done overnight; in particular, the growth of experience and expertise takes time. However, the management team feels that it now knows what techniques it must develop to provide the required information and control, where the main deficiencies are, and how they are to be overcome. The next few months will be a testing time with priority given to the improvement of communications at all levels. The Management Services and ADP Branch contribution will be to help create the conditions and proper climate for securing the improvements in view.

Implications and Questions

In this section we have reviewed types of computer applications supportive of management's role in public administration. The emphasis was on public management for two reasons: increasing demands for greater productivity are being made of public managers; and the scope of public services is increasing, but the increase in manpower is not keeping abreast of the increasing scope of activities even with increased productivity. This is creating a management gap which in part can be filled only by the computer. The computer's potential here stems from its capability to manage information more effectively than the human mind, and, derivatively, to aid in the planning, implementation, and evaluation of public services delivery. At this point, it is imperative to take stock of:

1. The particular benefits to be derived from the computer applications.
2. The organizational constraints that may be encountered.
3. What questions ought to be considered by the student of public administration in applying the material he or she has just completed reading.

A. BENEFITS

Mr. Østergaard in his article the *Design of Public Information Systems* aptly begins by noting that the dramatic increase in public spending has been due to the lack of managerial control, which stems from the decentralized nature of public administration. Supplementary departments even in smaller cities with populations of 250,000 or less, for example, are not aware of what the others are doing, although they may be serving common sets of clientele. The reason for this may be traceable to the status of information management: information files tend to be separate and uncoordinated; they tend to be stored in office basements and therefore inaccessible; they are often inconsistent and incompatible, and at time duplicate each other. In general, public agencies and departments try to become *totally* self-sufficient which becomes very expensive in terms of manpower and/or dollar requirements.

Computer-based information systems, in contrast, provide the only means for meaningfully organizing information into common bases which then can be shared by multiple users. How this may be accomplished is shown in the GIST and the city of Aalborg Public Information Systems.

Given this broad based utility of computers in the management of public agencies, the following are guidelines indicated for successful MIS programs in public management.*

(1) Management information systems should be designed primarily on jurisdictional as distinct from functional bases. That is, information which is at the core of management should focus on the needs of general purpose units of government rather than on the needs of functional departments. For when information is split along functional lines, it remains beyond the scope of top public management to maximize the computers utility for better management and therefore is dysfunctional for improved performance.

(2) Management information systems development should concentrate on developing improved data bases rather than exotic computer analysis techniques. This means that routine everyday jobs of government must be helped to gain improved performance. Although these applications are less attractive, their payoffs are much larger in terms of increased productivity.

(3) Systems design should be planned so that there is an incremental development of computerization. Building of systems needs begins with the utilization of basic data files that already exist—these may be manually or mechanically controlled at present. For example, the Aalborg system demonstrates how a single event, land registration, was used as the basic building block to construct a total MIS system for that city. Similarly, Mr Marks shows the successful growth of an incrementally built personnel system for the English Civil Service. In sum, it may be said that large scope turnkey systems should be avoided.

(4) In order to gain the expected benefit from computer utilization it is also essential to consider efficient operation of the computer itself. Mr. Tiffin's article proposes the following organizational devices to foster greater efficiencies in the research and development stages.

a. The formulation of training and computing standards.
b. The development of a management services unit to act as a bridge between administration and the computer center. This unit may serve in two capacities—planning and evaluating administrative tasks to be performed and training managers in the use of EDP.
c. The development of a basic financial analysis program to monitor the computer. The utilization of the hardware and the cost incurred

*Hearle, Edward F. R. Urban management information systems, *Journal of Socio-Economic Planning Sciences*, Vol. 1 (1968), pp. 215–221.

by different agency users should be the focal points of this accounting system.

B. ORGANIZATIONAL CONSTRAINTS

It is imperative to consider the organizational obstacles which may develop in the course of implementing a new or improved computer-based management information system. These considerations are often ignored and tend to complicate successful MIS implementation. The considerations raised here are not a comprehensive listing of all problems likely to be encountered; they are rather a sampling of organization problems of which to be cognizant.

(1) Technically competent manpower: Although many Public Management information systems are developed by private consulting firms who promise to package their program in a format that permits immediate integration with on-going systems, this promise should be closely examined. Experience has shown that this may not occur and that there are no short-cuts to in-house expert personnel.

(2) Information for Administrators: It is most important that any Management Information System incorporate management's needs as well as consider management's fears. Previously, we proposed that exotic applications and related data requirements be avoided. It is in this regard that we are similarly proposing MIS systems which provide an information format easily assimilated into the workings of management today. Hoping to revolutionize management with new systems or applications is like chasing clouds in the sky.

(3) Pursuant to this, it is proposed that a system for common communications in terms of administration and the computer be developed that permits the different functional agency heads participating in the system to be aware of what the other agencies are doing. This may be one of the first jobs for a management services unit of the type proposed by Mr. Tiffin.

(4) Lastly, a central committee has to be established to regulate MIS and to evaluate performance on an on-going basis. Emphasis on the latter is to show how the MIS helps management.

C. QUESTIONS

Integrating the above information for the student in public administration may be said to pose the following questions:

(1) In planning computer-based systems for improving management's internal operations, does a newly contemplated application increase the jurisdiction's capacity to govern? How?

(2) Where does the new application fit with on-going management systems: manual and computer-based? In this respect are there any comprehensive agency or supra-agency plans for system development?

(3) Where are the administrative efficiencies to be gained from a new computer system? Are these efficiencies complemented by efficiencies in the hardware (machine and peripherals) and software (systems and programs)?

(4) What routine and often time-consuming jobs are to be circumvented? If the application is exotic, a logical cost-benefit defense must be shown.

(5) Is there a clear, realistic, and viable timetable to which an internal manager or vendor may be held? Responsibility for planning, implementing, and evaluating must be squarely placed on a predetermined organizational entity subunit or person, and/or both.

With these concerns clearly described we now turn to considering computer applications involving the public agency's relationship to its clientele.

Selected Bibliography

ARTICLES

Balls, Herbert R. Computer utilization in support of better government, *Optimum*, Vol. 2, No. 4 (1971), pp. 15–24.

Bradburd, Arnold W. The relationship of systems work to administration, *Public Welfare*, Vol. 25, No. 2 (October 1967), 112–118.

Carlson, Walter M. A Management information system designed by managers, *Datamation*, Vol. 13, No. 5 (May 1967), 37–43.

Computers in public administration (Symposium), *Public Administration Review*, Vol. 28, No. 6 (November–December 1968), 487–552.

Computer simplifies welfare, *Business Week*, November 4, 1972, p. 87.

Cooperation as a model for municipal use of computers, *Institute of Public Service, University of Connecticut*, Municipal Information Technology Program, Series 3, 1968, 15 p.

Duff, Ian and Henry, Malcolm. Computer-aided management: A case study of Thos. Sim & Co., Ltd., a British textile firm, *Management Decision*, Vol. 9 (Winter 1971), pp. 204–12.

Electronic Data Processing as a Municipal Tool, *New Jersey Municipalities*, (February 1966), pp. 8–11.

Electronic data processing in urban government; Symposium, *American City*, Vol. 86 (May 1971), pp. 69–75.

Hanel, Richard S. Management systems analysis and urban data, *Management Information Service*, No. L-2 (February 1969), entire issue.

Hearle, Edward, F. R. Computers in Public Administration Symposium *Public Administration Review*, Vol. 28 (November–December 1968), pp. 487–488.

Hearle, Edward F. R. EDP: An evaluation of the use of computers by the city of New York, *Temporary Commission of City Finances, City of New York*, June 1966.

Hillegass, John R. Systematic Techniques for computer evaluation and selection, *Management Services*, Vol. 6 (July–August 1969), pp. 35–38.

Holler, J. N. and Updegraff, R. C. Punched cards hobble computer use; Computer-controlled data entry systems, *American City*, Vol. 87 (October 1972), pp. 99–100.

Jones, Curtis H. At last: Real computer power for decision makers: Interactive manager-computer systems meet the need of the executive who wants to solve a problem in his own way, *Harvard Business Review*, Vol. 48 (September–October 1970), pp. 75–89.

Jones, Malcolm, M. and McLean, Ephraim, R. Management problems in large-scale software development projects, *Indiana Management Review*, Vol. 11 (Spring 1970), pp. 1–15.

Kroeger, Louis J. The impact of computers on local governments, *Michigan Municipal Review*, Vol. 41, No. 6 (June 1968), 136–139.

McDonell, R. E. and Riordan, R. J. Computer aid for the small city, *American City*, Vol. 87 (May 1972), pp. 100–102.

Mensh, Michael, Organizing process computer software, *Automation* (February 1968), 57–60.

Parker, John K. Data services for local governments: To use or not to use, *Pennsylvanian*, Vol. 6, No. 7 (July 1967); 21–24.

Reilly, Frank W. Policy decisions and EDP system in the Federal government, *Public Administration Review*, Vol. 22, No. 2 (September 1962), p. 132.

Rhoads, M. N. Local governments share a computer, *American City*, Vol. 86 (February 1971), p. 52.

Ross, Joel E. Computers: Their use and misuse: Some do's and don'ts for management, *Business Horizons*, Vol. 15 (April 1972), pp. 55–60.

Soden, J. V. Planning for the computer services spinout, *Harvard Business Review*, Vol. 50 (September 1972), pp. 69–79.

Spiers, Maurice. The computer and the machinery of government, *Public Administration* (Journal of the Royal Institute of Public Administration, Great Britain), Vol. 46 (Winter 1968), 411–425.

Stragier, M. Commercially available computer programs, *American City*, Vol. 87 (September 1972), pp. 181–182.

Taft, Martin, I. On a Computer-aided systems approach to personnel administration, *Socio-Economic Planning Sciences*, Vol. 5 (December 1971), pp. 547–567.

Wear, J. W. Computerized total-cost bidding, *American City*, Vol. 86 (February 1971), pp. 60–61.

BOOKS

Brink, Victor Z. *Computers and Management: The Executive Viewpoint*, Englewood Cliffs, N.J.: Prentice-Hall, 1971.

Burck, Gilbert, ed. *Computer Age and Its Potential For Management*, New York, N.Y.: Harper-Row Torchbook.

Chacko, G. *Computer-Aided Decision-Making*, New York, N.Y.: American Elsevier, 1972.

Computers and Management: 1967 Leatherbee Lectures, Cambridge, Mass.: Harvard Business School, 1967.

Elizur, Dov, *Adapting to Innovation: A Facet Analysis of the Case of the Computer*, Jerusalem, Israel: Jerusalem Academic Press, 1970.

Foy, Nancy, *Computer Management: A Common Sense Approach*, Philadelphia, Penn.: Auerbach, 1972.

Harrison, Annette, *The Problem of Privacy in the Computer Age: An Annotated Bibliography*, U.S. Air Force Project Rand Memoranda, (RM-5495/1-PR/RC), December 1969.

Hearle, Edward, F. R. and Mason, Raymond, J. *Data Processing System for State and Local Governments*, Englewood Cliffs, N.J.: Prentice-Hall, 1965.

Higginson, Valliant M. *Managing with EDP: A Look at the State of the Art*, New York: American Management Association, 1965.

Hodge, Bartow and Hodgson, Robert N. *Management and the Computer in Information and Control Systems*, New York, N.Y.: McGraw-Hill Book Company, 1969.

Kanter, J. *Computer and the Executive*, Englewood Cliff, N.J.: Prentice-Hall, 1967.

Kelly, Joseph F. *Computerized Management Information Systems*, New York, N.Y.: Macmillan, 1970.

Morrill, Chester, Jr. *Computers and Data Processing: Information Sources: An Annotated Guide to the Literature, Associations and Institutions Concerned With Input, Throughput and Output of Data*, Detroit, Mich.: Gale, 1969.

Myers, Charles A., ed. *The Impact of Computers on Management*, Cambridge, Mass.: MIT Press, 1967.

Patmore, Ruth and Ross, Elizabeth, *Computerized Practice Set to Accompany Financial Accounting & Managerial Accounting*, New York, N.Y.: Macmillan, 1972.

Pescow, J. and Horn, J., eds. *Computerized Operations Research for Effective Decision Making*, Englewood Cliffs, N.J.: Prentice-Hall.

Sanders, D. H. *Computers and Management*, New York, N.Y.: McGraw-Hill, 1970.

Schlaifer, Robert, *Computer Programs for Elementary Decision Analysis*, Cambridge, Mass.: Division of Research, The Graduate School of Business Administration, Harvard University, 1971.

Sturt, Humphrey and Yearsley, Ronald, *Computers for Management*, New York, N.Y.: American Elsevier, 1970.

Tou, Julius T., ed. *Computer and Information Sciences: Proceedings, 2nd Battelle Memorial Institute*, New York, N.Y.: Academic Press, 1967.

Tyran, Michael, *Computerized Accounting Methods and Controls*, Englewood Cliffs, N.J.: Prentice-Hall, 1972.

Wheelwright, S. C. and Makridakis, S. G. *Computer-Aided Modeling for Managers*, Addison-Wesley, 1972.

MONOGRAPHS

Mumford, Enid, Computers, planning and personnel management, *Institute of Personnel Management*, London, England, July 1969.

Report to the President on the Management of Automatic Data Processing in the Federal Government, Washington, D.C., U.S. Printing Office.

Stevens, Mary Elizabeth, *U.S. National Bureau of Standards. Research and Development in the Computer and Information Sciences*, Superintendent of Documents # LC 70-603263, (Vol. 3 NBS Monograph 113), June 1970.

Use of Electronic Data Processing Equipment in the Federal Government, Washington, D.C.: U.S. Printing Office.

CHAPTER III

The Functional Administrative Areas

While initially state agencies turned to automated information systems to help expedite their administrative and internal management processes, today computers are being applied in all areas of state government. For example, the National Association of State Information Systems in the United States estimates that nearly 600 computers are currently installed in general state government agencies (excluding higher education).

A sampling of these functional applications are reviewed in the present chapter. Although it is impossible to report all functional achievements in the public sector, we have attempted to be comprehensive in our selections; to provide in-depth discussions of sample applications by devoting a separate section to each; to select reports of on-going systems that are general enough to hold out interest for concerned agencies and students of computer applications in the public sector.

The chapter begins with a major urban planning and management system that integrates models of urban growth processes of large metropolitan areas with financial policy planning aspects of municipal management. This was applied by the Decision Sciences Corporation to the city of Toronto.

From here we proceed to a discussion of departmental functional activities for local and municipal governments. The role of the computer in modern police work is described first by Melvin Bockelman, Chief of Computer Operations at the Missouri State Police Department at Kansas City, Missouri. Professors Soehngen and DeCicco of the Polytechnic Institute of New York report on a computerized sewage collection system which was applied in a subarea of Nassau County, New York

State. In a similar vein, Messrs, Szekely, Stankard, and Sisson describe an educational resource allocation model and simulation for Bucks County, Pennsylvania school districts.

Traffic management has always been a major urban problem even in the days of horse and carriage. Professor Cantilli of the Department of Transportation Planning and Engineering of the Polytechnic Institute of New York shows how computerized data processing in accident record handling leads to improved traffic management. Related to traffic management problems in the urban areas are transportation planning problems. Messrs. Dial and Bunyan, of Alan M. Vorhees and Associates, show an urban mass transit model that interfaces with highway planning to form a comprehensive urban transportation model for both planning and management purposes.

Housing poses a major problem for urban America today. Mr. Dodson, of Research Planning Corporation, describes a set of computer-based procedures which permit evaluating the effectiveness of experimental low-cost housing programs in terms of break-even-rent for the projected life of a housing development. Complementing the housing problem as a socially penetrating factor is that of welfare and its management. John David, of Systems RDI, reports on a computer-based public assistance system, which was successfully tested in New York City, although not implemented. The impact of the proposed PAPS approach would be to drastically improve the management of the existent welfare payment system.

The final two interrelated environmental problem areas to be covered include urban recreation and pollution. Dr. Dee, of the University of Illinois, and Professor Liebman, of Batelle Memorial Laboratories, describe how to more effectively plan and manage urban playgrounds and parks by interfacing public participation with computer planning tools which brings the readings full circle to the initial article on urban planning. The application of the approach is then reported for the city of Baltimore. In conclusion, Professors Koenig, Haynes and Fisher draw a comprehensive review of computer applications to date, emphasizing the urban environment.

9

Promus: An Urban Planning and Management System

DONALD F. BLUMBERG AND DILIP R. LIMAYE

Decision Sciences Corporation, Jenkintown, Pennsylvania

INTRODUCTION

The quality of decision-making of city and regional government and administrators is a topic of increasing concern. This has been spurred on by growing demands for current and capital expenditures for expanded or updated facilities, as well as education, health, welfare, and social services brought on by the general malaise of our cities including large-scale unemployment, poverty, and crime. This has been coupled with a decrease in revenues due to the egress from cities of many businesses and the decay in rateable land values.

There has slowly evolved an understanding that urban areas are, in fact, complex, dynamic systems, with many interrelationships existing between their various economic, social, and physical attributes. There has also been evolving an understanding that programs instituted in one functional segment of the city or metroplitan system (such as transportation) can have both direct and indirect effects, both productive and counter-productive, in other functional segments, especially over time. While many cities have responded by hiring specialist-experts in various disciplines such as transportation, facilities planning, education, health, and welfare to examine and evaluate these factors, many urban decisions are still often made on the basis of estimates of either the very short-term or very long-term direct effects of various programs.

In fact, the comprehensiveness of the options considered in making these decisions, the computation of risks and probabilities associated with these programs, and the cost-benefits of alternative programs are often not adequately evaluated prior to program selection. Beyond this, decisions are frequently made in a "vacuum," without considering the complementary (or disruptive) effects of other programs or policies in the mix of urban projects and programs. Finally, our urban managers and administrators fail to learn from past mistakes in decision making.

Urban planners and administrators are therefore faced with the need for better information, presented in more efficient and useful ways, and a means to analyze this information in a consistent and meaningful manner to assist in the decision-making process.

For example:

1. Planners want to improve their ability to analyze and project the rapidly changing socio-economic characteristics.
2. Decision makers need to acquire improved capability for examining the consequences of alternative program mixes.
3. Financial officers want better measures of program effectiveness and faster means of estimating future revenue and expenditure patterns.
4. Policy makers want the means to evaluate all issues quickly and consistently to select the optimum strategies.
5. Information-processing staff require more streamlined, sophisticated, and efficient tools for providing information to legislators and administrators.

What is required, therefore, is a systematic approach which can identify all the relevant interactions and interrelationships among the policies and programs of the city government and the community characteristics. This approach must be able to analyze not only the physical, social, and economic impact of alternative program mixes, but also evaluate the financial consequences.

The recognition of the need for comprehensive analysis of program alternatives and the availility of advanced data-processing techniques has prompted many efforts towards the development of urban planning and management systems. Starting with models of the specific elements of an urban system, such as land use, housing, transportation, etc., the state of the art has progressed towards models of urban growth.

A review of some of the models of elements of urban systems can be found in references 1 and 2. More recently, a few of these systems have been developed for PPBS type of analysis [3–6]. However, the first attempt at integrating the urban growth models with models of municipal financing and program planning is represented by the current efforts* to develop an advanced operational system for planning and management of large metropolitan areas. This system, called the Provincial Municipal Simulator (PROMUS), treats the city as a system comprising a set of interrelated subsystems, analyzed through the use of simulation models. Using these simulation models, PROMUS can evaluate the direct and indirect results of urban policies and programs on the physical, social, and economic characteristics of the community and develop a complete picture of the resulting revenues and expenditures to the local government.

This paper describes the concept of an integrated urban planning and management system, the evolution of the state of the art, and the operation of the PROMUS system.

THE CITY AS A SYSTEM

The urban area can be conceptualized as a complex system comprised of many interrelated elements. In order to understand this concept of the city/system, the types of functions or elements in the urban area must be defined. Four different subsystems can be easily identified[7]:

1. The Land Use Subsystem. This structure comprises the alternative uses of land for residential, commercial, industrial, or other purposes and the possibilities for change through time.
2. The Transportation and Communication Subsystem. The various networks within the urban area and links to points outside the area are included in this subsystem.
3. The Utilities and Services Subsystem. A wide variety of services including energy, water, waste disposal, as well as less obvious aspects of the economic infrastructure are included in this subsystem.
4. The Social and Economic Subsystem. The age, employment, income, and other basic demographic characteristics of the population, along with a wide variety of social characteristics comprise the social and economic subsystem.

These subsystems have been individually analyzed by planners and decision makers, but the interactions among them are rarely evaluated. In

*The work is being performed by Decision Sciences Corporation and P. S. Ross and Partners in conjunction with the city of Toronto and the province of Ontario.

an integrated urban planning and management system, these individual subsystems are brought together under one overall structure—the city viewed as a system.

Additionally, the urban planning and management system must also be able to assess the dynamically changing structure of the city. The basic problems of the urban area arise not only because of the complex interactions between the individual subsystems, but also because each of the subsystems is changing over time. Hence, the decision makers must develop an adaptive capability that can meet rapidly changing physical, social, economic, and technological requirements. This is a formidable task requiring the understanding and representation of the theoretical and practical structure explaining the interactions between the subsystems. Such a structure can be developed through mathematical modeling techniques forming the core of an integrated urban planning and management system.

HISTORICAL DEVELOPMENT OF PROMUS

The systems approach to urban problems was initiated in the early 1960s when the techniques of model building and simulation were first applied for urban planning techniques and analysis. One of the first attempts at this was represented by the Penn-Jersey Regional Planning Model[8] which was primarily a study of the requirements for new transportation facilities in the Delaware Valley. This model was designed to forecast the future in terms of new highway facilities to determine their effect on regional growth.

Two other studies were simultaneously being conducted, the first one in Pittsburgh[9] and the second one in San Francisco[10]. The Pittsburgh study was primarily a model of urban growth processes and the spatial allocation of growth. The model was oriented towards the land use and transportation system, and was later modified and updated to take care of certain aspects of the social and economic subsystems. The Lowry Model[11] and TOMM Model[12] were developed as the result of the Pittsburgh studies and later led to many other derivations in other cities.

The other study was being conducted in San Francisco and dealt primarily with the housing characteristics in the San Francisco area. The simulation model in San Francisco attempted to deal with the question of the effect of governmental policies and programs on the housing market in the San Francisco area.

The Penn-Jersey, Pittsburgh, and San Francisco studies formed the basis for future development of urban models and management systems.

During the last several years the number of different models of urban structures have evolved. Many authors have reviewed and compared the scope, structure, and application of these models. A list of some of the more well-known models is given in Fig. 1. References 13–15 describe a number of these models and their special features. Most of these models dealt with urban growth processes taking into account, primarily, the physical and economic characteristics of the community.

The evolution of the PROMUS system which includes all of the elements of the city/system, as well as their interaction with the revenues and expenditures of the local government, is shown in Fig. 2.

Learning from the experience of the other studies and models conducted during the early 1960s, and using demographic and socio-economic data from U.S. urban areas, the SCANCAP[16] Model was developed. The initial SCANCAP Model used a hypothetical community called CAPSBURG. This consisted of seven neighborhood areas representing typical neighborhood characteristics of U.S. urban communities. The major innovation in SCANCAP was the development of the community model which modified the TOMM Model into a small area model, and coupled this to the neighborhood and population distribution models.

In 1966 and 1967, the SCANCAP Model was revised and implemented using real data from the city of New Haven. This represented the first attempt at the application of community models for the evaluation of a specific U.S. urban area. Later, the SCANCAP Model was revised and applied to the city of Denver for educational planning. The revised model was called SCANPED and used the Denver data base. Attempts were also made to modify this model for the cities of San Diego and Saigon, but these attempts did not lead to any advancement in the state of the art.

In 1970, the Department of Housing and Urban Development expressed the need for the development of the capability to evaluate the economic and financial feasibility of new communities. The technology of urban planning and management systems was applied to this problem to develop the basic new community simulator (Basic NUCOMS[17]). This system is currently being considerably updated and modified to provide an integrated planning and evaluation system to assist HUD planners and decision makers in the evaluation of applications for financial guarantee assistance under Title VII of the Housing and Urban Development Act of 1970.

During the last two years, the city of Toronto and province of Ontario

NAME OF MODEL OR AUTHOR	DEVELOPMENT YEAR	AREA OF APPLICATION
1. Lowry	1963	Pittsburgh Community Renewal Project (CRP)
2. TOMM (Time Oriented Metropolitan Model)	1964	Pittsburgh CRP
3. Bass I, II, III	1965–1968	Bay Area Simulation Study
4. Plum (Projective Land Use Model)	1968	Bay Area Transportation Study Commission
5. Garin–Lowry	1966	Theoretical Extension of Lowry
6. Clug (Cornell Land use Game)	1966	Gaming Simulation Model for Educational Purposes
7. TOMM II	1968	Extension of TOMM
8. Wilson	1968	Theoretical Extension of Lowry
9. Cripps and Foot	1969	Bedford, Reading
10. Batty	1969–1970	Nottingham–Derby, Lancaster
11. SCANCAP	1965–1967	New Haven
12. SCANPED	1968–1969	Denver
13. NUCOMS (New Community Simulator)	1971–1972	Dept. of Housing and Urban Development, Park Forest South, Stansbury Park
14. PROMUS	1970–1972	Toronto
15. Nottinghamshire model	1971–1972	City of Nottingham and County of Nottinghamshire

Fig. 1 Representative list of urban models.

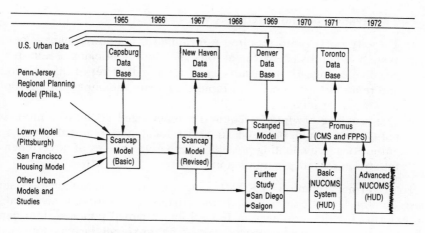

Fig. 2   Evolution of the PROMUS system.

embarked upon the development of the PROMUS system where the concept of the community model was considerably modified and updated, and then linked to the innovative Financial Policy Planning Subsystem, to provide a truly integrated urban planning and management system. PROMUS looks at both the changing characteristics of the community and the relationship of these to the municipal programs and services of the city government, taking into account cost and effectiveness of the programs as well as the level of service offered to the community.

THE PROMUS SYSTEM

PROMUS is a computer-based system that provides a systematic approach for the improvement of the quality of decision making at the local government level. PROMUS identifies relevant interrelationships and interactions between community attributes and determines the impact of community characteristics on the financial policies and programs of the local government and the financial and economic consequences of alternative programs and policies on the physical, economic, and social attributes of the community. PROMUS is designed to meet the needs of the city's financial, budgeting, and operational department administrators and to evaluate the direct and indirect result of urban programs before such programs are actually funded or instituted.

The motivation behind PROMUS was twofold:

1. The city of Toronto required a meaningful operating management system whereby department officials and politicians could test possible changes in programs against a standard set of information and relationships in order to rapidly evaluate the impact of alternative program mixes.
2. The province of Ontario required a generalized model of a municipality that could be used to assist local and regional planning authorities in evaluating possible alternative choices of governmental structure and programs and policies.

To perform its functions, PROMUS incorporates a comprehensive data base on all relevant community characteristics. In addition, it gives data on external factors—changes in federal and regional policies—that can affect a community. It provides a complete picture of all the expenditures, revenues, and cash flow of each major program within each city department. It also provides information on specific community attributes that affect the service levels of different programs, such as population, education levels, income levels, ethnic character and distribution, and area-by-area housing patterns.

The PROMUS system design is shown in Fig. 3. PROMUS is composed of two major subsystems, a Community Model (CMS) and a Financial Policy Planning Model (FPPS). The Community Model provides a logical structuring of a community at a particular point in time. It acts as the basis for predicting or forecasting the reaction and interaction of community attributes to community programs over a period of time. Even though the Community Model looks at the community in its entirety, it can also consider up to 25 individual small neighborhoods.

The Financial Policy Planning Model provides the base for analyzing the costs, cash flow, and revenue of community programs. It carries out full financial evaluations of community and area programs. It can measure present or future program costs, relate budget allocations to long-range plans beyond any one fiscal year, and establish a systematic budget review process.

The Community Model and the Financial Policy Planning Model are connected through a Policy Implementation Program. The Policy Implementation Program tests all community plans and programs in terms of community growth and change and its financial impact, considering both the internal and external demographic-economic structure.

Working in conjunction with elements of the Financial Planning Model,

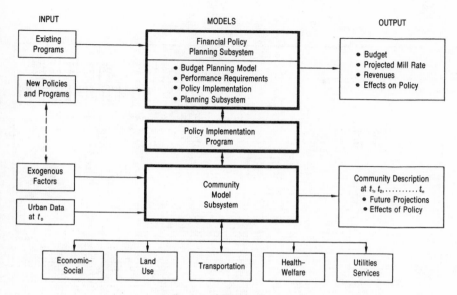

Fig. 3 PROMUS system.

the Policy Implementation Program evaluates, then projects the effect of the internal development plan on community factors. In this way, PROMUS has the capability to evaluate community plans, and their resulting economic, social, and industrial impact.

In use, PROMUS embraces practically all areas of city financial management, whether it be revenue, funds, or budget expenditures. It can analyze and evaluate taxation levels, project revenues from intergovernmental grants, from "self-sustaining" activities, and project total cash flow. It can also evaluate and forecast the source and allocation of funds on a city-wide or a department basis.

Besides incorporating a full urban data base, PROMUS also houses a subsystem called SYMAP, which was originally developed by the Harvard Computation Laboratory as a general graphics output system. SYMAP is capable of producing maps showing urban growth characteristics on regional and study-area levels. It can also display a wide variety of physical, economic, and social outputs. A SYMAP output for the city of Toronto is shown in Fig. 4.

The following sections of this paper briefly describe the major subsystems of PROMUS, the concept of the Program Matrices, and typical applications of PROMUS.

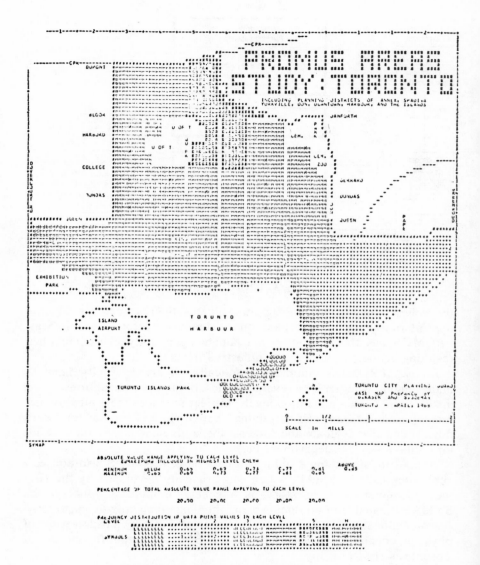

Fig. 4 Percentage of sound housing units, 1972.

THE COMMUNITY MODEL SUBSYSTEM (CMS)

The basic function of the Community Model is to simulate the reaction and interaction of community attributes to various community programs.

The Community Model, as the name implies, represents the community in which the programs are being executed and its evolution over time in terms of the development of demographic and socio-economic attributes. The community is subdivided into a number of small areas that may be thought of as neighborhoods. These are geographically contiguous units which are treated as homogeneous with respect to the attributes of significance. Since the number of attributes involved is large, an extremely large number of different neighborhood types can be represented. This is an essential feature if the many different types of urban communities found in the United States and Canada are to be capable of representation within the simulation model.

The Community Model Subsystem (Fig. 5) is subdivided into three major submodels:

1. Small Area Submodel.
2. Neighborhood Submodel.
3. Population and Income Distribution Submodel.

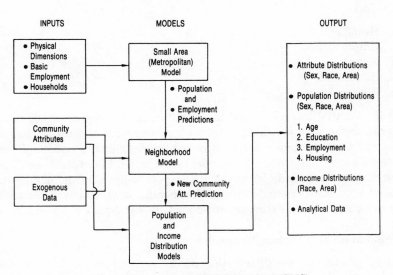

Fig. 5   Community Model Subsystem (CMS).

1. Small Area Submodel

This model allocates population growth and endogenous employment based on:

a. Exogenous employment (basic employment).
b. Distances between residential and industrial sectors.
c. Demand for various categories of occupational skills.
d. Land and household characteristics.

Basic employment for the metropolitan area as a whole is stated as an exogenous set of variables representing the level of employment in each of the basic industries of the community. The term "basic employment" is defined, consistent with the Lowry and TOMM Model definitions, as that portion of total employment within the community which is associated with the economic activity determined by factors outside of the community and its local economy.

2. The Neighborhood Submodel

On the basis of the outputs from the Small Area Submodel, the Neighborhood Submodel produces estimates of the most significant sociological characteristics in five categories for each neighborhood. These are:

a. Housing.
b. Employment.
c. Health.
d. Education.
e. Welfare.

It is essential to realize that the Small Area Submodel serves only to determine the way in which employment, business and residential construction and population are distributed throughout the community as a whole. The Neighborhood Submodel (see Fig. 6), in contrast, deals with each neighborhood individually. With respect to housing and employment in particular, it serves to determine the specific, detailed characteristics of the more aggregated estimates produced by the Small Area Submodel.

3. Population and Income Submodels

The age and income distribution of the population within each small area is computed in this submodel. The new age distribution is based upon

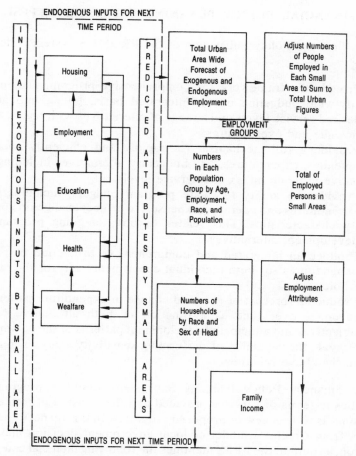

Fig. 6 Details of Neighborhood Submodel interaction in Community Model Subsystem.

the previous distribution aged by one period, and birth and death rates. Migration into a region is assumed to be similar to the estimated distribution. Estimates of male and female population within each age bracket are applied against the appropriate birth and death rate.

Family income is related to the age distribution of population, the occupational distribution of males and females, and the educational attainment distribution of the population.

THE FINANCIAL POLICY PLANNING SUBSYSTEM (FPPS)

The Financial Policy Subsystem of the PROMUS system is designed to:

1. Provide the framework for comprehensive program planning and city-wide budgeting on an integrated basis, taking into account desired service levels and a range of alternatives with regard to both revenue and expenditures.
2. Provide a full mechanism for rapidly and efficiently evaluating revenues, expenditures, and budgetary alternatives including alternative program mixes and service levels.
3. Provide the ability to relate program budgets, including capital expenditures and operating expenses, to project changes in community characteristics. This relates to both on-going programs and development alternatives.
4. Produce an integrated and comprehensive projection of program expenditures for both individual departments and for the city as a whole.
5. Produce a forecast of required change in expenditure patterns and revenues over time as a function of both alternative program objectives and anticipated development patterns of the community.
6. Provide the capability of performing sensitivity analyses in relation to the above functions.

The Financial Policy Planning Subsystem identifies programs and activities in terms of services provided and their costs for both existing programs as well as new or proposed programs. In this respect, the model differs from Crecine's model of local government decision making. In addition, as output, the FPPS identifies the following financial categories:

1. Expenditures.
2. Revenue forecasts.
3. Mill rate calculation.
4. Cash flow budget.

Figure 7 shows a flow chart of FPPS. The major output of the Financial Policy Planning Subsystem is a budget forecast detailing expenditure patterns as a result of both existing programs and activities as well as new program and activity mixes that are a result of community needs. There is a direct interface here between the two subsystems, the Community

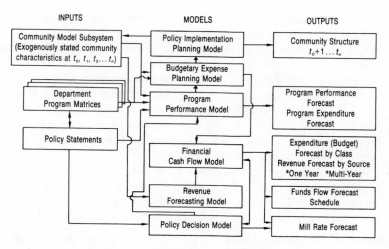

Fig. 7   Financial Policy Planning Subsystem.

Model and the FPPS, in terms of:

1. Computing revenues to the community based on the changing real property base, population, etc.
2. Computing expenditures due to the changing nature of the needs.
3. Computing effects of governmental policy action on the style, character, and structure of the community.

Program matrices set the context for the financial analysis of each department. Each department is divided into a number of programs. If appropriate, a program can be further structured into a number of activities. The process of disaggregation is constrained by the requirement that a comprehensive set of data be collected for each activity.

Program matrices have been developed for all departments of the city of Toronto. The most important departments in terms of dollars spent and services provided are the "delivery" departments, that is, Public Works, Fire, Public Health, Parks and Recreation, and Streets.

The program matrix for delivery departments contains the following information for each program/activity:

1. Service Level: The service level defines, in a quantitative measure, the means by which the activity level of a program can be altered to meet its objectives. For example, frequency of refuse collection, conditions of pavements and sidewalks, are the types of service levels considered.

2. Direct Workload: This is a measurement of the number of items which must be processed.
3. Workload Resources: These are the resources required to process the work of the program.
4. Community Characteristics: Community characteristics are factors outside of the control of the department that influence the direct workload. This would usually relate to community characteristics for those programs providing a deliverable product or service to the community. Other administrative programs would be related to the activity level of the delivery programs.
5. Observable Outputs: The observable outputs are any tangible products of the program. It should be noted that the outputs of one program may be the exogenously stated factors for another program. In these cases, the programs would be interrelated.

The set of information required by the program matrices, as outlined above, does not represent the total data requirements for each program/activity. Additional data is required by other submodels, particularly the Program Performance Model, the Budgetary Expense Planning Model, and the Policy Decision Model. Thus, the main contribution of the program matrices is to provide the framework for departmental analysis. An example of a Program Matrix for the Streets Department is shown in Fig. 8.

FINANCIAL AND BUDGETING APPLICATION OF THE PROMUS SYSTEM

The financial and budgeting applications of the PROMUS system can be divided into two main clusters. The first of these deals with applications associated with the financial management process. The second describes applications of a more general or policy oriented nature.

1. Financial Management Applications

The financial management function is concerned with the process of revenue generation and expenditure management. In fact, in the city of Toronto, these two functions are divided between two departments, Finance, and Budgets and Accounts.

In terms of the applications of the system, therefore, it is appropriate to discuss the Financial Management process under three subsections:

DEFINED PROGRAMS	ACTIVITIES	SERVICE LEVEL	INPUT		OBSERVABLE OUTPUT
			CONTROLLABLE	EXOGENOUS	
				Economic Development	
Refuse Collection	Bulk, household, and street refuse Daylight collection of refuse and combustibles Nighttime service	Frequency of pickups per week from residential, industrial, commercial Place of pickup (back of house or street)	Manpower Equipment Contract Service	Residential: Single family dwelling units Medium density dwelling units High-rise apartment units Commercial: Restaurants Office buildings Industrial: Heavy manufacturing	Observable Outputs: Tons of garbage collected Number of citizen complaints against department
Services					
Street Cleaning	Mechanical and manual Flushing and cleaning Clean catch basins Spring and fall leaf pick-up	Service frequency Main arteries—daily Others—weekly	Manpower Equipment	Weather Traffic Flow Road Mileage	Low nuisance Low dust pollution Low hazard
Snow Removal	Sand, salt, plow, and remove snow Contract for sidewalks— Hand shoveling of: Public transit stops, Main intersections, and Crosswalks	Minimum priorities Arteries to be bare Collectors center bare Locals ploughed as conditions permit	Manpower Equipment Contract Services	Weather, Traffic Patterns, Street mileage Statutory holidays, School term September start	Low hazard Low traffic flow delay interruption

Fig. 8 Program Matrix for Streets Department.

Budgetary Expenditure Management

The applications of the system to the budgetary expenditure management process includes the following:

1. Departmental estimate development.
2. Aggregation of current estimates.
3. Capital budget development.
4. Review and revise.
5. Research.

Figure 9 summarizes the FPPS applications in relationship to these elements.

It is clear, upon examining these applications, that a major concern of

FUNCTION	APPLICATION
Departmental estimate development	Establish program objectives
	Forecast long-term costs, service needs
	Select service levels, resource applications
	Apply program mix priorities
	Evaluate program cost-effectiveness
	Administrative cost projections
Aggregation of current estimates	Select program mix
	Evaluate mill rate impact of changes
	Forecast expenditure levels with community changes
Capital budget development	Forecast debt service and long-term funds flow
	Select mix, apply project priorities
	Evaluate current budgetary implications
Review and revise	Evaluate alternative priorities and program mixes
	Evaluate alternative resource applications, costs
	Evaluate alternative service levels
	Review interdepartmental linkages
Research	Identify program norms, cost patterns
	Examine new program options
	Assess development alternatives

Fig. 9 Summary of functional applications in support of budgetary expenditure management.

the budgetary expenditure management process is with the programs, their planning, operation, and management. PROMUS assists program supervisors and administrators in estimating the costs of delivery programs using a systematic approach based on defined program objectives and levels of service.

Source of Funds

Funds come from a variety of sources. By way of summary, revenue sources can be grouped as follows:

1. Taxation.
2. Intergovernmental transfer and grants.
3. Revenue from self-sustaining activities.
4. Debenture funds.
5. Financial revenues.
6. General miscellaneous revenues.

Potential applications of the PROMUS system in the revenue management activities in each of the above areas are summarized in Fig. 10.

FUNCTION	APPLICATION
Taxation	Assessment base forecasting Revenue need determination Mill rate calculation Long-term taxation policy Development
Intergovernmental transfers and grants	Payment base forecasting and evaluation Subsidy maximization planning Development of new sources and programs for revenue generation and possible subsidy
Self-sustaining activities	Forecast of present systems Projected budgets Research as to alternative rates Analysis of incidence of burden of payment Identify new areas of user charge application
Debenturing	Forecasts of debt service costs and patterns Debenture planning as to timing and amount Leverage control
General and miscellaneous revenues	Base forecasting and planning Rate analysis Incidence analysis New source development

Fig. 10 Summary of functional applications in support of revenue management.

Funds Management

The third element of the financial management process is funds management. This refers to the execution on a day-to-day basis of the financial management process. It is concerned with decisions regarding liquidity, the cost of money, financial revenues, cash management, and leverage. The FPPS provides support to the funds management process in the following decision areas:

1. Cash inflow forecasting.
2. Cash outflow forecasting.
3. Maintenance of desired liquidity.
4. Maximizing net financial revenues.

The applications of the FPPS in each of the above areas are summarized in Fig. 11.

FUNCTION	APPLICATION
Cash inflow management	Forecast cash inflow Evaluate timing options Evaluate revenue base changes
Cash outflow management	Forecast cash outflow Evaluate timing options Evaluate resource cost changes
Liquidity management	Establish cash minimum policies Evaluate alternative debt plans Smoothing inflows and outflows to eliminate peaks
Maximization of financial revenue	Evaluate short-term investment policy options Evaluate debenturing options as to timing and amount Review of interest rates Research into expanded investment portfolios

Fig. 11   Summary of functional applications in support of funds management.

2. Policy Applications

One of the most common types of policy applications is the Fiscal Impact Study. This is a special analysis of the financial effects on the community of changes in programs or policies. For example, there may be a change in a proposed development project, or a new municipal service may be introduced. There could be a major change in transportation networks or a major shift in the priorities among existing programs. Basically, it involves the potential effects on the community's financial structure as a result of a single decision or policy expression. It differs from the routine maintenance of programs primarily in that it represents not a continuation of past trends and practices, but rather a definite change in direction and break from the past.

Another area in which the system will offer support for policy development is the rapid analysis of new revenue forms. For example, characteristics of the community not now used as a base for taxation may be analyzed as to yield and impact with the aid of the FPPS and alternative rates and base classification examined rapidly based on consistent projections of community change.

The PROMUS system could well become an extremely powerful analytical tool when applied to this type of situation. Civic officials and planners charged with evaluating the particular policy choice in question benefit in a number of ways by using this approach:

1. The system calls upon a data base comprised of analytically derived "base values" which describe the city's characteristics in detail and make projections of revenue and expenditure on a consistent basis rapidly and efficiently.
2. The system then projects streams of revenues and expenditures over a long-time span.
3. The system will take more variables into account simultaneously than can be practically manipulated manually. Among these are:
   a. Community characteristics, changes and trends.
   b. Funding alternatives.
   c. Program characteristics.
   d. Resource costs.
   e. Cash flow patterns.
   f. Taxation policies, burdens and incidence.
4. Alternative assumptions and choices can be tested quickly and consistently to establish their significance to the policy choices under consideration.

Because of the speed and comprehensiveness of PROMUS, policy makers will be able to examine in detail, and project the financial consequences of, more variations of more alternatives. This will enable analysts to test and compare on a consistent basis alternatives proposed by groups within the community with a particular point of view in a given situation. Clearly displaying the different financial effects of various policy options, PROMUS will assist planners in processing decisions among alternatives on relative costs and benefits.

It should be emphasized here that PROMUS is not designed to assess social costs and benefits as distinct from economic costs and benefits. It merely projects observable and tangible factors in accordance with the definition of problems input into it. It serves to focus attention on the tangible and nonmeasurable qualitative factors, however, by providing a consistent analytical comparison among the measurable elements. For example, while PROMUS can evaluate the financial consequences of a particular development, it cannot assess the social values associated with it or its alternatives. On the other hand, by enabling consistent evaluations to be made of the fiscal impact of a variety of alternatives, it highlights the magnitude of relative costs involved in deciding for one alternative over others, and enables policy makers to focus on the trade-offs between social and economic values.

PROMUS does not relieve administrators of the final decision-making responsibility. What it does is arm them with valid data and meaningful analysis that will assist them in deciding on the best avenues to take to reach their expected goals.

SUMMARY

PROMUS can support not only the ongoing management process at the municipal level, but also the special studies necessary to evaluate major policy options. This latter application is becoming increasingly important as better informed and more outspoken groups within the community continue to grow in prominence.

Obviously, PROMUS suffers from some of the drawbacks and limitations of our large-scale urban models (see, for example, an excellent discussion of the problems in large-scale modeling in reference 18). A lot more research needs to be performed to improve the analytical methodology and representation of many of the complex interrelationships. However, by providing a mechanism for evaluating a number of "what if" questions and displaying the major variables pertinent to decision making, PROMUS provides a useful tool that can be continuously improved as better information and analyses are available.

In summary, PROMUS offers the potential of a sophisticated and powerful urban planning and management system to assist urban planners and administrators to rapidly evaluate alternative action plans in terms of financial implications and effects on community characteristics.

REFERENCES

1. Irwin, N. A. Review of existing land-use forecasting techniques, *Highway Review Board Record*, No. 88, pp. 182–216.
2. Decision Sciences Corporation, *New Communities: A Survey of the State of the Art*, Final Report submitted under Contract H-1496, U.S. Dept. of Housing and Urban Development, Washington, D.C., 1971, NTIS Access Number PB206-883.
3. Quade, E. S. *Systems Analysis Techniques for Planning—Programming—Budgeting*, Santa Monica, California: RAND Corporation, 1966.
4. McCullough, J. D. *Cost Analysis for Planning—Programming—Budgeting Cost-Benefit Studies*, Research Paper, Institute for Defense Analysis, undated.
5. Lyden, F. J. and Miller, E. G., (ed.) *Planning, Programming, Budgeting: A Systems Approach to Management*, Chicago: Markham, 1969.
6. Crecine, J. P. *Governmental Problem-Solving—A Computer Simulation of Municipal Budgeting*, Chicago: Rand-McNally, 1969.
7. Blumberg, D. F. The city as a system, *Simulation*, October 1971.
8. Harris, Britton, *The Penn-Jersey Regional Growth Model*, Penn-Jersey Transp. Study, Philadelphia, 1963.
9. Steger, Wilbur A. The Pittsburgh urban renewal simulation model, *Journal of the American Inst. of Planners*, Vol. XXXI, No. 2 (May 1965), pp. 144–150.
10. *Model of San Francisco Housing Market*, prepared by Arthur D. Little Inc. for the San Francisco Community Renewal Program, January 1966.
11. Lowry, Ira S. *A Model of Metropolis*, RM-435-RC, Santa Monica, Calif.: RAND Corporation, August 1964.
12. Crecine, J. P. *A Dynamic Model of Urban Structure*, Santa Monica, Calif.: RAND Corporation, 1968.
13. Harris, Britton, Quantitative models of urban development: Their role in metropolitan policy-making, in Perloff and Wringo, *Issues in Urban Economics*, Baltimore: John Hopkins Press, 1968.
14. Lowry, I. S. *Seven Models of Urban Development: A Structural Comparison*, Santa Monica, Calif.: RAND Corporation, 1967.
15. Goldner, W. The Lowry model heritage, *Journal of the American Institute of Planners*, March 1971, pp. 100–110.
16. Office of Economic Opportunity, *SCANCAP Program Development and New Haven Application*, Final Report, Contract No. OEO633, 1966.
17. Decision Sciences Corporation, *New Communities: Systems for Planning and Evaluation*, Final Report, Contract H-1496, U.S. Dept. of Housing and Urban Development, 1971, NTIS Access Number PB 206–882.
18. Lee, Douglas B. Requiem for large-scale models, *Journal of the American Institute of Planners*, May 1973.

10

The Computer—A Vital Element In Modern Day Police Operations*

M. BOCKELMAN

Missouri Police Department, Kansas City, Missouri

You and I live in a day and age when nine out of ten scientists who ever lived, live today; when man's ability to calculate has increased 500 million times faster than we could in the year 1945; where knowledge, prior to this century doubled every 50 years, it now doubles every five years.

We, in the Kansas City Missouri Police Department, know that the only permanent value of today is "change" in an ever-changing world. We are aware of the need not to stand still. Our policemen are tools of society and that society is more complex than it used to be, and it needs keener tools. Because of the complex interaction of our society, the police must tune themselves in to human relations as they exist today.

A rap on the noggin with a night stick, called a baton, is not the final answer. We know that we must be more sophisticated these days. It is a different world today and it requires a different sort of police department to cope with these problems. We subscribe to the theory that if we have been doing something the same way for five years we are probably doing it wrong. This is where the computer begins to play an effective part in modern day law enforcement operations.

Criminals do not bother to observe jurisdictional boundaries, but the police do. Computers with their vast capability for distance communication help the police to make up for this disadvantage. Whatever the cause for crime, it is up to the police to cope with it. The police must be responsive to society and since society has changed, so must the police.

---

*From the *Proceedings of the World Conference on Informatics in Government*, The IBI-ICC, Florence, Italy, October 1972, pp. 96–105.

Computers are helping the police to become aware of facts and theories hidden since the beginning of time.

Ours is a dynamic environment in which no two seconds in time are ever the same, and because we mortal humans cannot respond in time segments of less than one second, we have harnessed the power of computers to do what must be done in the smaller segments of time.

Computerized systems present a terrific advantage over manually based systems in that they enable us to bring together, promptly and accurately, all facets of information for an entire region into one common data bank. The fact that the participants are separated physically by geographic jurisdictional limits and political entities has no more meaning to the computer than if they were separated by a wall between rooms.

We are aware of the fact that the electronic computer will never arrest wanted felons nor protect us against the radical element committed to bombings, but it does have the capability to make us aware of potential problems before they occur and to retrieve within seconds all facets of a case hidden deeply within the volumes of archives of record systems.

In our environment, computerized information systems cannot be motionless and still be responsive. They are either progressing forward or disintegrating backwards. We also know that the computerized telecommunications systems are absolutely essential to police operations, that without them, we would evolve into a state of inefficiency and perhaps stagnation.

In a day and age when we hear of an uproar by many segments of our society regarding invasions of one's privacy by the computer, we have given great emphasis towards insuring that only documented information is recorded in the criminal data bank.

Law enforcement philosophy and policy require that computerized systems be established around the following concepts:

1. The computer system will be a slave to the needs of the officer in the field, rather than regimenting the officer to become a slave to computer systems.
2. The computer must function in a law enforcement environment, rather than attempting to orientate police operations into a computerized environment.
3. Computer technicians and hardware engineers will adjust their working hours to the needs of law enforcement operations.
4. A law enforcement officer is an extremely busy individual. Besides performing his basic duties of enforcing the law and resolving

crime incidents, he has many documented reports to prepare, some of which are required by law. Police record systems must first assist the officer in his informational needs, and these systems must operate efficiently and accurately in that environment.

5. At a time when society was restricting the powers of the law enforcement officer, it became necessary to develop the technological means by which the law enforcement officer could receive an immediate response to his informational needs, thus reducing or eliminating unnecessary periods in which the citizen is held. The system must, therefore, be designed to furnish responses within 10 seconds to inquiries initiated by the field forces.

6. The first basic category of information to be computerized to which the law enforcement officer needed immediate access was outstanding warrants and police pickup orders.

7. The second category of information needed by the field force was abstract data related to criminal convictions, parole status, penitentiary release, and other information relative to criminal records.

8. The third category of information needed was that which would forewarn the officer of impending danger, such as persons known to have been armed, considered dangerous, or those who have resisted arrest.

9. The data bank stored in the police computer system must be afforded security and protection of criminal records from access to unauthorized persons or agencies, as required by law enforcement ethics and state law.

10. The system must be validated as absolutely accurate since the citizen's freedom or detention may be involved. Every safeguard must be built into the system to insure the information is authentic and reliable.

11. Every category of information entered into the police computer's memory banks must be backed up by a legal document which, by law, authorizes police access to such information and empowers them to investigate and, where warranted, to arrest the citizen when the circumstances clearly indicate a violation of the law.

12. The system must employ the capability of transmitting "all points bulletin" and other administrative messages through a message switching system to any of the on-line Data Communication terminal devices. As a result of the expected high volume of inquiring traffic, the terminals must be buffered to provide for minimum line transmission time. System specifications require that

a minimum of ten terminals must be served efficiently with each terminal transmitting on the line for a maximum of eight seconds per transmission. The system would be designed for automatic numbering of messages thus reducing the administrative control of station clerks.

13. The hardware and software must be capable of operating in a multi-programming environment, with law enforcement telecommunications functioning in one partition and administrative report programs functioning simultaneously in a separate partition.
14. A technical position known as "Telecommunications Operations Specialists" was established in order to provide constant training of operations personnel who must have a thorough understanding of the theories and proper use of Police Computer Information Systems.
15. All action occurring on the telecommunications network must be logged in order that we may have the capability to review or extract any portion of telecommunications activity or to use on-line update activity to rebuild files should that requirement exist.

The conceptual systems study clearly showed that it was essential that the police must have access to a modern communications system in order to support a computerized teleprocessing system.

The on-line files are designed so that there will be three physical files, a name index, a general purpose index, and a master data file. The general index file will, by nature of the key, be subdivided into logical sub-files.

NAME INDEX FILE

The purpose of the Name Index File is to provide an alphabetic grouping of all names involved in any way with system participants. This file will contain true names, alias names, moniker names, and those business names that have reason to be in our files.

GENERAL PURPOSE INDEX FILE

The purpose of the General Purpose Index File is to maintain one central index file where a check can be made for any numeric identifier which may be associated with a person, address, automobile, offense or ticket, vehicle accident, and arrest. Also included will be index entries for

Court System purposes which will have court date and time as the key and Offense System entries which will be used for Daily Crime Summary (Part I: Offenses committed within past 24 hours), and Injury Accidents occurring within past 24 hours.

The types of data included in this file will be as follows:

1. License number.
2. Vehicle identification number.
3. Address.
4. Warrant number.
5. Free format information numbers.
6. Traffic ticket numbers.
7. Court date and time.
8. Case report number for arrest system/Civil Index (Case Number Index).
9. Four formats of an offense cross-index record.
10. Case report number for Vehicle Accident.
11. Arrest number index.

MASTER FILE

The purpose of the Master File is to provide one central file where all data concerning an individual or an automobile can be stored together. One seek by the 2314 can pick up all associated data.

The data in this file will be grouped together by an ALN (Alert Number). Within an ALN, several different suffixes will cause the data to be grouped and displayed in the sequence desired. The sequence of a complement of records will be as follows:

1. Name records.
2. Numeric identifier records.
3. Address records.
4. License records.
5. Warrants or Wants (In seriousness sequence).
6. Informational records.
7. Arrest information (abstract).
8. Prosecutor records.
9. Traffic arrest.
10. ASAP records.
11. Vehicle accidents.

12. Offense records.
13. Juvenile Court records.
14. Civil Index (Case Number Index).

In order to best use the record space available in our files, the records will be maintained in two parts. For example, the name record has certain data missing a large percentage of the time. Our solution to this was to divide the name record into one segment of data that is present most of the time, and another segment that is missing frequently. The second segment is called the numbers record and contains all numeric identification an individual normally uses. Another example of segmenting records is in the offense and traffic systems. These systems collect two types of data, statistical and historic. The historic data has to be retained for inquiry purposes for a period of one and two years respectively. Statistical data is necessary only long enough to run statistical reports. These records have been segmented on that basis, and the statistical records will be dumped into tape and purged from the Teleprocessing System as soon as the reports have been run.

One of the major problems confronting the computer technicians was developing a highly accurate technique by which the computer could search out and retrieve accurate information on a given person from other records with similar common names. The following explanation reflects the technique used by the ALERT System in the identification of correct names by the computer.

When the computer receives the name inquiry, the name is compacted to be used as the search key. The computer will retrieve all of the records with the same key as the search key. Comparison of the fields in the inquiry are then made against the equivalent fields in the records found. If the field in the inquiry and the equivalent field in the record are not blank, a positive value designated for that field is added to a total weight counter. If these fields contain matching information, the positive value is also added to the weight counter. When one or both fields are blank, no values are added to either counter. After all the fields have been compared, the weight counter is divided by the total weight counter giving a percent of hit. The records are then sorted so that the record with the highest percent will be displayed first. To be displayed, the record must match at a minimum of 40%. The following example portrays how the weighting table is used:

Data Element	Weight Factor Match	No Match
Last name	+ 180	− 20
First two characters first name	+ 80	− 30
Third character first name	+ 0	− 30
Remainder of first name	+ 80	− 20
Middle initial	+ 20	− 80
Race	+ 10	− 20
Sex	+ 0	− 160
Date of Birth—Month	+ 20	− 80
Day	+ 30	− 20
Year	+ 50	− 20

The name index is created by a process in which the vowels, the letters *w*, *h*, *y*, and any double letter are removed from the last name. The first character of the first name together with a maximum five characters of the last name, as defined above, form the name key for search purposes.

The system philosophy required "multi-threading" concepts, and a priority of processing actions must be implemented in order to guarantee the volume of "throughput" and processing of quantities of data proposed in this document.

To achieve this goal, the Real-Time Teleprocessing Program will consist of a main task and seven subtasks operating concurrently under control of the Disk Operating System. The seven subtasks are:

1. Line control program.
2. Output queue routine.
3. Input queue routine.
4. Faster transaction processor II.
5. Faster transaction processor I.
6. Source data collection processor.
7. Message switch/error handler.

These tasks are attached in that priority. That is, if two tasks require CPU Control, the task with the highest priority gets control and performs its function. When it no longer requires CPU Control, the other task takes over and performs its function. Under this arrangement, a task can interrupt a lower priority task or can be interrupted by a higher priority task.

Line control, input queuing, and output queuing are *low volume* processing service routines that require priority control in order to perform their services and keep the whole system running effectively.

The main task serves as the executive program of the ALERT System. It recognizes all seven subtasks and maintains control and priority assignments over the seven subtasks in their relations to each of the various tasks.

A technical capability was developed to reduce response time by recording the keys and addresses of major files in core in a process known as "Core Indexing."

Procedures were implemented to provide frequent backup of all on-line files. The capability was developed by which transactions could be extracted from the log files if recovery so required. One theory soon was verified. The moment the teleprocessing system became inoperative, the integrity of the system was seriously affected. Programs were developed to produce listings of "hot files" for use when the system was inoperative. Experience showed that inquiries from the field were greatly reduced when the field personnel knew they did not have access to the police teleprocessing system.

It was determined that data collection and processing of information into on-line files were a highly important element of real-time telecommunications systems, and that function was assigned to clerks highly trained in data entry techniques. All data entry for the Kansas City, Missouri Police Department was assigned to this unit which must man the on-line terminals on a 24-hour basis.

One of the major problems confronting police administrators was developing a system which would provide district officers with a compact, but meaningful, listing of subjects wanted who reside within the officer's district. A program was developed which contained an inventory of all wanted persons in street name and residence sequence within a district. The system proved extremely helpful in assisting the district officer in apprehending wanted subjects.

The Telecommunications System, while being responsive to the needs of law enforcement operations when requested, still lacked the capability of providing information to officers prior to arrival at a scene or incident. It was decided that the system must be cross indexed by street name and residence number, with capability of inquiry by street name and residence number for all persons wanted and those with active criminal records. An additional feature was added so that if no one lived at a specific address, the computer would supply names of those individuals who live on the street name within a two-block radius of the residence number. The Address Inquiry routine is generally used when police officers are called to a specific address on a disturbance call and the computer response is given by radio so that officers may be forwarned of wanted subjects or persons who live there and are known to be armed, dangerous, or resist arrest. Names and addresses of citizens with no criminal records were specifically excluded and the local chapter of the Civil Liberties Union was advised of that fact.

Successful automated information systems require a great deal of thought, foresight, and design effort. Equally important is the need for "user-participation" in the design of the system since, ultimately, the "user" must participate and utilize the system. Failing to fully involve the "user" and consider his operational requirements can only result in resentment, noncooperation, and lack of harmony in implementation of the operational system. The Command Staff decided that a Procedural Instruction should be published which contained Departmental Policy, Doctrine, and Procedures with respect to "Automated Information Systems." The document contained a list of terminology and definitions, many of which were new in the police environment, but which must be learned by law enforcement personnel involved in automated systems. Responsibilities applicable to various echelons of command were specifically outlined with respect to use and control of information systems within the police environment.

The system was given the acronym of ALERT, "Automated Law Enforcement Response Team," to denote the close relationship of the officer in the field to computer services. The ALERT System presently services an area comprised of 10,000 square miles of western Missouri and eastern Kansas. The network serves 24 police departments, six country sheriffs, the Kansas and Missouri Highway Patrols, the Kansas City FBI office, the Postal Inspector office, the Municipal Court of Kansas City, County Prosecuting Attorney, County Juvenile Court, and the Kansas City Parole and Prosecuting Attorney office. There are 115 on-line terminals involved in this network system.

A 2400 Band by-synchronous interface exists between the Kansas City Police Computer and the National Crime Information Center in Washington, D.C., where 4000 transmissions are exchanged each day concerning the nation's criminal element.

During the year 1971, the on-line files were accessed $5\frac{1}{2}$ million times, an increase of 2 million transactions over the previous year.

Utilizing the "Computerized Law Enforcement Resource Allocation System" the city of Kansas City, Missouri is recorded by the computer in 8000 workload areas. The Police Department is improving the effectiveness of current police resources by concentrating the available forces of some 1300 men throughout the 316 square miles of the city based on the greatest need of "Calls for Service." Studies made from the Police Computer Resource Allocation System have shown that metropolitan police solve two-thirds of the crimes they respond to within two minutes; however, less than one crime in five is solved if the response is delayed more than five minutes. Studies of "predicted" calls for service compared against actual events reveal that the computerized resource allocation system is effective in that the predicted statistics are about 95% accurate.

It is generally felt that the efficiency and productivity of the police force have been increased by 20% as a result of automation practices which have been implemented with the Police Department. The following specific instances are cited as examples where automation is improving the efficiency of law enforcement operations:

1. Reduction of a time span of from between 10 to 30 minutes to an average of 10 seconds, 90% of the operational time, in retrieving information as to "wants" status on the subject being checked by the officer in the field, and providing information which would "forewarn" the officer of contact with subject known to be armed, dangerous, or resist arrest.
2. The provision of instantaneous information to district officers and intelligence officers on movements of organized crime subjects.
3. The capability by law enforcement to be appraised of persons identified on parole status, with follow-up information submitted to the Parole Officers.
4. Development of the capability to provide statistical data related to vehicle accidents and enforcement by location, date, and time of occurrence.
5. Providing lists of wanted persons by residence within beat to reduce the amount of time for the law enforcement officer to get to each residence.
6. The provision of abstract criminal records for the district officer's informational and investigative purposes.
7. Production of summaries of investigator's work by case, by category of work within case, etc.
8. To provide police administrators with current information and projected cost of specific projects.
9. The preparation each day of listings of all outstanding wanted persons and stolen vehicles in the metropolitan area, which are disseminated to metropolitan area police operations.
10. The development of the capability to search computerized files by

"method of operation" or "method of commission of a crime incident" in an effort to identify likely suspects based upon previously established criminal patterns.

11. The ability to fulfill special requests for data on a timely basis from any of the real-time criminal files, or from the offense, arrest, vehicle accident, or traffic arrest files.
12. Preparation of uniform crime reports and National Safety Council reports for terminal users in the ALERT System.
13. Traffic ticket accountability from initial issue from the Municipal Court to the Police Department, through final disposition of the case.
14. On-line traffic arrest/conviction information for two years from the date of final disposition.
15. Assignment of patrol personnel to handle calls for service on the basis of resource allocation statistics.
16. Analysis of on duty patrol time spent in non-patrol functions, that is, vehicle and radio repair, administration activities, and on duty court appearances.
17. Analysis of effectiveness of foot patrol beats in areas previously covered by motorized patrol only.

The Police Department was anxious to implement the computer system in a manner to insure it was fully responsive to the information needs of the Criminal Justice Environment. The following management principles were implemented in an effort to guide the computer function:

1. Management cannot instruct a computer to perform properly until it first has a thorough understanding of what we want to do and how we want it done.
2. Management must be educated to become familiar with concepts of automation and techniques of computer technology. The system cannot be effective unless management is dedicated to its efficient use.
3. Computers are frequently resisted because they represent a catalyst toward "change." Commanders must exercise leadership to insure that subordinates accept this facet of technology.
4. Computers are too often regarded entirely as "a necessary evil," a "status symbol," "somebody else's responsibility," or really "nobody's responsibility at all." In this environment, the computer must be accepted as a tool of technology, one that is neutral in nature and will work obediently according to management's direction.

5. Computers must first be made a part of the organization they serve. If the computer is fully serving the mainstream of the organization it functions in, management is more likely to exercise greater control over the information processing system.
6. Computers help commanders understand their operations. This is a statement of fact submitted by leading consultant firms. The information systems provided by computers can help in understanding how a company functions, works, how its parts interrelate, and what factors can make a difference in performance.

Aware of the fact that not all of the department personnel would fully accept this facet of terminology, the Command Staff directed that each Recruit Class would be given two hours of class time in lecture and orientation into the concept, theory, and practical use of computers in police field operations.

It cost the Kansas City Missouri Police Department $85 an hour to operate the real-time system 24 hours a day. The total budget of the automation function amounts to $744,000 annually and represents about 5% of the total police budget. This cost factor is further equated to the support of 13 police officers on duty at all times or a total of 53 officers.

Computers represent the whole of technology and are resented by some because they are representative of pressure for "change" and "reform." It was vital that the computer must take its proper place as a tool in assisting police officers in their duties. In Service Training Courses are conducted in which the officer is reminded that the computer should be accepted for what it was created; information processing, recording, and calculation at great speeds and with perfection.

Administrators acknowledge the use of the computer as an instrument in the battle against crime. The Command Staff of the department readily admit that the computer's real potential remains untapped but one day will be used to analyze the underlying causes of crime outlined as follows:

1. Project patterns of criminal behavior and conditions which harbor such behavior.
2. Assist in the analysis of land usage and avoid development of unfavorable environmental conditions that promote and foster crime or conflict.
3. Development of trends that will predict future social problems, if not altered.
4. Creation of systems to deal with unacceptable behavior patterns before crimes or accidents are caused.

5. Analyzation of treatment and correctional programs and behavior patterns of individuals to determine the success of the correctional system.
6. Development of individual patterns of persons having trouble functioning in society.

This system cannot be adjudged a complete success until these objectives have been attained.

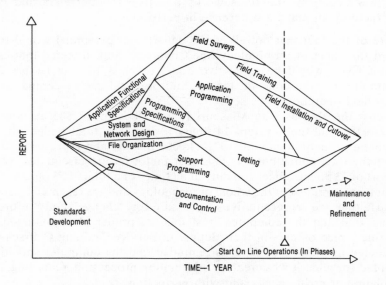

Fig. 1 Implementation of an "on-line telecommunication system" alert.

SANITATION AND WASTE MANAGEMENT

11

Design of Sanitary Sewage Collection System by Electronic Computer*

H. F. SOEHNGEN AND P. R. DeCICCO

Civil Engineering Dept., Polytechnic Institute of Brooklyn, Brooklyn, N.Y.

1. INTRODUCTION

The task of designing a sewage collection system for a municipality or sanitary district has always been a tedious and time consuming task requiring a certain degree of experience and engineering judgment for a satisfactory solution. While some practitioners have felt that the development of automatic sewer design by computer would defy solution because of the many decisions entering into a practical total solution, the problem of automation of sanitary sewer design by computer is an attractive challenge because of the magnitude of the present and future work loads for sewer designs facing sanitary engineers in urban and suburban environments throughout the country.

This paper describes a working and economical solution to the task of designing a sewage collection system by a series of integrated computer programs resulting in a simultaneous network solution for the design of sanitary sewers of a large area. One of the worthwhile features of the automated design approach is that it allows the sanitary engineer the opportunity of easily studying several solutions and iterating each to a minimum cost for a project.

The development of this systems approach to sanitary sewer design has taken three years of effort by a small group at the Polytechnic Institute of Brooklyn under the direction of the authors. A collection district in Nassau County (Inwood) previously designed by conventional methods was used as a check model for the computer design techniques. The

*From the *Journal of Socio-Economic Planning Sciences*, Vol. 1 (1968), pp. 391–403.

integrated computer systems developed, which include estimation of design flows, design of sewers, computation of partial flow characteristics, and estimate of cost, were applied to the design of the proposed Merrick Harbor Collection District in Nassau County in collaboration with Charles R. Velzy, Associates Inc., Consulting Sanitary Engineers.

This Collection District (Fig. 1) includes an area of approximately five square miles, with an ultimate population of 39,500 persons. The topography is typical of the Long Island south shore area and contains only minor relief. The sewage collection system designed by computer contains approximately 80 miles of sewer lines ranging from 8 in. to 36 in. in diameters (trunk interceptors in the district were not designed) and two pumping stations. The total number of sanitary sewer manholes required for the whole district is approximately 2000.

The computerized design solution of the Merrick Harbor Collection District described in this paper deals with the preliminary design as established in Nassau County in which designs are projected on 1 ft = 200 in. base maps for approval by County Public Works and Health Department officials before a final design is made at a scale of 1 in. = 50 ft. The integrated automatic design system which has been developed is, however, applicable to any stage of the total sanitary engineering process for a sewer project from a study stage to the final design stage. The computer solution does at least as much as the engineer would or could do with conventional procedures but in less time, with less cost and with a higher level of precision. Also, iterative computer techniques allow an opportunity for redesign with continuous monitoring of cost implications.

2. DESIGN CRITERIA AND STANDARDS

The bases for the computer oriented design for Sewage Collection District No. 3—Merrick Harbor—follow the general specifications for design of sanitary sewers of the New York State Department of Health and the additional requirements of the Nassau County Department of Public Works. *All* of the factors required in the design computations are treated as variables in the linked computer programs and are read-in as general data input. The use of a digitized Capacity-Population Curve in the computer design permits differentiation between lateral sewers and sub-main sewers.

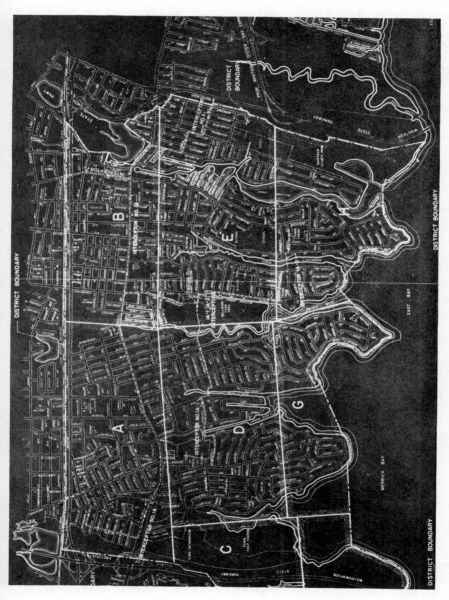

Fig. 1 Sewage collection district number 3—Merrick Harbor (MH).

Bases for computation and design
  1. *Design period.* 50 years.
  2. *Design flow.* (a) Average flows
       Domestic   100 gal/cap/day
       Commercial 3750 gal/acre/day = 37.5 persons/acre
       Industrial   5000 gal/acre/day = 50 persons/acre.
     (b) Maximum flows = average flow × capacity factor
       Capacity factor = 4 for flows less than 650,000 gal/day. Capacity
       factors for flows exceeding 650,000 gal/day as shown on Capacity-
       Population Curve (Fig. 2). All sewers are designed for a capacity,
       when running full, of not less than the maximum flows obtained
       from the Capacity Curve.

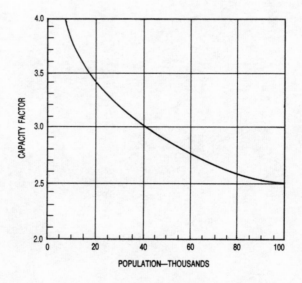

Fig. 2 Sewer design—capacity factors.

Pipe design factors
  3. *Minimum pipe size,* 8 in.
  4. *Minimum velocity,* 2 ft/sec (flowing full).
  5. *Maximum velocity,* 10 ft/sec (flowing full).
  6. *Flow formula,* Kutter's formula

$$V = \left[\frac{41.66 + \dfrac{0.00281}{s} + \dfrac{1.811}{n}}{1 + \left(41.66 + \dfrac{0.00281}{s}\right)\dfrac{n}{\sqrt{R}}} \right] \sqrt{RS}$$

where s = slope of hydraulic gradient = slope of invert (usually).

n = roughness factor (usually assumed at a value of 0.013 for clay pipe sewers).

R = hydraulic radius of wetted cross-section of a pipe ($d/4$ for pipes flowing full).

V = velocity of flow ft/sec.

$Q = (a)(V)(0.646)$ gives flow in millions of gal/day.

where a = area of the wetted cross-section of pipe in square feet.

7. *Roughness coefficients.* (a) $n = 0.013$ for general design. (b) $n = 0.0117$ for critical control lines.

8. *Permissible design diameters* (To allow use of asbestos cement pipe). 8 in., 10 in., 12 in., 14 in., 16 in., 18 in., 20 in., 24 in., 30 in., 36 in.

9. *Minimum slopes and pipe capacities,* velocity = 2.0 ft/sec.

Pipe diameter (in.)	Capacity = Q MGD	CFS	Percent min. slopes for n values 0.0017	0.013
8	0.45	0.70	0.30	0.40
10	0.70	1.09	0.22	0.28
12	1.01	1.57	0.17	0.22
14	1.38	2.14	0.13	0.17
16	1.80	2.79	0.12	0.14
18	2.28	3.53	0.09	0.12
20	2.82	4.36	0.080	0.10
24	4.06	6.28	0.061	0.08
30	6.34	9.82	0.053	0.057
36	9.13	14.14	—	0.043

10. *Minimum sewer depth.* 6.0 ft for dead end M.H., 6.5 ft otherwise.

11. *Maximum M.H. spacing.* 300 ft.

12. *Population contribution.* Four persons per residential dwelling = 400 gal/day average flow.

13. *Drop M.H. type.* Provide a drop pipe for a sewer entering a manhole at an elevation of 2.67 ft or more above the manhole invert and classify as drop M.H. In cases where drop is less than 2.67 ft bring crowns of pipes even during computer design.

3. DATA ORGANIZATION AND INPUT

The interrelationship of the key phases of the automated sanitary sewer design system are shown in Fig. 3. The major phases of the design system are: computation of contributary flows for each link, pipe design for each link of the network, cost estimates covering cost of constructing the entire network, critical control line determination, and redesign of the network and partial flow analysis of the designed system. The computer program for the computation of Contributing Flows (Phase 1) can be used independently. The Pipe Design Program (Phase 2) is dependent on

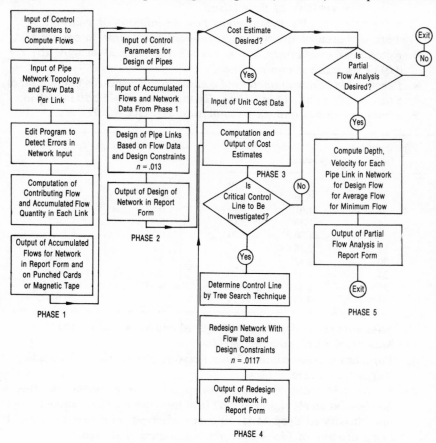

Fig. 3 Flow chart for automatic sewer design system.

output from Phase 1 and the remaining phases are essentially subroutine calls from the Pipe Design Program dependent, for execution, on options selected by the design engineer using the system.

Any systems solution for automatic sewer design must recognize the linked pipe lengths between manholes along the streets as describing a network and thus the proper network model must be adequately inputted for a simultaneous computer solution for an entire district or subdistrict.

To assist in defining the pipe network, each manhole of a proposed system is assigned a number (node number) by the engineer planning the layout. Because of the physical size of the Merrick Harbor Collection District (2000 manholes), it was decided to divide the total district into seven logical subdistricts (boundaries influenced mostly by the location of proposed pumping stations). A portion of the layout of Subdistrict 4, Merrick Harbor at a scale of 1 in. = 200 ft is shown in Fig. 4 which also indicates the topographical and subsurface information available to the designer at this stage as well as house, industrial, and commercial locations which help to establish flow contributions. The 1 in. = 200 ft base map used at this stage is prepared essentially from aerial photographs.

The role of an engineer is enhanced in the design process using this automatic design system. It is his skill and experience which is counted on to project a good sewer layout on the planning base maps. By use of the computer system being described, the engineer is freed however of all the tedious and repetitive computations and gains the ability to change a layout easily. Thus, he is able to compare alternate solutions and to make sound engineering judgments on the locations of pumping stations and other parts of the total system.

While it is possible to describe the terrain model in which the pipe network must fit in a three dimensional sense by use of X, Y, Z coordinate data of discrete points for input to the computer system which has been developed, it was found practical and expedient for the design of the Merrick Harbor Collection District to input only scaled pipe lengths from the base map layout and to derive the rim elevations of the proposed manholes for input to the computer by interpolation from contour information. For the final stage currently being carried out, a complete ground survey profile is inputted and utilized for the final sewer design by computer.

In addition to the pipe length of each link of the network and rim elevation data for each manhole, data on the contributary area to each link or number of homes serviced along each link must be inputted. For

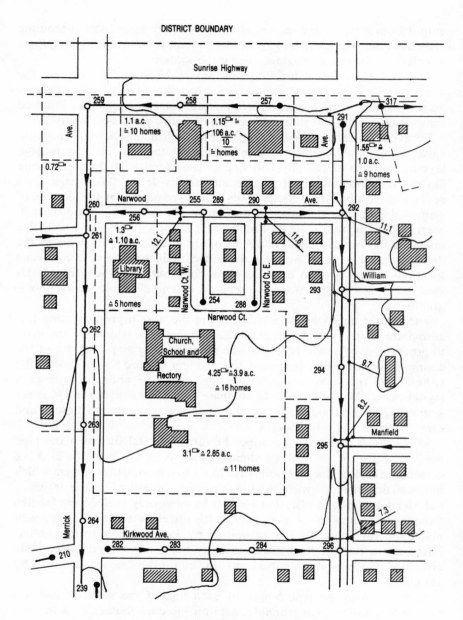

Fig. 4 Pipe network layout, 1 in. = 200 ft.

the Merrick Harbor project it was found expedient to input the number of homes serviced (equivalent to population served) by each link of the network. This was obtained from the 1 in. = 200 ft base maps as indicated in Fig. 4. Surcharge in flow due to the presence of industrial, commercial, or other special flow situations (such as schools) must be evaluated by an engineer based on knowledge of local conditions and can be inputted in Phase 1 of the automated system in terms of contributary area or expressed in terms of equivalent homes serviced.

To obtain annotated output, a dictionary of street names, together with an assigned code number for each street, is inputted in Phase 1 for each subdistrict. A typical street name dictionary is shown in Fig. 5.

Control parameters inputted for Phase 1 include the number of manholes in a subdistrict, the number of street names in a subdistrict, and

INPUT PRINTOUT			
Street Names	Code No.	Street Names	Code No.
Camden La.	1	Dorothy Ct.	25
Denton Dr.	2	Elizabeth Ct.	26
Shore Dr.	3	George Ct.	27
Clubhouse Rd.	4	Helen Ct.	28
Montery Dr.	5	Leonard La.	29
Lynn Ct.	6	Edward La.	30
Glenn La.	7	Leslie La.	31
Lonni Dr.	8	Beach Dr.	32
John St.	9	Montauk Av.	33
Ann Rd.	10	Ahlquist St.	34
Alexis Rd.	11	Rosebud Ave.	35
Cynthia La.	12	Brian Ct.	36
Bond Dr.	13	Echo Pl.	37
Beach Dr.	14	James St.	38
Holiday Park Dr.	15	Colonial Ave.	39
Barry Ct.	16	Riverside Ave.	40
Stanley Dr.	17	Bernard St.	41
Nelson Ct.	18	Florence St.	42
Julian La.	19	Irene St.	43
Joyce La.	20	Covered Br. Rd.	44
Preston La.	21	North Gate	45
Lowell La.	22	Lonni La.	46
Lindenmere Dr.	23	Kimberly Ct.	47
Charles St.	24		

Fig. 5   Street name dictionary for subdistrict.

a control indicator to determine the form of output (card or tape output) from Phase 1 in addition to a report listing.

An Edit Program, as indicated in the flow chart of the system (Fig. 3), automatically edits the input to Phase 1 to detect inadequate definition of the network of a subdistrict and also monitors input data to detect values which do not lie within expected bounds. The edit feature of Phase 1 of the total system has proved valuable in saving computer time in processing further phases with incorrect data.

The major input to Phase 2 (Pipe Design) is the accumulated flow output of Phase 1 as indicated in Fig. 3. Other major input data for Phase 2 concerns critical low basement elevations and data relating to drainage structures; features which impart constraints during the automatic design of pipe links in the subdistrict network. Other variables controlling pipe design inputted at this phase have been mentioned in Section 2 of this paper.

Control parameters inputted before execution of Phase 2 include indicators for executing any further phases of the system desired by the engineer such as Cost Estimates, Critical Line determination and redesign of the network, and Partial Flow Analysis of the designed network.

If the Cost Estimate Subroutine is called after execution of the Pipe Design phase, additional input relating to unit prices must be read-in. A table of depths of expected cut ranges for each pipe diameter is inputted together with an associated table of unit costs for each cut range and pipe diameter. Other cost estimate data to be supplied for a complete cost estimate for the major construction items of a subdistrict include information on House Connections and Assemblies, Manholes (standard and drop manholes), Removal of Concrete Pavement, Replacement of Pavement (up to 5 different types), and Maintenance of Trench.

The interrelation and sharing of input data between the various phases of the automatic design system has only been broadly described in this section. The organization of data input into the total automatic design system has required a good deal of time and thought on the part of the authors and others, but has accounted for much of the success of the computer oriented design of the Merrick Harbor Collection District.

4. EXECUTION AND OUTPUT

The linked computer programs for the total system have all been written in FORTRAN IV and have been compiled and executed to date on an IBM 7040 Computer at the Polytechnic Institute of Brooklyn with

8-729V Tape Drives and 32K core storage. A transition to execution of the system on IBM 360 Model 50 (256K core storage) at the Polytechnic is being made at this time which will improve execution times and allow even larger collection districts to be handled for a simultaneous design solution.

A sample of output from the Phase 1 main program (Accumulation of Flows) is shown in Fig. 6. A typical execution of Phase 1 for a subdistrict of approximately 300 manholes will take about 2 minutes on the IBM 7040. Therefore, the flow quantities for the entire network of pipes in the Merrick Harbor Collection District were obtained in report fashion in about 15 minutes of 7040 execution time. The output form adopted, as illustrated in Fig. 6, can easily easily be correlated to a plan showing the numbered manholes and closely resembles the traditional form sanitary engineers are accustomed to use in this phase of the design.

The actual design of the pipe network of a subdistrict is accomplished in Phase 2 of the total system (with modifications due to control lines in Phase 4). A sample of the report form output from the Pipe Design phase is shown in Fig. 7. Note the line-for-line correlation with the output from the first phase shown in Fig. 6. This organization of output greatly enhances the usefulness of the output reports.

A call to the Cost Estimate Subroutine (Phase 3) produces output illustrated by the sample shown in Fig. 8. As mentioned earlier, all major construction items for which unit prices are available are accumulated and summed by this program through a network analysis based upon the design of Phase 2 or Phase 4. Typical execution time for the design of a network consisting of 300 manholes and the development of a cost estimate for all possible construction items is about $2\frac{1}{2}$ minutes on the IBM 7040 computer.

For the Merrick Harbor project, the first design of a subdistrict network was always made on the basis of a roughness coefficient $n = 0.013$ in Kutter's formula. This is in accordance with usual practice. The algorithm for design utilized in the program has the goal of minimizing depths of cut for each pipe diameter, subject to low basement elevations and drainage structure constraints, and results in an economically designed network for $n = 0.013$. Experience with designs of sanitary sewer systems on the south shore of Long Island, however, indicates that the depth of cut of the low end of large pipe network often exceeds a desired maximum because of relatively flat terrain. Therefore, an attempt is made to "raise" the pipe network by designing the critical control line for more favorable n value, say $n = 0.0117$.

SEWAGE COLLECTION DISTRICT NO. 3—MERRICK HARBOR (MH), CHARLES R. VELZY ASSOC. INC. CONSULTING ENGINEERS

From MH	To MH On Street	Increments of Area and Population			Upstream Tributary Area and Population			Totals for Area and Population		Flows Average and Design		
		Area or Persons Populat. dwl. unt	per dwl.	pop. equiv.	or from area or pop. or MH	dwl. unt	pop. equ.	area or dwl. unt	population or pop. equ.	Avg. Flow at 100 GPCD	Cap. factor	Design Flow gal/day
1	2 Camden La.	6.	4.0	24.	1	0.	0.	6.	24.	2400.	4.0	9600.
2	3 Camden La.	3.	4.0	12.	2	6.	24.	9.	36.	1200.	4.0	14400.
4	5 Denton Dr.	8.	4.0	32.	4	0.	0.	8.	32.	3200.	4.0	12800.
5	6 Denton Dr.	8.	4.0	32.	5	8.	32.	16.	64.	6400.	4.0	25600.
3	6 Camden La.	1.	4.0	4.	3	9.	36.	10.	40.	4000.	4.0	16000.
	Totals	9.		36.		17.	68.	26.	104.	10400.		41600.
7	8 Shore Dr.	3.	4.0	12.	7	0.	0.	3.	12.	1200.	4.0	4800.
6	9 Denton Dr.	7.	4.0	28.	6	26.	104.	33.	132.	13200.	4.0	52800.
8	9 Shore Dr.	8.	4.0	32.	8	3.	12.	11.	44.	4400.	4.0	17600.
	Totals	15.		60.		29.	116.	44.	176.	17600.		70400.
9	10 Clubhouse Rd.	3.	4.0	12.	9	44.	176.	47.	188.	1200.	4.0	75200.
10	11 Clubhouse Rd.	6.	4.0	24.	10	47.	188.	53.	212.	2400.	4.0	84800.
12	13 Montery Dr.	7.	4.0	28.	12	0.	0.	7.	28.	2800.	4.0	11200.
13	14 Montery Dr.	1.	4.0	4.	13	7.	28.	8.	32.	400.	4.0	12800.
(1)		(2)	(3)	(4)	(5)	(6)	(7)	(8)	(9)	(10)	(11)	(12)

Fig. 6 Sample page of flow output.

SEWAGE COLLECTION DISTRICT NO. 3—MERRICK HARBOR (MH), CHARLES R. VELZY ASSOC. INC., CONSULTING ENGINEERS

From MH	To MH	Length (ft)	Diam. (in)	Slope percent	Capacity gal/day	Velocity ft/sec	Invert upper	Elevat'n lower	Sewer upper	Depth lower	Ground upper	Elevat'n lower	Design Flow gal/day
1	2	200.00	8	0.401	451306.	2.00	3.60	2.80	6.00*	6.00*	9.60	8.80	9600.
2	3	60.00	8	0.500	503946.	2.23	2.80	2.50	6.00*	6.00*	8.80	8.50	14400.
4	5	290.00	8	0.401	451306.	2.00	4.00	2.84	5.50†	5.76	9.50	8.60	12800.
5	6	290.00	8	0.427	466020.	2.07	2.84	1.60	5.76	6.00	8.60	7.60	25600.
3	6	175.00	8	0.514	511095.	2.27	2.50	1.60	6.00*	6.00$	8.50	7.60	16000.
7	8	100.00	8	0.401	451306.	2.00	2.80	2.40	6.00*	6.10	8.80	8.50	4800.
6	9	265.00	8	0.401	451306.	2.00	1.60	0.54	6.00	7.06	7.60	7.60	52800.
8	9	300.00	8	0.621	562850.	2.49	2.40	0.54	6.10	7.06	8.50	7.60	17600.
9	10	180.00	8	0.401	451306.	2.00	0.54	-0.19	7.06	8.49	7.60	8.30	75200.
10	11	185.00	8	0.401	451306.	2.00	-0.19	-0.93	8.49	9.43	8.30	8.50	84800.
12	13	210.00	8	0.401	451306.	2.00	3.50	2.66	6.50*	6.54	10.00	9.20	11200.
13	14	50.00	8	0.516	511946.	2.27	2.66	2.40	6.54	6.50*	9.20	8.90	12800.
		(13)	(14)	(15)	(16)	(17)	(18)	(19)	(20)	(21)	(22)	(23)	(24)

*Next to manhole number indicates that the pipe is on the critical path.
†Next to depth indicates pipe is set at minimum depth.

Fig. 7   Sample page of pipe design output.

215

SEWAGE COLLECTION DISTRICT NO. 3—MERRICK HARBOR (MH), CHARLES R.
VELZY ASSOC. INC. CONSULTING ENGINEERS

Estimates of Cost
Sub-district No. 1
Sewers

8 in. sewer Cut Range ft	Quantity L.F.	Unit Price $/ft	Amount $	
0–6	580.	8.80	5104.00	
6–8	30180.	11.00	331980.00	
8–10	11675.	13.75	160531.25	
10–12	8260.	17.05	140833.00	
12–14	2805.	22.00	61710.00	
14–16	1900.	26.15	49685.00	
16–18	765.	29.70	22720.50	
18–20	1090.	34.10	37169.00	
20–22	160.	37.00	5920.00	
Total 8 in.	57415. L.F.			$ 815652.73
10 in. Sewer				
18–20	590.	35.20	20768.00	
Total 10 in.	590. L.F.			$ 20768.00
12 in. Sewer				
20–22	95.	45.10	4284.50	
Total 12 in.	95. L.F.			$ 4284.50

Fig. 8   Sample page of cost estimate output.

If a designer desires a determination of a critical line he indicates this in
the input of Phase 2 of the system. He also specifies the low point critical
manhole. By means of a backward tree search through the already
designed network, a list of manholes on the critical line is determined by
the search algorithm in the Phase 4 subprogram. Figure 9 is an illustration
of a typical list of manholes on a critical line based on lowest invert
elevation of pipes at junction points (flows may also be used as a criterion
if desired). Having determined a critical line, a complete redesign of the
entire network of a subdistrict is now accomplished using $n = 0.0117$ for
design of pipe links on the critical line and $n = 0.013$ for the rest of the
network. Figure 10 is an illustration of the output from an iteration in this
redesign process. Note that manholes on the critical line are starred in the
output report for easy checking purposes. Since there may be more than
one branch to the critical line tree structure leading from the starting
manhole, the process of Phase 4 is an iterative procedure sometimes
requiring up to four iterations.

Critical Path Based on Lowest inv. el.	
Critical Path (Backward)	
M.H.	Dist. From Start
280	
279	60.
278	150.
277	360.
252	520.
251	805.
250	1090.
249	1195.
248	1480.
235	1620.
212	1880.
169	2000.
168	2300.
167	2600.
163	2750.
161	3005.
158	3225.
143	3260.
140	3395.
139	3490.
120	3585.
50	3665.
49	3745.
47	4000.
42	4235.
41	4485.
40	4725.
39	4965.
38	5090.
28	5330.
19	5590.
18	5800.
17	6015.
16	6265.
15	6415.
11	6600.
10	6785.
9	6965.
6	7230.
3	7405.
2	7465.
1	7665.
End of critical line	

Fig. 9 Critical path manhole list.

SEWAGE COLLECTION DISTRICT NO. 3—MERRICK HARBOR (MH), CHARLES R. VELZY ASSOC. INC. CONSULTING ENGINEERS

From MH	To MH	Length (ft)	Diam. (in)	Slope percent	Capacity gal/day	Velocity ft/sec	Invert upper	Elevat'n lower	Sewer upper	Depth lower	Ground upper	Elevat'n lower	Design Flow gal/day
1	2*	200.00	8	0.400	518026.	2.30	3.60	2.80	6.00*	6.00*	9.60	8.80	9600.
2	3*	60.00	8	0.500	579171.	2.57	2.80	2.50	6.00*	6.00*	8.80	8.50	14400.
4	5	290.00	8	0.401	451306.	2.00	4.00	2.84	5.50*	5.76	9.50	8.60	12800.
5	6	290.00	8	0.427	465640.	2.06	2.84	1.60	5.76	6.00	8.60	7.60	25600.
3	6*	175.00	8	0.514	587387.	2.60	2.50	1.60	6.00*	6.00*	8.50	7.60	16000.
7	8	100.00	8	0.401	451306.	2.00	2.80	2.40	6.00*	6.10	8.80	8.50	4800.
6	9*	265.00	8	0.304	451243.	2.00	1.60	0.80	6.00	6.80	7.60	7.60	52800.
8	9	300.00	8	0.534	521748.	2.31	2.40	0.80	6.10	6.80	8.50	7.60	17600.
9	10*	180.00	8	0.304	451243.	2.00	0.80	0.25	6.80	8.05	7.60	8.30	75200.
10	11*	185.00	8	0.304	451243.	2.00	0.25	-0.31	8.05	8.81	8.30	8.50	84800.
12	13	210.00	8	0.401	451306.	2.00	3.50	2.66	6.50*	6.54	10.00	9.20	11200.
13	14	50.00	8	0.516	511946.	2.27	2.66	2.40	6.54	6.50*	9.20	8.90	12800.
(13)		(13)	(14)	(15)	(16)	(17)	(18)	(19)	(20)	(21)	(22)	(23)	(24)

*Next to manhole number indicates that the pipe is on the critical path.

Fig. 10 Sample page of pipe design after iteration.

SEWAGE COLLECTION DISTRICT NO. 3—MERRICK HARBOR (MH), CHARLES R. VELZY ASSOC. INC. CONSULTING ENGINEERS

From MH	To MH	Diam. (in.)	Slope percent	Capacity gal/day	Velocity ft/sec	Design (avg.* cf.)			Average (100 GPCD)			Minimum (50 GPCD)		
						Flow gal/day	Depth (in.)	Velocity (ft/sec)	Flow gal/day	Depth (in.)	Velocity (ft/sec)	Flow gal/day	Depth (in.)	Velocity (ft/sec)
1790	1791	8	0.401	451306.	2.00	6400.	0.74	0.60	1600.	0.42	0.37	800.	0.31	0.29
1791	1792	8	0.401	451306.	2.00	16000.	1.11	0.84	4000.	0.61	0.51	2000.	0.45	0.40
1792	1793	8	0.401	451306.	2.00	20800.	1.25	0.92	5200.	0.67	0.56	2600.	0.50	0.43
1793	1794	8	0.401	451306.	2.00	30400.	1.49	1.05	7600.	0.80	0.64	3800.	0.59	0.50
1794	1795	8	0.401	451306.	2.00	41600.	1.72	1.17	10400.	0.93	0.73	5200.	0.68	0.56
1795	1796	8	0.401	451306.	2.00	56000.	1.97	1.29	14000.	1.04	0.80	7000.	0.78	0.63
1796	1797	8	0.401	451306.	2.00	68800.	2.17	1.38	17200.	1.15	0.87	8600.	0.85	0.68
1790	1798	8	0.550	528543.	2.34	11200.	0.89	0.83	2800.	0.49	0.50	1400.	0.36	0.39
1798	1799	8	0.401	451306.	2.00	16000.	1.11	0.84	4000.	0.61	0.51	2000.	0.45	0.40
1799	1800	8	0.401	451306.	2.00	25600.	1.38	0.99	6400.	0.75	0.61	3200.	0.55	0.47
1800	1801	8	0.401	451306.	2.00	35200.	1.60	1.11	8800.	0.85	0.68	4400.	0.63	0.53

Fig. 11 Sample page of partial flow analysis.

219

After each iteration and redesign, it is constructive for the designer to also specify that a cost estimate for the particular redesign be printed out (Fig. 8). A study of the successive cost estimates indicates the savings of many hundreds of thousands of dollars in construction costs for a collection district such as Merrick Harbor by the use of this technique.

A final optional subprogram for Partial Flow Analysis of the final design of a pipe network can be called if the engineer wishes a hydraulic review giving the actual velocities for various flow conditions. An illustrative page of output from this subprogram is shown in Fig. 11.

Execution of all of the phases for the total design of the Merrick Harbor Collection District took approximately 1 hour on the IBM 7040.

CONCLUSION

There are very definite economic advantages in using an automated design system such as that described. Not only are total construction costs minimized, but engineering design costs are also substantially reduced. The time required to obtain detailed designs is very significantly reduced over older methods.

Several useful by-products accompanying the application of the computer techniques include an increased insight by the engineer into the problems involved which is gained by the detailed systemization of the procedures, the improvement of both the quantity and the quality of output produced, and the release of engineering staff from the tedium associated with the repetitive compilation of data, the design of individual lines, and the estimation of costs.

The acceptance of the output from the computer for the design of the Merrick Harbor Collection District by county and health department officials has paved the way for more efficient and rapid design and review of sanitary sewer systems.

Acknowledgments—The authors wish to acknowledge the valuable programming assistance of Robert Jankowski, Instructor (Eve. School) Polytechnic Institute of Brooklyn during the development of the computer system.

The Merrick Harbor District was designed by computer in collaboration with the Consulting Engineering firm of Charles R. Velzy Associates, Inc., for Nassau County. We wish to express our appreciation to the management of this firm for the opportunity to test the development of the automatic sewer design system and for the invaluable assistance of their staff in checking all phases of input and output.

EDUCATION

12

Design of a Planning Model for an Urban School District*†

The S.D. Two Simulation Model

MIGUEL SZEKELY, MARTIN STANKARD, AND ROGER SISSON

Wharton School of Finance and Commerce, Philadelphia, Pa.

INTRODUCTION

A decision in an educational system is setting a policy for allocating resources. A variety of policies are possible; emphasizing, for example, a particular age group, particular subjects, staff selection and development, or advanced technology. A particular policy will lead to specific uses of resources for educational activities or programs. Thus, a policy causes the consumption of limited resources and influences the change in performance of the students.

This paper reports the design of a Simulation Model to aid in exploring the consequences of alternative allocation policies. It includes financial, operational, and student achievement factors. This model is the second to be developed in our research effort. The first model called S.D. 1, is a very aggregate model of the financial and operational aspects of a school district[3]. It estimates the costs of operating the district under an overall policy. The overall policy is defined by setting policy factors such as: staff-per-student, space-per-student, materials-per-student. Estimates of the effect of a policy on student behavior are not made explicitly in S.D. 1.

The objective of the educational system is basically, however, to

*This research was financed by the School District of Philadelphia and by the Intermediate Unit Planning Project operated by the Bucks County (Pennsylvania) Board of School Directors.

†From the *Journal of Socio-Economic Planning Sciences*, Vol. 1 (1968), pp. 231–242.

change the "potential behavior" of the students being educated. For example, it is hoped that a student who attends a high school civics program will exhibit desirable behavior some 5 years in the future by being a conscientious voter. Thus, models must contain representation of achievement.

S.D. 2 is an extension of S.D. 1 in several respects. First, student achievement is specifically represented, at least by an overall measure. Second, the model is more detailed. It contains specific representation of:

1. Areas within the district.
2. Grouping of students.
3. Grades.
4. Equipment types.
5. Educational programs.

It is believed that this model contains sufficient detail to be a specific tool to be used during the establishment of budgets in an urban school district. S.D. 2 permits the exploration of the effect of alternative educational program mixes or plans on both achievement and on the consumption of resources (Fig. 1).

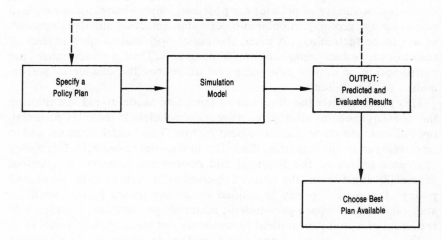

Fig. 1 Use of Simulation model.

Policies and plans are input to the simulator. As the simulator proceeds it carries out these policies and plans within appropriate constraints. Constraints include:

1. Operating budgets.
2. Capital budgets.
3. Limitation on teacher and staff availability.
4. Tenure.
5. Desire for continuity of programs.

The output of the simulator estimates the consequences of the policies in terms of:

1. Operating expenditures.
2. Capital expenditures.
3. Programs actually implemented.
4. Changes in student achievement.

Analysis of the output may suggest other alternatives. Thus, the model can be used iteratively to study alternatives until a decision must be made. Then the best available plan can be chosen for implementation.

The two most important features of S.D. 2 are:

1. It is a generalized model and can be modified to fit a district (or a county or intermediate unit) by use of data and parameters.
2. The model specifies the representation of policies and programs in enough detail to facilitate the achievement prediction procedure. (The details of the achievement prediction procedure are being developed on a separate research task; the approach only is summarized in this paper.)

Overview of the Model

The simulator is very simple in concept. It involves two files and a main program. The district is subdivided into a number of areas. The first files contain data about these areas. In principle, the area file contains all information which would be required for decision making in a particular area. It contains all demographic information as well as information about the current (in simulated time) resources of the school district in that area (number of schools by type, number of teachers, etc.). The second file contains all of the information required to make a decision concerning an educational program. This program file consists of technical and administrative data; for example, resources used by the program per student, percentage of students to receive the program by various categories of students. The main computer program then, in a very general process, takes the areas in turn and applies the programs to them.

This scheme provides great flexibility in use. It would be possible, at some cost in running time, to enlarge the number of areas represented, or the number of programs, or both. Similarly, it is possible to start running and testing the model on aggregate data, say using two or three areas and a similar number of programs, and expand as the facts are gathered and incorporated into the files (Fig. 2).

The level of aggregation we have selected requires a detailed description of the group of students to which a particular program is applied. Consequently, model S.D. 2 categorizes the student population by areas, age group (grade), ethnic group, socio-economic background, and "other characteristics" (regular student, disadvantaged student, or disabled student). In order to allow for the achievement submodel, the student population is further classified into five "achievement levels."

The model is structured so that educational achievement, as a result of participation in educational activities by student groups, can be estimated either within or outside the model.

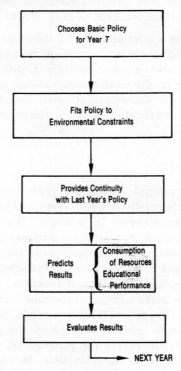

Fig. 2 Steps in Simulation model.

Policies are defined by describing the program mix for each year to be simulated and by stating the allocation rules for converting a proposed program mix into an operating program mix (meeting environmental constraints). Programs are described in terms of the resource requirements needed to implement the program in an area. Implementation of a program is specified by designating the group within each area to which a particular program applies.

The model has been designed so that certain areas may have first call on selected programs. This is accomplished by assigning a priority of 1, 2, or 3 to a program and by designating preferred areas as "key" (e.g., poverty) areas. These designations and priorities are all policy variables. Priority 1 programs are given full implementation in all areas of the system. Priority 2 programs are fully implemented in all "key" areas of the system, and priority 3 programs are implemented in all areas to the extent that remaining operating funds permit. A minimum level for each program for an area is set so that trivially small programs will not be funded.

Budget constraints are input for operating expenditures and for capital investments in building and equipment. (A separate funding level forecasting model is under development.) Provisions have been made so that funds may be committed for a certain program in a specified area. This enables the model to handle the real phenomenon of "committed" or "designated" funds.

Bussing of students from school to school does not quite fit into the framework of programs above. Thus, before the main routine performs the application of programs, the model performs the calculations necessary to implement bussing and other student transfer policy between areas. Educational parks may be represented.

The running sequence, while complicated in detail, is essentially simple. A first appraisal is made during which programs are applied to student populations in each area to determine resource needs. That is, the numbers of teachers, amounts of space, funds required, etc. are calculated as if all relevant educational programs are run. Then, if needs exceed the available budget, a second pass is made over programs and areas to adjust the degree of implementation in accordance with the rules stated in the allocation policy being used (Fig. 3).

Space and equipment needs are projected into the future and compared with the future availability of buildings and equipment (existing and to be completed). New schools and equipment are allocated to the different areas according to the results of the comparison above, and using the rules stated in the capital policy being implemented. Staff requirements and staff availability (existing staff minus attrition) are compared, and new staff are allocated to the different areas in accordance with policy rules.

Next, prediction of student achievement under the operating policy is made (inside or outside the model) and promotion of students is carried out. Finally, yearly operations are summarized and files are updated. This sequence is performed for each year to be simulated, with the output files of 1 year serving as input conditions to the next.

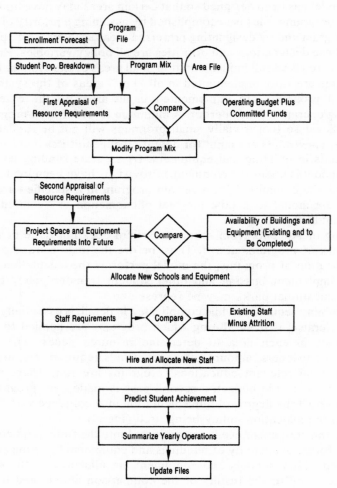

Fig. 3 Simulation model.

Detailed Description of Model S.D. 2

The main program mentioned earlier consists of 20 subroutines linked by a controlling program. A flow diagram of this program (MAIN), identifying the subroutines, is included in Appendix A. MAIN serves the purposes of controlling simulated time, positioning the tapes, zeroing accumulators, transferring control to subroutines while iterating on areas and/or programs, and making a few logical decisions. (Performing a set of operations on each area in the area file will be referred to as "looping on areas." The same terminology applies to programs.)

Subroutine INPUT reads in the information that describes the population characteristics, the existing facilities, and schedules for future acquisition of facilities in each area. It reads in the description of the educational programs as well as the policy rules which indicate where and to what extent the programs are to be applied. This subroutine also handles input of other parameters which are used in the simulator. After the initial pass INPUT reads in *changes* in these variables.

At the present, S.D. 2 uses the same set of policies and parameters throughout the time being simulated. Future versions will allow time dependent policies and parameters. The capital and operating funds available each year can vary and are read in MAIN.

Subroutine ENROLL breaks the student population into groups by area of residence, ethnic group, age (grade), socio-economic background, characteristics and achievement level. The fineness of this breakdown enables testing of different program mixes and of policies for bussing the students between schools. Specifically, the breakdown within areas by school area, age, characteristics (which includes disadvantaged) and achievement level is a sufficient description of groups for the application of educational programs; consequently, the breakdown by ethnic group and socio-economic background is dropped after the bussing transfer operation. The transfer of students makes it necessary to introduce the concept of "home areas" and "school areas."

The first four achievement levels are quartiles based on scores on appropriate tests. (Definition of the test battery implies defining the objectives of the schools. The separate task on achievement prediction is defining such a testing procedure.) The fifth level represents those students who were not promoted in any year. They are in this category only temporarily and are reassigned another level by a part of the achievement prediction submodel.

As a result of the yearly operation the students experience changes in grade (if promoted) and in achievement group, according to programs applied in their "school area." The need to have reports of achievement level by "home area" and the fact that transfer policies can change from grade to grade has made it necessary to keep records of each group of students (by home area, school area, age, characteristic and achievement level) as the group evolves through the system. The possibility of having new students in the intermediate grades (with different characteristics from those who have been exposed to the programs in previous years) made it necessary to treat separately the new students and the old students. The number of new students is obtained by interpolating the figures obtained from a demographic model maintained by the Philadelphia School District. For the first year being simulated the "new" students will be the estimated enrollment from the demographic model (who go to public school) and there will be no "old" students. Thereafter INPUT enters the new students. As it was pointed out previously, it was considered desirable to establish the policies for bussing students at a level of breakdown by home area, ethnic group, age, socio-economic background, characteristics, and achievement level. Of course, this does not mean that a different policy is applied to every different group; keeping this in mind, subroutine TR (called by subroutine ENROLL) works by exception applying a general bussing policy in all cases except in a few specifically indicated. (The general policy might be "no bussing.")

The simulator not only converts a set of programs and policies into needs (operating funds, capital funds, and manpower), but also checks them and modifies them to insure feasibility so that operations will be within the environmental constraints imposed by the availability of resources. This is done by computing first, the total amount of resources required, assuming full implementation of all policies (subroutine RQUIRE), and then allocating the resources available following a set of rules. The needs for teachers, paraprofessionals, materials, space, and equipment are computed from the educational program description, the applicable policies, and the number of students in each area. The overhead expenses are computed as a function of the number of students and of each of the basic resource needs previously calculated. The needs for operating funds are aggregated on a systemwide basis (subroutine AGFUND). Adjustments are made for the precommitted funds.

The simulator can run in two different modes: in Mode 1 there are enough operating funds for programs labeled as "necessary" (priority 1 programs and priority 2 programs in key areas) and priority 3 programs are implemented to the extent that the remaining funds permit. In Mode 2 operating funds are insufficient even for "necessary" programs; then priority 3 programs are dropped and "necessary" programs are implemented to the extent which the funds permit. The decision to use one mode or the other is made in MAIN. The percentage of applicability of priority 3 programs is computed by dividing available operating funds by funds needed. Then (while processing each area), a "share" is computed for each program (subroutine OPERA 1) and compared with a specified minimum allocation. In case the "share" does not meet the minimum, the program is dropped and the corresponding "share" is accumulated in a "pool." This pool is then distributed on a pro rata basis to the other programs applied. This reallocation (subroutine OPERA 2) is made within each area. This subroutine then converts needs into allocations using the percentage of applicability and aggregate requirements for each area.

The allocation of capital funds are made separately for each area, age group, and type (building space and equipment). First, subroutine AGGREI projects the needs for a number of years equal to the lead time (time necessary for the construction of a given type of school or for the delivery of a given type of equipment). Comparing the projected needs with the available facilities and the existing construction (or acquisition) programs, an estimate is made of the "gap" (unfulfilled equipment or space needs) in each area. The allocation procedure (subroutine ALOCAT) consists of assigning first one unit (when necessary) to each of the areas designated as "key" areas, in order of the size of the gap. When all the key areas have been treated once, the allocation is made by sorting areas for maximum gap. This technique represents a policy of satisfying needs in key areas first to some extent. The procedure is designed so that the needs of younger age groups are satisfied first. The allocation is carried on as long as there are funds left. Then the construction programs and equipment acquisition programs are updated (subroutine PROGUP). Policies can, of course, be changed.

The allocation of teaching manpower is done by first aggregating the needs on a system-wide basis, accounting for attrition of teachers and paraprofessionals. The attrition rate can be different for each area (Subroutine AGGRE 2). Once the total needs are known, the process of hiring professionals is represented by assuming that, up to a certain number, it is possible to hire all that are needed, but for higher numbers only a certain percentage can be hired (subroutine HIRE). (This method approximates the short supply of teachers.) After the hiring operation the total number of professionals available is known and the allocation scheme proceeds by satisfying first the needs of "selected" programs (priority 1 and 2 programs in key areas) and then allocating them on a pro rata basis for the rest of the programs (this allocation is done also in subroutine HIRE).

Prediction Achievement Changes

Subroutine EVALUA provides the structure necessary for the achievement evaluating submodel. Every group of students from every school area is treated first by representing the changes in achievement level resulting from the year's operation. This achievement prediction process is being developed on the basis of the following concept: Education is a communication process. The communication takes place both in school and at home. Achievement is related to the extent of the communication and to its quality (the latter being estimated at first by the cost per unit). The achievement prediction algorithm estimates a change in achievement for a group of similar students; that is, students in the same area for schooling, same ethnic group, and other characteristics, and who have been exposed to the same mix of educational programs. The change in achievement is hypothesized to be a function of the extent of communication resources applied (staff, materials), the space available, and the home support as measured by socio-economic factors in the students' home area. Still to be developed are the relationships to represent the interaction between programs. When achievement levels have been set, the appropriate year-end bookkeeping takes place; for example, promotions are represented.

In the first test runs, the following achievement process will be used. For a typical group, identified by a given school area, age group, characteristics, and achievement level, there will be a vector with five elements. Each element is the probability that a student of that group goes to each one of the five achievement levels as a result of the operations of the year being simulated. Drop-outs can be considered simply by making the sum of the five numbers less than one. The grouping for the next year can then be formed. The vector mentioned above will be obtained from empirical data. Subroutine EVALUA also includes the program for making changes on bussing transfers for groups moving beyond key grades (e.g., out of elementary school).

Programming Considerations

Model S.D. 2 has been programmed in FORTRAN IV. It consists of a main program and 20 subroutines. This arrangement has helped simplify the programming and made the debugging and testing much easier. Each subroutine has been tested individually with test data. Since the school district will be divided into about 20 areas, the requirements for memory space are large. Tapes are used continuously, and several tape units are used intermittently as scratch tapes and permanent files during the same run. This reduces core requirements but increases running time.

For the input data (INPUT subroutine) it was decided to use two different area files, one for the population characteristics and the other for the description of the facilities in each area. This was done in order to permit more efficient use of the core memory and a faster tape operation. System parameters and other data, which have to be used frequently, are kept in core.

Under the assumption of 20 areas, the information about students going from one specific area to all others requires an array with 4000 elements. This is large enough so that it was decided to make the computations individually for each area and then record it on a tape (writing in binary) (subroutine ENROLL). The updating of this tape requires that there be two such arrays in core at the same time, which still can be done within the core space available (512,000 bytes).

In order to identify the "special cases" in subroutine TR (for transfer policy) the indexes representing each one of the breakdowns are multiplied respectively by 1, 10, etc. and added up together so as to give one single and unique number for each group.

Subroutines OPERA 1 and OPERA 2 worked out (by using fixed point algebra) in such a way that the same scheme works for Mode 1 and Mode 2.

Subroutine EVALUA uses a scheme similar to the one used in subroutine TR for dealing with the special cases. In order to simplify the promotion procedure, it treats first the graduating students and then adds one to the age index of every group, except those in the fifth achievement level.

Status

This model is now programmed and is being tested. It is hoped that it will be sufficiently validated within a year so that the School District will begin to use it in its ongoing planning activities. The District is already gathering data about programs and about the system on an area basis. An instructional period is planned in order to let the managers learn about the model and to get their help in validating it.

REFERENCES

1. Sisson, Roger L. Applying operational analysis to urban educational systems, *Technical Memorandum*, University of Pennsylvania, Management Science Center, January 1967.
2. Stankard, Martin and Sisson, Roger. Operations research and improved planning for an urban school district, *Technical Memorandum*, University of Pennsylvania, Management Science Center, January 1967.
3. Sisson, Roger L. Some results of a simulation of an urban school district, *Technical Memorandum*, University of Pennsylvania, Management Science Center, March 1967.

Appendix A

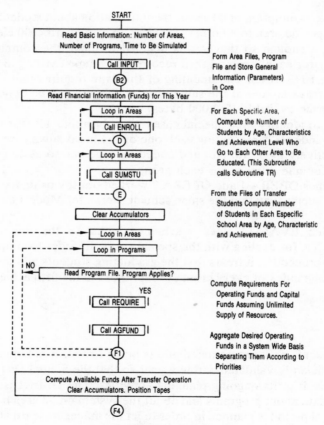

Fig. 4   Model S.D.2 flow chart.

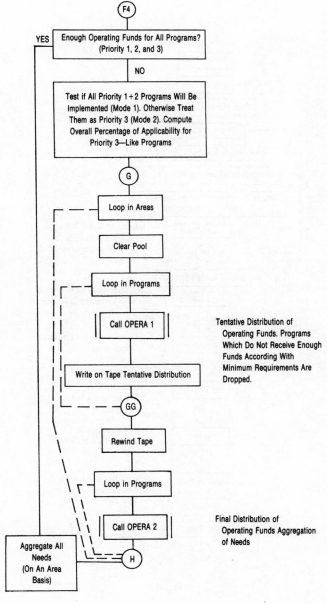

Fig. 5

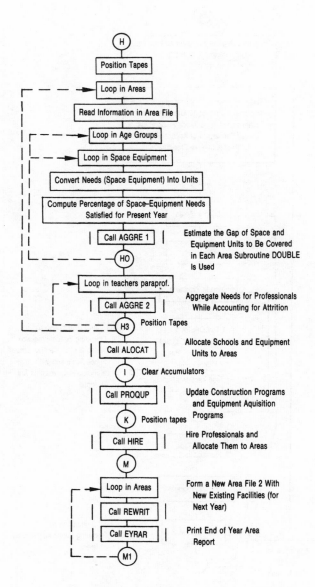

Fig. 6

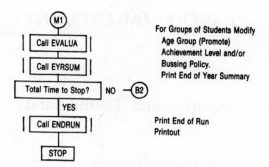

Fig. 7

TRAFFIC MANAGEMENT

13

Computers and Traffic Safety

EDMUND J. CANTILLI

Dept. of Transportation Planning and Engineering, Polytechnic Inst. of New York

Reducing injury and death, and accidents generally, in the current safety situation on streets and highways, devolves almost completely upon a piece of paper: the accident report. We have spent, and will spend, millions of dollars for driver improvement, vehicle design upgrading, and roadway reconstruction, all with a view to alleviation of the problem; but unless all these are based upon the data derived from that piece of paper, all our efforts will be in vain. And since a single state, like New York, can have as many as 450,000 accidents in a year, only through automatic means of extracting, analyzing, and interpreting the many items of data from those accident forms can we hope to bring the problem under control.

The traffic safety situation developed to the point of alerting Congress, in 1966, resulting in the Highway Safety Act, and consequently, the National Highway Traffic Safety Bureau, later upgraded to Department status. The new agency developed 16 Highway Safety Standards. Number 10 of those standards concerns Traffic Records, including, specifically, accident records and the development of accident record systems. Through the automated data processing capabilities of computer systems, the accident record handling procedure can reach its ultimate level of effectiveness.

GENERAL

The application of automated data processing to the traffic accident problem requires a review of the available methods of attack. Generally, a three-pronged program is required; each part of the man-machine-road environment system must be analyzed and improved.

The Man

Improvement in driver performance can come from more rigorous physical capability testing, psychological testing, increases in vehicle-to-vehicle communications, and refinement of driver advisory, informational, and warning methods. Data to be collected for these purposes includes:

Name.
Address.
Driver's License Number.
Physical and Psychological Testing Information.
Age, Sex.

Information to be developed includes:

Identification of drivers with high infraction-arrest-accident records.
Accident occurrence by age groups.
Relationship of accidents to physical capacities and to psychological test results.
Driver performance by areas of residence.

The Machine

Currently, the National Highway Traffic Safety Administration has concentrated on improving the safety characteristics of the vehicle. The data to be collected:

Make.
Year.
Model.
Weight.
Color.
Mileage.
Condition—especially of brakes, tires.

Information to be developed:

Accident occurrence related to each of above.
Severity, extent, and location of vehicle damage related to each of above.

Severity, extent, and location of injury to driver, passenger (by seat location related to each of above).

The Road

Data required for correction of deficiencies in the physical environment include:

Accident location geometry (vertical and horizontal).
Geometry of the specific accident location and physical features thereof.
Location and description of traffic control devices (signs, signals, markings, islands).
Regulations in force.
Road and traffic environmental conditions (extent of roadside access, advertising signs, volume, density, speed).

Information to be developed:

Relation of accident occurrence and severity to each of the above.
Relative value of changes to each (in terms of degree of effectiveness of change).

It has been recommended[1] that much more extensive data be collected (see Tables 1–4). While ideal, the difficulties inherent in the recording of much of this material by the recording officer are readily apparent.

LIMITATIONS

Considering the limitations of study of the three areas of analysis should help in deciding upon a course of action and an area of concentration.

The Driver's capabilities can be improved by more stringent testing, and/or the elimination of drivers with predetermined levels of infractions and accidents, or of certain age groups. But the elimination of any substantial proportions of the driving public will affect the numbers of vehicles sold, and its consequences (gasoline, oil, other auto-related industries) would adversely affect the economy of the country.

The vehicle can be improved a great deal, and this was the direction chosen by the new Department of Transportation. But beyond means of padding the interior, restraining the passengers, and creating a crashworthy, energy-absorbing vehicle construction (all of which have physical and economic limitations), such improvements will have no effect on *numbers* of accidents, which will continue to rise. And whatever effect on *severity* of accidents that develops will thereby be negated in a relatively short time. It may be argued that improvements in intervehicular and vehicle-road communications (requiring physical changes to the vehicle) will help reduce accident causation, but that discussion belongs with consideration of the *road environment*, below.

Improvement of the *road environment* has no such limitations as those outlined above in the foreseeable future. Elimination of confusion of the driver, removal of as much of the judgmental discretion and decision-making process required of the driver as possible, has a long way to go. And especially for this purpose, the study of accident reports is absolutely essential.

THE ACCIDENT RECORD

If this form were designed for one specific purpose and one specific user, the overall task would be simplified. But it is, for one purpose or another, of use and interest to many. For instance, Fig. 1 shows the many, varied, and often overlapping, interests related to the humble traffic accident report.

Consider the specific needs of the traffic engineer, the lawyer, the police, the administrator, and the medical doctor:

The Traffic Engineer

For the purpose of improving the road environment, the following data is required:

Time, date, day of accident.
Light, weather, road condition.
Type of accident.
Location—by facility, location within facility section within 2–3 feet.
Type of vehicle(s) involved, or fixed object.
Possible violation preceding accident.
Driver action preceding accident.
Nature, extent, and locations of vehicle damage.
Nature, extent, and locations of injuries incurred.
A diagram of the accident.
A verbal description of the accident.

USER AGENCY   INTEREST OR PURPOSE

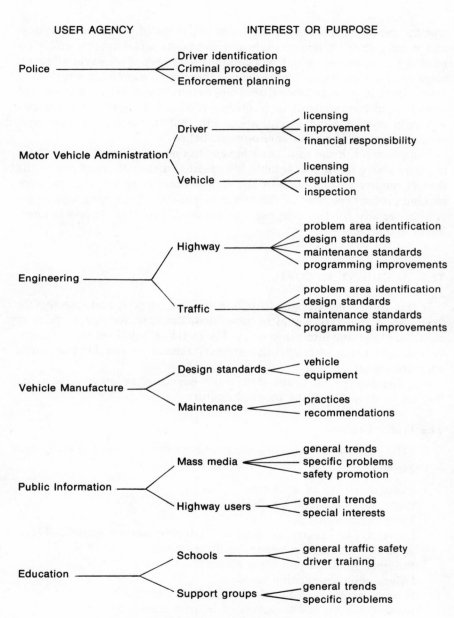

Fig. 1 Accident report users (Source: reference 2).

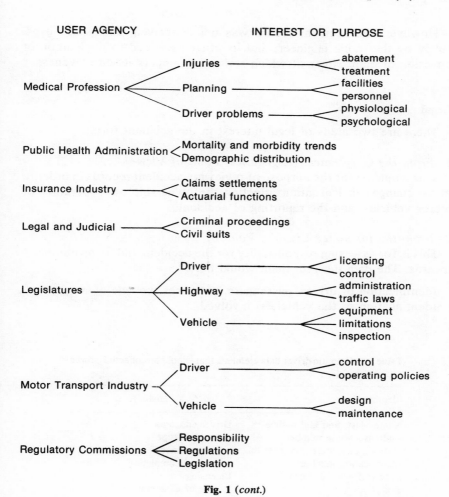

Fig. 1 (*cont.*)

In addition, the traffic engineer would have some interest in driver age, sex, and origin, for instance; vehicle make and model year; and other details not directly related to geometry and control of the road environment, since his purpose is to track down immediate contributory factors that can be corrected.

However, the accident record was not conceived, and is not used, solely by the traffic engineer; and its other uses lead to duplication or omission of data, either of which seriously hampers its effectiveness.

Legal

There are two areas of legal interest in the accident form:

1. From the Government (Legislative) Point of View

This would be for the purpose of reviewing accident records in order to make changes in legislation affecting the ownership and operation of motor vehicles, and the reporting of accidents.

2. From the Insurance Liability Point of View

This is for assessing responsibility for the accident and fixing monetary awards. The data desired, then, would be:

Identification of driver, passengers, witnesses, vehicle owner.
Identification of the vehicle(s) involved.

Table 1   Minimum driver data elements that should be collected, stored and retrievable.

Identification	History
Name—last, first and middle	Driver education
Address—house number,	Program type
street, city, state, zip code	Performance
Identification number	Year of completion
Date and place of birth	Licensing
Sex	Date of examination
Health	Restrictions
	Medical
	Physical deficiencies
	Mental or nervous impediments
	Driving performance
	Accident involvements
	Traffic violation convictions
	Department actions
	Driving exposure

Source: reference 1

Table 2 Minimum motor vehicle data elements that should be collected, stored, and retrievable.

Identification	Ownership	History
Model year	Owner identification (compatible with driver identification for retrieval of driver data)	Accident
Type (passenger car, truck, motorcycle, etc.)		Date of event
Model (SAE recommended passenger car identification terminology—SAE J218)	Address—house number, street, city, state, zip code	Severity
Make	Current registration plate number	Inspection
Car line	Previous ownership	Date
Series		Defects by category
Body type or style		Mileage or odometer reading
Vehicle identification number (VIN)		Stolen or abandoned
Measurements		Date of event
Empty weight—passenger car		Disposition
Engine cc's—motorcycle		Safety defect recall
Length, axles, empty weight—commercial vehicle		Nature of defect
Gross laden weight—commercial vehicle		Date of repair

Source: reference 1.

Table 3 Minimum highway data elements that should be collected, stored, and retrievable.

Identification	Physical Features Inventory	History
System name	Traffic control devices	Traffic violation convictions
Road/Street name	Design characteristics	Accidents
Location descriptor	Traffic characteristics	Road defects
		Maintenance and repairs

Source: reference 1.

Location.
Day, date, time.
Location and description of traffic control devices and ordinances in effect at the time of accident.

The Police

The accident record started as a police record, and the interest of the police is in:

1. Collecting data (from the insurance liability point of view) for the legal arm.
2. Enforcing existing laws, ordinances, regulations.

For this purpose, all of the data listed above is desired. In addition, knowledge of the concentrations and characteristics of accidents helps the police in assigning personnel.

Administrative

A state motor vehicle department retains the administrative interest in the registration of vehicles and drivers, and in the maintenance of a history of driver infractions and involvement in accidents. Data desired would be:

Name of driver.
Age, Sex.
Address.
License number.
Description and registration number of vehicle.
Date, circumstances, and general location of accident.
Whether driver was at fault.

Table 4 Minimum accident data elements that should be collected, stored, and retrievable.

Identification	Driver(s)/Pedestrian(s)	Vehicle(s)	Accident Severity
Accident identification number	Condition(s)	Defects	Property damage
Driver identification	Alcohol and drug involvement	Speed	Injury
Vehicle identification	Traffic law violation	Maneuver	Fatal
Road location descriptor	Intention	Point of impact	
Time of accident (month, week, day, time)		Damage severity	
		Object struck	
		Mileage or odometer reading	
Victims	*Environmental Conditions*	*Emergency Response*	
Injury type	Light	Time police notified	
Age	Weather	Time police arrived	
Sex	Condition of road surface	Time EMS notified	
Seating position/pedestrian	Maximum safe speed	Time EMS arrived	
Use of restraints	Road defects		
Cause of death	Physical features		
Blood alcohol concentration			
Ejection			
Date of death			
Extrication time			
Object struck in vehicle			

Source: reference 1.

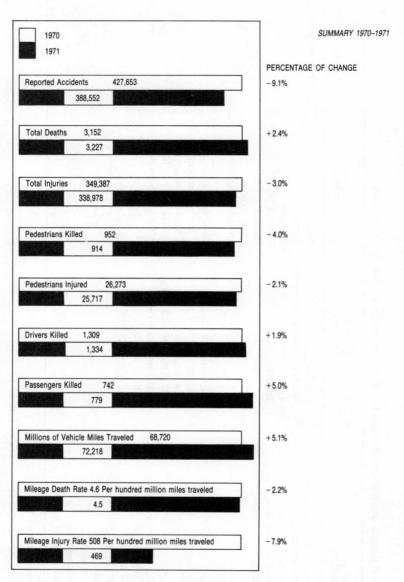

Fig. 2 Example of macro-statistical tabulation (Source: reference 3).

DEATH AND INJURY RATE

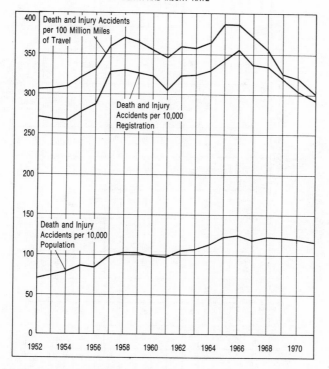

Fig. 3 Example of macro-statistical summary (Source: reference 3).

A state administrative unit would also want general data for the purpose of publishing statistics showing the overall extent of the problem, such as is shown in Figs. 2 and 3 and Table 5. A more specific breakdown is shown in Table 6. The flow chart producing such regular reports might be illustrated by Fig. 4.

Of course, details of the accident location can be fed into the computer record separately. In the Chicago Accident Information System[4] such data is basic. The data base file interrelationships are shown in Fig. 5. A typical report is shown in Fig. 6.

Medical

Authorities interested in the pathology of auto accidents may require detailed knowledge of location, appearance, and severity of injury, and

Table 5 Example of macro-statistical tabulation.

STATEWIDE TOTAL_____ PERIOD JAN/DEC 1971_____

		NUMBER OF ACCIDENTS				TOTAL KILLED	AGE							SEX		CLASS			
	TYPE OF ACCIDENT	TOTAL ACCIDENTS	FATAL	NON-FATAL	PROPERTY DAMAGE		0-4	5-14	15-24	25-44	45-64	65 & OVER	NOT STATED	MALE	FEMALE	DRIVER	PASSENGER	PEDES-TRIAN	OTHER
COLLISION WITH	Pedestrian	25368	896	24472		914	43	143	101	109	187	282	49	611	303			914	
	Other motor vehicle	302404	864	150262	151278	1026	12	40	292	272	228	167	15	677	349	628	397		1
	Other veh. & pedestrian	1541	101	1440		107	2	8	26	18	28	18	7	75	32	1		106	
	Railroad train	148	20	89	39	25	2	2	9	5	5	2		18	7	14	11		
	Animal	2138	3	489	1646	3		1	2					3		2			1
	Fixed object	29756	303	17361	12092	341	2	6	134	116	61	16	6	280	61	222	111	5	3
	Bicycle	6101	62	6030	9	63	1	43	12	4	1	1	1	51	12				63
	Other object	1670	12	882	776	12		2	3	3	3		1	8	4	7	5		
NON COLLISION	Overturned on road	2591	23	2028	540	24		1	14	5	3	1		21	3	14	10		
	Run off road	14398	604	9833	3961	683	4	15	287	192	139	38	8	530	153	441	221	21	
	Other non-collision	2437	29	1997	411	29	4	4	5	9	5	1	1	23	6	5	24		
	TOTAL ACCIDENTS	388552	2917	214883	170752	3227	70	265	885	733	660	527	87	2297	930	1334	779	1046	68
	PREVIOUS YEAR TOTALS	427653	2817	219382	205454	3152	80	264	834	730	631	533	80	2240	912	1309	742	1028	73

* DEFINITION OF INJURIES

Follow the Manual of Uniform Definitions of Motor Vehicle Accidents.

A. Bleeding member, distorted member or any condition that required victim to be carried from scene.

B. Other visible injuries such as bruises, swelling, limping or other painful movement.

C. Complaint of pain without visible signs of injury or momentary unconsciousness.

INJURIES BY TYPE OF ACCIDENT	TOTAL INJURED	AGE OF INJURED							SEX		CLASS				*NATURE OF INJURIES		
		0-4	5-14	15-24	25-44	45-46	65 & OVER	NOT STATED	MALE	FEMALE	DRIVER	PASSENGER	PEDESTRIAN	OTHER	A	B	C
Collision with: Pedestrian	25717	1546	8060	3303	3203	2598	1729	5278	16249	9468	105	104	25505	3	4809	6317	14591
Other motor vehicle	257617	7268	14123	66591	86430	50171	10304	22730	142145	115472	142418	114719	4	476	29814	45760	182043
Other veh. & pedestrian	2411	49	190	504	732	422	138	376	1609	802	333	354	1722	2	490	566	1355
Railroad train	145	5	10	49	54	23	3	1	88	57	93	51		1	64	36	45
Animal	624	12	35	260	201	66	19	31	402	222	388	214	1	21	180	234	210
Fixed object	24980	369	928	10691	7977	3273	650	1092	16479	8501	14878	9917	96	89	9415	6891	8674
Bicycle	6384	103	3607	1450	232	79	32	881	5099	1285	58	54	32	6240	1271	2297	2816
Other object	1292	36	75	423	438	191	26	103	850	442	636	581	21	54	330	366	596
Overturned on road	2880	28	129	1521	816	260	30	96	2079	801	1758	1116	1	5	905	942	1033
Ran off road	14563	239	667	7150	4000	1651	422	434	9647	4916	8731	5758	46	28	5590	4720	4253
Other non-collision	2365	121	301	420	531	348	209	435	1111	1254	433	1916	6	10	400	545	1420
TOTAL INJURIES	338978	9776	28125	92362	104614	59082	13562	31457	195758	143220	169831	134784	27434	6929	53268	68674	217036
PREVIOUS YEAR TOTALS	349387														51916	74989	222482

*Comparative figures not available.

Table 5 (cont.)

Pedestrian Actions by Age

PEDESTRIAN ACTIONS BY AGE	KILLED								INJURED							
	ALL AGES	0-4	5-14	15-24	25-44	45-64	65 & OVER	NOT STATED	ALL AGES	0-4	5-15	15-24	25-44	45-64	65 & OVER	NOT STATED
CROSSING AT INTER.																
With Signal	53	1	3	1	2	9	34	3	2713	45	306	351	505	520	382	604
Against Signal	115	1	12	1	17	26	45	9	2792	54	706	378	458	361	261	574
No Signal	45		5	5	4	11	17	3	1981	72	671	306	207	209	156	360
Diagonally	7			2		1	3	1	211	13	64	26	29	34	21	24
Between Intersections	194	9	31	36	22	31	49	16	1107	62	290	169	158	113	67	248
AT INTER.																
Getting on/off motor veh.									43		11	5	9	6	2	10
Pushing/working on veh. in road									31			6	10	5	2	8
Other—working in road	1				1				40	7	2	4	15	6	2	11
Not on road	17	2	3	1	2	5	3	1	230	101	35	38	38	41	19	52
Other	119	1	9	6	16	25	49	13	3082		763	377	423	338	214	866
BETWEEN INTERSECTIONS																
Walking with traffic	30		6	11	2	5	6		467	6	86	161	73	50	20	71
Walking against traffic	29	1	3	3	7	5	7	3	425	11	90	86	81	59	38	60
Standing/playing in Rd.	45	3	9	14	5	5	8	1	1341	94	456	202	187	109	63	230
Coming from behind parked car	82	12	22	9	7	11	17	4	5425	658	2850	391	341	214	140	831
Getting on/off motor vehicle	6		2		1	3			330	5	33	48	95	67	26	56
Pushing/working on veh. in road	18			2	3	11	2		246	1	6	61	92	30	4	53
Other—working in road	7			1	5	1			157	2	6	20	69	22	5	34
Lying in road	17			2	6	6	2	1	32			5	6	4		6
Not on road	51	12	5	5	8	14	6	1	796	54	115	122	128	124	54	199
Other	210	6	44	30	25	52	50	3	5985	388	1743	813	767	595	355	1324
TOTALS	1046	48	154	129	133	221	302	59	27434	1573	8242	3569	3691	2907	1831	5621

MILEAGE RATES

STATEWIDE	THIS YEAR TO DATE	LAST YEAR SAME PERIOD	PERCENT CHANGE
MOTOR VEHICLE DEATHS	3227	3152	+2.4
EST. MILEAGE (MILLIONS)	72218	68720	+5.1
DEATH RATE PER 100 MIL. VEHICLE MILES	4.5	4.6	-2.2
FATAL ACC. RATE PER 100 MIL. MILES	4.0	4.1	-2.5
Injuries per 100 Mil. Miles	469.4	508.5	-7.7

HOUR-DAY OF OCCURRENCE	SUNDAY			MONDAY			TUESDAY			WEDNESDAY			THURSDAY			FRIDAY			SATURDAY		
	FATAL	NON-FATAL	PROPERTY	FATAL	NON-FATAL	PROPERTY	FATAL	NON-FATAL	PROPERTY	FATAL	NON-FATAL	PROPERTY	FATAL	NON-FATAL	PROPERTY	FATAL	NON-FATAL	PROPERTY	FATAL	NON-FATAL	PROPERTY
From 12 MID	35	1388	742	11	666	371	13	516	311	10	505	326	20	705	388	18	867	549	37	1552	937
1 AM	39	1613	933	13	519	325	9	394	220	13	434	253	10	584	318	26	703	530	41	1666	957
2	47	1492	883	13	386	245	7	286	170	7	312	193	14	501	266	11	620	392	63	1542	875
3	38	1447	672	13	320	163	8	196	110	12	227	125	8	302	167	16	448	316	33	1214	659
4	21	839	369	4	220	139	4	142	101	2	159	98	4	212	139	6	318	192	18	767	361
5	17	457	202	5	183	148	1	147	102	6	139	111	5	192	120	10	233	193	17	476	253
6	8	337	226	13	419	403	6	389	354	5	358	347	8	380	434	8	437	396	13	401	314
7	6	365	266	11	1234	1243	8	1120	1188	4	1137	1146	8	1292	1308	12	1171	1263	8	559	491
8	7	378	293	11	1642	1573	8	1487	1410	6	1556	1575	13	1607	1561	9	1575	1585	8	739	771
9	6	516	462	9	1089	1091	11	1087	1046	8	1114	1117	12	1098	1141	4	1095	1052	10	935	959
10	15	774	656	15	1217	1145	7	1055	978	8	1086	1056	9	1079	1070	8	1155	1147	16	1271	1253
11	6	1072	883	10	1432	1295	8	1237	1157	8	1314	1329	15	1359	1255	9	1422	1398	18	1683	1586
12 NOON	8	1254	906	12	1630	1335	17	1306	1144	8	1469	1290	18	1507	1287	20	1719	1440	24	1862	1546
1 PM	12	1525	1098	19	1616	1338	12	1408	1199	18	1472	1211	12	1545	1249	13	1851	1484	12	2248	1721
2	14	1569	1125	15	1867	1616	17	1721	1402	18	1681	1389	22	1708	1531	14	2165	1813	18	2247	1774
3	10	1817	1221	28	2496	1923	22	2286	1792	24	2259	1887	22	2341	1937	29	2828	2320	25	2415	1753
4	26	1851	1251	16	2637	2140	23	2465	2118	22	2521	2061	27	2562	2310	17	3126	2634	28	2446	1816
5	21	1877	1108	26	2570	2009	29	2348	1812	23	2362	1973	24	2479	2078	32	3007	2320	34	2255	1536
6	26	1625	979	27	1798	1347	22	1614	1112	16	1665	1160	20	1825	1359	37	2274	1664	29	2111	1233
7	20	1481	968	16	1531	1106	14	1435	1025	22	1402	985	36	1687	1138	20	2084	1542	27	1938	1249
8	22	1368	889	25	1195	832	13	1086	787	20	1120	814	27	1357	971	27	1825	1291	29	1682	1158
9	18	1258	867	20	959	764	19	909	651	18	1017	765	13	1264	896	44	1644	1228	32	1584	1022
10	25	1163	810	21	806	576	10	792	568	16	943	702	21	1033	772	31	1538	1067	30	1492	989
11	25	1045	703	14	746	445	11	767	573	14	878	614	27	987	727	33	1779	1260	35	1660	1125
Not Stated	2	211	552	4	214	657		204	560	1	192	654	5	252	743	2	261	858	3	258	823
TOTAL ACC.	474	28722	19064	371	29392	24211	299	26397	21890	309	27322	23181	400	29858	25165	456	36145	29934	608	37003	27161

Source: reference 3.

Table 6 Example of micro-statistical summary.

MOTOR VEHICLE ACCIDENTS

	4TH QUARTER ENDED DEC 31, 1968								REPORTABLE		PREVIOUS QUARTER ACCIDENTS	
	REAR END	SIDE SWIPE	HD-ON, SD-SW OP-DI	ANG	FIX OBJ	PED	OTH	TOT	PERS INJ	PROP DAMG	TOTAL	PERS INJ
TERMINAL HIGHWAY-CENTRAL AREA												
13-LL TERM FRONTAGE RD-EAST END		2					1	3	2	2	3	1
14-LL TERM FRONTAGE RD-EAST HALF		2				2	1	5	2	2	5	
15-LL TERM FRONTAGE RD-WEST HALF	1					1	1	3			4	1
16-LL TERM FRONTAGE RD-WEST END	2					1	1	4		3	1	
17-TERMINAL PARKING ROAD											1	
18-LOT 2 CIRCLE ROAD-WEST SIDE							1	1			1	
19-LOT 2 CIRCLE RD-SD.WEST PORTION											1	
20-LOT 2 CIRCLE RD-SD.EAST PORTION											1	
25-RAMP FROM EB GC PKWY											1	
26-DIVERGE-MERGE UL RAMP												
27-UL TERM RD EAST HALF		2						2		1	4	1
28-UL TERM RD WEST HALF	2	2					2	6	1	5	3	1
29-UL TERM RD DOWN RAMP		1								1		
AREA TOTAL	5	9				4	7	25	5	14	25	4
TERMINAL HIGHWAY-EAST AREA												
01-WB EAST GC PKWY ENTRANCE ROAD												
02-INT EB TERM RD-E PKWAY ENT RD		1		1			1	3		2	4	2
04-WB TERM RD AMF TO HGR 8		1						1		1		
05-WB TERM RD HGR 8 TO HGR 6												
06-WB TERM RD HGR 6 TO HGR 2	1	1					1	3		2	3	1
07-EB TERM RD AT LOT 3		1		4				5		4	1	
08-EB TERM RD AT 102 ST BRIDGE	1		1	1			1	3	1	2		
09-EB TERM RD AT LOT 4 ENTRANCE												
10-WB TERM RD INTERSECTION AT HGR 2	1	2						3	2	4	2	
12-INTERSECT AT EAST END TERM BLDG		1						1		1	1	
22-EB RD SE OF LOT 2												
24-102 ST BRIDGE ON PROPERTY	1							1		1	1	
AREA TOTAL	4	7	1	6			3	21	3	17	13	3
TERMINAL HIGHWAY-WEST AREA												
30-WB TERM RD AT HGRS 1-3	2	1		1				4	1	2	2	
31-WB T RD INTERSECTIONS AT HGR 5	1			3			1	4	1	2	1	
33-ENTRANCE AT 94 STREET					1			1				
34-EB TERM RD OPPOSITE HGR 5												

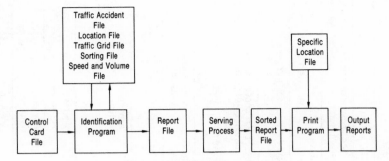

Fig. 4 Computer flow chart.

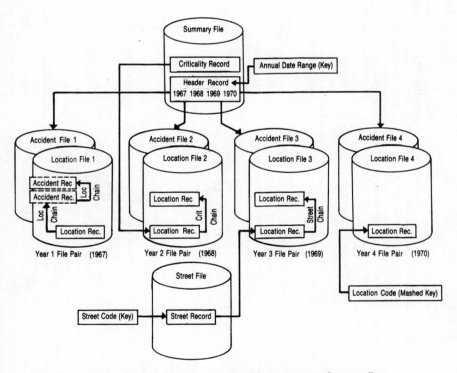

Fig. 5 Data case file interrelationships (source: reference 4).

CHICAGO ACCIDENT REPORTING SYSTEM --- LOCATION PROFILE REPORT

ACCIDENT OCCURRED AT STATE STREET AND MONROE STREET LOCN CODEO 1000-401-

DATE—30-03-68	TIME—4 PM	LIGHT COND—DAYLIGHT	LIGHTS—OFF	ACC LOCN—INTRSCTN	RD NOO 838564
WEATHER—CLEAR	STREET—DRY	ACC TYPE—IN TRAFFIC	COLL TYPE—TURNING	ARREST—NO	

ACC SEVERITY—PROPRTY L100   PED ACT—   PED STR—

VEH NO. 1	DR ACT—RIGHT TURN	VEH—PRIVTE CAR	DIR—NORTH	COND—NORMAL	VIOL—TOO CLOSE
VEH NO. 2	DR ACT—STOPPED	VEH—PRIVTE CAR	DIR—NORTH	COND—NORMAL	VIOL—NO VIOLATN

ACCIDENT OCCURRED AT STATE STREET AND MONROE STREET LOCN CODEO 1000-401-

DATE—26-04-68	TIME—5 PM	LIGHT COND—DAYLIGHT	LIGHTS—OFF	ACC LOCN—INTRSCTN	RD NOO 848623
WEATHER—CLEAR	STREET—DRY	ACC TYPE—IN TRAFFIC	COLL TYPE—SIDESWP SD	ARREST—NO	

ACC SEVERITY—PROPRTY L100   PED ACT—   PED STR—

VEH NO. 1	DR ACT—SLOWING	VEH—PRIVTE CAR	DIR—SOUTH	COND—NORMAL	VIOL—OTHER
VEH NO. 2	DR ACT—STOPPED	VEH—BUS	DIR—SOUTH	COND—NORMAL	VIOL—NO VIOLATN

ACCIDENT TYPE	NO.	%	COLLISION TYPE	NO.	%	DRIVER ACTION	NO.	%	DIRECTION	NO.	%	VIOLATION TYPE	NO.	%	PEDESTRIAN ACTION	NO.	%
PEDESTRIAN IN TRAFFIC	8	100	PARKING TURNING	2	25	STRAIGHT CHNGE LANE	5	29	NORTH SOUTH	5 5	29 29	RAN SIGNAL RAN STOP			X INTRSCTN BETWN CARS		
PARKED CAR RR TRAIN			REAR END HEAD ON	1	13	RIGHT TURN LEFT TURN	2	12	EAST WEST	7	41	WRONG SIDE BAD PASS			NOT AT INT WALK WITH		
BICYCLE ANIMAL			SIDESWP OD SIDESWP SD	4	50	U TURN SLOWING	2	12	NORTHEAST NORTHWEST	2	12	BAD TURN BAD BRAKES			WALK AGNST STANDING	1 6	

254

Detailed accident disclosure and location profile report

Collision / location / violation classification

FIXED OBJ OTHER OBJ	CUTTING IN MERGING	START UP UNPARKING	SOUTHEAST SOUTHWEST	BAD LIGHTS DDNT YIELD	ON OR OFF WORK VHCL
RAN OFF RD OVERTURNED	ANGLE BACKING — 1 13	STOPPED PARKED	UNKNOWN — 7 41	SPEEDING TOO CLOSE — 2 12	OTHER WORK PLAYING
NON-COLISN OTHER	OTHER UNKNOWN	BACKING NO DRIVER — 1 6		OTHER NO VIOLATN — 5 29 / 9 53	NOT IN RD OTHER&UNK
UNKNOWN		UNKNOWN			
TOTAL 8 100	TOTAL	TOTAL 8 100	TOTAL 17 100	TOTAL 17 100	TOTAL 17 100

Environmental conditions

WEATHER	NO. %	LIGHT CONDITION	NO. %	ROAD CONDITION	NO. %
CLEAR RAIN	8 100	DAYLIGHT DUSK/DAWN	7 88 / 1 13	DRY WET	8 100
SNOW FOG		NIGHT UNKNOWN		ICY REPAIR	
UNKNOWN				UNKNOWN	
TOTAL	8 100	TOTAL	8 100	TOTAL	8 100

ACCIDENT SEVERITY

PEDESTRN NO. %	MOTORIST NO. %	NON MTRVEH NO. %	OTHER NO. %	TOTAL KILLED	TOTAL INJURD
PEDS KILLD PEDS INJ A — 7 88	MTRS KILLD MTRS INJ A — 1 14	PROP<100		0 0%	
PEDS INJ B PEDS INJ C — 1 13	MTRS INJ B MTRS INJ C — 6 86	PROP≥100 UNKNOWN — 1 100			1 100%
UNKNOWN	UNKNOWN				
TOTAL 8 100	TOTAL 17 100	TOTAL 1 100			7 100

JOB COMPLETED

Fig. 6 Detailed accident disclosure and location profile report (source: reference 4).

information which might help in deciding exactly how such injuries came about. The physchology of the driver at the time of the accident, and just prior to it, would be of immense value. Simple equipment, easily operated by the police (like the "breathalyzer" for alcohol) would add extremely useful physiological and psychological data.

The quality and efficiency of emergency services rendered might also be information desired by a state medical agency charged with the evaluation and supervision of such service.

DIFFICULTIES CURRENTLY ENCOUNTERED

Traffic Engineering

The traffic engineer would like to have detailed information on the physical aspects of the area, including dimensions, location and timing of signals, radius of curvature, height of curb, etc. It is obvious that this cannot be regularly recorded by police dealing with many accidents. The traffic engineer would like great detail on what drivers and pedestrians were doing just before the accident. Again, this information must be reduced to a few broad categories (such as "cutting in" or "following too closely"), or nothing at all. In addition, opinions of the witnessing or reporting officer would be of considerable help to the engineer, but the officer would not volunteer opinions for which he might be held legally accountable.

Legal

Legally, culpability would ideally be assigned either by a witnessing officer or by a wealth of detail which obviously cannot be required of any but the most serious accidents.

Legislation would be aided by a detailed description of the behavior of drivers before the accident.

The Police

The police need a minimum of data for themselves, yet are saddled with the task of gathering data for all parties. The attitude of the data-collecting officer thereby suffers, and the quality of the data collected deteriorates. Complete instructions, such as might be made part of formal training and made continuously accessible in a guide book, would help to regularize entries and underscore the need for completeness and accuracy. Figure 7 shows sample pages from such a guide book.

DETAILED EXPLANATION OF ACCIDENT REPORT
GENERAL INSTRUCTIONS

<u>Print</u> all information <u>heavily</u> in <u>ink</u>. Make all check marks thick and dark.
Fill in <u>all</u> unshaded areas completely, using this manual as a guide for the proper information to be inserted in each category.
The use of the category OTHER should be avoided whenever possible and used only when none of the listed categories apply. When OTHER is used an explanation should be given.

DETAILED LOCATION

```
DETAILED LOCATION
-------------------------------------------------------------------
                                        □N.Y.   □N.J.
```

State precisely where accident occurred.
Be sure to check appropriate box to indicate State in which accident occurred.

Example: ON MARLIN ST, AT INTERSECTION WITH TRANSIT ST.

□N.Y. □N.J.

If not at intersection, specify in numerals the distance and state the direction from the nearest street, highway, bridge, or permanent landmark (preferably one shown on accident spot map) and identify said landmark.
If in tunnel, include nearest engineering marking.

Example: 20′ East of E.M. 31 + 00

FACILITY

```
FACILITY
```

Print out the name or accepted abbreviation of the P.A. facility at which accident occurred.

LOCATION (Boxes 5–9)

```
LOCATION
      (5)  (6)  (7)  (8)  (9)

-----------------------------------------
      SEE FACILITY MAP FOR
      APPROPRIATE CODING
```

Each facility or off-facility location has a specified code designation

Fig. 7 Sample page from a police accident report guide book (source: reference 5).

Administrative

Space and time consuming data on the driver and the vehicle is required (redundantly) here. There is some overlap with legal requirements.

Medical

The details of driver and passenger pathology can only be gotten for the few fatalities if a special police investigative squad exists.

Psychological data cannot be obtained at present except as the generalized opinion of the police officer concerning the appearance of the driver.

The impracticality of acquiring *all* desirable data on *all* accidents can be seen by inspecting the data sheets in a road research unit of the University of Birmingham, England, which seeks answers to 62 questions on costs, 31 of traffic engineering, 140 on the vehicle, 80 on medical and social factors. Obviously this data can be collected on only a small sample of accidents. Figure 8 shows the detail involved in such an effort.

"Fixed Data" Bank

There is no need for the duplication of the following data obtained previously:

Name.
Age.
Sex.
Residence address of driver.
Make.
Year.
Model.
Color.
Weight of vehicle.

These are on file at the motor vehicle department and identifiable by vehicle license number and registration number.

Indeed, passengers, driver, witnesses, and police officer could all be identified by Social Security number (which is fast becoming the universal number—the armed services have now switched to the Social Security instead of the special Service Serial number of yore). Reporting the officer's name, rank, and signature are unnecessary when the badge number is given.

63. Time off work—
- 1–3 days ☐ 1
- 4–7 days ☐ 2
- 8–14 days ☐ 3
- 15–21 days ☐ 4
- 22 days–1 month ☐ 5
- over 1 month ☐ 6
- none ☐ 7
- not known ☐ 8
- not applicable ☐ 9

64. Road surface—
- not impacted ☐ 1
- impacted with no injury ☐ 2
- impacted with minor injury ☐ 3
- impacted with moderate injury ☐ 4
- impacted with severe injury ☐ 5
- impacted with serious injury ☐ 6
- not known ☐ 7

65. Kerb—
- not impacted ☐ 1
- impacted with no injury ☐ 2
- impacted with minor injury ☐ 3
- impacted with moderate injury ☐ 4
- impacted with severe injury ☐ 5
- impacted with serious injury ☐ 6
- not known ☐ 7

66. Road furniture—
- not impacted ☐ 1
- impacted with no injury ☐ 2
- impacted with minor injury ☐ 3
- impacted with moderate injury ☐ 4
- impacted with severe injury ☐ 5
- impacted with serious injury ☐ 6
- not known ☐ 7

67. Types of road furniture impacted (exc. surface/kerb)
- lamp post ☐ 1
- tree ☐ 2
- road sign ☐ 3
- wall or fence ☐ 4
- bollard ☐ 5
- other ☐ 6
- not applicable ☐ 7

80. CARD CATEGORY—
- environmental factors ☐ 1
- vehicle engineering ☐ 2
- social factors ☐ 3
- medical factors ☐ 4

INJURIES CAUSED BY <u>OUTSIDE</u> COMPONENTS OF THE <u>VEHICLE</u>.

(1) Bumpers—
- not caused injury ☐ 1
- caused injury ☐ 2

(2) Grill—
- not caused injury ☐ 3
- caused injury ☐ 4

(3) Bonnet—
- not caused injury ☐ 5
- caused injury ☐ 6

(4) Insignia—
- not caused injury ☐ 7
- caused injury ☐ 8

(5) Wings—
- not caused injury ☐ 1
- caused injury ☐ 2

(6) Headlight—
- not caused injury ☐ 3
- caused injury ☐ 4

(7) Wing mirror—
- not caused injury ☐ 5
- caused injury ☐ 6

(8) Windscreen—
- not caused injury ☐ 7
- caused injury ☐ 8

(9) Windscreen frame—
- not caused injury ☐ 1
- caused injury ☐ 2

(10) Windscreen wipers—
- not caused injury ☐ 3
- caused injury ☐ 4

(11) Wheels—
- not caused injury ☐ 5
- caused injury ☐ 6

Fig. 8 Sample page from an extremely detailed accident report (source: reference 6).

Coding

Coding of the location down to the specific intersection or ramp (and knowledge of this coding by all officers) would eliminate another large time- and space-eating area. Location coding use can be facilitated by the marking of fixed objects (light poles, curbs, bridges, etc.) with code numbers.

POLICE ACCIDENT REPORT

| TIME & DATE OF ACCIDENT | MONTH | DAY | YEAR | DAY OF WEEK | HOUR | AM PM | INVESTIGATED AT SCENE? ☐ YES ☐ NO |

| LIGHT CONDITION | ☐ DAYLIGHT | ☐ DAWN | ☐ DUSK | ☐ DARK ROAD LIGHTED | ☐ DARK ROAD UNLIGHTED |

| ACCIDENT INVOLVED | No. KILLED | No. INJURED | No. OF VEHICLES | PROPERTY DAMAGE ☐ |

| LOCATION | ON | AT |

VEHICLE No. 1 / VEHICLE No. 2 sections each containing:

- DRIVER'S FIRST NAME, M.I., LAST NAME — MOTORIST IDENTIFICATION NUMBER
- ADDRESS — DATE OF BIRTH — SEX: MALE ☐ FEMALE ☐
- OWNER'S FIRST NAME, M.I., LAST NAME — STATE OF LICENSE (GIVE STATE IF OTHER): ☐ NEW YORK ☐ OTHER:
- ADDRESS — ☐ UNLICENSED ☐ NY LEARNERS PERMIT ☐ NY INTERIM PERMIT
- VEHICLE MAKE AND YEAR — BODY TYPE — VEHICLE I.D. NUMBER — APPARENT CONDITION OF DRIVER: ☐ NORMAL ☐ PHYSICAL DEFECT ☐ ILL ☐ FELL ASLEEP ☐ HAD BEEN DRINKING
- PLATE NUMBER — STATE OF REGISTRATION — EXPIRATION DATE — SEAT BELTS INSTALLED? ☐ YES ☐ NO ☐ FRONT ☐ REAR
- VEHICLE WAS DAMAGED? ☐ LEFT FRONT ☐ RIGHT FRONT ☐ LEFT REAR ☐ RIGHT REAR ☐ LEFT SIDE ☐ RIGHT SIDE OTHER: ☐
- CIRCLE POSITION OF UNINJURED

WEARING SEAT BELTS			NOT WEARING SEAT BELTS		
7	4	1	7	4	1
8	5	2	8	5	2
9	6	3	9	6	3

- VEHICLE TOWED AWAY? ☐ YES ☐ NO — BY WHOM?

KILLED OR INJURED

For each of 4 entries (numbered 1–4):

- NAME — ADDRESS — SEX — AGE — POSITION IN VEHICLE
- DESCRIBE INJURIES (STATE IF KILLED) — DATE OF DEATH — IN VEH. NO. — PEDESTRIAN ☐ MTCY. ☐ BICY. ☐
- PERSON WEARING SEAT BELT ☐ YES ☐ NO — INJURED TAKEN TO HOSPITAL ☐ YES ☐ NO — WAS PERSON EJECTED ☐ YES ☐ NO

1	2	3
4	5	6
7	8	9

(Left margin labels: DATE, SERIAL No.)

PRINT DO NOT WRITE   ●   DO NOT FOLD OR ROLL THIS REPORT

CONTINUED   COMPLETE ALL APPLICABLE SECTIONS ● CHECK APPROPRIATE BOX   SERIAL No.

ARRESTS: NAME OF PERSON   CHARGE   NAME AND LOCATION OF COURT

GIVE NAMES AND ADDRESSES OF UNINJURED PERSONS INVOLVED OR WITNESSES: (SPECIFY WHICH)

TYPE OF ACCIDENT COLLISION WITH:	TRAFFIC CONTROL:	WEATHER & ROAD CONDITIONS	ROAD CHARACTER	ROAD TYPE
☐ PEDESTRIAN	☐ NONE	☐ CLEAR/DRY	☐ STRAIGHT & LEVEL	NO. OF LANES
☐ OTHER MTR. VEH.	☐ POLICE OFFICER	☐ CLEAR/WET	☐ STRAIGHT/GRADE	☐ ONE WAY STREET
☐ OTHER MTR. VEH. AND PEDESTRIAN	☐ SIGNAL LIGHT IN OPERATION	☐ CLEAR-ICE/SNOW	☐ STRAIGHT AT HILLCREST	☐ TWO WAY STREET
☐ RAILROAD TRAIN	☐ SIGNAL LIGHT NOT IN OPERATION	☐ RAIN/WET	☐ CURVE AND LEVEL	☐ LANE DIVIDER
☐ ANIMAL OR ANIMAL DRAWN VEHICLE	☐ FLASHING LIGHT	☐ RAIN/ICE-SNOW	☐ CURVE WITH GRADE	☐ PAVEMENT MARKINGS
☐ FIXED OBJECT	☐ STOP SIGN	☐ SNOW-WET	☐ CURVE AT HILLCREST	☐ UNMARKED.
☐ BICYCLE	☐ WARNING SIGN	☐ SNOW/ICE-SNOW		☐ OTHER
☐ OTHER OBJECT	☐ YIELD SIGN	☐ FOG-DRY	**ROAD SURFACE**	
☐ MOTORCYCLE	☐ OTHER (INCLUDES R.R. CROSSING	☐ UNKNOWN	☐ CONCRETE	
NON-COLLISION	☐ UNKNOWN	☐ FOG-WET	☐ BLACKTOP	
☐ OVERTURNED IN ROAD	☐ SCHOOL CROSSING GUARD	☐ FOG/ICE-SNOW	☐ BRICK-BLOCK	
☐ RAN OFF ROAD		☐ FREEZING RAIN	☐ GRAVEL	
☐ OTHER		☐ ICE OR SNOW	☐ DIRT AND SAND	
		☐ MUDDY	☐ OTHER:	

ACTION OF PEDESTRIAN CROSSING AT INTERSECTION	ACTION OF PEDESTRIAN CROSSING NOT AT INTERSECTION	
☐ WITH SIGNAL	☐ WALKING IN ROAD WITH TRAFFIC	☐ PUSHING OR WORKING ON VEHICLE
☐ AGAINST SIGNAL	☐ WALKING IN ROAD AGAINST TRAFFIC	☐ OTHER WORKING IN ROADWAY
☐ NO SIGNAL	☐ STANDING OR PLAYING IN ROADWAY	☐ LYING IN ROADWAY
☐ DIAGONALLY	☐ COMING FROM BEHIND PARKED VEHICLE	☐ NOT IN ROADWAY
☐ OTHER	☐ GETTING IN OR OFF OTHER VEHICLE	☐ OTHER:

CONDITION OF PEDESTRIAN IF INVOLVED	☐ NORMAL	☐ PHYSICAL DEFECT	☐ VIEW OBSTRUCTED
	☐ HAD BEEN DRINKING	☐ CONFUSED BY TRAFFIC	

VEH. 1. 2.	APPARENT CONTRIBUTING CIRCUMSTANCES 1. 2.	1. 2.	VEH. 1. 2.	ACTIONS OF VEHICLE BEFORE ACCIDENT
☐☐ SPEED TOO FAST FOR CONDITIONS	☐☐ DRIVING WHILE ABILITY IS IMPAIRED	☐☐ GOING STRAIGHT AHEAD	☐☐	WRONG WAY, ONE-WAY THOROUGHFARE
☐☐ FAILING TO KEEP RIGHT	☐☐ IMPROPER PASSING	☐☐ OVERTAKING	☐☐	DEFECTIVE BRAKES
☐☐ FAILING TO YIELD RIGHT OF WAY TO VEHICLE	☐☐ IMPROPER TURNING	☐☐ MAKING RIGHT TURN	☐☐	IMPROPER PARKING
☐☐ FAILING TO YIELD RIGHT OF WAY TO PEDESTRIAN	☐☐ FAILING TO SIGNAL	☐☐ MAKING LEFT TURN	☐☐	ANIMAL ON HIGHWAY
☐☐ FOLLOWING TO CLOSELY	☐☐ UNATTENDED, ROLLING DOWN HILL	☐☐ MAKING A 'U' TURN	☐☐	DRIVING THROUGH PLAY STREET
☐☐ BACKING UNSAFELY	☐☐ FAILING TO OBEY SIGNAL	☐☐ BACKING	☐☐	PEDESTRIAN'S ACTIONS
☐☐ RECKLESS DRIVING	☐☐ DISREGARDED STOP SIGN	☐☐ STARTING IN TRAFFIC LANE	☐☐	UNSAFE EQUIPMENT
☐☐ DRIVING WHILE INTOXICATED	☐☐ DAZZLING, IMPROPER OR NO LIGHTS	☐☐ STOPPED IN TRAFFIC LANE	☐☐	NONE
		☐☐ STARTING FROM PARKING	☐☐	OTHER
		☐☐ SLOWING OR STOPPING		
		☐☐ SKIDDING		
		☐☐ PARKED		

DIAGRAM OF ACCIDENT

INSTRUCTIONS

USE SOLID LINE TO SHOW PATH OF VEHICLE OR PEDESTRIAN BEFORE ACCIDENT

NUMBER EACH VEHICLE AS ON FRONT OF REPORT. SHOW DIRECTION BY ARROW

USE DOTTED LINE TO SHOW PATH OF VEHICLE OR PEDESTRIAN AFTER ACCIDENT

SHOW VEHICLE BY

SHOW PEDESTRIAN BY

SHOW RAILROAD BY

INDICATE NORTH BY ARROW

DESCRIPTION OF ACCIDENT

SIGN HERE	OFFICER'S RANK AND NAME	SHIELD NO.	PCT/DIV.	CERTIFIED AS CORRECT	DESK LIEUTENANT

Fig. 9 Sample accident report form.

Other required data can be arranged for check-boxes, at least for the most common answers. This procedure is becoming more common (see Fig. 9).

Sampling Techniques

Concentration on different aspects of traffic accident data-gathering could be done on a sample basis, that is, for three months, extensive details of property damage are recorded; for the next three, extensive details of personal injury. In this way the overall onus on the reporting officer is smaller.

Optical Scanning

The "reading" of the original traffic accident report form by automatic means would obviate the need for keypunching, eliminating one source of delay and error.

Computer Diagramming

Easy availability of the diagram of high-accident-frequency locations, with attendant physical conditions, is a great need. Computer hardware is currently capable of such diagramming; another method involves the use of inset microfilm (aperture cards). An example of such an ultimate product is shown as Fig. 10. Figure 11 represents a summary means developed in San Jose[9].

REQUIREMENTS OF A TRAFFIC ACCIDENT ADP SYSTEM

There are two main purposes in studying accidents from the engineering point of view:

1. The correction of hazardous (high-accident-frequency) locations for a reduction in accident occurrence and accident severity.
2. The development of knowledge relating accident occurrence and accident severity to:
   a. Roadway geometrics.
   b. Roadside development.
   c. Access characteristics.
   d. Traffic flow characteristics (weaving, merging, speed).
   e. Traffic control measures and design (signs, signals, markings, islands).

Within these categories there are many additional variables.

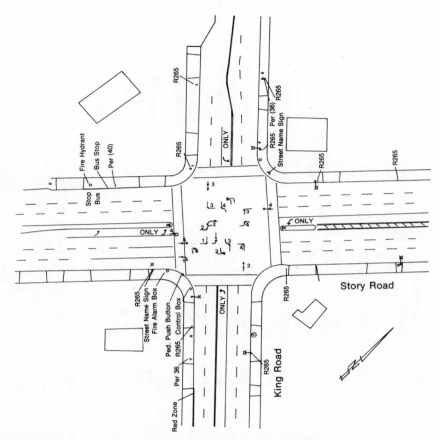

Fig. 10 Collision diagram superimposed on condition diagram (source: reference 9).

Correction of High-Accident-Frequency Locations

For correction of high-accident-frequency locations, the following procedure must be folllowed:

(1) Individual facilities (roads, routes, bridges, tunnel complexes) must be divided into *specific locations* identifiable by ADP code. An example is given in Fig. 12. Appropriate portions of an ADP coding book for these areas are shown in Fig. 13.

The location sizes and conformations must be determined by their homogeneity in terms of type of accident occurring, general speed range,

KING RD.—STORY RD. INTERSECTION

ACCIDENT NUMBER	DATE	DAY	HOUR	LIGHT COND.	WEATHER COND.	STREET COND.	DAMAGE TYPE
6840	31/ 8/67	THUR	2000	DARK	CLEAR	DRY	INJURY
7756	29/ 9/67	FRI	1700	DAY	CLEAR	DRY	PROPERTY
9344	1/12/67	FRI	1700	DARK	CLEAR	DRY	INJURY
3153	5/ 4/68	FRI	2200	DARK	CLEAR	DRY	PROPERTY
5459	16/ 6/68	SUN	2100	DARK	CLEAR	DRY	INJURY
6150	26/ 7/68	SUN	600	DAWN	CLEAR	DRY	INJURY
8566	16/ 9/68	MON	2300	DARK	CLEAR	DRY	PROPERTY
11182	22/11/68	FRI	900	DAY	FOG	WET	INJURY
6497	18/ 9/67	FRI	100	DARK	CLEAR	DRY	PROPERTY
7615	23/ 9/67	SAT	2100	DARK	CLEAR	DRY	PROPERTY
8092	9/10/67	MON	1300	DAY	CLEAR	DRY	PROPERTY
8193	12/10/67	THUR	2100	DARK	CLEAR	DRY	INJURY
8500	22/10/67	SUN	1600	DAY	CLEAR	DRY	INJURY
9414	19/11/67	SUN	1900	DARK	RAIN	WET	INJURY
3407	14/ 4/68	SUN	100	DARK	CLEAR	DRY	PROPERTY
8808	22/ 9/68	SUN	2100	DARK	CLEAR	DRY	PROPERTY
11474	30/11/68	SAT	2000	DARK	CLEAR	DRY	PROPERTY
11784	8/12/68	SUN	2300	DARK	CLEAR	WET	PROPERTY
12106	15/12/68	SUN	1400	DAY	CLEAR	WET	INJURY
1959	2/ 3/68	SAT	1500	DAY	CLEAR	DRY	INJURY
7290	11/ 8/68	SUN	100	DARK	CLEAR	DRY	PROPERTY
11658	6/12/68	FRI	100	DARK	CLEAR	DRY	PROPERTY
12527	24/12/68	TUE	2000	DARK	CLEAR	WET	PROPERTY

10438	17/12/67	SUN	200	DARK	CLEAR	DRY	INJURY
3531	18/ 4/68	THUR	300	DARK	CLEAR	DRY	INJURY
10480	4/11/68	MON	2300	DARK	CLEAR	DRY	INJURY
11210	23/11/68	SAT	500	DAWN	FOG	UKN	PROPERTY
5659	18/ 7/67	TUE	1700	DAY	CLEAR	DRY	PROPERTY
6348	12/ 8/67	SAT	1900	DUSK	CLEAR	DRY	INJURY
7373	17/ 9/67	SUN	200	DARK	CLEAR	DRY	INJURY
3373	13/ 4/68	SAT	1000	DAY	CLEAR	DRY	PROPERTY
501	21/ 1/67	SAT	2400	DARK	RAIN	WET	PROPERTY
1894	11/ 3/67	UKN	2400	UKN	OTHER	WET	INJURY
1042	2/ 2/68	FRI	1300	DAY	CLEAR	DRY	INJURY
4208	9/ 5/68	THUR	500	DAWN	CLEAR	DRY	FATALITY
3473	16/ 4/68	TUE	100	DARK	CLEAR	DRY	PROPERTY
5490	16/ 6/68	SUN	2100	DARK	CLEAR	DRY	PROPERTY
11774	8/12/68	SUN	400	DARK	RAIN	WET	INJURY
12397	22/12/68	SUN	1400	DAY	CLEAR	DRY	PROPERTY
10998	31/12/67	SUN	2400	DARK	CLEAR	DRY	INJURY
253	10/ 1/68	WED	700	DAY	RAIN	UKN	PROPERTY
6817	27/ 7/68	SAT	2200	DARK	CLEAR	DRY	PROPERTY

Fig. 11 Reproduction of computer printout (source: reference 9).

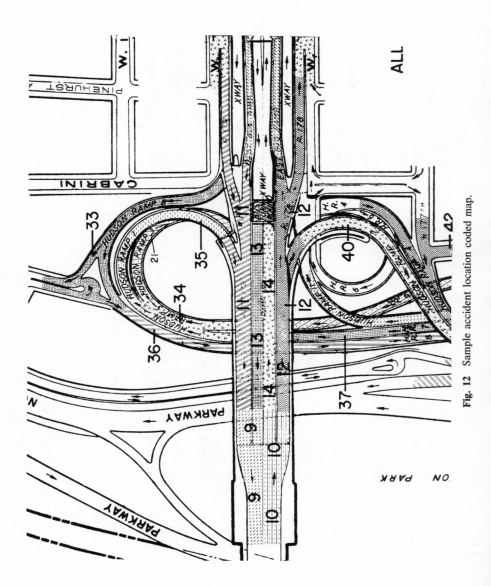

Fig. 12   Sample accident location coded map.

```
┌─────────────────────────────────────────────────────────────┐
│                         DRIVER ACTION                         │
│                                                               │
│                      (Column 39 & 40)                         │
│                                                               │
│                                                               │
│                                                               │
│     01 = Going straight ahead                                 │
│     02 = Turning                                              │
│     03 = Slowing or stopping                                  │
│     04 = Parking or Unparking                                 │
│     05 = Stopped by Traffic congestion                        │
│     06 = Stopped by Traffic Sign or Signal                    │
│     07 = Stopped by Traffic Officer                           │
│     08 = Merging                                              │
│     09 = Diverging                                            │
│     10 = Passing                                              │
│     11 = Lost Control                                         │
│     12 = Avoiding Vehicle, Object, Pedestrian                 │
│     13 = Changing Lanes                                       │
│     14 = Opening Door on Wrong Side                           │
│                                                               │
│                                                               │
│                                                               │
│     90 = Other                                                │
│                                                               │
│                                                               │
│     99 = Unknown                                              │
└─────────────────────────────────────────────────────────────┘
```

Fig. 13   Sample page from coding manual (source: reference 10).

maneuvering characteristics, driver choice, or discretion characteristics. It is not enough to divide a roadway into tenth-of-a-mile sections for ease of summary and calculation, as is done quite commonly [7, 8], and then to spot "clusters." A curve will have one set of characteristics, and a tangent section another. A divergence area will differ from a weaving section in type of accident.

(2) A method must be developed for attacking the *worst problem areas* first. Priority ratings have generally either been based purely on numbers of accidents occurring in a specified time period or numbers of fatalities.

The most commonly recommended[7] are:

$$R_m = \frac{N_x}{\Sigma \, L_i}$$

where R_m = average accident rate per mile.

N_x = number of accidents occurring on roadway sections of a during time t.

L_i = length in miles of the ith section.

$$R_{mvm} = \frac{N_x(1{,}000{,}000)}{365t \, \Sigma \, (ADT_iL_i)}$$

where R_{mvm} = average accident rate per million vehicle miles.

t = time period in years.

ADT_i = average annual daily traffic for the ith section.

$$R_{mv} = \frac{N_x(1{,}000{,}000)}{365t \, \Sigma \, ADT}$$

where R_{mv} = average accident rate per million vehicles.

Generally speaking this gives an inadequate or distorted rating. Numbers and rates of accidents do not reflect severity, and if numbers or rates of fatalities are used for this purpose, as they so often are, they are so small at a single study location as to be unrepresentative. A numerical severity rating system[11] is required. Again, numbers are not comparable between locations because of the many variables (volume of traffic being the most important), so that a measure of "exposure" is required. This has been the accident "rate" of accidents per some multiple of vehicle-miles (vehicles x miles driven), but this has rarely been applied to *specific locations*. ADP can facilitate this by eliminating the manual computations and adjustments required in interpolating between traffic counts made at a few locations on a facility for each specific study location. This produces an *accident rate* and a *severity rate* (using the method in reference 11), illustrated in Figs. 14 and 15. Figure 14 lists specific locations on a priority, based on accident rates; Fig. 15 is based on severity rates.

The procedures will produce listings of all areas (state or city wide) in order of size, and through statistical manipulation—setting of "normal" rates and quality-control procedures—the priority study locations can be identified. If, for instance, "critical" accident (or severity) rates are established (by determining state-wide or facility-wide averages) then highway locations with accident-severity rates in excess of the critical

CALCULATION OF ACCIDENT RATES FOR THE YEAR ENDED DECEMBER 31

PRIOR	LOCAT	ACC-RATE	ACC	VEH-MILES	LENGTH	VOLUME
1	22–06	718.75	23	.032	.151	210,910
2	24–04	521.74	12	.023	.113	204,980
3	22–04	472.22	17	.036	.151	236,586
4	14–01	254.39	29	.114	.019	5,984,250
5	14–03	227.27	30	.132	.033	3,989,500
6	22–08	218.75	7	.032	.151	210,910
7	22–01	173.08	18	.104	.294	352,128
8	15–21	120.96	116	.959	.090	10,652,527
9	15–34	106.24	46	.433	.039	11,110,372
10	23–01	103.45	3	.029	.034	865,340
11	14–10	102.13	24	.235	.024	9,776,250
12	03–65	94.34	5	.053	.095	562,032
13	13–60	90.61	83	.916	.085	10,779,594
14	13–57	63.12	89	1.410	.117	12,051,720
15	03–60	58.82	1	.017	.047	351,270
16	03–63	58.82	1	.017	.047	351,270
17	22–03	58.82	13	.221	.350	630,896
18	01–02	58.54	12	.205	.035	5,850,400

Fig. 14 Computer printout—accident rates.

19	22–05	55.56	2	.036	.085	421,820
20	12–01	54.55	3	.055	.029	1,903,382
21	14–05	51.78	32	.618	.062	9,973,750
22	03–33	51.72	9	.174	.095	1,826,604
23	03–31	51.69	23	.445	.161	2,763,324
24	03–64	50.00	1	.020	.053	374,688
25	14–08	39.94	25	.626	.050	12,521,500
26	13–58	39.46	41	1.039	.097	10,712,640
27	03–38	36.81	6	.163	.104	1,569,006
28	01–28	35.71	17	.476	.113	4,212,288
29	15–09	35.14	59	1.679	.110	15,261,500
30	13–68	35.05	36	1.027	.099	10,377,870
31	14–12	34.65	21	.606	.062	9,776,250
32	34–02	34.27	17	.496	.585	847,641
33	13–16	33.09	23	.695	.067	10,377,870
34	15–10	32.76	55	1.679	.110	15,261,500

35	14–23	32.75	32	.977	.083	11,771,000
36	14–27	32.73	36	1.100	.063	17,459,000
37	03–30	30.33	32	1.055	.181	5,831,082
38	15–08	29.90	47	1.572	.103	15,261,500
39	14–21	29.41	27	.918	.073	12,580,750
40	03–36	28.11	7	.249	.095	2,622,816
41	02–03	27.95	9	.322	.042	7,665,860
42	34–01	27.94	14	.501	.384	1,305,562
43	13–13	27.35	32	1,170	.104	11,248,272
44	12–10	27.03	3	.111	.057	1,949,618
45	03–16	25.55	37	1.448	.188	7,704,522
46	04–48	23.62	9	.381	.107	3,559,536
47	15–42	23.53	2	.085	.045	1,892,426
48	33–13	22.60	4	.177	.200	884,070
49	33–05	22.52	27	1.199	.211	5,680,620

Fig. 14 Computer printout—accident rates (*cont.*)

CALCULATION OF SEVERITY RATES FOR THE YEAR ENDED DECEMBER 31

PRIOR	LOCAT	SEV-RATE	SEVER	VEH-MILES	LENGTH	VOLUME
1	22–01	3769.23	392	.104	.294	352,128
2	23–02	1750.00	7	.004	.114	30.905
3	22–06	1343.75	43	.032	.151	210,910
4	24–04	1130.43	26	.023	.113	204,980
5	01–27	1000.00	351	.351	.200	1,755,120
6	22–04	888.89	32	.036	.151	236,586
7	34–02	818.55	406	.496	.585	847,641
8	14–01	605.26	69	.114	.019	5,984,250
9	14–03	507.58	67	.132	.033	3,989,500
10	04–14	362.79	393	1.131	.322	3,513,700
11	22–08	343.75	11	.032	.151	210,910
12	15–34	332.56	144	.433	.039	11,110,372
13	15–21	282.59	271	.959	.090	10,652,527
14	01–02	278.05	57	.205	.035	5,850,400
15	03–64	250.00	5	.020	.053	374,688
16	13–60	239.08	219	.916	.085	10,779,594
17	14–10	225.53	53	.235	.024	9,776,250
18	04–15	222.22	400	1.800	.420	4,285,494

19	03–65	188.68	10	.053	.095	562,032
20	03–68	184.05	30	.163	.104	1,569,006
21	03–33	183.91	32	.174	.095	1,826,604
22	23–01	172.41	5	.029	.034	865,340
23	22–05	166.67	6	.036	.085	421,820
24	13–57	164.54	232	1.410	.117	12,051,720
25	03–31	152.81	68	.445	.161	2,763,324
26	22–03	149.32	33	.221	.350	630,896
27	14–08	145.37	91	.826	.050	12,521,500
28	13–51	144.16	427	2.962	.140	21,157,464
29	04–10	143.52	559	3.895	.478	8,149,464
30	14–27	133.64	147	1.100	.068	17,459,000
31	13–18	129.50	90	.695	.067	10,377,870
32	03–30	118.48	125	1.055	.181	5,881,082
33	14–23	117.71	115	.977	.083	11,771,000
34	01–28	117.65	56	.476	.113	4,212,288
35	03–63	117.65	2	.017	.047	351,270
36	14–21	117.65	108	.918	.188	12,580,750
37	03–16	113.95	165	1.448	.188	7,704,522
38	13–58	113.57	118	1.039	.097	10,712,

Fig. 15 Computer printout—severity rates.

39	14-05	111.65	69	.618	.062	9,972,750
40	33-05	105.92	127	1.199	.211	5,680,620
41	34.01	105.79	53	.501	.384	1,305,562
42	13-13	104.27	122	1.170	.104	11,247,272
43	13-68	95.42	98	1.027	.099	10,377,870
44	15-09	91.72	154	1.679	.110	15,261,500
45	15-08	88.42	139	1.572	.103	15,261,500
46	03-36	88.35	22	.249	.095	2,622,816
47	04-48	83.99	32	.381	.107	3,559,536
48	03-20	82.76	48	.580	.125	4,636,764
49	11.08	81.89	354	4.323	.606	7,134,400

Fig. 15 Computer printout—severity rates (*cont.*)

rate are defined as hazardous:

$$\lambda c = \lambda a + k \sqrt{\frac{\lambda a}{m}} - \frac{1}{2m}$$

where λc = critical accident rate.

λa = average accident rate for the category or classification of highway being tested.

m = average vehicle exposure for the study period at the location.

k = constant; its value is set based on the number of hazardous locations it yields.

This is based on the method[12] set forth by the Office of Technical Services of the U.S. Department of Commerce:

Upper control limit = $\lambda + 2.576 \sqrt{\lambda/m} + 1/2m$

Lower control limit = $\lambda - 2.576 \sqrt{\lambda/m} - 1/2m$

where λ = overall accident rate for the highway.

m = number of vehicle-miles of travel on a control section.

This produces a "quality control" chart: but basing such identification on some acceptable "mean" of accident occurrence is erroneous to begin with. No absolute minimum "acceptable" accident number or rate has been established.

(3) *Information must be provided* for the local traffic engineer so that he can analyze the situation and develop recommendations for correction and improvement. The information includes:

Number of accidents (usually for a year).
Types of accidents (rear-end, head-on, etc.).
Time, day, month distributions.
Distribution by weather, road, light conditions, and by vehicle types.

A computer printout can provide much of this data. Figure 16 contains a sample of data for each accident, identified by a number.

In addition the engineer requires:

Location of individual accidents within the specific location (a "collision diagram").
A drawing showing geometry, buildings, trees, shrubs, curbs, walls, signs, signals, light poles, pavement markings (a "condition diagram").

Fig. 16 Computer printout—vehicle information.

CD NO.	—LOCAT—	DATE	QTR	HR	DAY	COND	SEV	INV	R & S	AP CS	TYP ACC	OBJ TB
481	01 02 B	2/08/69	1	15	6	111	2	2	2	1	03	00
481	01 02 B	2/08/69	1	15	6	111	2	2	2	1	03	00
741	01 02 B	3/09/69	1	01	7	114	4	1	2	1	80	00
101	01 02 B	3/20/69	1	15	4	311	3	2	2	1	04	00
101	01 02 B	3/20/69	1	15	4	311	3	2	2	1	04	00
11	01 03 B	1/09/69	1	19	4	344	2	2	4	1	04	00
11	01 03 B	1/09/69	1	19	4	344	2	2	4	1	04	00
416	01 04 B	2/01/69	1	17	6	523	2	2	4	1	04	00
416	01 04 B	2/01/69	1	17	6	523	2	2	4	1	04	00
602	01 04 B	2/19/69	1	19	3	424	4	2	2	1	04	00
602	01 04 B	2/19/69	1	19	3	424	4	2	2	1	04	00
743	01 05 B	3/07/69	1	16	5	121	4	2	2	1	04	00
743	01 05 B	3/07/69	1	16	5	121	4	2	2	1	04	00
825	01 05 B	3/07/69	1	08	5	621	1	2	4	1	04	00
825	01 05 B	3/07/69	1	08	5	621	1	2	4	1	04	00
415	01 06 B	1/23/69	1	16	4	523	3	2	2	1	02	00
415	01 06 B	1/23/69	1	16	4	523	3	2	2	1	02	00
437	01 06 B	2/12/69	1	04	3	964	1	1	4	1	05	12
578	01 06 B	2/04/69	1	23	2	664	2	2	4	1	03	00
578	01 06 B	2/04/69	1	23	2	664	2	2	4	1	03	00
604	01 06 B	2/18/69	1	08	2	321	4	2	2	1	02	00
604	01 06 B	2/16/69	1	08	2	321	4	2	2	1	02	00
480	01 07 B	2/16/69	1	21	7	114	3	2	2	1	02	00
480	01 07 B	2/16/69	1	21	7	114	3	2	2	1	02	00
587	01 07 B	2/19/69	1	11	3	521	3	2	2	1	04	00
587	01 07 B	2/19/69	1	11	3	521	3	2	2	1	04	00
122	01 07 B	3/23/69	1	13	7	111	4	2	2	1	04	02
122	01 07 B	3/23/69	1	13	7	111	4	2	2	1	04	02
146	01 07 B	3/23/69	1	15	7	111	3	2	2	1	04	00
146	01 07 B	3/23/69	1	15	7	111	3	2	2	1	04	00
122	01 08 B	1/17/69	1	20	5	114	2	2	4	1	03	00
122	01 08 B	1/17/69	1	20	5	114	2	2	4	1	03	00
107	01 09 B	3/16/69	1	15	7	111	4	2	1	1	02	02
107	01 09 B	3/16/69	1	15	7	111	4	2	1	1	02	02
123	01 09 B	3/23/69	1	17	7	111	4	2	2	1	03	00
123	01 09 B	3/23/69	1	17	7	111	4	2	2	1	03	00
280	01 11 B	1/03/69	1	20	5	114	3	2	2	1	03	00
260	01 11 B	1/03/69	1	20	5	114	3	2	2	1	03	00
177	01 12 B	3/19/69	1	04	3	114	2	2	4	1	14	12
177	01 12 B	3/19/69	1	04	3	114	2	2	4	1	14	12
482	01 13 A	2/07/69	1	18	5	113	2	2	4	1	03	00
482	01 13 A	2/07/69	1	18	5	113	2	2	4	1	03	00
630	01 13 A	3/02/69	1	11	7	321	4	2	2	1	02	00
630	01 13 A	3/02/69	1	11	7	321	4	2	2	1	02	00

VEHICLE INFORMATION														
	—DRIVER—			VEH	PERSONAL INJ.				—PA	VEH.—	PEDESTRIAN			VE
VL	AC	A&S	C	DAMG	DR	WST	A&S	NO	VEH.	ORG.	ACT	A&S	INJ	NO
06	01	6	1	75										1
06	01	5	1	250										2
00	12	2	1	100								2	2	1
00	01	3	1	500										1
02	01	K	1	125										2
00	01	4	1	50					1357	304				1
06	01	2	1	125										2
00	01	3	1	125										1
02	01	9	9	9999										2
06	01	4	1	200		1	M	1						1
06	08	6	1	125										2
02	08	7	1	475		1	3	1						1
00	01	6	1	125										2
02	08	4	1	50										1
00	01	2	1	50										2
00	03	4	1											1
07	01	5	1	600										2
90	90	2	1						3901	304				1
00	01	3	1	150										1
06	13	9	1	9999										2
00	03	5	1	125	1	1	3	6						1
07	01	3	1	355										2
00	01	4	1	350										1
07	01	5	1	600										2
06	08	4	1	200										1
00	03	4	1	500										2
05	01	5	1	600	2			1						1
06	08	7	1	9999										2
00	01	4	1	350										1
06	08	5	1											2
01	01	3	1	125										1
01	02	4	1											2
00	01	L	1	475	2			1						1
07	01	3	1	400										2
00	01	3	1	125	2			1						1
06	08	R	1	125										2
01	09	3	1	350										1
01	09	7	1	200										2
00	90	4	1	125					5205	302				1
00	11	2	1	75										2
06	02	7	1	125										1
06	02	M	1	125										2
00	01	3	1	350	2	9	2							1
07	01	3	1	600										2

Traffic volumes through the section (for the same time distributions).

Average or 85th-percentile speeds through the section (for the same time distributions).

It is obvious that any of the above data that must be collected or developed by the engineer will delay his analysis of the problem.

(4) *A method of attack* must be provided, standardized for use by the engineers. This should include:

Study and correlation of traffic variables to accident data.

Inspection of site under conditions approximating high-accident-frequency conditions.

Relation of accident types to physical and psychological conditions.

(5) *The weighing of corrective measures* must be systematized. The costs of accidents at the location to the national economy, the state, the individual and his family, and employer must be compared to the costs of proposed corrective measures, with alternatives if there are any.

A means of predicting the *results* of proposed corrective measures must be devised so that the cost may be compared to expected benefit.

(6) *Correlation of accidents and roadway environmental characteristics.* Knowledge developed through such analysis will provide two main tools:

1. The relative *safety* (or hazard) of each variable in an overall situation.
2. The relative *value* of each corrective measure, both tools sadly lacking from the repertoire of the planner, highway designer, and traffic engineer.

A multivariate correlation analysis would involve the following variables at an accident location:

1. *Number of accidents* by time of day, day of week, month of year; by type of accident.
2. *Severity of accidents* numerically expressed[11], by time of day, day of week, month of year; by type of accident.
3. *Traffic volume*, by the same time division, by type of vehicle.
4. *Traffic characteristics*, which would include: speeds; densities; weaving; passing; stopping time and distance; start-up time (at lights); observance of traffic regulations; and observance of traffic signs, signals, markings, etc.
5. *Roadway configuration*: the main groupings would be the following: tangent section; curved section; merge; diverge; and weaving section.

These will be further qualified by: percent upgrade (or downgrade); width of roadway; width of lanes: degree (or radius) of curve (left or right); merge left (or right); equal diverge; skewed diverge left (or right); off-ramp; on-ramp; length of weaving section; type of weaving section and divided-undivided-width of median.

6. *Roadside environment* would cover shoulders, curbs, recovery area, roadside development (by type, extent, density), type, position, size of traffic control devices.

CONCLUSION

ADP Traffic Safety Systems developed schematically, integrating all elements for purposes of comparison and correlation (see Fig. 17), are of great importance to the improvement of the urban traffic safety situation.

It is obvious that the automatic extraction of data from source documents such as the traffic accident report is the only hope for long-range solution of the traffic accident problem. The myriad variables, and their many forms, associated with a transportation system made up of individual units guided by nonprofessional drivers, where discretion is almost limitless in control of vehicular speed, direction, and maneuvera-

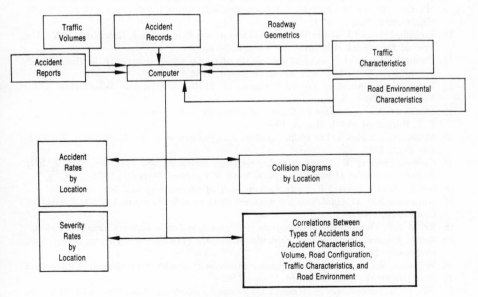

Fig. 17 ADP traffic safety analysis system.

bility, can *only* be analyzed and reduced to comprehensive information by automatic and electronic means.

Only the thinnest surface of the accident-data reduction and interpretation problem has been skimmed. The greater part (and the most interesting) remains to be explored.

REFERENCES

1. Jordan, A. D. and Wilson, J. E. Traffic records—A conceptual view, in *Traffic Engineering*, July 1971.
2. Michalski, Charles S. Current trends in accident analysis (monograph), *National Safety Council*, Chicago, Ill., 1966.
3. *Accident Facts*, Albany, N.Y.: New York State Department of Motor Vehicles, 1972.
4. Dial, R. B. The Chicago accident information system, in *Traffic Engineering*, January 1972.
5. Cantilli, Edmund J. *Guidebook for Completing the Motor Vehicle Accident Report*, New York, N.Y.: The Port of New York Authority, 1966 (unpublished).
6. Mackay, G. M. *Road Accident Research*, University of Birmingham, England: Dept. of Transportation and Environmental Planning, 1967.
7. Roy Jorgensen Associates, *Evaluation of Criteria for Safety Improvements on the Highway*, Washington D.C.: Office of Highway Safety, Bureau of Public Roads, U.S. Dept. of Transportation, 1969.
8. Smith, A. B. Surveillance of accident locations by electronic data processing methods (unpublished monograph), *California Transportation Agency*, Sacramento, Calif., 1965.
9. Hindiyeh, O. and Muchowski, S. J. User-selected information retrieval system, in *Traffic Engineering*, August 1971.
10. Cantilli, Edmund J. *Motor Vehicle Accident Report Coding Book*, New York, N.Y.: The Port of New York Authority, 1965 (unpublished).
11. Cantilli, Edmund J. Statistical evaluation of traffic accident severity, in *Bulletin 205*, Washington, D.C.: Highway Research Board, 1958.
12. Rowe, S. E. Accident record systems, in *Traffic Engineering*, Washington, D.C., February 1970.
13. Morin, D. A. *Application of Statistical Concepts to Accident Data*, Washington, D.C.: U.S. Bureau of Public Roads, 1968.
14. Michalski, Charles S. The traffic accident data project, in *Traffic Engineering*, Washington, D.C., 1967.
15. Cornag, Jeoffrey Y., Scott, Ellis L., Kenney, James B., and Connelly, John J. *EDP Systems in Public Management*, New York N.Y.: Rand McNally, 1968.
16. Segal, M. D. *Accident Records System-State of Maine*, Augusta, Me., 1966.
17. Jorgensen, Roy D. *Guidelines for Accident Reduction*, Washington, D.C.: U.S. Dept. of Commerce, 1964.
18. Recht, J. L. The accident count—How NSC gets it, in *Traffic Safety*, Chicago, Ill., 1968.
19. Reilly, Eugene, *Weather and Vehicular Accidents* (Thesis), New Haven, Conn.: Yale University, May 1966.
20. Williston, R. M. Electronic computer in accident studies (monograph), *Connecticut State Highway Dept.*, Stamford, Conn., 1966.
21. Hill, G. A. *Surveillance of Accident Locations by Electronic Data Processing Methods*, Sacramento, Calif.: Division of Highways, 1968.

14

Public Transit Planning System*

ROBERT B. DIAL AND RICHARD E. BUNYAN

Alan M. Voorhees and Associates, Inc., McLean, Virginia

FOREWORD

The United States Department of Housing and Urban Development contracted Alan M. Voorhees and Associates, Inc. to design and write a system of Computer Programs to assist in long-range mass transit planning. This paper is a description of these programs. Any ideas expressed or implied are not intended to reflect the policy of HUD.

SECTION I: INTRODUCTION

The Problem

Urban mass transit has been receiving increasing attention in recent years as an important element in any possible solution to the urban transportation problem. In 1964, the Urban Mass Transportation Act was signed into law. The Act provides for federal assistance to urban areas for planning mass transit systems. This furnishes the fiscal wherewithal for carrying out transportation studies in which "balanced" transportation systems may be planned.

The heavy operating expense of any bus system and the enormous capital cost of even a modest rapid rail system necessitate cautious and exhaustive planning to guarantee that the millions of dollars spent are allocated in a near optimal manner. In particular, computer programs are necessary to assist in this planning effort. Such programs have long been in use for highway planning.

*From the *Journal of Socio-Economic Planning Sciences*, Vol. 1, 1968, pp 345–362.

The computer programs described below were developed specifically to assist in the long-range planning of urban mass transit. They provide the planner of any urban area with the ability to evaluate conveniently and economically a proposed system. With a minimum of data requirements, the programs furnish analyses of both the supply and demand sides of urban mass transportation as well as their interactions. Through the use of these programs, along with existing programs for highway planning, the expected economic and social costs and benefits of a proposed transportation system can be inferred with an accuracy heretofore unattainable.

Content of This Paper

The next section of this paper describes the overall concept and model framework of the program package. It lists each program separately and briefly discusses its functions and interrelationships with other programs in (and out of) the battery.

The last two sections discuss in some detail the most interesting of the individual programs. Section III describes the analyses performed by the Network Analysis Program, AVNET. Section IV exemplifies the capabilities of the Transit Pathfinder Program, AVPATH, and describes its enabling algorithm.

For the reader who wishes a more detailed description of the conceptual and programming aspects of the Public Transit Planning System than this summary report provides, the following technical reports are recommended:

> *Urban Mass Transit Planning Project, Technical Report no. 1: Factors Influencing Transit.* Alan M. Voorhees and Associates, Inc., McLean, Virginia, 1966.
> *Urban Mass Transit Planning Project, Technical Report no. 2: Computer Program Specifications.* Alan M. Voorhees and Associates, Inc., McLean, Virginia, 1966.
> *Urban Mass Transit Planning Project, Technical Report no. 3, Vol. I: I.B.M. 7090/94 Computer Programs, General Information Manual.* Alan M. Voorhees and Associates, Inc., McLean, Virginia, 1967.
> *Urban Mass Transit Planning Project, Technical Report no. 3, Vol. II: I.B.M. 7090/94 Computer Programs, Users' Reference Manual.* Alan M. Voorhees and Associates, Inc., McLean, Virginia, 1967.

SECTION II: THE SYSTEM

The transportation planning process can be pictured as the flow chart in Fig. 1. The programs described in this report figure significantly in the first six of the seven activities charted. Figure 2 depicts the inputs, outputs,

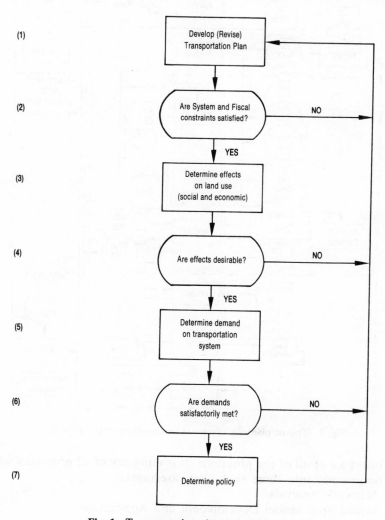

Fig. 1 Transportation planning process.

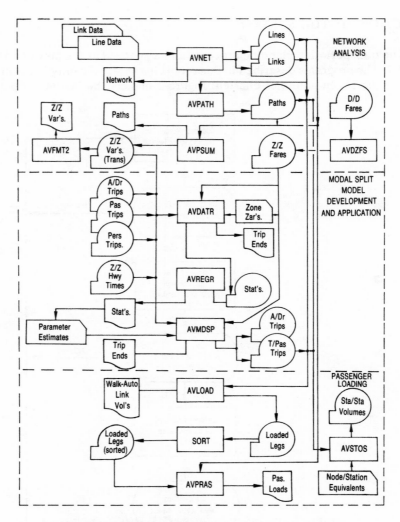

Fig. 2   Transit planning system (Line numbers in parenthesis.)

and interface of all of the programs. It is a battery of 12 programs which can be grouped into three analytical categories:

1. Network Analysis.
2. Modal Split Model Development and Application.
3. Passenger Loading.

Network Analysis

This category consists of five programs which are concerned solely with the supply side of the problem:

(1) AVNET creates or updates a magnetic tape description of the transit system. Its inputs are link data, which describes the physical network, and line data, which describe routes and headways. The program's functions vary from the checking for network coding errors to analyses of the network's operating costs. Section III discusses this important program and network coding in greater detail.

(2) AVPATH reads the network description output by AVNET and outputs a description of minimum cost (disutility) paths between all (or selected) analysis zones in the system. Knowledge of these paths is valuable in at least three ways:

1. An examination of a few of them can uncover many network coding errors otherwise unnoticeable.
2. They provide a necessary element for inferring passenger loadings.
3. They convey the components of the relative disutility associated with each zone-to-zone movement. This is needed in modal split analysis.

AVPATH is discussed in detail in section IV.

(3) AVPSUM reads the paths output by AVPATH and outputs up to 12 interzonal matrices. Each cell in each matrix is a quantification of a characteristic of a zone-to-zone trip via the transit system. Among the outputs are the number of transfers required for each zone-to-zone movement and the length of time spent traveling on each mode. A second function of AVPSUM is the printing of a description of the paths themselves for plotting or analysis purposes. The format of this description as well as an explicit listing of AVPSUM's outputs are presented in section IV.

(4) AVFMT 2 merely prints selected portions of AVPSUM's output, in order that elements of the 12 possible matrices of interzonal disutility may be examined in detail.

(5) AVDZFS reads a description of a fare structure in terms of a matrix of district-to-district costs. It transforms it to a zone-to-zone matrix for purposes of compatibility throughout the remainder of the process.

Modal Split Model Development and Application

A basic step in transportation planning procedure is the division of travel demand into two components: demand for private transport and demand for public transport. The procedure has come to be known as "modal split."

There are many factors to be considered in modal split. Some apply to all trips produced by a zone, such as car ownership; others apply to all trips destined to a zone, such as parking costs; and, others apply to the specific zone-to-zone pair, such as the travel time via transit versus that via auto. The analyst must examine these factors and express their effects in terms of a "model." The model is then calibrated, tested, and finally applied to obtain estimates of future demand on the transit and highway systems.

Three programs in the system aid the analyst in the development and application of a modal split model:

1. AVDATR reduces the huge quantities of data output by AVDZFS, AVPSUM, and analogous programs in the highway planning battery [3] into a small and efficient file for use in regression analysis. Many measures of interzonal system effectiveness (both transit and highway), as well as land use and socio-economic characteristics, may be required in the formulation of a realistic model of demand. AVDATR reads these many files and outputs summary information and statistical values necessary for parameter estimation via regression analysis.
2. AVREGR performs multiple regression on selected variables read by AVDATR. It is at this point that the model builder obtains his parameter estimates.
3. AVMDSP applies the modal split model developed through the use of AVDATR and AVREGR. It outputs a forecast of interzonal transit trips and auto driver trips. This is accomplished by reading a forecasted (total) person trips matrix and splitting it into two matrices on the basis of interzonal and zonal characteristics as interpreted by the model. Figure 3 depicts the inputs and outputs of the modal split programs.

Passenger Loading

This category consists of combining the forecasted volumes with the description of the transit system to determine the demand on each element of the system. There are three programs (plus SORT) within this category. Their use depends on the demands of the analyst:

1. AVLOAD reads the zone-to-zone transit volume matrix and assigns its elements to the corresponding minimum paths output by AV-

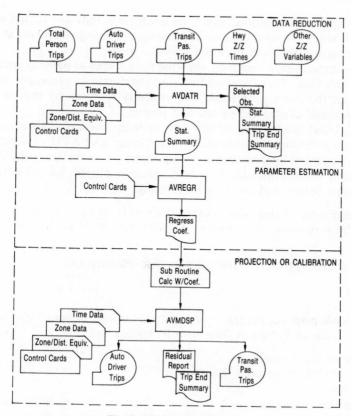

Fig. 3   Model split program.

PATH. It assigns a passenger to the line(s) which serves him best with respect to his initial origin and ultimate destination. It writes a tape which, when sorted, can be input to AVPRAS to provide reports on ridership and line and mode loadings. Among AVLOAD's printed outputs are:

a. Volumes on walk and auto connector links.

b. A summary of mode-to-mode transfers.

c. Total trips assigned and unassigned by zone of origin.

2. AVPRAS reads AVLOAD's output after it has been sorted and prints the following reports pertaining to system usage:

   a. A node-to-node volume summary for selected lines within modes which tabulate the total volume for each on-off node combination of a given line.

b. A passenger loading report for each (selected) line within mode showing the total number of passengers getting on and off at each stop and the load between stops.

c. A transit usage summary showing the number of passengers using each line, the corresponding passenger miles, passenger hours, and the line's peak load. The headway required by the inferred demand is also calculated and posted.

3. AVSTOS* reads a list of selected node numbers and their corresponding "station" numbers. By combining AVPATH's output and the projected interzonal transit trip matrix, it compiles a station-to-station volume matrix. This is a valuable output for purposes of station design and revenue forecasting.

The remainder of this paper details the nature of the use and utility of two of the programs listed above, AVNET and AVPATH.

SECTION III: AVNET: THE NETWORK PROGRAM

Input

The transit planning programs read a coded transit system, described in terms of *links* and *lines*. A link (arc) is defined by:

1. The nodes at each end.
2. The distance between the nodes.
3. A mode.
4. The time (disutility) to traverse the link via the specified mode.

A transit line describes a route and its level of service. Its description contains:

1. A mode designation.
2. A line number.
3. A headway (frequency).
4. A sequence of node numbers, describing the line's route as an ordered set of transfer points.

Mode designators on both the line and link data must agree for lines traversing the link. They represent transit categories such as local bus, express bus, rapid transit, commuter rail, etc. (see Table 1). In addition,

---

*This program was developed under the sponsorship of the National Capital Transportation Agency, Washington, D.C.

walk links and auto connector links are considered mode types which cannot have any associated lines. They are normally used to connect zone centroids (nodes which represent origins (sources) and destinations (sinks) of the system) to the transit system. They represent the walk or drive to or from the bus stops and transit stations. Walk links are also used to connect bus stops to permit "walking transfers."

Table 1 Mode categories—An example.

Mode		
0	Walk	Fixed
1	Auto connector	categories
2	Surface transit	
3	Express surface transit	
4	Other surface transit	Flexible
5	Rapid transit	categories
6	Commuter railroad	
7	Other	

Headways are given as estimates of levels of service. They permit approximation of expected wait and transfer times by AVPATH. They are also needed to estimate capital and operating expenditures.

Maximum Program Parameters

Much of the problem of urban transportation network analysis is the problem of scale. The systems analyzed are very large, and the analyst needs information at a very fine level of detail. The usefulness of a computer program in this area is largely determined by the size of the problem it can handle.

The Transit Planning Programs can accommodate a very large system. The systems of Washington, and Detroit are, for example, well within the program's limits. The program can handle a system with as many as 2800 transfer points. There can be as many as 11,000 links. Each link can carry up to 31 lines. Six transit modes (plus walk links and auto connectors) are possible, and each may have as many as 255 lines (see Table 2).

An Example

An artificial example of a coded transit network is illustrated in Fig. 4. This network has four centroids (numbered 1–4), and a total of 13 nodes.

Table 2   IBM 7090 transit planning programs.

Parameter	Maximum
Number of zones (centroids)	999
Number of nodes, including centroids	2800
Unweighted time	63
Distance	25.5
Auto connectors and walk links	2800
Number of links, including auto connectors and walk links	11,000
Number of links exiting a node	31
Number of lines for each mode	255
Number of transit modes	6
Total number of lines	1530
Maximum headway	60
Minimum headway	1
Number of lines on a link	31
Number of links (i.e. stops − 1) on a line	99

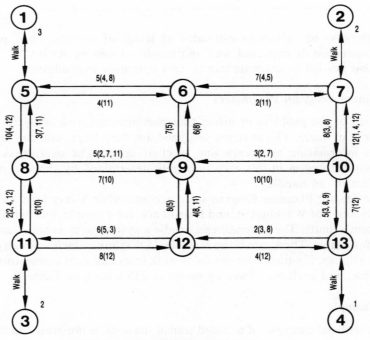

Fig. 4 Hypothetical transit network.

The network has only two modes, walk (0) and transit (2). The circles represent nodes, and the lines drawn between them are one-way links whose arrowheads signify direction. On each link is a number outside parentheses representing time (or cost) to traverse the link, and (except for the walk connectors) one or more numbers in parentheses denoting transit lines. These line numbers correspond to the table at the bottom of the figure which indicates the frequency of service in buses per hour.

It takes 10 minutes to travel from node 5 to node 8. The rider has a choice of either line 4, which runs every $\frac{1}{2}$ hour, or line 12 which runs every 20 minutes. If a passenger wishes to go from centroid 1 towards centroid 3, he might use this link. If so, he would have a choice of five buses per hour, assuming it is irrelevant to him which line he takes.

The two code sheets in Figs. 5 and 6 show how the analyst would code the network in Fig. 4.

Table 3 Line frequencies.

Line No. 1	1	2	3	4	5	6	7	8	9	10	11	12
Frequency (1) Buses/hr.	6	10	5	2	6	5	3	3	10	6	6	3

Output

AVNET produces a report which lists the links coded by the planner to enable him to conveniently check his network and to use it for future reference. In addition to listing the input data, it summarizes the frequency of vehicles on each link and shows the number of lines on the link.

The program also furnishes statistics concerning the transit lines. A "Transit Line Summary" report shows the amounts of time each vehicle on a line spends running and standing for each period (A.M., P.M., midday, and night) of a day. This report can reveal situations where different scheduling or routing of lines could result in providing better service with the same number of required vehicles or the same service with fewer vehicles.

The number of vehicle hours and miles of operation for each line is also given. From these can be calculated a figure which approximates the cost of each line's operation.

AVNET allows the transit planner to test alternate routes very easily. Once the physical network description is laid out, the difficult work is done. To revise the routing and/or frequency of service of a line, he only

AMV ALAN M. VOORHEES & ASSOCIATES, INC.

PROJECT **HYPO.NET**   W.R. NUMBER _____   CONTENTS _____   DECK NUMBER _____   DATE _____   PAGE ____ OF ____

HUD TRANSIT NETWORK—LINK DATA CARD

CARD NUMBER	JURISDICTION	A NODE	B NODE	UPDATE CODE / MODE (col 13)	DIST. MILES	A→B A.M. SPEED TIME	FABRA	B→A A.M. SPEED TIME
1	1	1	5	0	5	3	2	
1	1	2	7	0	4	2	2	
1	1	3	11	0	5	1	2	
1	1	4	13	0	3	4	2	
1	1	5	6	2	7	10		5
1	1	5	8	2	10	2		3
1	1	6	7	2	14	7		7
1	1	6	9	2	26	8		6
1	1	7	10	2	20	7		12
1	1	8	9	2	12	2		5
1	1	8	11	2	31	10		6
1	1	9	12	2	10	8		3
1	1	9	13	2	17	5		4
1	1	10	12	2	10	8		7
1	1	11	13	2	25	4		6
1	1	12	13	2	18			2

IDENTIFICATION

UPDATE CODE (COL. 13)   JURISDICTION

BLANK   ADD   1   0.

NONBLANK DELETE   2

           3

DATA PROCESSING   HUD TRANSIT LINE DATA CARD

WORK REQUEST
SEQUENCE

ROUTE DESCRIPTION AS A SEQUENCE OF NODE NUMBERS

'T' IF LAST CARD

CARD NO	TRANSIT CO	MODE	LINE NUMBER	CARD SEQ. DIRECTION	HEADWAY A.M.	P.M.	MID NITE	MINIMUM	1st NODE	2nd NODE	3rd NODE	4th NODE	5th NODE	6th NODE	7th NODE	8th NODE	9th NODE	10th NODE	11th NODE	12th NODE

Fig. 6 Line data coding form.

DIRECTION CODE
0 DELETE
1 1-WAY L-R
2 2-WAY
3 = 1-WAY R-L
4 = CODE 1 W ONE STAND
5 = CODE 2 W ONE STAND
6 = CODE 3 W ONE STAND

has to change one card. Other changes can be made which will affect the paths taken by passengers going between points in the system. These changes are input as parameters to the Pathfinding Program, AVPATH, and they are discussed in the next section.

SECTION IV: AVPATH: THE PATHFINDER PROGRAM

The purpose of this section is to exemplify the mechanics and capability of the program AVPATH, which finds minimum weighted time paths between zones via a transit system. Also discussed briefly is the program AVPSUM which provides summaries and traces of AVPATH's output. The section ends with a description of AVPATH's pathfinding algorithm.

AVPATH

AVPATH's job is to find for each pair of zones an expected path to be taken by passengers making that interzonal trip. Knowledge of these paths is helpful in at least two respects: first, it provides the means for projecting passenger loadings, and, second, it furnishes information on the amount of time the traveler would probably spend on various modes if he were to choose to travel between two given zones by transit. Such data are necessary for modal split purposes.

Example

A discussion of minimum time transit paths begins best with an example. Referring to Fig. 4 the fastest way to go from node 1 to node 4 is the following:

1. Walk from node 1 to node 5:		3 minutes
2. Wait for line 11:		5 minutes
3. Ride to node 7 $(4 + 2 = 6)$:		6 minutes
4. Wait to transfer to line 3 or 8:		3 minutes
5. Ride to node 13 $(8 + 5 = 13)$:		13 minutes
6. Walk to node 4:		1 minute
Total time to go from node 1 to node 4:		31 minutes
Time walking:		4 minutes
Time waiting:		5 minutes
Time riding on mode 2:		19 minutes
Time transferring:		3 minutes

Transfer time and wait time were both calculated using one-half the inverted sum of the frequencies of the lines available. In our example, the transfer time X to get on lines 3 and 8 was calculated as follows:

$$X = 1/2 \left(\frac{1}{\text{frequency of line 3} + \text{frequency of line 8}}\right)$$

$$= 1/2 \left(\frac{1}{5+3}\right)$$

$$= 1/16 \text{ hour}$$

$$\cong 3 \text{ minutes}$$

The computations of the riding and walking times are obvious from Fig. 4.

Weighted Time Paths

A better approximation of the "expected interzonal path" might be a minimum *weighted* time path wherein the times to transverse various link types are weighted to reflect differences in the values the passenger places on the time he spends walking, waiting, transferring, and riding on each mode. While it is unknown at this time what these weights should be for any particular area, AVPATH allows the user to experiment by permitting their introduction at execution time. If no weights are specified, they are assumed, as in the above example, to be unity.

The effect of factoring the wait or transfer times is the same as dividing the frequency by the weighting factor. The effect of specifying a factor for a given mode is the multiplication of the time of all links of the mode by the specified factor. The user of AVPATH can manipulate these weights so as to make certain modes more or less attractive to the path-finding algorithm.

Constrained Paths

Paths can also be made to satisfy certain constraints. One such constraint is that the total number of transfers on a path be limited to a user-specified maximum. For example, if the user specified a maximum of zero transfers, then AVPATH's minimum time path from node 1 to node 4 satisfying this constraint would be:

1. Walk from node 1 to node 5:   3 minutes
2. Wait for line 12 at node 5:   10 minutes
3. Ride line 12 from 5 to 13:   24 minutes
4. Walk from node 13 to node 4:   1 minute
    Total time to go from node 1 to node 4:   38 minutes

It is sometimes too unrealistic to flatly assess a transfer or wait penalty of one-half a (combined) headway. For example, a passenger who rides a bus which arrives on the hour seldom stands in the cold for 30 minutes. He has better sense. Therefore, the user is permitted to specify the maximum transfer or wait penalty to be assessed for waiting for or transferring to each mode. Whenever a calculated transfer or wait time exceeds the maximum, AVPATH will reset it to the maximum.

Obviously, different values for these maximums can alter paths. For example, the unconstrained minimum path from node 4 to node 2 is:

1. Walk from node 4 to node 13:   1 minute
2. Wait to catch line 3 or line 8:   3 minutes
3. Ride from node 13 to node 12:   2 minutes
4. Wait to transfer to line 11:   5 minutes
5. Ride from node 12 to node 7 $(4+5+3+4+2=18)$:   18 minutes
6. Walk from node 7 to node 2:   2 minutes
   Total time to go from node 4 to node 2:   31 minutes

Total time via this (absurd) path is 31 minutes. The time required via the more obvious path is 32 minutes:

1. Walk from 4 to 13:   1 minute
2. Wait to catch line 12:   10 minutes
3. Ride from 13 to 7:   19 minutes
4. Walk from 7 to 2:   2 minutes
   Total time to go from node 4 to node 2:   32 minutes

Although this example is artificial, it nonetheless shows that if the maximum wait were constrained to 5 minutes, the time to catch line 12 would be reduced by 5 minutes. Then the more direct path would require 27 minutes instead of 32 and thus would become the "best" path.

The remaining constraint that the user can impose is a blanket penalty for selected mode-to-mode transfers, or he can preclude transferring between selected mode pairs. As an example, when finding minimum paths for the morning network, the user might permit transfers *from* auto connectors (mode 1) but not *to* auto connectors, indicating the availability of a car at the origin end of the trip only, for example, kiss-and-ride.

Example of Transit Paths

Figure 7 is a plot of the (unconstrained) minimum paths from node 1 to all other nodes. In it, the paths which go through nodes without transfer-

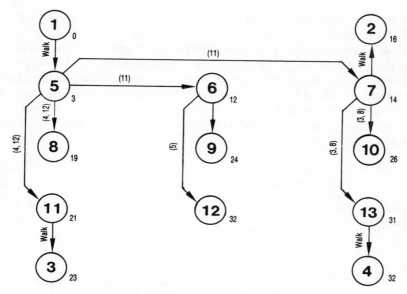

Fig. 7   Minimum paths from node 1.

ring are drawn to the side of the node. A path drawn into a node indicates a transfer must be made to exit the node. The number posted beside each node is the total time to go from node 1 to that node via the minimum time path. The numbers in parentheses are the line numbers providing the minimum time service.

AVPSUM

This program has two functions related to the analysis of minimum transit paths:

1. To write a "skim trees" tape which is a matrix giving for each zonal interchange the following 12 values, as taken over their minimum weighted time path:
   a. Unweighted running time by mode (0 through 7).
   b. Number of transfers (excluding the first).
   c. Unweighted transfer time.
   d. Unweighted wait time.
   e. Total weighted time.
2. A print-out of selected paths.

The first item, the "Skim Trees" tape, is used by AVDATR and AVMDSP and will not be discussed here. The second is used by the analyst to examine paths found by AVPATH. It prints a path as a list of transfer points. These points are given as node numbers and have posted with them the total weighted and unweighted time from the origin node, as well as the mode and line(s) which are ridden from that node to the next. For example, the path from node 1 to node 4 would be listed on a page whose heading would say that the origin zone was 1 and in whose text would somewhere appear:

				Minimum Weighted Time Paths From Zone 1				
Dest	Node	WT	T	M	$L1$	$L2$	$L3$	$L4$
4		32	32	0				
	13	31	31	2	3	8		
	7	14	14	2	11			
	5	3	3	0				

In this table, only the transfer points are listed, and they are given in reverse order. The total weighted (WT) and unweighted (T) times from the origin node to the transfer (or terminal) point are posted on the same line as the transfer point. The above example describes the following path:

> From node 1 (Home) walk ($M = 0$) to node 5. When you arrive at node 5 you will be 3 minutes ($WT = T = 3$ minutes) from node 1. At node 5 catch line 11 ($L1 = 11$) of mode 2 ($M = 2$) and ride it to node 7. At node 7 you will be 14 minutes from node 1. There you should transfer to either line 3 or line 8 ($L1 = 3$, $L2 = 8$), and ride to node 13. You will arrive at node 13, 31 minutes after leaving node 1. Finally, walk ($M = 0$) from node 13 to node 4. All told, your journey will require 32 minutes. (Note that in the above example all of the weighting factors are unity, and the weighted time (WT) always equals the actual time (T).)

AVPATH's Algorithm

By ignoring considerations made for computer running time and user-specified constraints on paths, AVPATH's algorithm can be simply described as an extension of the wellknown Moore tree building al-

gorithm, which finds the set of minimum paths from a given home node
(1, 2) to all other nodes in the system. The extension accommodates the
peculiarities of transit trees and appropriately considers transfer and wait
times as functions of combined frequencies. The algorithm proceeds by
finding minimum paths to nodes in the order of their total time from the
home node.

Notation

A description of the algorithm is facilitated by using set notation:
Let N be a set which describes a transit network of d arcs and e nodes:

$N = \{n_k = (i_k, j_k, c_k, L_k): k = 1, 2, \ldots, d\}$ where
n_k = the k'th arc in the network, described by four elements.
i_k = the arc's i-node,
j_k = the arc's j-node,
c_k = the time (cost) to traverse arc n_l,
L_k = the set of line numbers of all routes which go from node i_k to
node j_k in c_k units of time (or cost).

Let T be a set describing the algorithm's output. It is a description of a
tree from the home node h to the other e-1 nodes in the network. T has e
elements, including a "dummy" arc from h to h via a null line set in zero
minutes:

$T = \{t_k = (a_k, b_k, y_k, P_k): k = 1, 2, \ldots, e\}$ where
t_k = the k'th arc in the tree, described by four elements.
a_k = the arc's i-node,
b_k = the arc's j-node,
y_k = the time to go from node h to node b_k,
P_k = the set of line numbers of routes going from a_k to b_k
in the minimum time.

The set S is a "sequencing table." It is a set of arcs ordered on the basis
of the time associated with the arc, representing the time to go from the
home node to the arc's j-node. From S the algorithm extracts candidates
for the tree.

$S = \{s_k = (u_k, v_k, r_k, M_k): k = 1, 2, \ldots\}$, where
s_k = the k'th arc in S, described by four elements.
u_k = the arc's i-node,
v_k = the arc's j-node,
r_k = the time to go from h to v_k on a path whose final leg
originates at u_k.

M_k = a set of line numbers designating a subset of those routes which a passenger can ride from u_k to v_k.

Let the set W be a function defined for all nodes. Its value is equal to the time to go from the home node to the argument node via some feasible path:

$$W = \{w(a_k): a_k \epsilon N\}$$

Finally, define the set function f as the transfer time function. For any combination of line numbers in the system, it furnishes the appropriate transfer penalty. In the examples above, f was one-half the inverted sum of the lines' combined frequencies. The function can have any form provided it is nonincreasing in the sense that the more buses that the passenger can choose from, the less he waits.

$$F = \{f(L): L \text{ is any line number set}\}$$

Procedure

Following initialization the algorithm proceeds by extracting arcs from the sequencing table S and placing them in the tree T whenever an arc represents the final leg of a minimum path to its j-node v_k. For each arc extracted, one or two arcs are created and entered into the sequencing table. The first arc is always entered. It represents the paths which go *through* the extracted arc's j-node without transferring at v_k. The second arc is only generated when the extracted arc is placed in the tree. It represents all paths which require a transfer at node v_k. The entire process can be described in seven steps:

1. Initialize: $\forall q \neq k$, $w(q) = \infty$; $w(h) = 0$; $S = (h, h, 0, \Phi)$.
2. Extract arc from sequencing table: Find $s_k \ni r_k \leq r_q \forall s_k \epsilon S$.
3. Determine if the extracted arc is the terminal arc of a minimum path: Does $r_k = w(v_k)$? If yes, go to Step 4. If no, go to Step 6.
4. Enter extracted arc into tree: $T = T \vee s_k$. If tree is complete, that is, there are e arcs in the tree, stop. Otherwise go to Step 5.
5. Enter "transfer arc" into sequencing table: $\forall n_q \epsilon N \ni i_q = v_k$ and $L_q \setminus M_k \neq \Phi$:

$$S = S \vee (v_k, j_q, t_k + c_q + f(M_k), M_q)$$

6. Enter "through arc" into sequencing table: $\forall n_q \epsilon N \ni i_q = v_k$ and $L_q \wedge M_k \neq \Phi$:

$$S = S \vee (u_k, j_q, t_k + c_q + f(L_q \wedge M_k) - f(L_q), L_q \wedge M_k)$$

7. Erase extracted link from sequencing table, update minimum time to entered arc's j-node and continue:
   $$S = S \setminus s_k$$

   $$w(j_q) = \min \{w(j_q), t_k + c_q + f(M_k), t_k + c_q + f(L_q \wedge M_k) - f(L_q)\}$$

   Go to Step 2.

AVPATH's algorithm guarantees minimum paths to all nodes in a connected network. It reports all lines which provide the "best" service between any two nodes. Whenever there is more than one path which provides minimum time service, the one is selected which requires the fewest transfers.

REFERENCES

1. Dial, R. B. Transit pathfinder algorithm, *Proc. Highw. Res. Bd 46th Ann. Meet.* Washington, D.C., January 1967.
2. Moore, E. F. The shortest path through a maze, *Int. Symp. Theory Switch., Process.* Harvard University, April 2–5, 1957.
3. *Traffic Assignment Manual.* U.S. Department of Commerce, Bureau of Public Roads, Office of Planning, Urban Planning Division, June 1964.

HOUSING

15

COST-EFFECTIVENESS IN EXPERIMENTAL, LOW-COST HOUSING PROGRAMS*

E. N. DODSON

Associate Director, Economics Department, General Research Corporation, Santa Barbara, California

INTRODUCTION

The need for an increase in the supply of adequate, low-cost housing has been widely discussed and documented. The Housing and Urban Development Act of 1968 set a national goal of 26 million housing units to be constructed over the next ten years, with 6 million of these units for low and moderate-income families. Since passage of the Act, there has been some testimony that even this ambitious goal is short of actual needs[1]. Further complicating the achievement of this objective is the general failure of previous attempts at low-cost housing to actually provide adequate housing at truly reduced cost[2]. Thus, there is considerable interest in experimental programs designed to test and demonstrate new approaches to meeting this national goal.

The stated objective of *low-cost* housing is more nearly straightforward than that of more broadly oriented urban renewal projects. This is not to say that the qualitative amenities of urban living are unimportant to residents in low-cost housing, only that the focus upon low cost is paramount. Low rent or ownership payments are not solely a matter of reducing construction costs—numerous other expenses covering operation, maintenance, financing, and replacement must be considered. Since these expenses are incurred at various times in the life of a building

*From the *Proceedings of the Urban Symposium*, The Association for Computing Machinery, New York, 1970, pp. 158–169.

project, they must be taken into account with proper concern for their timing.

To provide a better understanding of the relationships among the various expenses and to assess their individual impacts upon total cost, we have—in effect—simulated the cash flows associated with the entire life cycle of a housing project. The summary measure of the numerous costs in this simulation model is "break-even rent," that is, the revenue per dwelling unit required to just cover life-cycle costs. Costs must be met in one way or another—if not as rental or purchase payments by the occupant, then by a direct or indirect subsidy. With a simulation of total costs, any subsidy required to keep actual monthly payments within specified limits can be readily identified (payment by the occupant plus the subsidy equals the "break-even rent"), and the costs of alternative design, construction, and maintenance, as well as all other costs of a housing program can be evaluated as they contribute to reducing the "break-even rent."

Numerous experimental projects have been proposed to prove and demonstrate particular construction techniques and administrative procedures. The simulation model*—henceforth referred to as the "Housing Model"—can be used to assess the comparative benefit (i.e., reduction in break-even rent) if the experiment succeeds, or to identify the key cost-determinants upon which experimental efforts to reduce costs should be focused.

The qualification of *comparative* benefits should be emphasized; that is, the procedures set forth here are useful only for selecting among alternative experimental projects. They establish no absolute merits—the primary reason being that low-cost housing projects serve more purposes than the single one of economic efficiency.† Also involved is the governmental role of redistribution of income. Benefits stem from objectives, and with multiple and incommensurable objectives—absolute net benefit cannot be determined.

The cost-effectiveness of experimental housing programs can be compared in terms of the following "scenario": alternative experiments have been proposed to establish the feasibility and costs of new techniques and

---

*The basic elements of this model were first reported in reference 3, which includes the complete computer code.

†Another reason why absolute benefits cannot be *measured* is the prominence of non-quantifiable externalities associated with adequate housing. These externalities, or "spill-over" effects, are widely discussed in the literature (see, for example, references 4 and 5).

procedures; when the experiments are concluded, large-scale housing projects will probably implement the newly proved approaches. The key elements, then, in a cost-effectiveness analysis are the cost of the experiment itself, the probability of experimental success, and the actual reduction of break-even rent upon implementation of the experimental technique.

In describing this analysis, details of the Housing Model are set forth first. Then several factors bearing upon use of the model in cost-effectiveness studies are considered.

THE HOUSING MODEL

Part of the inherent difficulty in providing adequate, low-cost housing stems from the long time between planning and eventual operation. During this period, financial responsibility often rests with several organizations. Even for a single organization, the financial terms and conditions during succeeding phases of a project differ, as do the several categories of cost (investment, operating, etc.) for individual components of a dwelling unit. While initial investment costs for housing components are generally evident to the investor, the longer-term costs for maintenance and replacement are not so clearly indicated nor is their impact upon total project costs well understood.

In addition to the tangible costs for the physical elements of a housing project, there are other less tangible costs, such as planning, relocating residents, and borrowing money. All of these must be combined to compare the cost-effectiveness of alternative techniques and procedures. Accordingly, a Housing Model has been formulated to provide a comprehensive structure for these comparisons.

The Housing Model is a simulation of the entire life cycle of a housing project, from the initial organization to the final residual salvage. Needed first is "seed money" to cover all preconstruction costs except those for the project site and existing properties, which are financed with an acquisition loan. Then a construction loan is obtained for demolition and clearance, as well as for construction (or for selective cleanup and rehabilitation). When construction is complete, the property is mortgaged to repay the seed money and to pay off the acquisition and construction loans.

During operation of the project, various administrative, maintenance, and replacement costs are incurred. At the end of its economic life, the property has some residual salvage value. Cash deficits during the life of the project are met with intermediate loans (at interest), while any cash surplus is invested (at interest). The final salvage receipts will be applied to the intermediate cash-deficit loans. Break-even rent, the amount that must be received per month per dwelling unit to cover life-cycle costs, is calculated by assuming a nominal rental appreciation rate per year, then equating the discounted present value of rental receipts and salvage value with the discounted present value of incurred costs. The project's final cash balance, then, will equal zero. The Housing Model provides complete flexibility in the specification of input parameters; hence, the sensitivity of the break-even rent to specific cost factors can be readily determined.

Inputs and Outputs

In its present form,* the model requires as input quantities the descriptors of the housing project listed in Table 1, plus a "component list" in the form shown in Table 2 (which may include up to 100 items). The values shown in Tables 1 and 2 will serve as a "base case" to demonstrate use of the model in cost-effectiveness studies.

The component list covers all furnishings and structures in each dwelling unit. The level of detail need only be sufficient to account for differences among the alternatives being evaluated.† These inputs are used to compute total life-cycle cost, which is then translated into a rental schedule that will just cover the costs (i.e., break even).

Outputs from the Housing Model include the identification of the required loans; a year-to-year tally of break-even rents, operating costs, and cumulative cash balances; and a tabulation of the break-even rent in percentage per attributable source. These outputs are illustrated for a representative case in Tables 3–5. Note in Table 3 that the final cash position is zero; that is, as defined here, the project breaks even. The

---

*There are a great variety of institutional arrangements under which low-cost housing projects can be financed and operated. The Housing Model in the particular form illustrated here is based upon limited dividend sponsorship and the below-market-interest-rate (BMIR) program under Section 221(d)(3) of the National Housing Act.

†To elaborate: particular experiments may be directed to reducing construction and maintenance costs for interior plumbing. The components identified in Table 2 must then differentiate among the various types of interior plumbing. Whereas, parts that may be common to all alternatives, such as interior walls, floors, and ceilings, may be aggregated as one "component" (with care being exercised to account for the time phasing of maintenance and replacement).

Table 1 Model inputs: General descriptions.

COST ANAL RUN	10-STORIE APARTMENT PROJECT

PREACQUISITION PHASE-

ANNUAL INTEREST ON SEED MONEY, PERCENT	0.0000
SCHEMATIC DRAWINGS (PRELIM. PLANS)	1000.0000
SITE EVALUATION AND SOILS ENGINEERING	500.0000
OPTION ON SITE, COST PER YEAR	0.0000
ADMINISTRATIVE EXPENSES, COST PER MONTH	1000.0000
SITE ACQUISITION LOAN FEE (POINTS)	0.0000
ANNUAL INTEREST, ACQ, LOAN, PERCENT	4.5000
MONTHS FROM SEED MONEY TO SITE ACQUIRED	3.0000

PRECONSTRUCTION PHASE-

LAND COST (PER OLD DWELLING UNIT)	30188.0000
FHA FEES, PERMITS, PERCENT CONSTR. COST	1.9000
ADMINISTRATIVE COST PER MONTH THIS PHASE	2000.0000
RELOCATION COST (PER OLD DWELLING UNIT)	0.0000
NUMBER OF OLD DWELLING UNITS ON SITE	1.0000
TITLE, LEGAL, ETC., PERCENT CONSTR. COST	3.5000
COST OF QUANTITY SURVEY AND BID EXPENSE	700.0000
CONSTRUCTION LOAN FEE (POINTS)	0.0000
ANNUAL INTEREST ON CONSTR. LOAN, PERCENT	6.7500
MONTHS FROM ACQUIRE TO GROUND-BREAKING	1.0000

CONSTRUCTION PHASE-

SITE DEVELOPMENT COSTS (TOTAL)	48000.0000
ADMINISTRATION, OVERHEAD COST PER MONTH	1000.0000
NUMBER OF NEW DWELLING UNITS TO BE BUILT	80.0000
MONTHS FROM GROUND-BREAKING TO MOVE-IN	12.0000
JOB OVERHEAD, PERCENT CONSTRUCTION COST	1.5000
JOB OVERHEAD AND PROFIT, PCT CONST. COST	10.0000
ARCH. AND ENGRG. FEE PERCENT CONST. COST	5.5000
REGIONAL CONSTR. COST VARIATION, PERCENT	−1.0000

OPERATIONS PHASE-

ECONOMIC DISCOUNT RATE, PERCENT PER YEAR	6.0000
WORKING CAPITAL, PERCENT OF TOTAL COST	2.0000
MORTGAGE LOAN FEE (POINTS)	1.0000
BMIR LOAN ANNUAL INTEREST RATE, PERCENT	3.0000
MORTGAGE REPAYMENT PERIOD, YEARS	40.0000
RELOCATION COST/NEW DWLG UNIT (ONE TIME)	0.0000
GENERAL INFLATION RATE, PERCENT PER YEAR	2.5000
SALVAGE VALUE OF PROJECT (END MORTGAGE)	30188.0000
RENT APPRECIATION RATE, PERCENT PER YEAR	2.5000
OCCUPANCY FACTOR, PERCENT	95.0000
INSURANCE, PERCENT OF MORTGAGE, FIRST YR	.3000
ADMIN. ACCTG. MGMT. COST/YEAR INITIALLY	10000.0000
OPER. AND UTILITY COST/DWLG UNIT/YEAR	250.0000
UNACCOUNTED MAINTENANCE/DWLG UNIT/YEAR	20.0000
ANNUAL TAXES, PERCENT OF ORIG. MORTGAGE	1.5000
ANNUAL DIVIDEND, PERCENT ORIG. MORTGAGE	0.0000

Table 2 Model inputs: Component list.

COST ANAL RUN	EXAMPLE NO. 1			08/30/69 TIME	0.00.00 PAGE 2
RESOURCE LIST—					
	NUMBER ITEMS REQUIRED PER DWLG. UNIT	COST/ITEM $ EACH (INSTALLED)	USEFUL LIFE OF EACH ITEM IN YEARS	REPLACEMENT* (REFURBISH) $ EA ITEM	MAINTENANCE $/YEAR PER DWLG. UNIT
SUBSTRUCTURE COST	1.000	168.750	50.000	0.000	0.000
STRUCTURAL FRAME	1.000	2518.750	50.000	0.000	1.250
EXTERIOR WALLS TOTAL	1.000	725.000	50.000	0.000	6.250
ROOF COVER	1.000	56.250	21.000	56.250	0.000
INTERIOR PARTITIONS	1.000	1293.750	50.000	0.000	9.380
FLOOR FINISHING	1.000	187.500	15.000	0.000	0.000
CEILING FINISHING	1.000	62.500	50.000	100.000	3.130
HEATING, VENTILATION	1.000	225.000	21.000	62.500	1.880
ELECT., INCL. FIXTRS	1.000	516.250	50.000	0.000	1.880
PLMBG., INCL. FIXTRS	1.000	1000.000	50.000	0.000	1.880
ELEVATORS (SHARED)	1.000	1275.000	50.000	0.000	0.000
CABINETS, WARDROBES	1.000	55.000	50.000	0.000	2.750
FURNISHED EQUIPMENT	1.000	75.000	15.000	75.000	8.000

*Note: replacement cost not entered where useful life is greater than the 40-year project life.

Table 3 Model outputs: Summary of costs and break-even rent.

COST ANAL RUN	10-STORIE APARTMENT PROJECT		06/11/68 TIME 0.00.01 PAGE 3
SEED MONEY 7311	ACQUISITION 30188	CONSTRUCTION 993062	TOTAL COST 1030561

MORTGAGE ASSUMED = 1061790.10

FIRST YEAR VALUES OF ANNUAL PAYMENTS FOR—

MORTGAGE 45936	TAXES 15927	INSURANCE 3185	DIVIDENDS 0

OPERATING FINANCIAL QUANTITIES—

YEAR FROM OPENING	BREAK-EVEN RECEIPTS PER UNIT/MONTH	OPERATING COST/UNIT PER MONTH	CUMULATIVE PROJECT INCOME	ACTUAL YEAR-END NET CASH
0	94.240	103.708	6999	6999
1	96.596	105.105	−5806	−5386
2	99.011	106.536	−17782	−17685
3	101.487	108.003	−28909	−29874
4	104.024	109.507	−39166	−41923
5	106.624	111.048	−48531	−53804
6	109.290	112.628	−56982	−65483
7	112.022	114.248	−64496	−76925
8	114.823	115.908	−71049	−88094
9	117.693	117.609	−76618	−98948
10	120.636	119.353	−81177	−109444
11	123.652	121.141	−84702	−119536
12	126.743	122.973	−87167	−129173
13	129.911	124.851	−88545	−138301
14	133.159	126.776	−88809	−146863

15	136.488	149.870	-108207	-175074
16	139.900	130.772	-106159	-183530
17	143.398	132.845	-102911	-191294
18	146.983	134.970	-98434	-198294
19	150.657	137.148	-92697	-204454
20	154.424	139.380	-85667	-209692
21	158.284	158.289	-93270	-229876
22	162.242	144.014	-83559	-233958
23	166.298	146.418	-72457	-236894
24	170.455	148.882	-59929	-238579
25	174.716	151.408	-45940	-238905
26	179.084	153.997	-30452	-237752
27	183.561	156.651	-13429	-234993
28	188.150	159.371	5168	-230496
29	192.854	162.159	25379	-224115
30	197.676	195.606	17877	-245064
31	202.617	167.946	41436	-236209
32	207.683	170.948	66732	-225085
33	212.875	174.026	93810	-211513
34	218.197	177.180	122712	-195301
35	223.652	180.413	153486	-176245
36	229.243	183.727	186177	-154129
37	234.974	187.124	220834	-128720
38	240.848	190.606	257506	-99771
39	246.870	194.175	296243	-67020
40	253.041	197.833	367284	-0

Table 4 Model outputs: Apportionment of break-even rent.

COST ANAL RUN EXAMPLE NO. 1		08/30/69 TIME 0.00.01 PAGE 4

PERCENTAGE OF RENT DUE TO—

PRECONSTRUCTION COSTS—	=	6.030
OPTION COST—	=	0.000
LAND PURCHASE—	=	5.525
ADMINISTRATION—	=	.123
SERVICES HIRED—	=	.014
RELOCATIONS—	=	0.000
UNACCOUNTED—	=	.369
CONSTRUCTION COSTS—	=	38.073
SITE DEVELOPMENT—	=	.307
ADMINISTRATION—	=	.295
TAXES, INSURANCE—	=	1.028
PROFIT AND OVERHEAD—	=	3.807
ARCH. AND ENGRG. FEES—	=	2.094
FHA FEES AND PERMITS—	=	.723
TITLE, LEGAL FEES—	=	1.333
CONSTRUCTION LOAN FEE—	=	.952
CONST. LOAN INTEREST—	=	2.494
INSTALLED RESOURCES—	=	25.041
UNACCOUNTED—	=	− .000
POSTCONSTRUCTION COSTS—	=	55.897
RELOCATIONS—	=	0.000
ADMINISTRATION—	=	4.683
OPER. AND UTILITY—	=	14.049
UNASSIGNED MAINTENANCE—	=	0.000
TAXES—	=	28.017
INSURANCE—	=	7.004
DIVIDENDS—	=	0.000
ASSIGNABLE MAINTENANCE—	=	3.409
REPLACEMENTS—	=	.895
SALVAGE RETURN—	=	− 2.161

Table 5 Model outputs: Apportionment of break-even rent (continued).

COST ANAL RUN   EXAMPLE NO. 1   08/30/69   TIME   0.00.01   PAGE 5
BREAKDOWN BY CONSTRUCTION ITEMS USED—

| | FRACTION OF RENT DUE TO EACH ITEMS | | |
	INSTALLATION	REPLACEMENT	MAINTENANCE
SUBSTRUCTURE COST	.005	0.000	0.000
STRUCTURAL FRAME	.077	0.000	.001
EXTERIOR WALLS TOTAL	.022	0.000	.006
ROOF COVER	.002	.001	0.000
INTERIOR PARTITIONS	.040	0.000	.009
FLOOR FINISHING	.006	.004	0.000
CEILING FINISHING	.002	0.000	.003
HEATING, VENTILATION	.007	.001	.002
ELECT., INCL. FIXTRS	.016	0.000	.002
PLMBG., INCL. FIXTRS	.031	0.000	.002
ELEVATORS (SHARED)	.039	0.000	0.000
CABINETS, WARDROBES	.002	0.000	.003
FURNISHED EQUIPMENT	.002	.003	.007

succession of negative cash balances reflects the need for interim financing, undertaken with the foreknowledge that, in this example, "salvage" proceeds will just meet all final expenses.

Table 3 also indicates steadily increasing break-even rents or receipts. The change from year to year is input as a specified rent-appreciation rate (in this case, for example, 2.5% per year). Operating costs include maintenance, replacement, taxes, and other recurring expenditures; the irregularities in this column are due to replacement items, such as "heating, ventilation" units. Tables 4 and 5 indicate proportionate sources of life-cycle cost (hence of break-even rent) for items in Tables 1 and 2.

COST-EFFECTIVENESS ANALYSES

Cost-effectiveness analysis requires some systematic means to relate the costs associated with particular undertakings to their consequences. The "undertakings" in question here are various procedural, administrative, and technical experiments directed to the goal of large-scale low-cost housing. If successful, the experiments will establish the technical feasibility of the approach together with an indication of costs. For example, an experimental program might show that a modular plumbing unit can be made and installed, and that installed-unit costs (in large quantities) could be $400.

The Housing Model provides a structure within which changes in activity costs or time can be related to changes in break-even rent. The key to useful application of the comparatively straightforward procedure is, of course, the specification of all the input parameters. Unit costs for various resources and activities are affected by such factors as the scale (or magnitude) of the eventual implementation, the geographic region, climatic conditions, business conditions, etc.[6]. Each one of these must be included in a comprehensive assessment of costs. Cost factors can easily be found for geographic and climatic variations[6, 7]. Little or no data is published in the open literature about the effects of project scale and general business conditions, but discussions with appraisers and construction personnel indicate that while these considerations cannot be directly modeled, neither can they be overlooked. They remain as a major element of the "art" of project cost estimation which must be included as a subjective input.

As noted previously, the required level of detail for the input parameters need only be such that distinctions can be made among the alternatives under review. Thus, *if* the effects of business conditions are common to all the alternatives they need not be considered in detail. In general, the effects on different kinds of labor and material are believed to be distinctly different. Thus, in a variety of alternative experiments, changing business conditions could be suspected to carry varying impacts. Nevertheless, to forecast *differences* in economic conditions for various classes of labor, material, and financing to the time when large-scale implementation of new approaches is actually undertaken is such a formidable task that it has not been attempted (although the simpler sensitivity analyses to test the effect of individual deviations from a general forecast of economic conditions might be useful).

Experimental Data

Some of the required input data may be obtained from field experiments which serve either of two purposes: (1) establishing feasibility (and costs) for new methods which would not otherwise be tried, or (2) serving as a "proving ground" to establish the best use of new methods which might otherwise be implemented but presumably on a less efficient basis.

The approach to cost-effectiveness analyses for the first case is comparatively straightforward. Computing the benefit of any particular experiment is based upon the "with and without" principle, that is, upon the difference between the break-even rent using normal, or "base case," procedures, and the presumably lower rent following the experiment.

There are, however, serious practical problems in extrapolating from experimental observations to actual costs in large-scale implementation of the experimental technique. One conceptual approach which reflects economies of scale is the widely employed "learning curve," or "progress function" that depicts the effect upon unit costs of variations in the total quantity produced [8, 9]. In concept, costs observed in an experimental project of ten dwelling units, for instance, can be translated into corresponding costs in an eventual implementation of a thousand units. In practice, there is considerable variation in the applicable slope of the learning curve and in the quantities, or scale, over which the slope applies. Consequently, the analyst must rely upon the judgments of experts in each field.

As an example, suppose the observed unit cost of an experimental plumbing module was $1600. A knowledgeable manufacturer might estimate that in mass quantities the cost of each unit would be $400. This is the figure that would be used in the cost-effectiveness study; that is, it would be an input in the Resource List of Table 2. The "base case" of Table 2 included an installed plumbing cost of $1000 per dwelling unit. If the reduction to $400 is the only change derived from the experiment (i.e., plumbing maintenance and all other inputs remain the same), break-even rent is reduced from the $88.97 shown in Table 3 to $84.68. This difference of $4.29 per month per dwelling unit for the initial year is the indicator of effectiveness.

Similarly, some procedural innovation might permit a reduction in "months from groundbreaking to move in" (see Table 1) from 12 months to 5 months. The Housing Model indicates that this would bring the break-even rent down to $85.38, a reduction of $3.59. Note that individual changes are not additive because of the interacting effects of time and cost. To illustrate: the actual effect of combining the two examples is a rent reduction of $7.64, which is less than the sum of the individual figures. (The Housing Model's ability to account for these "non-additive" effects of multiple changes is an important feature for the study of prospective housing innovations.)

These indicators of effectiveness should then be related to the cost of conducting the experiment and to the probability of achieving the indicated reductions in unit cost or time.* Procedures for estimating the cost of experiments are not included here; to the extent that the experiments represent advances in the state of the housing art, cost estimation presents some conceptual problems which must be left for further study. In the illustrations thus far, the new cost and time figures have been single-valued, representing expected values. Perhaps, a more sophisticated approach would be to incorporate subjective probabilities in the estimates of post-experiment costs and times. An approach is indicated in Fig. 1 in which a probability density function (pdf) of achievable plumbing unit cost is superimposed upon the direct output of the Housing Model. The result, a pdf of achievable break-even rent, shown along the y-axis, can then be translated to a pdf of rent reduction. The literature of Statistical Decision Theory presents a comprehensive means of dealing with uncertainties in such effectiveness measures. For most purposes, however, the expected values of rent reduction suffice.

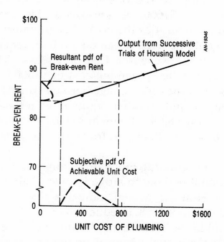

Fig. 1 Probability density functions of unit cost and break-even rent.

---

*Multiplication of the indicated reductions in break-even rent by the total number of dwelling units to be constructed will establish total "savings" per month. (If desired, this figure could be discounted to a present value.) For a constant number of dwelling units in the implementation phase, this procedure will not change the relative ranking of alternatives. Hence, *comparative* effectiveness can be left simply in terms of change in break-even rent per dwelling unit.

Recall that the second use of field experiments was to test various uses of new procedures that would be less readily developed and tested during a standard construction project. The experiment thus leads to greater efficiencies from the outset of actual projects. Although the same learning would eventually take place during large-scale construction, without prior experimentation, the same economies would take longer to achieve. In terms of learning curves, this effect can be shown graphically, as follows:

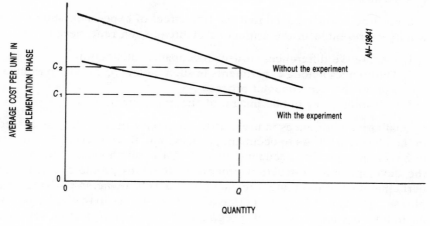

Fig. 2

To appraise the effect of the experiment, two trials with the Housing Model should be conducted, one with the appropriate "resource input" at cost C_1, and the other at cost C_2. The difference in resulting break-even rents is the indicator of effectiveness.

As an example, assume that a new construction technique for structural frames has been proposed. After some experimental trials, the expected unit cost for structural frame is $1000 (cf., $2518.75 in Table 2); whereas, without the experiment, the average unit cost would be $1600. From exercises of the Housing Model, the resulting break-even rents are $78.11 and $82.04, respectively, and their difference is the effectiveness indicator for this experimental project, or $3.93.

With these indicators of comparative effectiveness, completion of the cost-effectiveness analysis and selection of "best" experiments from among the alternatives follow conventional guidelines. However, one departure from classical procedures arises because of the general indivisibility of experiments—that is, half an experiment may not provide any results; hence, marginal analysis cannot be fully employed. The fact that many prospective time and cost changes are not additive also complicates the analysis somewhat. Thus, implementation of combined time- and cost-saving innovations must be examined as *combinations* to ensure proper account of their actual effect, combined, in reducing break-even rent.

In Conclusion

It must be acknowledged that the true effect of experimentation is not wholly represented in the arithmetic of break-even rent, because of:

1. Qualitative differences in user (occupant) satisfaction.
2. Differences among experiments in such factors as dweller participation in the experimental process.
3. "Visibility," or public image, of the experiment.

Qualitative differences in user satisfaction have been widely discussed in the literature [5]. As to occupant participation, there is growing interest in having prospective occupants of low-cost public housing take part in the development-construction process in order to promote a sense of participation and to create a feeling (or a fact) of ownership—hence the phrase, "sweat equity." The notion of visibility refers to the real need for an innovative *image* in such programs. Public administrators reveal a strong need to have visible, tangible evidence of new developments in order to sustain public interest and support. Furthermore, procedural innovations may require a special "visibility" to establish their benefits in the face of opposition by particular groups profiting from older procedures. These special factors must be considered along with the estimates of reduction in break-even rent if cost-effectiveness is to be truly comprehensive.

REFERENCES

1. Romney, George, speaking to the U.S. Conference of Mayors, May 1969. Secretary Romney said, "As far as I'm concerned the national goals as declared by Congress underestimated the need rather than overstated the need, because we've lost ground since the goals were established."
2. See, for example, J. F. Bernheisel, Drummond, K. R., Ifft, J., Johnson, A. C., Nicholls, J., Radner, L., Roach, J. W. *An Analysis of Twelve Experimental Housing Projects*, Bedford, Mass., The Mitre Corporation, McLean, Va., Report # MTP 324, Jan. 1969.

3. Dodson, E. N. and Albini, F. A. *A Planning Model for Low-Cost Housing Projects*, Santa Barbara, Calif.: General Research Corporation IMR-913, June 1968.
4. Rothenberg, J. *Economic Evaluation of Urban Renewal*, Brookings Institution, Washington, D.C. 1967.
5. Frieden, B. and Morris, R. *Urban Planning and Social Policy*, Basic Books, New York, 1968.
6. Eaves, Elsie, How the many costs of housing fit together, *Research Report No. 16*, prepared for the National Commission on Urban Problems, Washington, D.C., 1969.
7. Moselle, G. (ed.), *National Construction Estimator*, Craftsman Book Co., Los Angeles, Cal., 1968.
8. Asher, H. *Cost Quantity Relationships in the Airframe Industry*, The RAND Corporation, R-291, July 1956.
9. Conway, R. and Schultz, A. The manufacturing progress function, *Journal of Industrial Engineering*, January–February 1959.

16

PAPS—The Public Assistance Processing System*

JON R. DAVID

Systems RDI Corporation, Lodi, New Jersey

Abstract—The volume of paper and the incidence of fraud in public assistance program areas—Welfare, Medicare, Medicaid—is so great that government agencies find themselves with ever-increasing work backlogs, without current information, and losing millions of dollars each month. Public assistance recipients, check cashers, Medicaid/Medicare vendors, and local, state, and federal agencies are all dissatisfied with the present situation. The introduction of properly designed identification cards, in combination with standard terminals, imprinters, computer processing, and optical scanning, will immediately resolve the above problems, and offer great benefits in other areas, both in the present and in the future.

INTRODUCTION

The Public Assistance Processing System was designed to eliminate the specific problems of check cashing, Welfare check thefts, and delayed Medicaid vendor payments. As the system design matured it became obvious that the System would offer additional immediate advantages, and other optional or future benefits.

In its final form the basic System will:

1. Guarantee that no "bad" (i.e., forged, stolen, duplicate, etc.) Welfare checks can be cashed.
2. Enable prompt (within a few days) payment of Medicaid vendors (doctors, druggists, etc.).

---

*From the *Proceedings of the Urban Symposium*, of the Association of Computing Machinery, New York, October 1971, pp. 16–26.

3. Give up-to-date information regarding what is going on in Medicaid areas, for example, what goods and services are being dispensed, at what price, where, when, and by whom.
4. Serve as the backbone for a Hospital Information and Control system.
5. Coordinate with, and/or expand into, Employment, Unemployment, and/or Eligibility systems.
6. Integrate with nongovernment systems (e.g., Blue Cross/Blue Shield) presently operational or being developed.
7. Facilitate both interarea movements of public assistance recipients, and "federalization" of public assistance programs.

The first three capabilities are immediate, the second three are optional, and the last is future.

The situation in New York City is used for reference throughout this system description, and while it is true that it is an extreme case, this in no way alters the relative value of the system in other locales. Descriptive figures come from cognizant government personnel and/or newspapers, and equipment prices were obtained from the manufacturers. The Medicaid or Medicare names, although used individually, signifiy both programs.

PRESENT SITUATION

New York City has about 1 million public assistance recipients, issues more than a half million public assistance checks per month, and receives about 23 million Medicaid vendor statements per year from close to 40,000 vendors. The magnitude of this leaves New York unable to readily process eligibility applications, months behind in processing Medicaid vendor statements, without up-to-date information about what is going on, and with dissatisfaction both on the part of private sectors such as Medicaid vendors (because of the indefinite time to get paid), and public assistance recipients (because of the delays and unwelcome receptions they often experience). Further, it is estimated that the Federal government spends about a quarter of a million dollars per year to inhibit Welfare check thefts by double-teaming mail routes on check delivery days (the 1st and 16th of each month) in just two of New York City's five boroughs (Brooklyn and the Bronx); about 1 million dollars of bad checks get cashed in the City each month, with one-third of this absorbed by the government, and the rest absorbed by the private sector.

Some steps have been or are being planned or taken to remedy some of the above, but their approach is on an item-by-item basis. Not only do these individual programs ignore all relationships between the problems encountered in the public assistance situation, they seem to be ineffective within the area they try to treat, and are often doomed to failure before they start. For example:

1. Thin plastic picture identification cards were used in an attempt to minimize the cashing of bad Welfare checks. This program is, by definition, ineffective since the main problem is reported not to be identification, but recipients getting checks, reporting them lost, getting second checks, and cashing both, resulting in the first being stopped at the bank. Further, the Check Cashiers Association, handling about 80% of the Welfare checks mailed each month, refused to accept these cards for check cashing identification.
2. A "checkless" system is now being considered. This, as above, may quite possibly be doomed to failure. Beyond any technical and administrative difficulties is the point that Welfare recipients well may not stand for this approach, and while one can argue that public assistance recipients should accept what they get, it would be a fatal error to assume you can readily initiate programs that may strip away more of what little dignity these people have left. Arguments about funds transferred directly into a bank account actually adding dignity (since nobody outside the bank can know the source of the money) can be countered with the funds transfer being the first step in a total (food, clothing, residence, etc.) allotment system.

It is worth repeating again that programs such as those cited above attack only individual problems and are, even at best, virtually worthless beyond this point.

BASIC SYSTEM

The basic system requires the issuance of identification cards to public assistance recipients. These cards will be used in Welfare check cashing to:

1. Identify the cardholder.
2. Certify that the check belongs to the cardholder.
3. Guarantee that the check is not forged, stolen, etc.

In the Medicaid area the cards will be used to:

1. Record all billable transactions.
2. Provide detailed descriptive information describing the transaction.
3. Produce the documents assuring prompt vendor payment.

The identification cards should be of an American Express/Diners Club quality, and should have at least the cardholder's individual identification number embossed. For check cashing purposes these cards should be used with standard telephone company equipment such as a touch-tone phone or touch-tone "pad" coupled to a dial phone; for Medicaid transactions these cards should be used with standard imprinters such as those used in restaurants, gasoline stations, etc.

SYSTEM OPERATION

For Welfare cashing the Public Assistance Processing System will operate as follows:

1. Identification card will be presented along with any check to be cashed.
2. Check number, check amount, and cardholder identification number will be input, at touch-tone speed, to a central data file verification program.
3. Check number, check amount, and identification number will be cross checked at computer speed and a "Yes"/"No"/"Repeat" response given.

The "central data file" mentioned in item 2 can, and most probably will, be the same as the one used to generate the checks.

Inspecting the above sequence shows:

1. Forged or altered checks will be rejected.
2. Forged or altered identification cards will be rejected.
3. Checks reported lost, stolen, etc., will be rejected.
4. Checks lost, stolen, etc., but not reported will be worthless to anybody possessing them.
5. A lost, stolen, etc., card would be worthless because either it would be reported as such and rejected, or, if not reported, would not be matched with a check (forged or stolen, of course) with both the correct check number and check amount.

322 J. R. DAVID

The only way left to cash a "bad" check is to steal both the check and corresponding identification card at the same time, and cash the check before the theft is reported. This would have to be done after mail delivery yet before the check is rightfully cashed; the identification card would be worthless thereafter, and the time interval would be so short that the risk should very greatly outweigh the unlikely possible "gain"; this, therefore, should present, at most, a negligible problem. It will be shown in the next section that even this possible minimal trouble area can easily be eliminated.

Third-party check cashing, that is, the cashing of a check by an individual other than the person named on the check, can be accommodated in several ways: "Deposit Only" requirements coupled with properly signed bank withdrawal slips, authorized signature cards at banks, and professional check cashers, identification cards for third parties who would be registered at the central office and verified on-line, etc. Whatever method is used to treat this situation, it should be noted that third-party check cashing is fairly uncommon.

For Medicaid transactions the System will operate as follows:

1. Medicaid recipients will present their identification card to "pay" for goods and/or services (drugs, medical, dental, hospital, clinic, etc.) they receive.
2. "Vendor" will imprint a "chit," as now done by restaurants, gasoline stations, etc., using the identification card; vendor will include a "Class of Service" code to describe the charge.
3. Once per month, or other time period, each vendor will send copies of chits for the preceding period to a central office. (It does not matter whether all chits for an area are submitted on the same date, say the 1st of each month, or on billing cycle days throughout the period.)
4. At the central office these chits will be optically scanned, the data therein being put on magnetic tape.
5. The magnetic tape will be sorted by a computer.
6. Minimal computer processing will produce check tapes, report tapes, etc.
7. These tapes will be printed as desired.

Examining the above sequence shows:

1. Vendors perform minimal work.
2. Vendors retain a copy of all Medicaid transactions since multipart chits, like those of Diners Club, will be used.

3. Payment to vendors, generation of reports, etc., can be as fast as desired since the scanning/sorting/processing is relatively fast.

Misuse of a stolen (or found) identification card at Medicaid vendors is not treated above. This area is felt to be both minimal and unimportant because:

1. Lists of bad cards could be regularly issued.
2. Periodic issuance of verification cards, or reissuance of the plastic cards, would severely limit potential losses.
3. Probably most important is the fact that cognizant officials feel that any misuse of this type by an individual must in and of itself be minimal, and, moreover, the misuser probably is getting drugs or what-have-you for someone (himself included) "deserving," that is, close to eligibility.

This unimportant potential trouble area, although minimal, can, as in the case of the simultaneous check/card theft and rapid cashing mentioned above, also be easily eliminated by the same methods alluded to above and set forth in the next section.

Within the comments on misuse, item 2 bears further discussion. Public assistance identification cards are now reissued at various intervals in different areas of the country; this, as mentioned in item 2, can still be done with the Public Assistance Processing System's plastic identification cards, but the alternative, also mentioned, may be more attractive, that is, issue the plastic cards on a permanent basis, and reissue only paper verification cards that are, of course, dated.

The last item to be noted is that Medicaid vendors indicate "Class of Service" upon transaction chits. Herein lies the key to a data bank giving needed information, much of which is not only presently unavailable, but inconceivable. This "Class of Service" code is optically scanned, along with amount, date, and vendor number, on each transaction chit, and, if we assume that chits are sent in on the first of every month, we get data an average of a half month old which would contain the following types of information:

1. What goods and services are being given.
2. Where and when these goods and services are being given.
3. How much these good and services cost.
4. To whom these goods and services are being given.

In addition to enabling government agencies to become aware of specific needs in the Medicaid sector, both as a whole and by area, this information can readily be used to:

1. Determine, project, and/or analyze trends.
2. Do cost comparisions to indicate possible overcharges and/or areas the government might efficiently assist.
3. Perform internal audits to check things like multiple vendor charges and/or cardholder "purchases."

These nominal applications in no way limit the uses that this information has, and should not be considered all-encompassing. They are given merely to indicate the inherent power of the Public Assistance Processing System, and to suggest possible benefits. For example, it would be trivial to include prescription number on doctor and druggist chits, and a computer cross check could be made to insure a prescription filled has been issued, and prescriptions refilled are properly so done.

SYSTEM "HARDWARE"

The key item in the Public Assistance Processing System set forth herein is an identification card compatible with both data transmission and imprinting. The other major items are the data transmitters and imprinters, with opical scanning and computer equipment filling out the system "hardware." These items will now be discussed, but there is no attempt, either explicit of implicit, to specify, or even imply, particular manufacturers, except Telephone Company equipment for data transmission.

The identification card, as mentioned earlier, should be plastic, of American Express/Diners Club quality, with the identification number embossed. This is all that is required for the basic system. Other items, however, may be considered, namely:

1. Additional embossing of cardholder's name. Strongly recommended, this facilitates identification by the government and in the field, and is also a security feature.
2. Dial-a-phone punching, in addition to embossing, of identification number. This is recommended since it enables check cashers to more rapidly input cardholder's number, while minimizing chance of input error; also a security feature.

3. In addition to the identification number, an origin code defining locale can be used. This would be helpful in various analyses, and also useful in expanding the system beyond the local level. This is strongly recommended.
4. An issue (sequence) character to be used so that lost, stolen, etc., cards can be reissued without changing the basic identification number. This is strongly recommended.
5. Signature panel. This is recommended as a security feature.
6. Picture of cardholder. This is another security feature, but has concomitant administrative and acceptance troubles. While not recommended, it is also not recommended against, and should be left to the individual locale.
7. Unique color(s). Another security feature, apparently not worth too much.
8. Patterned plastic. Another security feature, again apparently not too valuable.
9. Seals, crests, etc. Still more security, still not recommended.
10. Coded (hidden, secret) numbers. This is the feature alluded to in the previous section to handle simultaneous check/card theft, and to handle stolen, found, etc., cards at Medicaid vendors, and is worth considering. Cards would be coded, at issuance, with several random digits known only to the cardholder. Vendors and check cashers could, at their option, use small keyboard devices like a touch-tone phone into which the card is placed and the cardholder keys in this coded number. A red/green light then indicates whether he is wrong or not.
11. Coded characteristics. Instead of using coded numbers, palm characteristics could be used for local verification. While this should give additional security beyond coded numbers, the concomitant implementation problems makes it not recommended.

Each of the above items, whether recommended or not, contributes to card security. Security is measured by both ability to tamper with (alter) a card, and ability to produce a new (forged) card; while system security is a strong point, it has been shown that a bad card is worthless for check cashing, and worth at most very little in producing Medicaid goods and services.

On the following page is a picture of a nominal identification card. A basic punched/embossed card was provided as a standard product, and then, here at our offices, a color picture and signature panel were added for illustration. This layout is not necessarily recommended, and is used merely to get all visible features on the same side of the card.

Examining this card we see:

1. The embossed number, which could be ID/Origin/Sequence, happens to be the Systems RDI Corporation telephone number, and the punched holes are a dial-a-phone representation of this number.
2. The embossed and signed name is that of this author, as is the picture.
3. While the card is colored, the plastic is not patterned.
4. There is room for a seal or crest in the upper right corner of the card, and coded numbers or palm characteristics are not visible.

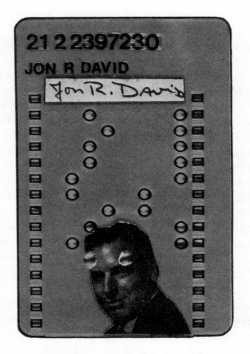

Fig. 1 Nominal identification card.

Data transmission which, for all practical purposes, must use phone lines, should logically use phone company equipment, and either a touch-tone phone or a touch-tone pad coupled to a standard dial phone is recommended. Other things to consider are:

1. Automatic dialing. This is strongly recommended. Check cashers must connect to a computer, and input check number, check amount, and cardholder number; two of these functions will be automatic, saving time and eliminating errors, if phones (or pads) with a dial-a-phone slots are used.
2. Printed records. It is felt that some check cashers would like to have immediate computer printed records of information regarding checks they cash, and these people can use touch-tone devices with printer attachments. These are not yet made by the Telephone Company, but various manufacturers produce devices of this sort compatible with phone company systems. As a more complex piece of equipment than a simple phone or pad, reliability should be lower; maintenance, too, may well not equal that of the Telephone Company. Since system operation is not effected either way, and printed records versus reliability/maintenance is a question of values, this should be left to the individual check cashers.
3. An alternative method of approach: an imprinter can be used to describe the check and cardholder, and the chit produced can be immediately scanned and the information sent over phone lines. Although this is not as expensive as it sounds, it seems inferior to the approach to printed records indicated above in item 2, and is not recommended.

The imprinters for the Public Assistance Processing System should be OCR (optical character recognition) variable-amount dating imprinters with vendor identification plates. Imprinters of this type are seen throughout the country, particularly at gasoline stations. While alternatives to vendor plate, data, and even amount and class of service imprinting are available, they are more work, create possible errors, and often complicate optical scanning. These alternatives, not even detailed herein, are recommended against; worldwide use of standard imprinters should indicate this is wise.

If the recommendation for a standard imprinter as described above is followed, the optical scanning gear can be single font. This will be both common and inexpensive, and the load will be light. If, however, things like handwritten digits are introduced as standard, the equipment will be much more complex and expensive, and the choice of equipment much narrower. Whatever equipment is used should have a reject bin. Scanning directly to magnetic tape would be an attractive feature.

The computer requirements are minimal, namely:

1. A dedicated disc for the data file.
2. A computer with foreground/background capabilities to accommodate the check cashers.
3. Computer time to run the computer sort and perform minimal processing.
4. An off-line print station, or additional computer time, to print the report and check tapes.

It should be noted that the computer requirements most probably can be met with existing equipment, scheduled or spare-time, and both the computer and optical scanning requirements should be able to be satisfied by relatively inexpensive equipment purchased or rented for those functions, or by various private service bureaus.

SYSTEM COSTS

There are both initizalization and operational costs involved in the Public Assistance Processing System. Initial costs are primarily made up of the identification cards and any equipment it is elected to purchase; operational costs include the imprinters, data transmission and optical scanning equipment, and the computer time and data file storage.

In New York City, where about 1 million cards will be initially required, the card price can be from about $0.07 to about $1.00 per card, depending on the options incorporated. For example, punched/embossed cards with signature panels and coded numbers should be less than $0.15 per card; the addition of the picture option would easily raise the price $0.25–$0.50 per card, whereas other options would be less than $0.01 per card extra.

The imprinters and phone company data transmission equipment should be from $0.50 to $7.00 per month; if the phone/printer option is effected the cost will be at least $30.00 per month. A good imprinter should be available at a monthly cost of about $2.00, a touch-tone pad for $1.90, and the automatic dialer option for less than $5.00. It is felt that the vendors and check cashers will gladly pay for this equipment on a monthly basis, since, above and beyond the public relations pressure that would be put on them (pleas by top officials through organizations such as the AMA, literature mailed to the individuals, etc.), they would receive considerable benefits, such as:

1. Check cashers, for as little as $1.90 per month, would be assured that all checks were "good." When one considers the $670,000 (more or less) loss currently absorbed by the private sector in cashing bad checks, and the fact that the Check Cashiers Association, currently handling about 80% of the checks, only has 200–300 members, one gets an average monthly loss per member of more than $1,500 (80% of $670,000 is $536,000; assume 300 members), which is significantly greater than $1.90 or even $30.00 (for the phone/printer option). Further, if any cashed checks were later lost by, or stolen from, the check cashers, there would be a record of the transaction logged in the data file.

2. Medicaid vendors, many of whom now factor their receivables at a 10% discount, would be guaranteed almost immediate payment. Further, it would be trivial to supply them with regular (say monthly) chronological listings of their Medicaid transactions, thereby simplifying their bookkeeping and accounting. If necessary, if a vendor is willing to generate a "cardless" chit for all non-Medicaid transactions, his (monthly) statement could include a chronological listing of all his income. Another "bribe" could easily be direct credits to a vendor's bank account if he so desires. The above seems well worth $2.00 per month.

The optical scanning equipment will have low-level use, and an intelligent selection of imprinters could bring the cost below $100 per month. Similarly, the cost could also easily be at least $10,000 per month, depending on the requirements placed on the equipment by both the imprinters and the system operation. In any event, this cost is much less than the six-figure monthly amount currently lost by the City via bad checks, is less than the money the Federal government devotes to double teaming mail routes as earlier mentioned, and should be a lot less than the manpower saved by automating the Medicaid vendor statement processing.

The computer power required should, as mentioned above, be available with present equipment, scheduled or spare-time, and would therefore be free. Puchasing the equipment could run from about $30,000, and a private service bureau would charge about $500 per month (for disc storage) plus computer time, where computer time should be from $30 to $300 per hour.

Conservative total (nominal) system cost for the New York City situation (with lesser requirements costing less, of course) is (at most) $200,000 down and (at most) $15,000 per month; this should save the City at least $10 million per year, while giving much greater power (such as the Medicaid data bank), and both increasing services to, and improving relations with, the public and private sectors involved in the public assistance situation.

It is worth noting that the Federal government has indicated a willingness to assume, under certain reasonable circumstances, at least the start-up costs.

OTHER CONSIDERATIONS

There are certain miscellaneous points worth discussion, namely:

1. A system the size of New York City's can easily take up to six months to set up. While 40,000 imprinters alone can make this period mandatory, coding and/or pictures for 1 million cards could also produce this delay.
2. It is assumed that information for initial cards will come from an (possibly augmented) existing data file.
3. Some chits submitted to the central agency for processing may prove unintelligible to the optical scanning equipment. Provision must therefore be made for the input of compatible (equivalent to a chit) data, and it is recommened that punch cards be used.
4. The identification cards can be used in connection with a modified central data file for credit checks of the cardholder, (future) allotment systems, etc. This is not important for the present, and while it is well within the System potential, it is beyond the scope of this description.
5. Storage of the Medicaid vendor chits for audit and/or other later inspection can be accommodated as paper is now stored, that is, in boxes, files, etc. The possibility of microfilming them in conjunction with the optical scanning offers several advantages, such as:
   a. Storage space is minimal.
   b. Retrieval of a chit (image) is achieved within a few seconds.
   c. Examination can be simultaneously performed by many people at various locations remote from the microfilm file.
6. Rather than spend money, little though it may be, for the advantages and powers of the Public Assistance Processing System, New York City (or any other locale) can actually make money while enjoying

all benefits by merely buying the imprinters and/or data transmission equipment and in turn "renting" it to the vendors and check cashers. (Actually, it would not be a true rental, but a payment for additional services and assurances above and beyond what is now available). A variation would be the vendors and check cashers individually paying the list price individual rental, while the City receives a volume discount based on the total amount of equipment in use.

OPTIONAL AND FUTURE SYSTEM EXPANSION

The following brief descriptions are set forth to give an indication of the potential inherent in the Public Assistance Processing System, above and beyond it's basic uses.

Hospital Systems

In New York City we have about 19 virtually autonomous City hospitals, relatively uncoordinated in spite of the Health Services Administration "super-agency." Identification cards in the hands of public assistance recipients would be an information link uniting these hospitals, and any individual without a card would be issued a plastic card (to become his permanent card) upon being admitted to any hospital. These cards could be coded for class of payment (e.g., fully insured, partially insured, uninsured, etc.) and, along with public assistance recipients' cards, become the basis for billing systems (the card identifies the individual; his number is the index for payment/treatment charges; the payment code allocates these charges) and/or patient monitoring and control systems (the card identifies the individual; his number is the index to record prescribed medications/treatments, and then verify them before they are administered). Further, once all (or even most) hospitals have implemented these systems, an immediate extension would be areawide bed, medical history, etc. systems.

Employment/Unemployment Systems

Individuals seeking unemployment benefits, or seeking employment through the government, would be issued cards if they did not already have one from another source. Each individual would be assigned job codes and capability codes based on his desires, education and experience (if any), references (when available), salary history and requirements, time available to work, etc. These codes would be in, or input into, a relatively permanent master file indexed by card number, and referenced against available job openings which would be coded by type of work, experience and education required, salary, hours, etc., to immediately find possible work compatible with the applicant. Payments of unemployment benefits could easily be recorded and indexed by the card number.

Eligibility Systems

The eligibility requirements for various public assistance programs can easily be represented in terms readily ingested by current automation techniques. To be specific, they are combinations of numeric, "Yes/No," and choice (e.g., one of a range of five) parameters. A computer program can accept this data and immediately combine it to determine eligibility or, where applicable, degree of eligibility. This could be done immediately upon application (with later verification) or based on some schedule, say within a week. A combination of the two is probably best. Upon application, the data would be input using a teletypewriter or some such device to a computer; any extraordinary data could be questioned by the computer via the teletype, and confirmed or changed; likewise, if a person misses eligibility by only one or two points, these can be questioned. This would, of course, eliminate unfair errors due to misunderstanding, handwriting, or other input errors, etc. The system would, after some predetermined time (immediately, a day, a week, etc.), process this data as follows:

1. A number would be assigned and provision would be made for a card to be generated. This number, to appear on the card, would index the disposition of the case and all other business.
2. If eligible, a regular card would be made and sent as soon as possible. Immediately, however, the applicant would be notified of eligibility and issued a temporary card, both performed by the computer.
3. If ineligible, the applicant would immediately get (computer-generated) notification of this, with reasons for this ineligibility. The card mentioned in item 1 would be of plain type (such as that mentioned above under "Hospital Systems") with a letter informing him to use the card for future applications (and possibly for hospital stays, seeking employment, etc.).

If a person is unemployed and/or seeking employment at the time of application, and if employment systems such as described above exist, the applicant, if not yet coded, can be coded and immediately referred to potential jobs. (This is, of course, independent of whether or not he is eligible.) Similarly, the applicant could be sent to (or scheduled for) a special employment section for this service.

Integration With Other Systems

Several nongovernment organizations such as Blue Cross/Blue Shield are presently experimenting with limited identification card applications in areas such as prescription filling. These organizations could immediately use Public Assistance Processing System identification cards, and could issue their future cards compatible with them. These cards would then not only be the basis for these private systems, but would allow extensive information communication and internal cross checking within and between both public and private programs at all levels.

Federalization and Interarea Movements

It should be obvious that the basic Public Assistance Processing System will work in any locale. If the origin code option is effected it would be trivial for one locality to honor requests from public assistance recipient cardholders who are the responsibility of other localities; the origin code would enable immediate routing of whatever charges are to be transferred. Further, it can be used to route any medical inquiry to the individual's home area (if that home area has a card-indexed medical history system as described above). Another possibility, that of national public assistance programs, would use these cards, already in the field, as the backbone of information processing for these systems, thereby minimizing many administrative problems inherent in such a transition.

SUMMARY

It has been shown that the Public Assistance Processing System is not only a great asset to the programs that inspired its design, but to other important and far-reaching programs. For a relatively small cost it saves millions of dollars while solving many specific problems and providing both immediate and potential powers for both present and future operations.

17

A Model for Selection of Urban Recreation Facilities*

NORBERT DEE AND JON C. LIEBMAN

Senior Environmental Planner, Battelle, Columbus Laboratories, Columbus, Ohio

Professor of Environmental Engineering, University of Illinois, Urbana, Illinois

INTRODUCTION

In many cities of the United States, the urban recreation needs of the population are not being adequately met by the existing supply of urban recreation facilities. Overcrowded facilities exist in some areas while in others facilities are vacant, and individuals are using the streets for recreation[2, 5].

There are many reasons for the existence of recreation facility maldistribution. Certainly budgetary limitations of the cities play an important part in the creation and the subsequent lack of response to these problems. However, the authors feel that many of these problems can, in part, be alleviated and deficiencies corrected by a rational resource allocation procedure supported with citizen participation.

These two elements of approaching solutions to current recreation problems are combined in the recreation model presented in this paper. Resource allocation is treated in detail and has been tested in principle in Baltimore, Maryland. Citizen participation, on the other hand, is in the conceptual stage of development.

---

*From the *Proceedings of the Urban Symposium*, of the Association of Computing Machinery, New York, 1972, pp. 233–240.

URBAN RECREATION MODEL

If the recreation problems of the cities are to be ameliorated, solutions that are acceptable to the population must be implemented. Little is gained if the resource allocation is acceptable to the city planner, and other city offices, but unacceptable to those who have been "selected" to use the facility. Therefore, it is important to generate solutions that are both efficient in the allocation of the cities' resources and are desired by the population.

A model that includes both of these components is illustrated in Fig. 1. Resource allocation is the core of this model. For a given set of conditions, it is possible to compute an "optimal" allocation of recreation facility type, integer groupings of recreation activities, and site locations that maximize facility attendence. Inputs to the resource analysis and to the comparison of alternatives are performed through "interaction of the citizens with the computer" along with technical input from the planning agencies.

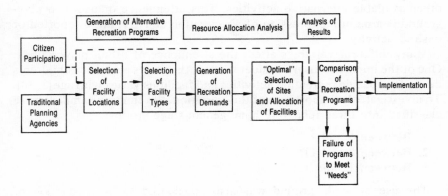

Fig. 1   Urban recreation model.

The best forms of citizen interaction are in the process of development. It may be achieved through the use of computer games which sample various neighborhoods by using teletype equipment or through the responses of the various neighborhoods' elected or appointed representatives. The form of the interface is important but the lack of the desired form should not be used as an excuse to avoid this necessary linkage. The authors feel that any reasonable "visible" linkage is better than none.

RESOURCE ALLOCATION ANALYSIS

In the development and testing of this component of the urban recreation model, the inputs assigned to the people were generated by the researchers. These inputs were based, in part, on Baltimore City's recreation program. In addition, the scope of the study was limited to urban playgrounds as recreation facilities and to children's usage of these facilities. Although the scope was limited to a specific type of urban recreation, it is felt the procedure is applicable to other types of urban recreation.

Demand Analysis

Variables Affecting Urban Recreation

The demand for recreation supplied by urban playgrounds was measured by attendence at the playgrounds. Attendence at these playgrounds is an output measure of the desire for recreation in competition with all other available alternative activities. This attendence or use of a playground is a natural expression of a recreation activity, not a reported or desired activity.

Many different variables affect the attendence of urban playgrounds. One of the important user considerations is the user's age, since children's desire for specific recreation activities and facilities varies with age [3, 10]. To investigate the importance of this variation, the children sampled were classified into three relatively homogeneous age groups:

1. Between 5 and 7.
2. Between 8 and 11.
3. Between 12 and 15.

The use of a playground was also considered to be a function of alternative recreational activities available to the children. These activities could take place at "competing" public playgrounds or in the children's neighborhood. The approach used in the study was to consider both private and public competition. The distance between the nearest alternative public playground was used as a measure of the playground's public competition, and the total number of swings and swimming or wading pools in the children's neighborhood was used as a measure of the playground's private competition. Another variable thought to be important in the attendance at playgrounds was the child's family income.

Income is often used as a surrogate for measuring the socio-economic characteristics of individuals and groups [2, 3, 10, 12].

The location of the user with respect to the playground is an important consideration in determining recreation demand; distance provides the necessary linkage between the user and the recreation activity. In past studies of recreation demand, the distance from the facility to the user has been shown to be the most important variable, and usage has been found to vary inversely with distance.

The quality of the facility also influences one's use of that facility. Quality was measured by the type of playground, its size, and whether it has supervision [12]. The three types of playgrounds that existed in Baltimore, Maryland, were:

1. An "asphalt jungle"—playground with an asphalt surface and a few swings and slides
2. A type 1 playground with a recreation center offering activities such as arts and crafts, movies, and passive games
3. A type 2 playground with a swimming pool.

The playgrounds were grouped into two sizes: small (less than two acres) and large (greater than two acres but less than six acres). Supervision at a playground is another measurement of a playground's quality. This supervision allows the children's parents to permit their children to use the playground with some confidence of their children's safety. It also minimizes unnecessary confrontation between children of different ages, sex, and race. A preliminary survey of Baltimore's playgrounds revealed that playgrounds without supervision were used sparingly and in many cases not at all. Because it would be difficult to obtain data from these nonsupervised playgrounds, only supervised playgrounds were used in the study.

Demand Submodel

The data used in the development of the demand submodel were gathered from 24 playgrounds during the summers of 1968 and 1969. These playgrounds were cross-classified according to their type (three types) and size (two sizes), with four playgrounds for each cell of this 2×3 cross-classification. To obtain a cross-section of the population of Baltimore, Maryland, locations of these playgrounds were selected from several socio-economic areas of Baltimore.

The regression formulation, Eq. 1, was used to determine the demand for recreation at urban playgrounds. Distance is measured by the number of street crossings between the playground and the population areas. It is expressed in the formulation as "rings" of equal distance surrounding the playground.

$$Y_{ij} = b_0 + b_1 X_{ij}^{-a} + b_2 X_{2i} + b_3 X_{3i} + b_4 X_{4i} + b_5 X_{5j} + e \qquad (1)$$

where i = population or area index.

$\quad j$ = playground location index.

$\quad Y_{ij}$ = rate of attendance from i to j or [(number of children per day in area i who came to playground j)/(total number of children in area i)].

$\quad X_{ij}$ = distance from area i to playground j.

$\quad X_{2i}$ = average income of area i as expressed in the 1960 Census.

$\quad X_{3i}$ = number of swimming pools in area i.

$\quad X_{4i}$ = number of swing and slide sets in area i.

$\quad X_{5j}$ = distance from j to the closest playground.

$\quad b_i$ = coefficients.

$\quad a$ = distance coefficient.

$\quad e$ = error term.

Over 2000 samples were taken during the summers of 1968 and 1969. This information was used to develop 18 demand equations, each specific to age, type, and sizes—$3 \times 3 \times 2$. A statistical analysis was run on the individual demand models and a covariance analysis was conducted on the grouping parameters of age, type, and size[4].

A summary of the results of a statistical analysis of the demand models are:

1. The distance variable—measured by the minimum number of street crossings and expressed as $1/d^2$—is the most important variable in determining the rate of attendance for urban playgrounds. Information obtained from these demand equations indicate that a threshold distance exists beyond which no one uses the playground.
2. Other variables in the regression model are less significant than the distance variable, but in many cases do contain a significant amount of the variance.
3. The income variable was found to be correlated with the recreation alternatives and not statistically significant.
4. The R^2's of all demand equations were significant at the 0.001 level and ranged in value from 0.4 to 0.9. The F values of all equations were also significant at the 0.001 level.

The results of the covariance analysis are:

1. The rate of attendance at the playgrounds is significantly (0.001) dependent on the size and type of playground.
2. The rate of attendance at the playgrounds is significantly (0.05) dependent on the age groupings.

Site Location Submodel

Submodel Formulation

Formulation of a mathematical model for optimal location of public facilities is often difficult. The objective function and the constraint set are not always easily defined in quantifiable terms or measurable in commensurate units. Consequently, surrogates are often used in place of the desired variables. Some of the surrogates that have been used in the public facility location models are minimum time traveled by the users, average distance traveled by the users, and the maximum distance or time between facilities [9, 11, 14].

The objective function of the playground location model is the maximization of playground usage in the entire system. Sites which are to be considered for possible playground development are identified prior to using the model. At each of these potential playground sites it is possible to build one of three types of playgrounds. The relationship between playground location and usage of the playgrounds is obtained by dividing the study area into discrete population centers and applying the demand model to these areas to obtain the estimate of usage.

To avoid the interaction problem that exists between two neighboring playground sites, each population center was allowed to assign itself to only one potential playground site—the nearest one. This limitation did not seem to be a serious problem, because the data on existing use patterns supported the closest playground assumption, and it also allowed an easier model formulation. Budget restrictions on the model are handled by specifying the number of playgrounds of each type that are to be constructed.

Location Submodel

The model developed for the location of urban playgrounds is

$$\text{Maximize facility use} = \sum_{k=1}^{3} \sum_{j=1}^{n} \sum_{i=1}^{m} S_{ij}^{k} X_{ij}^{k}$$

subject to

1. $\sum_{k=1}^{3} \sum_{j=1}^{n} X_{ij}^{k} = 1 \qquad i = 1, 2, 3, \ldots\ldots\ldots\ldots, m$

2. $\sum_{k=1}^{3} Y_{j}^{k} \leqslant 1 \qquad j = 1, 2, 3, \ldots\ldots\ldots\ldots, n$

3. $\sum_{j=1}^{n} Y_{j}^{k} = M^{k} \qquad k = 1, 2, 3$

4. $X_{ij}^{k} \leqslant Y_{j}^{k} \qquad \begin{aligned} & i = 1, 2, 3, \ldots\ldots\ldots\ldots, m \\ & j = 1, 2, 3, \ldots\ldots\ldots\ldots, n \\ & k = 1, 2, 3 \end{aligned}$

5. $X_{ij}^{k}, Y_{j}^{k} \{0, 1\} \qquad \begin{aligned} & i = 1, 2, \ldots\ldots\ldots\ldots, m \\ & j = 1, 2, \ldots\ldots\ldots\ldots, n \\ & k = 1, 2, 3 \end{aligned}$

where i = population index.
  j = facility site index.
  k = facility type index.
  m = number of population nodes (centers).
  M^{k} = number of facilities of type k to be constructed.
  n = number of facility locations.
  S_{ij}^{k} = number of individuals expected to go from population center i to facility of type k at location j, if j is the facility which serves center i.
  X_{ij}^{k} = 1 if population node i assigns to type k facility at location j;
      = 0 otherwise.
  Y_{j}^{k} = 1 if there is a facility of type k at location j;
      = 0 otherwise.

The objective function coefficients, S_{ij}^{k}, are determined from the demand model. The first constraint requires the population center to be assigned to only one playground, and the next constraint allows only one type of playground to exist at a specific location. The budget constraint which is the third constraint, is exogenous to the model and is expressed in the number of playgrounds to be built instead of in dollars available [7, 13]. The final constraint provides the linkage between the demand for and supply of playgrounds. It states that a playground must exist in order for an assignment to be made to it.

Analysis of the Results of the Location Model Application

The location model was tested on 3800 acres in Baltimore, Maryland containing 767 city blocks. This area was selected because of the minimum movement across the boundaries due to major highways, railroads, and other flow restrictive developments, and includes both high and low income population centers.

Twenty existing and potential playground locations were selected for verification of the model and application of alternative methods of development. Specifically, five existing playgrounds were tested to verify the model. Of these five, two playgrounds showed estimated usage that differed significantly from existing attendance. Further investigation revealed that the difference was due to the grouping of city blocks into population centers. Because relative attendance figures were sufficient for testing development alternatives, the grouping of city blocks was not altered.

The development alternatives investigated for 17 out of 20 playgrounds were:

1. Optimal distribution of the playgrounds.
2. Optimal distribution of 6 playgrounds to existing distribution of 11 playgrounds.
3. Optimal distribution of 6 playgrounds with political constraints to existing distribution of 11 playgrounds.
4. Optimal reassignment of existing 11 sites (maintain the same playground sites, but reassign types).
5. Optimal assignment of 11 playgrounds iteratively to an optimal location of 6 playgrounds.

The model was run on an IBM 7094 using an implicit enumeration algorithm with an imbedded transportation algorithm [1, 8]. The running time for 200 population centers and 20 potential locations with three types ranged between 30 and 88 seconds with 8–19 iterations.

The results of testing these four alternatives on the study area for two playgrounds of each type are given in Table 1 [6].

The optimal location, Alternative 1, would result in 160,940 children attending the area's playgrounds annually. Because no estimate was made on a projected existing trend, it is not possible to estimate the improvement for the entire system. However, by comparing the other alternatives with the existing 11 playgrounds and the optimal 17 playgrounds, a good relative understanding of the system is possible. Alternative 2 is probably

Table 1   Annual attendance for different alternative developments.

		Number of Playgrounds	
		11	17
Alternative			
Existing		81,148	
Alternative 1	Optimal location		160,940
Alternative 2	Optimal location/existing base		130,622
Alternative 3	Optimal location/existing base/supervisory		112,500
Alternative 4	Reassignment of existing	115,650	
Alternative 5	Optimal location iteratively/optimal base	138,927	155,104

the most realistic approach because it adds to the existing playground distribution and does not start from a "no" playground situation. The improvement in attendance of over 59,000 is about 19% from the optimal attendance. Alternative 3 requires that an equal number of playgrounds be assigned in each political area. As a result of this constraint, there is only an increase of about 31,000 children which is about 32% below optimal and a loss of 18,000 children from Alternative 2—a loss of 13% to satisfy a political requirement. In Alternative 4, the existing distribution of playground types are reassigned to the existing 11 locations, resulting in a 42% increase of over 34,000 children. The last alternative was studied to compare the results of starting with an optimal base and then adding to it with those from just optimally locating all the playgrounds. The results showed a loss of only 5000 children or 3% for the stepwise approach. Therefore, for this study there seems to be little difference between optimally solving the system in stages and optimally solving the entire system.

SUMMARY

The regression analysis has indicated that it is possible to predict with reasonable success the demand for various types of urban recreation. By using demand submodels and other statistical techniques, it is possible to gain much information on the users of recreation facilities.

The resource allocation submodel has indicated that mathematical techniques exist that can aid in the efficient allocation of recreation resources. The technique developed in this paper is relatively efficient and is structured to input various types of input constraints and policies.

However, both of these techniques are only parts of the overall recreation model. It is necessary to include with these mathematical techniques a method of determining the needs and desires of the citizens so that this information can become inputs to the mathematical models and be used in analysis of alternative recreation programs. Citizen participation is also necessary in the often forgotten implementation phase.

REFERENCES

1. Balas, E. An additive algorithm for solving linear programs with zero-one variables, *Operations Research*, Vol. 13 (July–August 1965), 517–546.
2. Battelle Memorial Institute, Columbus Laboratories, *Evaluating Urban Core Usage of Waterways and Shorelines*, Office of Water Resources Research, U.S. Department of the Interior, 1971.
3. Cicchetti, C. J., Seneca, J. J., and Davidson, P. *The Demand and Supply of Outdoor Recreation*, Bureau of Economic Research, New Brunswick, N.J.: Rutgers, The State University, 1969.
4. Dee, N. and Liebman, J. C. A statistical study of attendance at urban playgrounds, *Journal of Leisure Research*, Vol. 2, No. 3, (Summer 1970).
5. Dee, N. *Urban Playgrounds: An Optimal Location Model* (unpublished Doctoral Thesis), Baltimore, M.; John Hopkins University, 1970.
6. Dee, N. and Liebman, J. C. Urban recreation: Demand analysis and site selection, presented at the 12th American meeting of the *Institute of Management Sciences*, October 1971.
7. Efroymson, M. A. and Ray, T. L. A branch and bound algorithm for plant location, *Operations Research*, Vol. 4 (3), (1966).
8. Geoffrion, A. M. *An Improved Implicit Enumeration Approach for Integer Programming*, RM-5644-PR, Santa Monica, Calif.: Rand Corporation, 1968.
9. Marks, D. H., ReVelle, C. S., and Liebman, J. C. Mathematical models of location: A review, *Journal of Urban Planning and Development Division*, American Society of Civil Engineering, Vol. 96, (March 1970).
10. Planning Foundation of America, *Modeling Recreation for Use in a Metropolitan Region*, U.S. Department of Housing and Urban Development, 1969.
11. ReVelle, C. S., Marks, D. H., and Liebman, J. C. An analysis of private and public sector location models, *Management Science*, Vol. 16 (11), (July 1970).
12. Seneca, J. J., Davidson, P., and Gerard, A. F. An analysis of recreational use of the TVA lakes, *Land Economics*, Vol. 44, (1968).
13. Spielburg, K. Plant location with generalized search origin, *Journal of the Institute of Management Sciences*, Vol. 16, No. 3, (1969).
14. Teitz, M. *Toward a Theory of Urban Public Facility Location*, Working Paper 65, prepared for the 14th annual meeting of the R.S.A., 1967.

POLLUTION

18

Management of the Environment

HERMAN E. KOENIG, DEAN L. HAYNES, AND P. DAVID FISHER

Dept. of Electrical Engineering, Michigan State University, East Lansing, Michigan

1. INTRODUCTION

The environment may be defined as the complex of biotic, climatic, edaphic, hydrologic, social, and cultural factors that act upon an ecological community and ultimately determines its form and survival. Because of his intellect, man is capable of significantly modifying his environment. On one hand he strives to improve the human habitat, while on the other hand these very activities often contribute to its subtle degradation. These degradations usually result from the general lack of concern for the delicate balances that often exist within ecological communities.

Only when these disruptions to the environment pose an immediate threat does man seem to become alarmed. For example, it became apparent in the 1950s that fallout from nuclear weapons tests might result in worldwide genetic mutations. The partial test-ban treaty adopted in 1964 was a direct result of governments being sufficiently concerned about radiation hazards to seek some common policy of self-restraint. Governments responded because of public anxiety about the prospect of these genetic mutations[1].

Before the test-ban treaty was signed, Carson's *Silent Spring* [2] drew attention to the extravagent use of pesticides in American agriculture. Carson described how these pesticides were at times both counterproductive and the cause of unexpected damage to various ecological communities that man traditionally counted on for his survival. Although the long-term effects of the excessive use of certain pesticides were potentially as damaging as radiation from nuclear weapons tests, public apathy kept governments from responding as they did with respect to the adoption of the test-ban treaty. This public apathy was due in part to the fact that the ill effects of pollutants, such as pesticides, are generally first apparent in wildlife, unlike the prospect of immediate genetic mutations in humans.

Man's vantage point by 1972 was completely different from what it was in 1962 when *Silent Spring* was first published because the effects of widespread misuse and mismanagement of the environment by then were reaching crisis proportions in many regions of the earth. Excessive noise, eye-watering exhaust fumes, respiratory ailments, dwindling freshwater supplies, overharvesting of renewable resources, and the exhausting of traditional energy sources made people aware and alarmed about the deteriorating state of the environment. Public anxiety led the United States Government and other governments of the world to become sufficiently concerned so as to initiate the establishment of national policies designed to regulate activities which could cause either short-term or long-range damage to the environment.

The nuclear test-ban treaty was relatively easy to implement because the decision to violate the treaty rested in the hands of only a few people. Also, monitoring the atmosphere to detect violators was also relatively easy because of the nature and source of the contaminant. Legislation regulating pollution from factories, power plants, sewage treatment plants, automobiles, ships, etc. is not nearly as easy to enforce because of the exceedingly large number of individuals and institutions responsible for polluting, as well as the spatial distribution of the sources of pollution. Furthermore, a more complex set of social, political, and economic factors complicate matters. A sophisticated environmental monitoring communication and data management network is required to properly manage man's ecosystem.

2. A SURVEY OF THE CURRENT ROLE OF COMPUTERS IN ENVIRONMENTAL MANAGEMENT

Computers are playing an auspicious role in managing the environment since man is finding applications for them in virtually every aspect of ecosystem design and management. For example, computers are used to control the sequencing and timing of on-line data acquisition tasks and for reducing and storing the resulting data; they control analytic laboratory instruments such as gas chromatographs and spectrophotometers and then manage the voluminous data derived from the instruments. Predictive, computer-based models accept the real-time information required to understand the state of an ecosystem, and then, these same models are used to provide both early warnings of adverse trends and a summary of the most probable effects different management strategy alternatives will have on the ecosystem.

In the area of environmental management, the computer is used by basic and applied researchers, by governmental policy making and regulatory groups, and of course, by both the public and private sectors of society involved in the day-to-day, on-line management of the environment. The purpose of this section is to review a few representative applications computers have found in the area of environmental management.

Monitoring and Managing Waste Water Sewer Systems [3]

San Francisco, like many of the older cities in the United States, has a combined sewer system; that is, domestic and industrial waste water and the runoff from rainfall are transported in one set of pipes. The basic system is depicted in Fig. 1. When there is no runoff due to rainfall, the waste water moves from its sources into collector sewers, then into interceptor sewers, and finally into one of three sewage treatment plants. These plants nominally handle 39 billion gallons of dry-weather waste per year, while their capacity is well over 100 billion gallons per year. This safety factor was included to account for rainstorm runoff. But during a rainstorm the quantity of sewage may rise to a rate that is as much as 100 times the average rate for the dry-weather volume, resulting in massive overflows of raw sewage into San Francisco Bay and the Pacific Ocean. On the average, such overflows occur 82 times during the year.

The disheartening fact is that when the sewer system was modernized and the sewage treatment plants built, engineers designed the system so that only on rare occasions would the total flow exceed the capacity of the system. This error was due to an invalid assumption on the part of the engineers. The design was based on a determination of instantaneous rainfall intensities, how long rain falls, and how often particular combinations of rainfall intensities and durations occur. Once these facts were known, a statistical analysis resulted in a recommendation for the total specifications for the sewer system. In the case of San Francisco, data for making this analysis was obtained from a single rain gage which sat on top

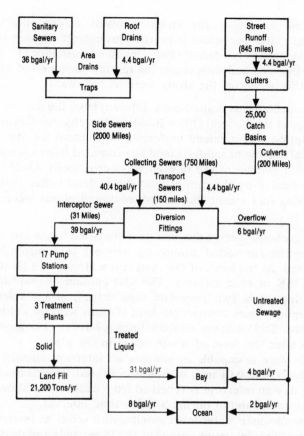

Fig. 1 A block diagram illustrating the sewer system in San Francisco (Giessner et al., 1973).

of the Federal Office Building. Data had been collected at this one site for 62 years and the rainfall model used assumed that rain falls uniformly over the entire area drained by the sewers.

Before trying to correct the defects in the system, the city's sanitary planning and studies engineers set out to determine what kinds of waste flow were involved. One aspect of the study involved a computer analysis of 60 years of data from the single rain gage coupled with sewage volume data. This analysis led them to conclude that rainfall intensity turned out to be far less important than knowledge of the relation between volume of storage to treatment capacity in a given period of time.

The second aspect of the study involved determining the actual temporal and spatial variations in rainfall throughout the area serviced by the sewer system. This latter study involved installing 17 rain gages throughout the area and then recording rainfall for a period of one year. Results of this aspect of the study were as follows:

1. Data collected was dramatically different from the data derived from the gage at the Federal Office Building, thereby invalidating both the assumption that it rained uniformly throughout the area, and that, the total volume of rainfall could be estimated from a single gage.
2. The total volume of the rainfall was consistently 15–25% less than that indicated by the rain gage at the Federal Office Building. This surprising fact meant that added treatment plants were not necessary.

The data gathered during this one-year study led to the implementation of the computer-controlled monitoring network that currently exists in San Francisco. At the heart of the system is a Honeywell H316 minicomputer with 16K of core memory. The unit contains a real-time clock, a power-fail interrupt, two magnetic tape drives, and a teletypewriter. Leased telephone lines connect the field stations with the central facility. Thirty of the field stations contain tipping-bucket rain gages and 120 stations monitor the level of waste water in the pipes.

Each rain gage is capable of sending an interrupt signal back to the computer each time 0.01 inch of rain is collected. The computer records the time of day an interrupt is received from each field station and keeps track of the total rainfall during a given time interval.

Each remote waste-water-level monitor also sends an interrupt back to the computer. This interrupt arrives every 15 seconds and its duration is a measure of the level of waste water in a given sewer line.

This 15 second cycle establishes the raw data recording cycle. From the 120 waste-water monitors come 480 measurements each and every minute. At the end of each minute this information is written in a single record on magnetic tape, and at the end of this record, the accumulated rainfall data is also written. In addition, five-minute data summaries are stored on magnetic tape along with hourly summaries of sewer levels, accumulated rainfall, and peak rainfall intensities. Even with all this information, the computer is busy only 10% of the time.

Computer generated maps are regular output of the computer. These maps graphically illustrate how rainstorms move across the city with time and how the sewer system is responding with time in different parts of the city. This data base is currently being used to develop predictive models that will eventually be suitable for real-time management of the sewer system.

The basic management strategy now under development is the following: the total treatment capacity of the city will be allocated to different segments of the city at different times. Decisions will be based upon the way rainfall varies with time at any given point and from point to point at any given time during a storm. This approach will maximize the effectiveness of the existing storage and treatment facility and will serve as a sound basis for determining future waste-water storage and treatment needs.

An Integrated Monitoring System for Water Quality Management in the Ohio Valley [4]

In the early 1950s, the Ohio River Valley Water Sanitation Commission (ORSANCO) inaugurated a manually operated river quality monitoring program [4]. Water samples were analyzed using conventional analytical laboratory instruments, and although the program systematically compiled and evaluated river data on a regional basis, it left much to be desired. The average cost of collecting and analyzing a single sample was $2.20, thereby making the cost of effectively operating the monitoring network unrealistically high in terms of the willingness of state governments to fund the operation. This limited the frequency with which samples could be collected and analyzed. Second, the time lag between sample collection and the time analytical results were summarized, prohibited the use of the monitoring system in the on-line management of the river. The data could only be used to chart the long-term deterioration of the river and not for rapidly identifying pollution and taking corrective action.

By the late 1950s, ORSANCO began to consider alternate monitoring systems and, after two years of research and development, built a prototype field monitor and a central receiving station. The objective of the prototype was to overcome the deficiencies of the earlier monitoring schemes by measuring water quality characteristics automatically and then by telemetering the results to the central receiving station for further analysis, as well as for decision making.

This prototype installation clearly demonstrated the feasibility of the approach, and by 1968, the monitoring system consisted of eight field stations on the Ohio River, six field stations on its tributaries, a central receiving station, and a data-processing center. This network is still operating today. All field stations communicate with the central receiving station over leased teletype-grade lines. Each of the field stations is capable of automatically collecting data for the purposes of determining the following water quality characteristics: pH, oxidation-reduction potential (redox), chloride, dissolved oxygen, conductivity, water temperature, and solar radiation.

ORSANCO headquarters automatically interrogates each field station on an hourly basis. This sampling interval was selected as adequate for evaluating the variations in water quality on the basis of analyzing over 2 million data samples. Seven years experience lead ORSANCO to conclude that computer-controlled telemetering of the data back to the central receiving station has two distinct advantages over on-site recording. First, the data are ready for processing and decision making as soon as received. Second, the method enables the immediate detection of equipment malfunctions and automatically alerts maintenance personnel to potential problems.

In order to automatically troubleshoot the system, each time a field station is interrogated several tests are made by the central computer:

1. Every transmission from a remote station includes a series of test signals. These signals are used to determine if the various components of a given field station and communication equipment are functioning properly. From these test signals, it is determined if the power supplies at the field station are operating at their proper levels, if the communication equipment transmission lines are functioning properly, if water is passing through the flow cell of the monitor at a proper rate, and whether there are any calibration adjustments which must be made in software with the incoming data.
2. A station check insures that appropriate limits of data acceptibility have been selected for data from a particular station. This check includes both absolute limits as well as proper monthly limits.
3. Once a decision has been made to accept the data, each sensor is read three times to insure repeatability.

At the heart of the monitoring system is an IBM 1130 computing system with 8K of memory, a disk pack, an 1134 paper tape reader, a 1055 paper tape punch, a 1442 card real-punch unit, an 1132 medium speed printer, and a 029 interpreting key punch. The total cost of leasing the data-processing equipment, leasing the telephone lines, and maintaining and servicing the complete monitoring and data reduction facility is 11 cents per data item. This compares with the $2.20 per data item for the manual data acquisition and data-processing approach.

Over the past decade, ORSANCO has used this integrated monitoring system to develop a better understanding of the total ecology of the Ohio River watershed. They are finding that very subtle relationships exist between downstream and upstream water conditions. For example, a certain city was having difficulty maintaining desired dissolved oxygen levels in the Ohio River below the outfall from its sewage treatment plant. The city spent a considerable amount of money to upgrade its sewage treatment facility but to no avail. Further studies found that upriver water conditions coupled with the outfall made it impossible to meet the standards set. In another case, a slug of acid from a reservoir moved more than 100 miles downriver before there was a fish kill. A combination of factors, not just the presence of the acid, led to the fish kill. In fact, had it not been for the monitoring system following the movement of the acid downriver, the blame for this kill might have been laid to the wrong parties.

Results to date from this automated monitoring facility on the Ohio River seem to indicate that before the network can be used routinely as a component in the on-line management of the watershed, much work must be done in modeling and simulating the Ohio River system so that the total effects of both man and nature are understood.

Remote Sensing the Environment

As described previously, the Ohio River Valley Water Sanitary Commission's water quality monitoring system is comprised of a network of field stations; each station samples one point along the River or along one of its tributaries. In order to properly characterize the state of the River—both spatially and temporally—two important questions must be answered: How many independent sampling points must exist along the River and how often must each of these points be interrogated? OR-SANCO determined that sampling intervals of one hour was sufficient[4] and Anderson[5] drew similar conclusions in his studies of the Mississippi River. The question of how many sites are required is not as easy to answer; in fact, the siting of remote stations would have to be determined by the terrain, by the number of towns, the hydrological conditions of the river basin, the climate, the amount and type of industry along the river, as well as by the basic objectives of the monitoring network.

Remote sensing of the waterway would tend to overcome this spatial sampling problem. When remote sensing from either an airplane or satellite is utilized, the user takes advantage of the following: remote sensing provides a detailed overall view of the system under observation, usually from a distant vantage point; it provides a detailed image record to be used to detect changes in selected regions with time; it can expand the limits of the human eye by sensing parts of the electromagnetic spectrum not utilized in human vision[6].

Because of the disproportionately large role the eye of man plays in his experiences, a natural desire on his part would be to sense pollutants with an appropriate imaging apparatus and then translate this two-dimensional signal into a picture that could either by interpreted manually or automatically by a machine. This desire has led to the development of an entire family of computer-based image acquisition and image processing systems, as well as a full range of sensors capable of detecting everything from oil slicks (Munday and Penncy, 1971) to thermal plumes[6]. These sensors are capable of obtaining distinct signatures for various classes of pollutants. These signatures are obtained using passive or active radiometeoric techniques at either radio, microwave, infrared, visible, or ultraviolet wavelengths. Regardless of the portion of the spectrum used, the data acquisition approach is always the same: a certain region is scanned by the sensor and the information is stored on magnetic tapes. The information is then fed into a computer and a "visual" image is constructed for interpretation by either man or a machine. Details of sensor theory and sensor systems are described in a book edited by the National Research Council[7], and a good review of picture processing is presented in a book by Rosenfeld[8]. Because remote sensing, as we know it today, would be impossible without the data processing and storage capabilities of the digital computer, it would be worthwhile to consider the function of the computer in analyzing the voluminous data derived from remote sensing systems.

This role is reviewed by Andrews *et al.*[9] and by Nagy[10]. Andrews *et al.* are principally concerned with image restoration so that a trained observer can manually interpret the resultant images. Nagy[10] spends little time discussing these issues but rather outlines the types of computer algorithms required to replace the trained observer by a machine.

Andrews *et al.*[9] partition the image restoration problem into four distinct parts: computer image coding; computer image detection; computer image restoration; and finally, computer image enhancement.

The principal goal in image coding is to remove any redundancies in the image before transmitting it across a digital communication link and before storing the image in computer memory. This image coding step is critical because of the vast amount of information contained in just a single raw image. For example, consider just a single frame with spatial resolution and contrast, roughly equivalent to an image on a television set. Over 10^6 data bits would be required to adequately characterize such a raw image. Bits of information discarded at the outset due to redundancy, would not only save valuable storage space, but also would reduce the overall computation time required for the computer to analyze a given data set.

The image detection process involves passing the coded signal through a matched filter. This signal processing step maximizes the signal-to-noise ratios for processing purposes. The objective of image restoration is to recover losses suffered in the imaging and sending system due to unavoidable degradations. These degradations must, of course, be fully understood ahead of time. Image enhancement, although having similar goals as image restoration, attempts to improve the quality of the image without prior knowledge of any degrading phenomena. Image enhancement might involve sharpening or dulling edges in an image or artifically coloring an image to achieve certain desired effects.

Image enhancement, as defined above, is a heuristic tool often used to highlight certain features in an image. At this point, the restored and enhanced image is either turned over to a trained observer for analysis or a computer is utilized to extract information from the picture.

Nagy[10] divides the process of classifying objects in an image using a machine into four steps: preprocessing (image restoration and enhancement); object isolation; feature extraction; and, finally, application of a decision scheme. Preprocessing is normally necessary to put the raw input data into a suitable form for the steps that follow. Object isolation separates the image into regions containing one object or a portion of an object. This step will allow the "background" to be discarded, thus potentially saving much computer storage and computation later in the object classification procedure. The feature extraction procedure extracts information useful in classifying the objects, and the decision scheme determines the classification of each object.

To utilize remotely sensed data in environmental monitoring an a priori body of knowledge must exist concerning the general features of the system under observation; for example, the general characteristics of discharges from various sources adjacent to a body of water[11]. The problem of remote identification is thus one of detecting a given substance or condition among known ambient contaminants. Because of the high technology level and high cost currently required, remote sensing is only a viable data source if no alternate technique is feasible. Some of the problems associated with using remote sensing in managing the environment are described in a later section.

Computer Simulations

In the three examples presented in the previous section, computers were used extensively for timing and sequencing data acquisition tasks, for manipulating raw data, for storing data and data summaries, and for outputting, in a convenient form, data summaries for inspection and interpretation by trained observers. In each case, the data acquisition and data management tasks performed by the computer proved cost effective and enabled the data summaries to be available in time for real-time control strategies to be implemented.

Successful implementation of control strategy alternatives is impossible unless predictive models are available, which are capable of accepting real-time data that characterizes the current state of the particular ecosystem. The model must then provide both early warnings of adverse trends as well as a summary of the most probable effects different management strategy alternatives will have on the future state of the ecosystem.

Because of the complexity of the ecosystem these predictive—or forecasting—models are themselves computer-based. Furthermore, the spectrum of most probable effects of different management strategies are often only understood through the collection of vast amounts of actual data, coupled with computer simulation designed to verify the "goodness" and predictive capabilities of the models. The simulations often speed up the process of developing and implementing the management plan because simulations replace the need for certain field experiments— experiments that might require months or even years of field testing. Representative examples illustrating the utility of computer simulations in developing predictive models are presented below.

Behar[12] has developed a model that simulates the distribution of total oxidants in California's South Coast Air Basin. As a result of these simulations, knowledge of the spatial distribution of pollutants allows calculation of dose rates for the entire population within the region, thereby eliminating the important constraint that in the past required that the sample population be located within a certain radius of an air-monitoring station. These simulations, in effect, helped define the optimal set of air-monitoring stations as well as the minimal set of the sample population which must be observed.

Malin[13] developed two models—EXPLOR and NEXUS—to simulate air pollution over roads. The simulation models account for the topography, road beds, and weather conditions. The movement of particulate matter was studied under various topological and climatic conditions along with the dispersal of carbon monoxide, unburned hydrocarbon, nitrogen oxide, and lead. The results of the simulation compared favorably with actual roadway conditions on a Los Angeles street. Ultimately, this type of simulation will be used in the design of new streets and highways since knowledge gained through the computer simulations will be used to design highway systems to maximize the dispersal of pollutants that might exist.

The NEXUS simulation model was further refined by Sklarew *et al.*[14] and applied to the study of photochemical fog in Los Angeles. Demergian *et al.*[15] also conducted simulation on photochemical smog but their emphasis was to uncover the relative importance of the various intermediate compounds in photochemical smog reactions.

The above examples dealt with computer simulations that were designed to provide a better understanding of processes which contribute to undesirable concentration of pollutants in the atmosphere. Each of the simulations was first used to mimic an existing aspect of the ecosystem and then each was used in a predictive mode to suggest methods of redesigning aspects of the ecosystem in order to minimize the adverse effects due to man-made air pollution. Simulations dealing with virtually every aspect of air pollution can be found in the literature. Most of these deal with modeling the sources of pollution and the dispersal of pollutants under various topographic and climatic conditions. Similar computer simulations are being used in studying both noise pollution and water pollution.

3. THE APPLICATION OF COMPUTER-BASED MODELS IN THE DESIGN AND MANAGEMENT OF THE ENVIRONMENT

The computer-based models discussed briefly in the previous section dealt primarily with the simulation of specific aspects of man's environment. There are, in fact, several broad application areas for ecosystem models in the design and management of the environment.

Initially, the model is used as a research tool to acquire a comprehensive understanding of an ecosystem. The "goodness" of the model is judged ultimately in terms of its ability to describe the observable relationships that exist between a given species and its biotic and abiotic environment. In effect, the model summarizes the degree of understanding that has been acquired concerning a particular ecosystem. As a research tool, the predictive capabilities of the model are used to suggest additional experiments, which must be conducted in order to properly establish all of the basic mechanisms responsible for determining the state of the ecosystem at any point in time. In short, the first application of a model is to provide the foundation for conceptualizing the theoretical principles that govern the behavior of the specific ecosystem and then motivate their generalization to encompass other similar types of ecosystems.

In the second application, the predictive capabilities of the model are used as a guide to understand the consequences of artificial perturbations on the ecosystem. For example, suppose that a certain insect pest is accidentally introduced into a region and begins to multiply rapidly. In a few years the past might reach such numbers that it could have a serious economic impact on agriculture in the region. The ecosystem model for this pest could be used to test the effects of introducing a parasite which would attack the larvae of the pest. If models exist for both the parasite and pest, then computer simulations could be used to determine the feasibility of using the parasite to control the pest population. The parasite would represent an artificial perturbation to the pest's ecosystem. If the parasite was clearly an unacceptable form of control, good pest and parasite ecosystem models would so indicate, thereby saving both a substantial amount of time (usually it takes years to establish a parasite population) and money. This condition might result because either climatic or soil conditions are not amenable to the establishment of the parasite population or because of climatic factors, the time synchronisms of the pest and parasite are such as to prohibit significant parasitization. The purpose of models in this second set of applications would then be to test the feasibility (or consequences) of introducing various artificial perturbations into the ecosystem. These perturbations may represent events or combinations of events that have never formally been observed but yet have a non-zero probability of occurring, or they may represent control options that might ultimately be used to manage the ecosystem.

Many ecological communities are strongly affected by minor changes in the environment; in particular, climatic factors often dramatically affect the developmental rates and survival rates of many species. Therefore, because of the stochastic nature of the environment, predictive models characterizing these ecosystems will only have a capability of providing insight into the short-term trajectory of the ecosystem. To properly track the ecosystem with time, the models must be repeatedly resynchronized with the actual ecosystem; consequently, the ecosystems must be placed periodically under surveillance. The problem of ascertaining the current state of such an ecosystem is not an easy task, principally because of the time required to conduct a biological survey. The third important aspect of the computer-based models is as follows: the models must be structured so that only sparse information concerning the current state of the ecosystem need be collected. Then, with the aid of the model, this limited set of data could be used to determine the complete state of the ecosystem. In general, abiotic aspects of the ecosystem are easily obtained. Hence, if possible, the models should be capable of being synchronized with abiotic information. The biological survey would only be used over the longer term for purposes of verifying the basic "goodness" of the model and for improving it.

The ultimate objective of developing the ecosystem models and the control strategy options is to manage the ecosystem. Successful management of any ecosystem is based on several factors. First, a viable set of control strategy options must be available for implementation. Second, the current state of the ecosystem must be known so that the predictive model and the actual ecosystem can be properly synchronized. Finally, these models must be capable of providing both early warnings of adverse trends and a summary of the most probable effects different management strategy alternatives will have on the ecosystem. Once management decisions have been made then the appropriate control measures must be implemented and at the proper time in order to be effective. This on-line ecosystem management system is schematically depicted in Fig. 2. Predictive models would also be required by government agencies involved in both policy making and regulation.

4. THE ON-LINE MANAGEMENT OF INSECTS PESTS

A detailed example is presented in this section to illustrate the vital role computer systems can play in the control of man's environment. The example deals with the problem of controlling insect pests. At the outset, it is important to note that pest management contains the salient features of numerous environmental questions facing society today since efficient

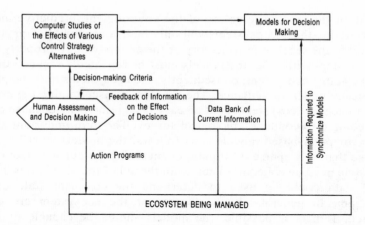

Fig. 2   Schematic diagram of an on-line ecosystem management system.

pest management embodies many of the complex interactions that characterize man's activity in his biotic and abiotic environment. As such, it has tremendous potential to lead the way into the future where environmental problems are considered as primary concerns rather than the primary product of man's activity.

The approach to pest management, which will be described, is being developed, implemented, and refined by scientists at Michigan State University. This coordinated research and development program was initiated in 1970 and has relied on the cooperative interactions of scientists in the various disciplines from agriculture, engineering, and natural science with endorsement and support from the Center for Environmental Quality, the Agricultural Experiment Station, the Agricultural Extension Service, the Division of Engineering Research at Michigan State University, the National Science Foundation, and the United States Department of Agriculture.

Multifactor Control of Insect Pests

The control of pest populations is an important aspect of agricultural production, forest management, and improvement of human habitats. Many biological organisms become pests only in response to man's activities. For example, the modern agricultural practice of planting large acreages of monoculture, often with crop species bred for a specific purpose, such as increased yields or ease of machine harvesting, frequently has led to outbreaks of damaging biological populations. When a potential pest is accidentally introduced from another geographical region into such an ecosystem, the absence of natural enemies and host resistance combined with the availability of an abundant food supply can lead to disastrous effects on the agricultural production. Certain cultural practices in agriculture can also aid a pest species by inhibiting its natural enemies.

The use of pesticides is only a short-run solution since the pests commonly build up a resistance to the chemicals in a relatively short time[15a]. This results in the need for a continuous development of new chemicals with a concomitant heavy economic investment in industrial research. A current estimate for development of a new pesticide is 10 million dollars. This represents an increase of about 6 million dollars over the estimated developmental cost for the year 1969[16]. This high cost necessitates the development of broad-spectrum compounds to ensure sufficient volume of sales to return the investment. Unfortunately, such compounds also ensure greater environmental damage by destroying natural enemies of the pests and other beneficial organisms, as well as by polluting the soil and nearby streams. Pesticides entering human food chains constitute another undesirable feature. Failure of current pesticide policies clearly suggest the need for integrated control strategies as discussed at length by Conway[17] and Pimentel[18].

There exist many alternatives to pesticides as pest management tools. These include the development of plant resistances, control by parasites, predators and competitors, microbial controls, viruses, cultural controls such as crop rotation, planting schemes (temporal and spatial) and fertilization, chemical attractants and repellants, feeding deterrents, and sterilization. These individual control programs have evolved over the years into the classical approach to pest management schematically depicted in Fig. 3[19]. With this approach, the particulars of an existing or potential pest problem are first identified and then resources are directed into discipline-oriented research programs to screen chemical compounds for toxicity, prepare spray calendars, develop resistant host varieties, release parasites or predators, etc. Each technique is researched as if it singularly were, or must be, the total and ultimate solution to the particular pest problem. Extension workers recommend the technique which shows the greatest promise for achieving the control. If a particular technique fails, the alternatives are reevaluated and the research is continued. If secondary pests develop, a new program of research is initiated. The end result for any given pest situation is a set of recommen-

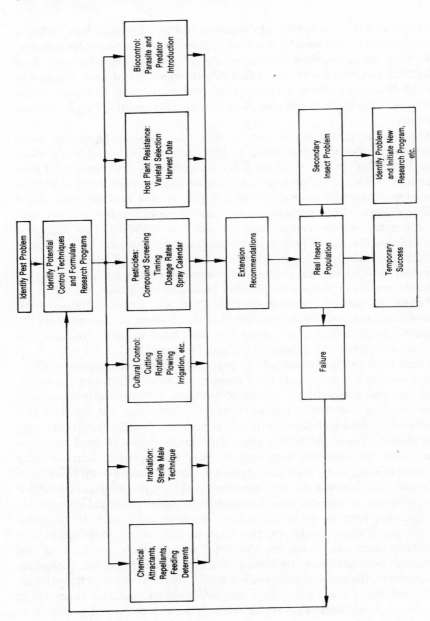

Fig. 3 Block diagram illustrating a classical approach to pest management.

dations with little or no flexibility to account for stochastic and regional variations in weather and field conditions or for biological variability and adaptability. No provision is made for integrating the various techniques of control into more comprehensive strategies based on the ecological characteristics of the total ecosystem. Evaluation of the alternative control techniques often ignores the dynamic interactions between the pest and its environment. The static recommendations that are specified, in addition to lacking flexibility, do not consider the age structures and time synchronisms of the interacting populations or the long-term economical and ecological constraints on the ecosystem. In many pest situations, the practical limits of such solutions have been reached. By its very nature, the classical approach to pest management research cannot fully exploit the potential of integrated strategies of control for improving reliability, as well as ecological and economical effectiveness.

An approach to pest management is depicted in Fig. 4 through which multifactor control strategies can be systematically developed and modified from region to region according to day-to-day changes in weather, field, and economic factors [19]. This on-line pest management system has the following essential operating features. Environmental data are obtained at selected sites around the state or region of interest. Summaries of this information are sent instantaneously, via communication channel A, to appropriate users for insertion into their predictive pest management models. This information together with the biological data obtained from communication channel C serves as the basis for synchronizing these models with the actual pest ecosystem and for refining parameter estimates. The models, which incorporate the dynamics of the interacting populations, the quantitative features of the various management strategies, and the economical and ecological constraints, are then used to identify both the control strategy alternatives and the points in time when critical biological measurements (communication channel B) are to be made on the pest ecosystem. These measurements characterize the state of the ecosystem and are used to periodically update the models and to monitor the effectiveness of the previous control strategies. Agricultural extension personnel in the pest management decision-making unit interrogate the management models (communication channel D) and then, on the basis of the output (communication channel E), alert growers (communication channel F) to the various control strategy options. This system must be capable of functioning in such a manner as to guarantee that recommendations can be quickly transferred to growers so that appropriate action programs can be implemented.

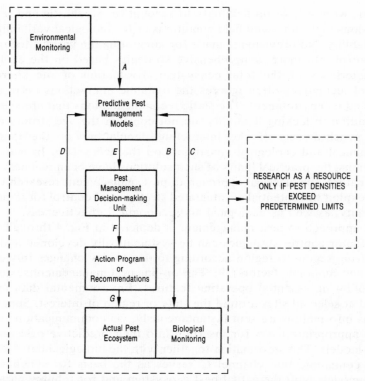

Fig. 4 Block diagram illustrating the basic components of a fully operational on-line pest management system.

The ultimate objective in managing any pest ecosystem is to maintain it, through selected controls, in such a state that the interactions of man, pests, and the environment are ecologically compatible and economically and socially feasible. This goal is achieved through the development and implementation of a series of dynamic models which use on-line measurements of selected biotic and abiotic features of the pest ecosystem to predict the effect of various control strategies, thus enabling agricultural scientists to obtain a quantitative evaluation of possible management alternatives. These models represent the keystone of the pest management decision-making unit, have high short-term predictability (three days or less) but considerably lower long-term predictability. This lower long-term predictability is due to the stochastic nature of the microclimate; consequently, it will be necessary to periodically update the models with current climatological and biological information. The principal functions of the pest management decision-making unit are as follows:

1. To take the real-time climatological and biological information required to describe the current state of the pest ecosystem and update the computer-based predictive pest management models.
2. To interrogate the models in order to determine the acceptable near-term control strategy options.
3. To communicate these options to growers in such a manner that the control measures can be properly implemented.

The problem of updating the models with current biological information is not simple. If a trained entomologist can look at a potential problem frequently during a season, he can evaluate population buildup of the pest and parasites, plant growth response, and the progression of damage. On the basis of these observations he can make highly accurate predictions. In any survey of pest numbers, the timing, the distribution of ages in the population, the width of the age classes, and distribution of mortality within age classes all affect the proportion of individuals counted in the population. If enough is known about these pest-specific factors, the proportion counted can be determined and the population level estimated. The time lag inherent in processing and interpreting biological information greatly limits the opportunity to implement an on-line pest management system. This point can be driven home by considering the following example.

Biological surveys associated with pest control and crop loss appraisal have traditionally been conducted manually by Survey Entomologists in cooperation with various state and federal agencies. At predetermined intervals of time throughout the growing season, workers collect selected samples of crops, pests, parasites, and predators. These samples are then brought back into the laboratory along with the abiotic data for analysis. Consider the biological survey currently associated with cereal leaf beetle ecosystem in North America[20]. Geographically, this survey included the states of Michigan, Ohio, Pennsylvania, Indiana, and Wisconsin, as well as the province of Ontario. There were a total of 26 test sites distributed throughout this geographical region. Each site contained 60 fields with the size of each field ranging between 5 and 50 acres. Six man-days per year were required for collecting the necessary field samples at each site. Biotic material collected included leaves, cereal leaf beetle larva, and adults, as well as parasites of the cereal leaf beetle. Two thousand man hours were required to analyze these samples and then one-man year for data reduction. After data reduction was completed, the information related to the biotic survey was ready for insertion into the predictive pest management models. The cost of this survey was approximately $35,000, and it was supported by the operating budget of numerous federal and state agencies.

The principal deficiencies with this method of data collection and analysis are as follows: long time delays—typically six months to a year—exist between the time data are collected and the results of the reduced data are inserted into the models; consequently, these delays make it impossible to use this information in order to properly characterize the current state of the pest-crop-parasite ecosystem. In most cases, the analyzed data cannot be used in the decision process until the next growing season. Furthermore, because of these lengthy delays, existing techniques for investigating the dynamic behavior of the pest-crop-parasite ecosystem cannot be used in the eventual "on-line" control of the ecosystem. The other major deficiency with this method of conducting the biotic survey is the uncertainty surrounding the validity of the data. This uncertainty arises due to the subjective techniques used to estimate leaf damage (Fig. 5), age distribution of the larval population,

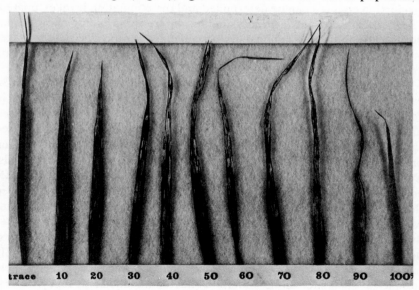

Fig. 5 Subjective classification of leaf damage caused by feeding cereal leaf beetles. (Photograph by C. Wilson, Purdue University.)

and the parasitization rate. Hence, it was not possible to assess the impact of this uncertainty on cereal leaf beetle pest management; however, strong evidence exists that indicates that the implementation of the on-line pest management program for the European red mite in Michigan was limited by "human" errors on the part of the technicians who analyzed the field samples[21].

These deficiencies in the historical approach to the biological survey render the pest management system, depicted in Fig. 4, virtually useless as far as on-line multifactor pest control within a given growing season at either the state or regional level is concerned. Several new approaches to the biological survey or combinations of approaches hold promise to overcoming these deficiencies. Each approach involves the application of sophisticated computer systems.

One possibility would be to improve the manual data collection and analysis procedures, thereby speeding up the process of collecting, analyzing, and reducing the data and by increasing, through cross-checking and correlation studies, the accuracy of the analyzed data. These improvements in the manual collection methods might be accomplished by defining a new and expanded role for Agricultural Extension. The extension component might include such diverse groups as vocational agriculture, Future Farmers of America (FFA), 4-H, sportsman's clubs, and biology classes, along with the traditional state and federal agencies. All of these groups are potential resources to help implement pest management programs, particularly, the biological survey aspect of the program. Because of the new demands placed upon this modified classical approach to the biological survey, an elaborate communication network would have to be established connecting these survey groups with a central data bank, as well as to the pest management decision-making unit. Specialists in the decision-making unit would be responsible for telling the survey personnel in the field what biological data must be collected and at what time and under what conditions. After the data has been collected and reduced, it would be immediately inserted in a centralized data bank. Specialists in the pest management decision-making unit would interrogate the data bank and update the predictive pest ecosystem models.

A second approach to overcoming the deficiencies in the present method of conducting the biological survey would be to automate portions of the survey. For example, field samples could be collected manually and then prepared for analysis; however, automated instruments could then be used to estimate leaf damage and crop development, to determine the age distribution of larval pest and predator populations and the parasitization rate. Output from these instruments would be coded electrical impulses which would be stored on paper or magnetic tape and then automatically inserted into a digital computer for analysis and data reduction. This approach has the potential of speeding up both the time required to analyze the field samples and the time required for data reduction. Furthermore, this approach has the additional advantage that, since machines and not people would be analyzing the data, subjective evaluation of the field samples would no longer interject unknown errors. Errors associated with the machines would, in principle, be well understood, provided, of course, the machines are always properly calibrated.

Synoptic evaluation of each field at each test site could be the key to acquiring, analyzing, and reducing the data so as to meet all of the practical constraints placed on the biological monitoring network by the actual pest ecosystem.

This synoptic approach would involve remotely sensing selected fields or agricultural regions from either elevated positions, airplanes, or satellites. Although this approach seems to hold great promise, several deficiencies—in terms of immediate utility—are evident. First, the predictive pest-crop-parasite ecosystem models currently under development for prototype pest management systems [22, 23] require pest, predator, and parasite population estimates as inputs to the predictive models, while the synoptic approach to the biological survey admits only crop damage estimates [24]. Therefore, if the synoptic approach is to have merit, the predictive models must be structured to accept crop damage as the principal biotic input from which the various population densities would be derived. Second, the remote sensors must be calibrated and must be reasonably accurate. Doubts concerning the accuracy of such a system are increased when one considers the natural variability of the fields due to cloud shadows, angle of the sun, moisture content of the atmosphere, biological variability due to the different types of vegetation, crop maturity, soil characteristics, crop row spacing, wind direction, and velocity, etc. [25]. Calibration of the remote sensor would require the acquisition of ground truth information. One haunting fear is that more data might have to be hand collected and analyzed in order to calibrate the remote sensing system than would actually be required for the biological survey itself. This, of course, is unknown at this time. Finally, it is apparent that the synoptic approach to data acquisition would imply that vast amounts of data would be at our disposal. Very large and fast computers coupled with sophisticated data management techniques would be required to efficiently store, retrieve, and analyze this voluminous data in order to extract the required information about the ecosystem under surveillance so that appropriate pest management strategies could be implemented.

The prospect of doing biological pattern recognition presents some formidable problems. The most obvious of these is shared by all image recognition systems: The raw data in the form of a large matrix is not suitable input for recognition algorithms. Initially, groups of points, which represent object shadows in the image plane, must be detected. Often it is necessary to massage the raw image using filtering or image enhancement techniques before the presence of an object can be established. Next, these objects must be subjected to various measurements so that they can be assigned to unlabeled pattern classes, and then, the identity of the pattern classes must be discovered using a pattern classification algorithm. Practical limitations on the size of the computer being used often forces one to relinquish image quality by lowering the planar and/or intensity resolution. This, in turn, has a concomitant effect on the ability to render and identify classes of objects. When an attempt is made to classify objects that are principally biotic, account must be taken of minor inhomogeneities implicit in any class owing to physiological and behavioral variances.

The success of any classification algorithm employed hinges upon those information compression techniques that preprocess the Quantized, Digital Picture Function (QDPF). Consequently, strong emphasis must be placed on research toward the development of flexible data structure analysis methods tailored to biological classificatory problems. To analyze the structure of the data, a multistage sequential feedback process that incorporates two clustering methods is usually employed[10]. The first method clusters in the image plane, I, and the second clusters in a multidimensional representation space, Z. This type of process is in line with the basic CPU memory constraints because it allows unnecessary portions of the QDPF to be discarded immediately after objects in the image plane are isolated. As seen later, this isolation generally requires only a very low resolution image while object classification generally requires a much higher resolution.

Figure 6 illustrates the various stages in the entire data management strategy. At the user's discretion, the QDPF, designated here by f_I, is subject to image enhancement and/or filtering to accentuate certain features such as edges and to remove spurious noise. The "massaged" QDPF, denoted $\hat{f}_I$, is then restricted, via an object isolation method, to a

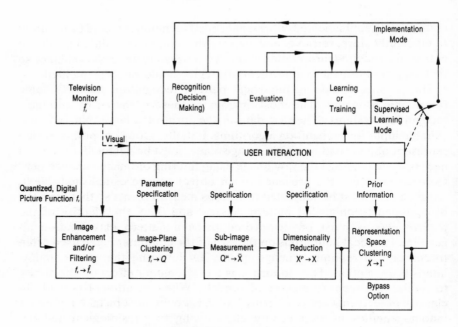

Fig. 6   The data management strategy.

collection of subsets representing "object shadows." The result is a collection of subimages Q. Next, each subimage is subjected to a single-valued measurement transformation $\mu : Q \to \bar{Z}$ where $\bar{Z}$ is a multidimensional measurement space. The user may also choose to reduce the dimensionality of $\bar{Z}$ by introducing a mapping $\rho : \bar{Z} \to Z$, where $\dim Z \leqslant \dim \bar{Z}$. For example, ρ might result from the application of a multidimensional scaling technique such as that given by Sammon (1969). The data structure analysis process may either terminate at this stage or the user may opt to subject the set X to a hierarchical clustering Γ or both are input to the classification process. This portion of the data management strategy operates in two modes: the supervised learning mode is to calibrate the entire pattern-recognition system. This is accomplished by evaluating the performance of the decision maker using video images of known classifications. On the basis of each evaluation, certain parameters in the decision maker are updated, and when no appreciable improvement results, the user may resort to interaction with the data structure analysis process. Once the decision maker begins to perform satisfactorily in the supervised learning mode, the classification process is switched to the implementation mode whereupon unclassified data is presented for classification.

The image processing and pattern recognition approach described, of course, need not be limited to the synoptic evaluation of an entire field. Atmar *et al.*[26] have developed and are using an automated image processing system to classify and count field-gathered biotic samples. The backbone of their system is a 16K Hewlett Packard 2116C minicomputer which addresses a 1.2 megaword disc. Using the Bayesian decision rule they are able to classify and count nine different common insects found in New Mexico. The percentage of each specie, correctly classified, is as follows: Lady beetle (92%), Collops (91%), Big-eyed bug (90%), Alfalfa hopper (85%), Lygus adults (84%), Lygus nymphs (94%), Nabid (88%), Cucumber beetle (91%), and Brown lady beetle (94%). Although man could obviously do a much better job at classifying these insects, these results are significant in that they indicate the current state of development of the techniques that will make the biological survey amenable to the on-line control of insect pests.

From the above discussion it should be obvious that implementation of the on-line pest management system depicted in Fig. 4 would be impossible without major changes taking place in the method of conducting the biological survey. Certainly, the biological survey will always be important in that it will confirm the basic reliability of the predictive pest ecosystem models, and furthermore, will provide information concerning refining and optimizing the models. There is no doubt, however, that it would be extremely advantageous to minimize the amount of data required in the biological survey. This can be accomplished by recognizing that the pest ecosystem unfolds during a given year according to physiological time. Hence, care must be taken that the biological rate functions controlled by their time-temperature dependency on the environment are effectively quantified. From this type of information, management models can be formulated with the need for a minimum amount of real-time updating via biological observations. Biological observations can be accurately interpreted with a population model, however, only if the data can be placed on a time-temperature scale. Often the first biological event (the first insect to emerge, the first parasite to attack, etc.) cannot be observed. There is a need of a method to estimate and/or calibrate the observation in order to effectively use the model. In Fig. 7, a density observation taken at time t_1 will be identical to an estimate taken at t_2 but will have a vastly different meaning in terms of a model predicting plant damage. At t_1 most of the insect damage has not occurred yet, and at

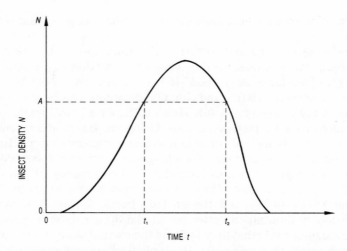

Fig. 7 Hypothetical total population incidence curve for an insect, where $N(t_1) = N(t_2)$.

t_2 damage is well past the peak. When the estimates are taken from separate fields at two different times, there is no way to accurately assess the ultimate outcome in terms of crop damage caused by the pest population without the aid of a synchronized population model.

This approach shifts the emphasis from making numerous biological observations throughout the year to the requirement that real-time microclimatic information is known. This is precisely the approach being taken. The predictive pest ecosystem models are being structured to accept climatological data as the principal real-time input. This information is used to synchronize the models with the actual pest ecosystems. These predictive models then inform the extension specialist in the pest management decision-making unit of the key time(s) during the year when certain biological samples should be collected and analyzed, and the principal purpose of the biological survey would be to verify the predictive models. Hence, heavy reliance need not in general be placed on receiving the results of the biological survey in "real time." But how is real-time climatological data obtained? Historically, agricultural scientists have relied on a national climatic summary for weather data. This monthly summary is typically available three months late while the pest management models obviously require real-time data. Consequently, a weather-monitoring network must be defined which is capable of providing this critical information.

The simplest and least expensive method of obtaining real-time remote-site environmental data would be to tie the central data acquisition center into one or more of the existing national weather service networks. One of the most promising of the services is the U. S. Department of Commerce's "Aviation Weather Network" (AWN) since it provides hourly weather summaries for hundreds of selected locations around the country and since its format is computer compatible [19]. In the past, this network has been used almost exclusively for air-traffic control and weather forecasting; thus, the environmental monitoring stations are located at airports. Data disseminated to users, therefore, is not exactly the type required by agricultural scientists since data transmitted over this network include ceiling, visibility, obstructions to vision, sea-level pressure, temperature, dew point, wind velocity, altimeter setting, and runway visual range. Only four of these nine parameters are of general interest to agricultural scientists. This contrasts sharply with the types of environmental data typically required (Table 1).

After scanning the list of required parameters given in Table 1 and the list of what is available from AWN, first impressions are that this network is inadequate as far as the needs of agricultural scientists are concerned. However, cost factors involved with alternate schemes, coupled with the fact that this method of acquiring environmental data is quite inexpensive, causes reconsideration of the options more carefully. For example, there is no charge for connecting into AWN and the network is fully maintained by the National Weather Service. Furthermore, the cost of a dedicated telephone line, which is required in order to bring the data to the Central Data Acquisition site, is very low ($8.25 per month from the Lansing Airport to Michigan State University), and the local telephone company maintains the line at no additional cost.

Aviation Weather Network would look much more attractive if the data bank did not have to record and process all of the unwanted data. This unwanted data falls basically into two categories. First, because of their location, many of the remote sites reporting would be of no interest to agricultural scientists; hence, they would want to disregard data derived from these sites. Second, only a fraction of the environmental data collected from even a desired site is useful (e.g., no use would exist for altimeter setting or runway visibility). Thus, it would be desirable to name only the required data from a given station. Finally, the format of the incoming data, although computer compatible, is suboptimal since it is in a five bit Baudot code. Therefore, it would be desirable to reformat the data before it is stored.

Table 1 Representative environmental data required.

Parameter	Number of Measurements Required per Site	Range	Accuracy	Threshold	Maximum Rate of Change of the Parameter per Unit of Time
Air temperature	1	−55–120°F	±2°F	—	2°F/min
Soil temperature	4 (0, 1, 3, 5 in.)	28–130°F	±2°F	—	2°F/min (surface) 2°F/hr (subsurface)
Wind speed	1	0–50 mph	±1 mph	1 mph	30 mph/sec
Wind direction	1	0–360°	±10°	1 mph	180°/min
Barometric pressure	1	27.0–31.5 in. Hg	±0.2 in. Hg	27 in. Hg	.33 in. Hg/hr
Humidity	1	0–95%	±1%	5%	20%/hr
Precipitation	1	0–4 in. rainfall	0.1 in.	0.1 in.	15–20 in./hr
Soil moisture	1	0–100% field capacity	±17%	0%	33%/hr
Light intensity					
Low	1	0–300 cal/cm^2/d	±5 cal/cm^2/d	0	—
High	1	0–10^4 ft/candles	20%	—	—

A simple system for performing these data conversion tasks is depicted in Fig. 8. The direct current loop, which is nothing more than a two-terminal connection block at the customer's end, is provided by the telephone company. The marking signal provided by the telephone company is 62.5 ± 2.5 mA; the spacing signal is no current[27]. The I-V converter translates this current into a voltage. The input of the I-V converter should have a fixed resistance of less than 150 ohms and an inductance of less than 0.5 henry. It should also be isolated from the ground by at least 1 megohm and should not impress foreign voltages in excess of $\frac{1}{2}$ volt on the telephone line. The interface conditions the electrical signals and converts them from a bit-serial to a bit-parallel code. The minicomputer performs several important tasks. It decodes the information and extracts the required data from useful sites and discards

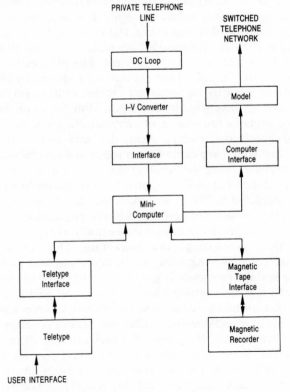

Fig. 8 Block diagram of the data conversion system.

the rest. It then formats the retained data, codes it, and outputs it to the data storage unit and/or to the pest management decision-making units. Obviously, this conversion system is quite flexible since sites or data can be added or discarded by merely altering the software in the minicomputer. Furthermore, with this system, exclusive use of one national weather service is not required; any computer compatible service or a combination of services could be used. The teletype is used primarily for user interaction in adding or deleting weather stations, debugging the system, etc. The system and user programs would be stored on magnetic tape along with data summaries. At routine intervals, a subroutine would be executed in the minicomputer that would initiate a call to the data bank over the switched telephone network and climatological information gathered would be conveyed to the data bank.

The advantages of using this approach are as follows: The initial cost of implementing this system would be quite low and the operating and maintenance costs would be negligible. Data derived from such a network could be used to predict near-term local weather patterns. In addition, the approach would be very easy to implement. The principal disadvantages of this approach are: Not all of the parameters required by the predictive models would necessarily be furnished by the weather service; the user would be forced to "take what he could get." Furthermore, data collected by the service might be too sparse, thereby resulting in unacceptably large errors in the predictive models. Also, the data would, in general, be collected at sites which are distant from the actual agricultural area being managed, thereby making the weather data difficult to use.

Consider the following specific applications of the on-line pest management system depicted in Fig. 4. Although the specific example presented related to the management of cereal leaf beetle populations, the principles illustrated can be generalized to include virtually every aspect of agricultural production, processing, and marketing. The cereal leaf beetle emerges from overwintering sites during late April and early May. The timing of this spring emergence is a critical event in the life system of this economic pest; it is the starting point of a series of highly synchronized interactions that ultimately determine the degree of crop damage over a very wide range of insect densities. Adult emergence is determined by soil and air temperature at the sites of overwintering. The relationship between emergence and temperature is not a direct one, but one in which the insect integrates those air temperatures above 48°F in each of several different microhabitats (Helgesen and Haynes, 1972). The net result is an emergence curve over a two to three week interval which can be skewed either early or late, depending on the overall weather of the particular year. The crop responds to a second threshold temperature (Gage, 1972) and the parasites[28] of the cereal leaf beetle to a third threshold temperature.

Predictive models have been developed for the cereal leaf beetle. One aspect of these models is the following: the models are capable of predicting the age class, or maturity, of individuals in the population at any time of the year. Eight such stages are identified in Fig. 9. Figures 10–12 represent the output of the predictive models for selected dates throughout the year 1971. Weather information at selected climatological stations throughout Michigan was inserted into a computer on a daily basis. This information was used to update the time-synchrony predictive

ABSOLUTE VALUE RANGE APPLYING TO EACH LEVEL

(# Maximum # Included in Highest Level Only)

Minimum	0.00	100.00	275.00	425.00
Maximum	100.00	275.00	425.00	545.00
	1	2	3	4

```
==========  ===============  ============  ============
.........   + + + + + + + + +  000000000   PPPPPPPPP
.........   + + + + + + + + +  000000000   PPPPPPPPP
....1....   + + + + 2 + + + +  000030000   PPPP4PPPP
.........   + + + + + + + + +  000000000   PPPPPPPPP
.........   + + + + + + + + +  000000000   PPPPPPPPP
==========  ===============  ============  ============
```

Minimum	545.00	605.00	665.00	1065.00
Maximum	605.00	665.00	1065.00	5000.00
	5	6	7	8

```
==========  ============  ============  ============
TTTTTTTTT   AAAAAAAAA     888888888     888888888
TTTTTTTTT   AAAAAAAAA     888888888     888888888
TTTT5TTTT   AAAA6AAAA     8888788888    88888888888
TTTTTTTTT   AAAAAAAAA     888888888     888888888
TTTTTTTTT   AAAAAAAAA     888888888     888888888
==========  ============  ============  ============
```

Fig. 9 Key to interpreting the cereal leaf beetle maturity maps. Level:
1. To the midpoint of emergence of over-wintering adult cereal leaf beetles.
2. Feeding-out in fields and oviposition.
3. Egg development.
4. Small larval stages.
5. Intermediate larval stage.
6. Large larval stage.
7. Pupal stage.
8. New adults.

Fig. 10 Distribution of cereal leaf beetles throughout the state of Michigan on May 10, 1971, based on predictive cereal leaf beetle population models.

Fig. 11 Distribution of cereal leaf beetles throughout the state of Michigan on June 9, 1971, based on predictive cereal leaf beetle population models.

Fig. 12 Distribution of cereal leaf beetles throughout the state of Michigan on July 9, 1971, based on predictive cereal leaf beetle population models.

model for the cereal leaf beetle. From the maps it is obvious that this output was region specific. Other outputs from the models could have been maps illustrating population densities, overwintering mortality rates, anticipated crop damage, etc.

The information contained in these maps would be used to time the biological survey in each region and to identify and time the appropriate pest control strategies. Benefits derived from this approach to pest management include the following:

1. By reducing (minimizing) the number of spray applications required, production costs would drop without sacrificing yield.
2. Damage to the environment due to insecticides would be minimized.
3. Multifactor control strategies would be more realistic.
4. Agricultural extension and/or private consulting firms would be used more effectively.

5. CONCLUSIONS

The overall requirements for the on-line management of insect pests clearly illustrate the vital role computers will play in the management of man's environment. The complexity of almost any ecological community is such that sophisticated, computer-based models will be an essential ingredient in on-line control. Furthermore, because of the stochastic nature of the environment, the models will usually only have a short-term predictability and, consequently, will have to be routinely updated with current data and continuously resynchronized with the actual ecosystem. Vast amounts of data will be collected, analyzed, stored, and automatically inserted into the models.

The data acquisition system will automatically perform calibration checks on remote-station monitoring instruments as well as on the data communication network. Potential problems would be identified and repair personnel automatically alerted since mismanagement of an ecosystem for even only a couple of days could have long-term damaging effects on the ecosystem.

Federal, state, and local governmental agencies will draw upon the predictive models, the historical data, and the data bank of current facts and trends for the purpose of both policy making and regulation.

The success of these various programs will only be measured in terms of the degree to which long-range improvements can be made in the human habitat.

REFERENCES

1. Maddox, J. Pollution and worldwide catastrophe, *Nature*, Vol. 236 (1972), 433–436.
2. Carson, R. *Silent Spring* (Alfred A. Knoph), 1962.
3. Giessner, W. R., Moss, F. H., and Cockburn, R. T. Minicomputer points the way to sewer system improvements, *Electronics*, Vol. 46 (1973), 114–118.
4. Klein, W. L., Dunsmore, D. A., and Horton, R. K. An integrated monitoring system for water quality management in the Ohio valley, *Environmental Science and Technology*, Vol. 2 (1968), 764–771.
5. Anderson, J. J. Minicomputers and water quality surveillance, *Proceedings of the National Symposium on Data and Instrumentation for Water Quality Management*, (1970) 420–429.
6. Scherz, J. P. Remote sensing considerations for water quality monitoring, *Proceedings of the Seventh International Symposium on Remote Sensing of the Environment*, Vol. 2 (1971), 1071–1092.
7. National Research Council, *Remote Sensing*, National Academy of Sciences, 1970.
8. Rosenfeld, A. *Picture Processing by Computer*, Academic Press, 1969.
9. Andrews, H. C., Tescher, A. G., and Kruger, R. P. Image processing by digital computer, *IEEE Spectrum*, Vol. 9 (1972), 20–32.
10. Nagy, G. State of the art in pattern recognition, *Proc. I.E.E.E.*, Vol. 56 (1968), 836–862.
11. Gilliland, B. E. Feasibility study of water resource pollutant identification by digital computer identification of remote infrared spectral signatures, *Final Report Project No. S-016-SC*, of the South Carolina Water Resources Research Institute, 1972.
12. Behar, J. V. Application of computer simulation techniques to problems in air pollution, *Proceeding of the Sixth Berkley Symposium on Mathematical Statistics and Probability*, Vol. 6 (1971), 29–69.
13. Malin, H. M. Computer model simulates air pollution over roads, *Environmental Science and Technology*, Vol. 6 (1972), 1071–1075.
14. Sklarew, R. C., Fabrick, A. J., and Prager, J. E. A particle-in-cell method for numerical solution of the atmospheric diffusion equation, and applications to air pollution problems, *U.S. Environmental Protection Agency, Publication No. APTD-0952*, 1972.
15. Demergian, K. L., Kerr, J. A. and Calvert, J. G. The relative importance of the various intermediate species in the removal reactions in photochemical smog, *Environmental Letters*, Vol. 3 (1972), 137–149.
15a. Brown, A. W. A. *Insecticide Resistance in Arthropods*, Geneva: World Health Organization, 1958.
16. Johnson, J. E. and Blair, E. H. Cost, time, and pesticide safety, *Chemtech.*, Vol. 2 (1972), 666–669.
17. Conway, G. R. Better methods of pest control, in *Environment—Resources, Pollution and Society*, (Murdoch, W. W., ed.), Stamford, Conn.: Sinauer Associates. (1971), 302–325.
18. Pimentel, D. Complexity of ecological systems and problems in their study and management, in *Systems Analysis in Ecology*, (Watt, K. E. F., ed.), Academic Press: New York: 15–35, 1966.
19. Haynes, D. L., Brandenburg, R. K., and Fisher, P. D. Environmental monitoring network for pest management system, *J. of Environ. Entomology*, 1973.
20. Fisher, P. D., Caron, R. H., Walton, R. L., and Haynes, D. L. Automated approach to

the biological survey for peest management systems. *Second Annual Remote Sensing of Earth Resources Conference*, Univ. of Tenn. Space Institute, 1973.

21. Croft, B. A. Private communication, 1973.
22. Koenig, H. E. *et al.* Design and management of environmental systems, *Second Annual Report. NSF GI-20*, Vol. 1, (1972).
23. Croft, B. A. and Nelson, E. E. An index to precict efficient interactions of Typhlodromus occidentalis in control of Tetranychus mcdanieli in Southern California apple trees, *J. Econ. Entomology*, Vol. 65, No. 1 (1972), 310–312.
24. Frey, H. T. Agricultural applications of remote sensing—the potential from space platforms, *Agricultural Information Bulletin N-328*, USDA, Washington, D.C., 1967.
25. Nagy, G. and Tolaba, J. Nonsupervised crop classification through airborne multispectral observations, *IBM J. Res. Develop.*, (1972), 138–153.
26. Atmar, J. W., Pooler, J. L., Webb, F. C., Flachs, G. M., and Ellington, J. J. Construction of a device to identify and count insects automatically, *J. Environmental Entomology*, Vol. 2 (1973), 713–715.
27. Bell Report. 44-55- and 75-Baud Private Line Channels: Interface Specifications, *Bell System Data Communication Technical Reference*, 1967.
28. Gage, S. H. *The Dynamic Interaction Between the Cereal Leaf Beetle Population and Its Significant Parasites*, Ph.D. thesis, Michigan State University, East Lansing, 1974.

Implications and Questions

In contrast to the previous chapter, which emphasized improved internal administrative processes through the computer, the present chapter emphasizes the improved public services delivery through the computer. To this end, more than ten computer applications in ten substantive areas of administration were shown. This included a representative sampling of governmental functions extending from criminal intelligence and environmental protection to urban and transportation planning. The underlying perspective in each was to show *what* improvements in service delivery or planning could be expected through computers. For the student of public administration there was the added perspective: to show *how* the objective of improved service delivery was achieved in each of the ten sample cases.

An overview of the readings in this Chapter, which constitute the bulk of the material presented, reveals that the range of the computer's role in improving the delivery of public services is almost infinite. Although this is not an indication of the quality of particular applications, each shows a set of parameters for thinking about service delivery problems in terms of effectiveness in achieving improved public service performance and efficiency and in achieving savings for the taxpayer. For example, the Dee and Liebman study on the selection of urban recreation facilities demonstrates how a parks department may predict with reasonable accuracy the demand for urban recreation facilities in various neighborhood areas. This computer-based model also describes how to match the park department's resources with the demand, thus, it may be said to accomplish the dual goals of efficient and effective service delivery. Similar dual objectives may be obtained from the studies of Dial and Bunyan on a computer-based planning system for urban mass-transit; David on the public assistance processing system (PAPS); Dodson on experimental housing, etc. The question that remains to be answered, however, concerns improved participation of the citizenry. In the previous chapters this question did not surface because we were dealing with internal administrative matters generally beyond the scope of citizen interest. Here, in contrast, we have dealt with the functions of government with direct impact on the quality of citizen life.

One of the major problems facing democratic governments in most all-industrialized societies is alienation. Without going into the deep-rooted causes of this phenomenon, it is reasonable to assume that large-scale bureaucratic organizations characteristic of modern-day governments are in part responsible. Granted this, it becomes the obligation of public agencies to develop systems that involve citizens in planning as well as in program evaluation. To do this, the technical information utilized in computer-based models for improving services delivery must be framed in a format understood by the layman. In the previous chapter we argued for a "soft communication system" as a prerequisite to successful implementation of internal management systems. A similar concept is being proposed here in conjunction with an organizational mechanism (such as a board of directors) for planning and evaluating new as well as on-going functional administrative applications.

Although this proposal may seem to imply a dramatic change in existing public sector computer applications, it does not. Rather, it is in keeping with the policy guidelines developed in Chapters I and II which call for centralized direction of computer systems and applications development as well as broad based agency participation within jurisdictional lines. The present scheme for function management extends the agency participation argument by incorporating citizen participation.

Other operational changes may be expected as a result of this organizational change. Some of these include:

1. The consideration of clientele groups' priorities in administrative decision making, which, in turn, may lead to greater organizational responsibility to the public.
2. The organizational decentralization of public service agencies around broadly based representative interagency or interdepartment computer utilization committees that do not lead to administrative inefficiencies.
3. The creation of an ombudsman's office along jurisdictional lines allowing for easy access to necessary organizational information bases to effectively represent citizen interests; this ease of access is gained as a result of the relative speed with which information is retrieved from computerized data storages. Ample evidence for this may be seen in the Cantilli article on *Computers and Traffic Safety* in the present chapter as well as the GIST and city of Aalborg data systems reported in Chapter II.

Improved service delivery and organizational effectiveness and efficiency are intertwined. The connecting point is the computer. For the purpose of highlighting the different areas of management's concern in the public sector we have thus far distinguished two types of computer applications: those concerned with internal management (Chapter II) and those concerned with functions management (Chapter III). Actually, both are interconnected, being two parts of the same problem of administration. Awareness of this interrelationship is a prerequisite for learning computer utilization and its attendant problems which is the topic considered in the following chapters.

Selected Bibliography

ARTICLES

American Public Welfare Association, A compilation of papers presented at national conference on public welfare data processing, APWA, Chicago; 1968, 76 pp.

Bargman, Robert D. SANMIS (Sanitation Management Information System) is the latest improvement in the Los Angeles refuse collection program, *Western City*, Vol. 45, No. 2 (February 1969), 19–20.

Bartol, Kathryn M. Soviet computer centres: Network or tangle?, *Soviet Studies*, Vol. 23 (April 1972), pp. 608–618.

Black, Donald, Library information system time sharing, system development corporation's LISTS project, *California School Libraries*, (March 1969).

Black, Guy, *The Application of Systems Analysis to Government Operations*, New York: Frederick A. Praeger, 1968.

Black, Harold and Shaw, Edward, Computers in the service of ekistics, *Ekistics*, Vol. 28, No. 164 (July 1969), entire issue.

Black, J. F. You can forecast CO concentrations: Use of mathematical model, *American City*, Vol. 87 (June 1972), pp. 71–72.

Blaine, S. Computer based information systems can help solve urban court problems, *Judicature*, Vol. 54 (November 1970), pp. 149–153.

Blake, Edward, J. and Polansky, Larry, Computer streamlines caseload at Philadelphia common pleas court, *Judicature*, Vol. 53 (December 1969), pp. 205–209.

Blubaum, Paul E. and Pasquan, Albert L. Phoenix applies modern technology to police records management, *Western City*, Vol. 43, No. 7 (July 1967), 20.

Bowne, Norman E. Simulating air pollution, an "Output" article in *Public Automation*, Vol. 5, No. 6 (June 1969), insert.

Broadbent, A. and Barras, R. Planning and the computer: A national computer for agency planners?, *Journal of the Town Planning Institute*, Vol. 57 (March 1971), pp. 111–113.

Bruns, William J. and Snyder, Robert J. Management information for community action programs, *Management Services*, Vol. 6, No. 4 (July–August 1969), 15–22.

Bugby, David J. and Schwitter, Joseph P. Conversion to computerized inventory control, *DPMA Quarterly* (Data Processing Management Association), Vol. 2, No. 3 (April 1966), 2–13.

Burton, Ellison S. and Sanjour, William, A simulation approach to air pollution abatement program planning, *Socio-Economic Planning Sciences*, Vol. 4 (March 1970), pp. 147–159.

Can computerized signal controls be improved?, *American City*, Vol. 87 (August 1972), p. 82.

Carabillo, Virginia, EDP for urban planning systems, *SDC Magazine*, February 1965.

Chartrand, Robert L. Computer-oriented information for the U.S. Congress, *Law and Computer Technology*, Vol. 1, No. 2 (February 1968), 2–7.

Computer-assisted instruction and cable television, *Intellect*, Vol. 101 (October 1972), p. 13.

Computer communications for fire, police, utilities; San Diego, Calif., *American City*, Vol. 87 (March 1972), pp. 106–107.

Conceptual design of a regional information system, *Denver Regional Council of Governments*, March 1970.

Computerized police communications, *American City*, Vol. 86 (May 1971), p. 32.

Computerized signal settings speed traffic flow, Kansas City, Mo., *American City*, Vol. 86 (April 1971), p. 126.

Crecine, John P. Computer simulation in urban research, *Michigan Municipal Review*, Vol. 41, No. 6 (June 1968), 144–148.

Crecine, John P. *Computer Simulation in Urban Research*, Santa Monica, Calif.: *Rand Corporation*, 1967.

Dakin, John, Models and computers in planning, *Planning*, July 1965.

Davies, Ross, Computer graphic techniques in planning, *Planning Outlook*, Vol. 8 (Spring 1970), pp. 24–39.

De Gennaro, Richard, The development and administration of automated systems in academic libraries, *Journal of Library Automation*, Vol. 1, No. 1 (March 1968), 75–91.

Derry, John R. and others. An information system for health facilities planning, *American Journal of Public Health*, Vol. 58, No. 8 (August 1968), 1414–1420.

Dillingham, James H. Computer analysis of water distribution systems, *Water and Sewage Works*, Vol. 114, Nos. 1, 2, 3 (January, February, March 1967), 1–3; 43–45; 96–100.

Dorosh, W. N. Calgary–Urban planning and a computer, *Urban Renewal and Public Housing in Canada*, Vol. I (1966), pp. 7–10.

Doud, Charles W. How the personnel function looks from the information system approach, *Public Personnel Review*, Vol. 29, No. 3 (July 1968), 164–167.

Dudkin, L. Computers and optimal planning, (Translated and condensed from Pravda, Oct. 12, 1971), *Current Digest Soviet Press*, Vol. 23 (November 9, 1971), pp. 15–16.

Dueker, Kenneth, J. Application of information system concepts to transportation planning, *Highway Research Record*, No. 194, 1967.

Durning, Danny, Organizational implications of advanced computer-use for state government, *Arkansas Business Review*, Vol. 4 (August 1971), pp. 23–27.

Electronic traffic cops take on bigger jobs, *Business Week* (July 10, 1971), pp. 51–52.

Elias, Samy E. G. *Mathematical Model for Optimizing the Assignment of Man and Machine in Public Transit "Run-Cutting."* Morgantown, W. Va.: West Virginia University, Industrial Engineering Department, 1966.

Enthoven, Alain C. Analysis, judgment and computers: Their use in complex problems, *Business Horizons*, Vol. 12 (August 1969), pp. 29–36.

Evans, Alfred S. Development of a computer program for the public health laboratory, *Public Health Reports*, Vol. 82, No. 7 (February 1967), 169–179.

Fitzgerald, J. E. Code inspectors and computers work well together, *American City*, Vol. 86 (April 1972), p. 42.

Forsyth, G. C. and Thomas, D. G. Models for financially healthy hospitals, *Harvard Business Review*, Vol. 49 (July 1971), pp. 106–117.

Freed, Roy N. Computers in judicial administration, *Journal of the American Judicature Society*, Vol. 52, No. 10 (May 1969), 419–422.

Fuller, F. J. and others. Computerized traffic control, *American City*, Vol. 86 (October 1971), pp. 109–111.

Gallati, Robert R. J. Criminal justice systems and the right to privacy, *Public Automation*, Vol. 3, No. 7 (July 1967), insert.

Gallati, Robert R. J. The role of the courts in a state-wide criminal justice information system, *Police*, Vol. 16 (May 1972), pp. 18–23.

Gazis, Denos C. A computer model for the financial analysis of urban housing projects, *Socio-Economic Planning Sciences*, Vol. 5 (April 1971), pp. 125–144.

Gazis, Denos C. and Weiss, George H. Effects of random travel times on the design of traffic light progressions, *Journal of the Franklin Institute*, Vol. 282, No. 1 (July 1966), 1–8.

Grayson, Lawrence P. and Robbins, Janet B. United States office of education support of computer projects, 1965–71, *U.S. Superintendent of Documents*, 1972.

Greenwood, P. W. Potential uses of the computer in criminal courts, *Rand Corporation, Document No. P-4581*, Fall 1971.

Grundstein, Nathan D. Urban information systems and urban management decisions and control, *Urban Affairs Quarterly*, Vol. 1, No. 4 (June 1966), 20–32.

Hammond, A. L. Computer-assisted instruction: Many efforts, mixed results, *Science*, Vol. 176 (June 2, 1972), pp. 1005–1006.

Hammond, A. L. Computer-assisted instructions: two major demonstrations, *Science*, Vol. 176 (June 9, 1972), pp. 1110–1112.

Helgesen, R. G. and Haynes, D. L. Population dynamics of the cereal leaf beetle, Oulema Melanopus (L) and its interaction with two primary hosts: Winter Wheat and Spring Oats, M.S. thesis, Michigan State University, 1972.

Hemmens, George C. Survey of planning agency experience with urban development models, data processing, and computers, Conference on Urban Development Models, *Highway Research Board*, Dartmouth College, June 26–30, 1967.

Henderson, Hazel, The computer in social planning, *Wharton MBA*, Vol. 6 (December 1971), pp. 14–16.

Herrmann, Cyril C. Systems approach to city planning: San Francisco applies management techniques to urban redevelopment, *Harvard Business Review*, Vol. 44, No. 5 (September–October 1966), 71–80.

Holtzman, Wayne H. Conference on computer assisted instruction, testing and guidance, *Items*, Vol. 22, No. 4 (December 1968), 43–48.

Hoover, Edgar, M. Computerized location models for assessing of indirect impact of water resources projects, *Washington University*, St. Louis, Mo., May 1966.

Horinek, Ernest E. Electronic data processes in highway operations, *Civil Engineering*, Vol. 39, No. 2 (February 1969), 46–48.

House, Peter, Environmental pollution: More problems without solutions, (Conference paper), 1970, 13p. *Applied Simulations International Inc.*, 1100 17th St., N.W., Suite 900, Washington, D.C. 20036.

Jeffus, Pepita O. Tax accounting by computer, an "Output" article in *Public Automation*, Vol. 5, No. 9 (September 1969), insert.

Lamb, W. D. Computers put efficiency in refuse collection; Nashville, Tenn., *American City*, Vol. 87 (September 1972), pp. 151–152.

Maxman, Robert J. and Greco, William L. Description of a data system for small urban areas, *Purdue Road School*, 1968, 97–107.

Meehan, James B. Modernized computerized communications in aid in crime prevention, *Police*, Vol. 15 (May–June 1971), pp. 39–43.

Meihls, Archie, Automated legislation, *Law and Computer Technology*, Vol. 1, No. 1 (January 1968), 19–21.

Meyer, John R. and Kain, John, Computer simulation, physio-economic systems and intra-regional models, *American Economic Review*, Vol. LVIII, May 1968, pp. 171–181.

Mitchel, William H. SOGAMMIS, a systems approach to city administration, an "Output" article in *Public Automation*, Vol. 2, No. 4 (April 1966), insert.

Montijo, R. E., Jr. California DMV goes on-line, *Datamation*, Vol. 13, No. 5 (May 1967), 31–36.

Moravec, Adolph F. Using simulation to design a management information system, *Management Services*, Vol. 3, No. 3 (May–June 1966), 50–58.

Munday, J. R. and Penney, R. D. Remote sensing of oil slicks, Proceedings of the Seventh International Symposium on Remote Sensing of the Environment, Vol. II, p. 1015–1032, 1971.

Nejelski, Paul, Computer simulation: An aid to court study, *Judicature*, Vol. 55 (June–July 1971), pp. 17–20.

Packer, A. H. Simulation and adaptive forecasting as applies to inventory control, *Operations Research*, Vol. 15, No. 4 (July–August 1967), 660–679.

Penberthy, William R. Computerized voter registration, *American City*, Vol. 82, No. 11 (November 1967), 78–79.

Public Administration Service, A computer-based payroll system for the city of Wilmington, Delaware, Mimeographed, *PAS*, Chicago, 1966, Var. pages.

Ramo, Dr. Simon. The systems approach: Automated common sense, *The Nation's Cities*, Vol. 6, No. 3 (March 1968), 14–19.

Raphael, David L. Computer models for institutional planning and control, an "Output" article in *Public Automation*, Vol. 3, No. 4 (April 1967), insert.

Rhornton, O. Frank and Ellisor, James B. Computerized voter registration in South Carolina, *State Government*, Vol. 42 (Summer 1969), pp. 190–193.

Rosenthal, A. H. Admatch, A computer tool for urban studies, *Rand Corporation, Document No. P-4532*, December 1970.

Rourke, Francis and Brooks, Glenn E. Computers and university administration, *Administrative Science Quarterly*, Vol. 11, No. 4 (March 1967), 575–600.

Sammon, J. W. A nonlinear mapping for data structure analysis, *IEEE Trans. Comp.*, Vol. C-18, pp. 401–409, 1969.

Sandman, Cal M. *An Information File for a Municipal Income Tax System*, 1969. Available from the author at: Commissioners of the Sinking Fund, 617 W. Jefferson St., Louisville, Ky.

Savas, Emanuel S. Preparing for information systems in New York City, an "Output" article in *Public Automation*, Vol. 4, No. 2 (February 1968), insert.

Second generation traffic control by computer; Project of Los Angeles County, *American City*, Vol. 87 (April 1972), p. 112.

Shulman, Harry Manuel, Success of NCIC systems, *FBI Law Enforcement Bulletin*, Vol. 37, No. 10 (October 1968), 7–11, 23.

Simmie, J. M. Electronic data processing applied to town planning, *Journal of the Town Planning Institute*, (January 1967), pp. 11–14.

Sorkin, Michael, The FBI's Big Brother Computer, *Washington Monthly*, Vol. 4 (September 1972), pp. 24–30.

Suppes, Patrick, The uses of computers in education, *Scientific American*, Vol. 215, No. 3 (September 1966), 206–208.

Tabb, William K. Data retrival systems, the university, and state decision making, *Public Administration Review*, Vol. 31 (July–August 1971), pp. 435–440.

Taylor, Jean G. and Navarro, Joseph A., Simulation of a court system for the processing of criminal cases, *Simulation*, Vol. 10, No. 5 (May 1968), 235–240.

Trafficking by computer; Washington, D.C., *Time*, Vol. 100 (July 3, 1972), p. 56.

Turner, E. D. A computerized system for road accident statistics in London: development and use, *Greater London Council Intelligence Unit Quarterly Bulletin* (March 1972), pp. 22–37.

United States House Committee on Government Operations, Intergovernmental Relations Subcommittee Administration of Federal Health Benefit Programs, September 28–December 1, 1971, 92nd Congress, 1st Session.

Videtti, Joseph A., Jr. Application of computers in law enforcement, *Police*, Vol. 13 (July–August 1969), pp. 33–39.

Vincent, J. Richard, *Criteria for Linking Functional to Jurisdictional Systems*, Municipal Information Technology Program, Series No. 4. Storrs, Conn.: University of Connecticut Institute of Public Service, 1968.

Vinsomhaler, John and Noon, Robert. Information systems applications in education. Annual Review of Information Science and Technology, Vol. 8 (1973), pp. 277–318.

Vrecion, Vladimir, An automated method of logical analysis of socio-legal phenomena, *Law and Computer Technology*, Vol. 1, No. 12 (December 1968), 7–11.

Wardell, Edward J. and Murray, Roger J. Computerized traffic signal system maximizes roadway network capacity and improves pedestrian safety, (John F. Kennedy International Airport) *Traffic Engineering*, Vol. 38, No. 12 (September 1968), 26–28.

Whittaker, William L. and McDermott, John T. Computer technology in an appellate court, *Judicature*, Vol. 54 (August 15, 1970), pp. 73–78.

Willis, George L., Electronic Vote-Counting in a Metroplitan Area, *Public Administration Review*, Vol. 26, No. 1 (March 1966), 25–30.

Wilkins, R. Threat of law enforcement technology, *Current*, Vol. 139 (April 1972), pp. 15–18.

Wood, Peter, The use of computers in town planning, *Long Range Planning*, Vol. 3 (April 1971), pp. 59–64.

BOOKS

Bower, James B. and Welke, William R., eds. *Financial Information Systems: Selected Readings*. Boston: Houghton Mifflin & Co., 1968.

Cox, Nigel S. *et al. Computer and the Library; The Role of the Computer in the Organization and Handling of Information in Libraries*, Hamden, Conn.: Shoe String Press, 1967.

Crecine, John P. *A Computer Simulation of Municipal Budgeting*, Chicago, Ill.: Rand-McNally, 1969.

Dukes, C. W. *Computerizing Personnel Resource Data*, New York: American Management Association, 1971.

Fitz, Harry H. *The Computer Challenge to Urban Planners and State Administrators*, Washington, D.C.: Spartan Books, 1965.

Goodlad, John I. *Computers and Information Systems in Education*, New York, N.Y.: Harcourt Brace Jovanovich Publ., 1966.

Haga, Enoch, ed. *Automated Educational Systems*, Elmhurst, Ill.: The Business Press, 1967.

Hall, J. A., ed. *Computers in Education*, Elmsford, N.Y.: Pergamon Press, 1963.

Lindberg, Donald A. *Computer and Medical Care*, Springfield, Ill.: C. C. Thomas, 1971.

Lithtwood, Martha B., ed. *Public and Business Planning in the United States*, Detroit, Mich.: Gale Publ., 1972.

Milliman, Gordon, *Urban and Regional Information System for Social Programs*, Papers from the Fifth Annual Conference of the Urban and Regional Systems Association, September 7–9, 1967, Garden City, New York, Kent, Ohio: Center for Urban Regionalism, Kent State University, 1968.

National Academy of Sciences. Highway Research Board, *Improved Street Utilization through Traffic Engineering*, Special Report No. 93, Washington, D.C.: The Academy, 1967.

Naylor, Thomas H. *Computer Simulation Experiments with Models of Economic Systems*, New York, N.Y.: Wiley, 1971.

Oettinger, Anthony G. *Run, Computer, Run*, Cambridge, Mass.: Harvard University Press, 1969.

Rose, J. *Computers in Medicine*, Baltimore, Md.: Williams and Wilkins, 1969.

Schroeder, Earl W. A metropolitan government information system, *Data Processing*, Vol. XXII, 1967 International Data Processing Conference. Park Ridge, Ill.: Data Processing Management Association, 1967.

Sharkansky, Ira, *Public Administration: Policy-Making in Government Agencies*, Chicago, Ill.: Markham, 1972.

The Computer in the Public Service: An Annotated Bibliography 1966–69, Public Administration Service, 1970.

Whisenand, Paul M. and Tamaru, Tug T. *Automated Police Information Systems*, New York, N.Y.: Wiley, 1970.

Wren, A. *Computers in Transport Planning and Operation*, New York, N.Y.: Gordon and Breach, 1971.

MONOGRAPHS

Arnstein, George E. *Design for an Academic Matching Service*, Washington, D.C.: National Education Association, Association for Higher Education, 1967.

Curran, A. T. and Avram, H. D. *The Identification of Data Elements in Bibliographic Records*, AD-666-47, Springfield, Va.: Clearinghouse, U.S. Department of Commerce, 1967.

Duke, Richard, and Burkhalter, Barton R. *The Application of Heuristic Gaming to Urban Problems*, Tech. Bull. B-52, East Lansing, Mich.: Michigan State University, Institute for Community Development, January 1966, 13 pp.

Feasibility Analysis of a Public Investment Data System, Vols. 1 and 2, Prepared by Operations Research, Inc. Springfield, Va.: Clearinghouse, U.S. Department of Commerce, 1968.

Hamblen, John W. *Computers in Higher Education*. Atlanta, Ga.: Southern Regional Education Board, August 1968.

Hann, Roy W., Jr. and Sparr, Ted, Computer selection by water utilities, *Journal American Water Works Association*, Vol. 61, No. 2 (February 1969), 89–96.

Information systems in public health, Second Annual Joint Conference, American Statistical Association, New York Area Chapter, and the Public Health Association of New York City, *Public Health Report*, Vol. 83, No. 5 (May 1968), entire issue.

Institute of Municipal Treasurers and Accountants, *Computers in Local Government*, London: IMTA, 1964, 66 pp. 15 s.

Kevang, M. J. *An Information System for Urban Transportation Planning: The BATSC Approach*, PB-180-224, Springfield, Va.: Clearinghouse, U.S. Department of Commerce. microfiche.

Public Administration Service, *An Approach to Developing and Installing a Financial Management Information System for Mankato (Minn.) State College*. Mimeographed. Chicago: PAS, 1969, 27 pp.

Public Automated Systems Service, *ADP in Public Personnel Administration*, Publ. No. 186, Chicago: Public Administration Service, 1969, 40 pp.

Public Automated Systems Service, *Governmental ADP: The Practitioners Speak*, Publ. No. 182. Chicago: Public Administration Service, 1968.

Ross, Daniel. *Highway Engineering Advanced Computer Systems*. PB-180-761. Springfield, Va.: Clearinghouse, U.S. Department of Commerce, 1968.

U.S. Department of Health, Education, and Welfare, Office of State Merit Systems, *Survey of Automatic Data Processing in State Personnel Agencies*, Washington, D.C.: Government Printing Office, 1968, 38 pp.

Vincent, J. Richard, *Municipal Information Systems' Concepts*, Storrs, Conn.: University of Connecticut Institute of Public Service, Municipal Information Technology Program, 1967, 60 pp.

Weiner, Myron E. *Concepts and Techniques of Automation for Management*, Storrs, Conn.: University of Connecticut Institute of Public Service, Municipal Information Technology Program, 1966, 79 pp., appendices.

Willis, Charles R. Computers in production control, *The Tool and Manufacturing Engineer*, (August 1968), 46–49.

CHAPTER IV

The Learning and Utilization of the Computer

The previous chapters have explored specific computer applications, first, in the internal management environment of the public organization and then, in the external environment within which the public organization plays its role. In the present chapter we turn our attention to the complementary educational area of teaching computers to executives in public service. A major part of the education process involves the formulation of strategies of introduction. Two significant reasons for giving careful attention to the strategy of introduction are that: (1) the computer deals with the sensitive inner workings—the guts—of a government or business organization. The most careful of EDP efforts may be expected to be confronted with resistance by individuals or groups affected. Resistance, further, is complicated by the fact that it is generally camouflaged, difficult to identify, and even more difficult to cope with. (2) Even assuming organizational consensus and a willingness for subgroups to accommodate change, only limited amounts of change at any one time may be expected to be absorbed without serious organizational stress.

An overall strategy for the "introduction of computerization" should be one of evolutionary advance, not revolutionary change. (See Chapters I and II.) The differences between the terms "evolutionary" and "revolutionary" as used here have to do with the speed, breadth and depth of implementation, and the extent of detail of long-range planning. With respect to implementation, there are simply too many technical as well as organizational complexities and too many uncertainties to justify more than a carefully paced growth curve. As to long-range planning for computerization, the technology is moving too rapidly, our mastery of it is assuming new dimensions, and the dynamic nature of modern organization life precludes planning much beyond a year or two.

Grandiose objectives, therefore, should be avoided. The worst analogue of this—the classic proposals for a "total single integrated system" or "turn-key operation"—coming before management is prepared. Such systems are dangerous illusions that live more on paper than in complex organizations. Computer systems—both hardware and software—for an entire organization must be visualized not as a supersystem of systems, but as a federation of information subsystems built around department or agency structure in an organization. Each system should be built in a modular fashion, suited to the organizational fabric and should yield results concurrent with the development of additional modules. Only in the most monolithic organizations can a single total system be considered a realistic endeavor.

One caveat must be raised: we hardly want islands of mechanization. What we do desire, however, by a "federation" is cost-feasible "commonalities," where budgeting and personnel subsystems, which cannot be integrated into a single tightly fitted system for an entire organization, can be integrated into a loosely knit structure which must be developed. Within government this is essential, for public agencies are generally highly decentralized with pluralistic management forms. This type of federated information system can be achieved only within a centralized planning and management approach as proposed in Chapters I and II.

Given that governments at both national and local levels will continue to introduce larger computers with greater information capacities incorporating greater flexibility for developing new applications, it is imperative that we focus on the educational material for training public executives in the use of computers, their potential and problems.

An overall educational framework for teaching the public executive a role in planning, implementing, and managing EDP operations is presented by Mr. I. L. Auerbach of Auerbach Corporation. Professors Blanning, Lewin, and Uretsky of New York University describe an educational game, similar to the "Carnegie-Mellon" management game, for highly sophisticated public executives. The authors show how this technique may be utilized to improve both computer utilization and decision making.

19

Educating Executives about EDP*

I. L. AUERBACH

Auerbach Corporation, Philadelphia, Penn.

Synopsis. Executives in government must understand both the problems and the potential benefits of EDP. They must be actively involved with the definition of the tasks to be performed and must know how to interact with the EDP operation in their organization if the desired benefits are to be derived.

The executive's role and his involvement are defined, with emphasis on what the executive really needs to know. This knowledge will help him fulfill his responsibility confidently and effectively. The concept of the steering committee is described, which makes it possible for the executive to actively participate in EDP decisions.

The executive must be prepared to learn quickly. Special educational techniques must be employed to enable the executive to acquire the proper attitude toward the EDP function, toward creation of the proper environment, and to understand the part the computer plays in achieving an effective information system.

1. INTRODUCTION

Educating executives about EDP is a topic of critical importance. This is an area of extreme need, even in the countries which have been using computers for some time. Most executives have some information about computers, but few know how to use computers effectively.

A senior financial executive of a major U.S. government agency recently addressed this subject and made the following observation: "It is rare indeed that top executives know so little about a major financial commitment, that in addition implies so much organizationally." And I believe we would all have to agree that most executives have always made sure that they are rather intimately familiar with the implications of

*Reprinted from the *Proceedings of the World Conference On Informatics in Government*, The IBI-ICC, Florence Italy, October 1972.

a major acquisiton of equipment, and as a result know something about how it works, the kinds of people needed to make it operate properly, its anticipated economic payoff, and the secondary implications use of the equipment will have for the other parts of the organization. And most important, hardly any executive would willingly agree to a major acquisition of equipment unless he was reasonably certain that it would bring positive results to his organization.

All of us know that this is the way executives operate, so it is all the more mystifying, and perhaps troubling, that they have not acted this way about their computers. The age range of most modern top executives in government and business—in their early or late fifties—is a contributing factor. They have been trained and attained success in their careers without experiencing the need or opportunity to become familiar with the intimate working details of modern information technology. And, confronted by the spectre of EDP in their own operation and decisions regarding its acquisition and use, they are often persuaded by glib salesmen or overenthusiastic technicians to make decisions that are not in their organization's best interests.

The obvious remedy to this problem is education. Inform the user and the decision maker. Equip him to cope with the perplexing issues that he must face. Enable him to live comfortably in the environment of modern information technology. But how?

In my country there has been a proliferation of computer appreciation courses which—call them what you may—have rarely lived up to their billing. In too many cases they have served only to further confuse those they have promised to enlighten.

It is not an easy task. The executive, this manager of management, has gained respect for his performance as the leader of his organization, has professional stature in his own field, and is usually unwilling—at least reluctant—to reveal his ignorance of the exotic world of EDP. In defense, he may have totally withdrawn from the scene, trusting that the experts he hires will work their magic to produce a successful EDP operation. He may have relegated the computer and its concomitants to the status of operational backup; like the elevator and the air conditioner, they will function and serve the organization because people are charged with making them run.

But it is safe to assume that the executive who is conscientiously discharging his responsibilities will also recognize the need to expand his horizon to include the computer and all it entails. Further, that such recognition will not place his organization status in jeopardy.

All of this simply reinforces the importance of the subject we are discussing at this symposium. I should like to hope that you may benefit from the experiences that many of us have already had, and thus avoid some of the pitfalls encountered in the establishment of computer operations. To accomplish this, however, it will indeed be necessary to provide education about EDP to executives.

In dealing with this subject I want to address three major areas. First, the objectives for the use of EDP. Second, what the executive really needs to know, and finally, some of the techniques and methods that can be used in developing a productive educational program.

2. SETTING THE OBJECTIVES FOR EDP

Just how concerned should an executive be about this EDP operation? In my opinion he should be very concerned, because most management authorities agree that failure of many EDP systems has been the direct result of top management's failing to set the goals for computer use. From the top, down through the upper level of management, there must be an active concern and participation in establishing the purpose and priorities for computer use.

The cost of EDP equipment and the recurring costs of systems analysts, programmers, and operating personnel are very large. In fact, in most organizations, computers will represent the largest single capital expenditure, except in heavy industry where equipment needs are very large.

In addition to the operational costs, an EDP center has a tremendous impact on the structure of an organization. The entire operation will have to adjust to using the information that is derived from the computer.

These kinds of traumatic costs and organization impact make it absolutely imperative for top management to be personally involved in the decisions and policymaking processes that relate to a computer installation.

The way top management becomes involved will vary from organization to organization. In a very authoritarian environment, the chief executive may make the decisions and issue decrees. In a very free and participative kind of organization the decisions may emanate from further down, or be the result of joint effort of much of the management team.

Regardless of the kind of organization, the method which I believe is most desirable is the "steering committee" approach. A number of organizations use the steering committee to direct their entire data-processing effort. A logical step is to charge the EDP steering committee with setting objectives for the EDP activities. Initially, a steering committee may only act in a judicial role deciding the merits and priority of applications. As expertise is gained, a steering committee should provide the direction of the EDP activity and adopt a more aggressive role. I am not suggesting that the steering committee should run the EDP department. I do not think a committee should run anything. The EDP department should be clearly in the hands of an EDP manager.

I want to expand on the steering committee for a few moments because I do believe it is the best approach in most cases, and because I think a full understanding of it is required to formulate an effective educational program for executives.

If a steering committee is to be used, the crux of the issue is the committee membership. Top management must be involved and I believe the senior executive should be the committee chairman. In this way the steering committee can speak with the authority and power of the senior executive. The other members should include the senior financial executive, the EDP manager, and a knowledgeable key executive from each major function of the organization that may use the computer facility.

The purpose of the steering committee should be to provide guidance to line management to optimize the utilization of EDP, thereby insuring a better tool for control and planning of each operation.

The duties of the committee will include:

1. Providing an overview of future plans that may involve EDP support.
2. Monitoring EDP expenses.
3. Establishing priorities for implementation of extensive system analysis and programming specifications.
4. Advising in the resolution of obvious conflicts in operating schedules.
5. Making recommendations for system modification and upgrading of the hardware and software systems when appropriate.
6. Making recommendations to improve application areas that can result in reduced expenses.
7. Providing liaison with operating management so that application can be mutually identified and their needs satisfied.
8. Providing liaison functions between the EDP center and its users pertaining to problems and/or future needs.

9. Making recommendations as to the membership of task forces to perform detailed systems analysis within a specific user area.
10. Authorizing new applications based on estimated costs and delivery schedules versus benefits to be derived.
11. Reviewing monthly EDP progress reports and making recommendations if and when appropriate.

The steering committee should meet monthly and should have a preissued agenda. The recommendations of the committee should be recorded in minutes of the meeting and the resulting action items should be clearly identified with responsibility assigned to named individuals and deadline dates for action completion indicated.

An early agenda item for the steering committee, prior to commitment to purchase EDP equipment should be the establishment of criteria for evaluating proposals of managers and vendors. The objectives should be directed toward:

1. Smallest possible capital investment.
2. Minimization of effects of technological obsolescence.
3. Lowest possible net cost of computer system use.
4. Greatest possible privacy and security of records.
5. Maximum ability to enlarge or improve the system.
6. Protection against losses from data-processing error.
7. Selection of the "main-line applications" that have real economic or operational payoff in the organization's future, rather than those that merely simplify a clerical or accounting function.

Too frequently the applications that are programmed for a computer are those that have the least economic payoff. For example, most companies program their payroll operations as one of their initial entries to the computer. Very few companies in the world have ever had economic payoff from running payroll on a computer unless the company is extremely large. The reason it is done is that the procedures have been so well documented and organized that the logical sequence is easily transferred into computer language.

By "mainline applications" I mean those areas of activity that have the maximum impact on its success or profitability; for example, to a major manufacturing company production control, machine loading, inventory control, and distribution are vital; in public administration, planning, personnel skills inventory, contract funding and administration. In a university, utilization of resources, both the physical plant and the teaching resources, in an optimum manner requires great attention to scheduling of both classrooms, professors and students in an extremely short period of time. Likewise, the creation of reports has saved teachers many hours of drudgery.

A recent survey of the FORTUNE 500 largest firms in the United States shows the following distribution of computer applications.

	Currently Implemented			Planned		
	Mfg.	Non-Mfg.	Total	Mfg.	Non-Mfg.	Total
Accounting/bookkeeping	38	20	58	7	2	9
Production	34	11	45	15	6	21
Sales analysis	35	15	50	5	4	9
Marketing	28	11	39	17	8	25
Distribution	29	12	41	12	3	15
Materials management	22	7	29	14	5	19
Planning	19	12	31	13	7	20

Utilization of computer time is distributed as shown in the chart below.

Heavy usage (70%–80%)	Receivables Billing Payroll
Moderate usage (30%–60%)	Inventory General ledger Sales analysis Payables
Light usage (2%–10%)	Forecasting Market analysis Engineering Calculations

For each using organization a careful introspective search of the "mainline application" is both important and worthy of considerable time and attention before dashing into an EDP installation.

Now, what I have really described here is the process that any organization should go through prior to making a commitment to EDP operations, whether or not a steering committee is used. What you have just heard is the environment within which any educational program for executives must fit, and obviously there are differing levels of needs for education.

3. EDUCATIONAL NEEDS

Which brings me to my second point. What do executives need to know about computers and modern information technologies?

The first educational need for any executive involves attitude, and this may cover a wide range depending on the executive's previous exposure to EDP.

But the first attitude that must be established is that the computer is a tool and as such must contribute to the organization just as any other tool is expected to do. The computer is not a magic box, but it is very easy for executives to view it as such and therefore devise all kinds of interesting but not necessarily valuable things for the magic box to do. We have all seen this happen. And this kind of reaction by executives is the product of the wrong attitude.

Therefore any education about computers for executives should start from that point. The computer is a machine and it must contribute to the purpose and objectives of the organization.

Once the purpose motive is established, then executives will need to be exposed to the kinds of things EDP can do for them. And these applications must be presented in such a way that they can be related to the executive's own operation. He must begin thinking about the "main-line applications" that exist in his organization.

Then he must learn about the organizational impact the computer may have. He must be aware that organizationally he may not be able to handle the information the computer produces. He should begin to look very carefully at his organizational structure and realize that if necessary, he must reorganize to get the optimum efficiency from his EDP operation.

The average executive, given sufficient training in those three areas, should be well equipped to attack the computer problem. You might be inclined to say, "But that's not enough, you haven't given him enough facts, you haven't covered enough subjects." But if you look back to my discussion of the steering committee you will see that these three areas are the biggest problems he will face.

The EDP education you want to give an executive has nothing to do with how a computer operates. Effective education should not fill his head with details about programs and hardware.

Perhaps the best way to describe effective EDP education for executives is that it should be purpose oriented and not bit oriented.

Granted, I have oversimplified to stress the point that attitude is the most important thing. But if you as an educator approach the education process with that same attitude then I believe you will be better equipped to comprehend the proper balance between what a computer can do, the effect of the computer on the organization, and how a computer does it. The EDP manager and his staff are the only ones who need to completely understand how a computer does it. The rest of management on the other hand need know only about how it works to ‘keep what it does in perspective.

In concluding this portion of my talk, let me say that the computer should be only a part of a total information system, and top management must develop the information system. The full realization of this will benefit any organization that is concerned with EDP operations.

4. EDUCATIONAL TECHNIQUES

Now, let us turn to the third point, and that is some of the techniques and methods that can be used in EDP education for executives.

To begin at the beginning, it is imperative that schools of business and administration and professional schools offer a well-rounded education on the use of EDP in their area of specialization. The executive over 50 may be excused from having a personal knowledge of EDP because through most of his working life EDP was not a consideration. But now, every graduate of any business or professional school should have a basic education which in general terms teaches him how computers work, what they are capable of doing and the organizational structure that is required to take advantage of them. For students today, EDP education should be a requirement regardless of the specialty that the student is studying.

It will be years, however, before we gain the benefit of these school graduates who are well-rounded in the uses of EDP, so it is essential that we look at means of educating experienced executives who may be looking forward to their first personal involvement with the computer.

If the business and professional schools have good courses on the use of EDP, then it will be possible to cycle many executives through these, utilizing a week-long total immersion kind of training, or through night classes.

We have to recognize a natural resistance to this kind of education, particularly by the experienced executive who has long been away from the classroom. This man, and he is the most important to us today because he must carry the burden of decision making during the next several years, will probably respond better to the kind of training found in seminars where he can be learning with his peers. These seminars must have a high degree of participation by the executives and the seminars should be led by educators who have had hands-on experience and who can relate to the seminar participants on their own terms. These seminars should utilize case studies and there should be actual problem-solving taking place in the class.

Obviously, it will be impossible for an organization to expose its entire executive and management staff to this kind of training, but at a minimum the group selected as the steering committee should have this training as soon as possible, and ideally the entire top management group should be included.

Since an organization cannot rely on outside seminars for all of its managers, it should seriously consider some form of in-house training. This should be a responsibility of the steering committee, and the committee members should themselves be working within the organization to shape the attitudes of other managers to accept EDP and use it in the most efficient manner.

In each of the educational steps, we must keep in mind the mental attitude of the executives and managers we are trying to reach. We have to realize that management often does not know which way to turn, perhaps through fear of showing their ignorance or of being drawn into a pit with jargon-jabbering eggheads. Computer experts, like all other professional experts, frequently lapse into a mode of conversation using what appear to be ordinary words that have taken on a special meaning in the data-processing field. When this happens it is not possible to convey information to an already fearful executive.

The executive may be fearful for more than one reason. He does not understand the vocabulary, but he may also be resentful of the computer because he may feel that it will diminish his role. He will naturally be reluctant to fully embrace the computer because it represents change, and just as naturally he will be inclined to view the computer as some dark mystique. These attitudes have to be overcome, therefore, the first role of the educator will be to persuade modern executives and management staffs to come to terms with the computer. This places a special burden on the instructor and the successful educator in this situation will be one who has the ability to generate enthusiasm among his students. Getting executives and managers emotionally ready to learn may be the hardest task. Once accomplished then the educator may use proven educational methods.

The important traits that the instructor should possess are:

1. Enthusiasm for his subject and an ability to transmit this enthusiasm to others.
2. Outgoing personality.
3. Well developed sense of humor.
4. Sensitivity and perception.
5. Ability to communicate verbally.

The training and experience that the instructor should possess should include, though not be limited to:

1. Familiarity with and understanding of computer hardware and systems.
2. Awareness of current state of the art.
3. Hands-on experience in the computer field.
4. Fluency in the language in which the course is given and that spoken by the students.
5. Knowledge of teaching methods.

In our own training work we have found that when confronted with something new, something of which he is perhaps a little frightened, the manager can quickly become distracted or bored. Therefore I suggest that audiovisual aids be used and that personal involvement of the student be sought constantly. One simple rule is that any instructor who spends more than five minutes talking to executives without inviting any kind of reaction or participation is failing in his job.

In conclusion, I should like to summarize briefly some of the key points which I want to leave with you.

1. Educating executives about EDP is desperately needed.
2. Developing the right attitudes is a more important educational task than imparting a large number of facts.
3. Executives and management staffs need to know very little about how a computer works, but they need to know a lot about what the computer can do and the effect that will have on their organizations.
4. Organizational structures must be examined, and executives and managers must be urged to view the computer as only part of a total information system which they themselves must develop. And finally, preparing the executive to learn may be the most important contribution educational programs can make.

BIBLIOGRAPHY

Auerbach EDP Users' Notebook, Philadelphia, Pa.: Auerbach Publ. Inc., 1972.

Brink, Victor Z. *Computers and Management: The Executive Viewpoint*, Englewood Cliffs, N.J.: Prentice-Hall, Inc. 1971.

Davis, Gordon B. *Introduction to Electronic Computers*, 2nd ed., New York: McGraw-Hill, 1972.

Fletcher, Allan, *Computer Science for Management*, Philadelphia, Pa.: Auerbach Publ. Inc., 1968.

Harold, Frederick G. *A Handbook for Orienting the Manager to the Computer*, Philadelphia, Pa.: Auerbach Publ. Inc., 1971.

Heany, Donald F. *Development of Information Systems: What Management Needs to Know*, New York: Ronald Press, 1968.

Hertz, David B. *New Power for Management: Computer Systems and Management Science*, New York: McGraw-Hill, 1969.

House, William. *The Impact of Information Technology on Management Operations*, Philadelphia, Pa.: Auerbach Publ. Inc., 1970.

Joslin, Edward O. *Computer Selection*, Reading, Mass.: Addison-Wesly, 1968.

Kanter, Jerome, *Management Guide to Computer System Selection and Use*, Englewood Cliffs, N.J.: Prentice-Hall, Inc., 1970.

McCarn, David. Getting ready: The seemingly irrational effects of introducing a computer must be recognized and dealt with in preparing the organization for automation, *Datamation*, August 1, 1970.

Orlicky, Joseph, *The Successful Computer System: Its Planning, Development and Management in a Business Enterprise*, New York: McGraw-Hill, 1969.

Szweda, Ralph A. *Information Processing Management*, Philadelphia, Pa.: Auerbach Publ. Inc., 1972.

Wilson, Ira G. and Wilson, Marthann E. *Management Innovation and System Design*, Philadelphia, Pa.: Auerbach Publ. Inc., 1971.

20
Issues in the Design of an Urban Game

ROBERT W. BLANNING, ARIE Y. LEWIN and MYRON URETSKY

The Wharton School of the University of Pennsylvania, Philadelphia, Pa.

Graduate School of Business Administration
New York University, New York, N.Y.

INTRODUCTION

During the past two decades, gaming has been widely used to train decision makers in military, government, and business organizations. Its principal advantage is that it allows the student to experience, under relatively controlled conditions, the real world in which the academic theories and perspectives of the classroom will be applied.

Gaming has been most frequently used in the training of military and business executives. (See, for example, Kibbee *et al.*[9], Rowland and Gardner[16], and Wilson[18].) In part, this has resulted from a general appreciation of the need for skilled decision makers in these organizations and the consequent availability of funds for both academic and professional executive development programs. This, in turn, has stimulated the construction of models that make it possible to simulate the consequences of the decisions of game participants. Such models constitute a significant part of any business or military game.

These advantages do not accrue to the designers of urban games. It is only during the past five years that the "crises of the cities" has been recognized by those with the resources to support the education of urban planners and administrators. This would not be a major concern if the problems confronting urban managers were merely a strightforward extension of the problems confronting business and military managers. But as we will see in this paper, the problems are different.

404

The principal differences are:

1. The relative lack of control by the top decision makers over their bureaucracy.
2. The interaction of economic, social, and political variables.
3. Ill-defined performance measurements.
4. Explicit consideration of the politics of the system.

In the following sections we outline the special problems faced by urban managers, examine the ways in which these problems affect the design of an urban game, and present a design for a proposed urban game. The proposed design is based on our experience in developing and implementing a large, complex management game at the Graduate School of Business Administration at New York University[11] and on our analysis of the principal differences between management decision making and urban decision making. The purpose of this paper is both to examine the principles that govern the design of urban games and to suggest how these principles might be applied.

URBAN DECISION MAKING

As the deteriorating quality of life in the cities is becoming of national concern, so also are the special difficulties confronting urban managers: the deteriorating tax base in the cities, the rise of social problems, the increasing demands by city residents for improved social services, and the restrictions on city policies imposed by state and federal governments. Although managers in other types of organizations must face similar problems, their problems are not nearly as severe.

From the perspective of the designer of an urban game there is one principal distinction between the problems faced by urban managers and the problems confronting the managers of other organizations. This is the relative lack of control by the city managers over the performance of the city government. Specifically, there are a large number of decisions that determine the quality of life in the cities, and most are made by people other than the senior decision makers in the city government. These decisions can be grouped into four categories: economic decision; social decisions; political decisions; and government decisions. Although other organizations must suffer a lack of complete control over the consequences of their decisions (e.g., a large corporation must contend with suppliers, consumers, and competitors), these organizations have far greater control over their environment. (As Galbraith[8] suggests, "The genius of the industrial system lies in its organized use of capital and technology. This is made possible ... by replacing the market with planning" (p. 354).) As we will see in the following sections, one of the critical issues in the design of an urban game is the extent to which the game must make explicit the lack of control by the urban manager over many economic, social, political, and government decisions.

The *economic* decisions not controlled by the urban manager fall into two categories: land use, and the production and distribution of most goods and many services. These include decisions to:

1. Buy and sell land and hence to establish prices for land parcels.
2. Construct buildings on the land and establish rents or prices.
3. Produce goods, hire and fire (or layoff) employees, and mitigate the adverse environmental effects of such production (including air pollution, water pollution, noise pollution, and the construction of unsightly facilities—"visual pollution").
4. Distribute and market products (this includes the prices charged to consumers and the responsiveness of product and service characteristics to consumer demand).

All of these decisions can be regulated or influenced by law and by executive action, but the economic community can bring powerful political pressures (discussed below) to bear on the regulators. (For a more complete discussion of these decisions and their consequences see Netzer[13] and Perloff and Wingo[14].)

The *social* decisions not controlled by the urban manager fall into three categories: selection of a place to live (which may be outside the city); selection of a job and a place to work; and participation in socially dysfunctional and in some cases, criminal behavior. (In addition to references [13, 14], see Chapter 7, "The Metropolitan Community" in Dobringer[6] and the chapters "Urban Crime" and "Rioting Mainly for Fun and Profit" in Wilson[19].) The first of these decisions, residential location, is partly economic. It is described here as a social decision because of the importance of noneconomic factors (crime rates, quality of public education, social class of neighbors) in the selection of a place to live. The second decision, selection of occupation and job location, has a larger economic component but is also partly social. For example, many people (including urban planners) attach considerable importance to such social factors as the social acceptability of a job and the work surroundings. The third category of decisions—which includes strikes, boycotts, and riots—has economic, social, and political components.

Thus, the "social" decisions not under the control of the urban manager overlap into the economic and political areas.

The third class of decisions not under the control of the urban manager are *political* decisions. In most major cities, the senior member of the executive branch and all members of the legislature are periodically elected by the residents of the city. One test of the performance of an urban manager is whether he is in office, that is, whether he is elected to public office or appointed by an elected official. This means that an urban manager must respond to political pressures from the electorate, even when he is convinced that his responses are not in the best interests of the city residents. Although the urban manager can attempt to influence political pressures and can sometimes safely ignore them, they constitute a major force that he cannot control. (See, for example, Baker[2] and Banfield and Wilson[3], who describe these pressures in detail.)

Although an urban manager makes *government* decisions (since he is a member of an urban government), there are many government decisions over which he has little control. These include certain decisions within the urban government and decisions made at higher levels of government. The internal decisions are those made by subordinates who are unresponsive to the policies of senior managers. The higher-level decisions are those made by federal and state officials. These decisions are primarily financial, but they also include restrictions on the use of urban resources. (See, for example, Linsay[12], who describes the problems of a big-city mayor constrained by state and federal policies.)

This fragmentation and decentralization of urban decision making affects the stability and responsiveness of urban governments. In private organizations the existence of such measures of performance as profit, growth, rate of return, and market share make it possible for the decision makers to compare their actual performance with desired (or planned) performance and with the performance of other organizations which are in similar lines of business or are competing for similar resources (primarily capital and managerial talent). This type of feedback lends a certain stability to the growth of private organizations, for it allows lower-level managers a limited ability to infer the effect of their decisions on the well-being of the enterprise without detailed top-level guidance. The decentralization of goals and decisons in cities also lends a stability to the growth of urban governments, but it is static stability that leads many urban managers to "play it safe" by making only marginal modifications in existing policies, even when it is clear that the problems faced by the government require bold progressive action. (See, for example,

Braybrooke and Lindbloom[5], who describe the "strategy of disjointed incrementalism," and Schultz[17], who suggests that "the pernicious practice of incremental budgeting" can be mitigated if not eliminated in public organizations by the use of comprehensive planning and budgeting systems.) This lack of responsiveness of many city governments makes it far more difficult for the senior managers to "turn the organization around" to meet major challenges and problems.

THE PURPOSES OF GAMING

The special problems facing urban managers outlined above give rise to special issues in the design of an urban game. Before we examine these issues, it is appropriate to outline the general purposes of gaming. By a game we mean an educational process with the following characteristics:

1. The one or more participants in the game make a sequence of decisions corresponding to the problems placed before them by a Game Director.
2. The consequences of these decisions are calculated by hand or by a computer, and are generally communicated to the participants after each set of decisions in the sequence. (They are not always communicated to the participants, and where they are communicated there may be some time lag—this depends upon the objectives of the particular game).
3. The calculations are performed by means of an explicitly defined model. (The model does not necessarily have to be one of the real world. For example, the model in the New York University Management Game does not correspond directly to any specific real world corporation or industry.)
4. The participants are evaluated on the basis of their decisions, and the evaluations may consist of narrative discussions on the decisions and their consequences, or they may consist of formal grades.

In this type of learning experience, the students learn by doing. Rather than being told about the real world, they experience it vicariously, by actively participating in the educational process. They can make mistakes and observe the consequences of their mistakes without incurring many of the real-world penalties of the mistakes. Thus, they can experiment with their own theories, hypotheses, and hunches to obtain some insight into their validity and relevance. Furthermore, the use of a model may make it possible to collapse the time frame of the decisions and their consequences, so that the participants may obtain many years of vicarious experience (with respect to the specific issues described by the game) in a few weeks or months.

In addition to these general purposes and advantages of gaming, there are four specific objectives to be satisfied. These objectives apply not only to the training of business and military managers but also—and with possibly greater relevance—to the training of urban managers.

First, a properly designed game often serves as an eclectic experience—it forces the participant to integrate the lessons learned in several separate courses or programs. Thus, the participant in a business game may be required to apply lessons learned in courses on accounting, finance, and statistics; and the participant in a military game may apply lessons learned in courses on strategy, tactics, and logistics. The participant in an urban game may make use of material learned in courses on urban sociology, economics, and politics, and on municipal administration.

The use of gaming in integrating the subject matter of related disciplines is becoming increasingly important. Schools of business and public administration are becoming more professionalized, with the result that the separate departments in these schools have become academically self-sufficient and to some extent, isolated. Thus, a game that allows the student to synthesize the techniques, approaches, and perspectives learned in different courses can lead to a valuable learning experience. This is especially important in training urban managers, who must have some understanding not only of management principles and methods, but also of subdisciplines such as urban sociology, urban economics, and urban politics.

The *second* objective of gaming is to give students an opportunity to obtain simulated real-world experience while still in school. In the past obtaining experience of this type was merely a convenience that helped to prepare a student for his first job. But the rapid advances in knowledge relevant to management decision making make such "in-school" experience even more important, for it forces the student to learn to teach himself. Since the useful life of lessons learned in school is becoming shorter and shorter, it is as important for students to *learn to acquire* new information as it is to *acquire* existing information. Nowhere is this more true than in the behavioral sciences and in the disciplines related to the management of public organizations. Thus, a learning experience that requires the student of urban management to teach himself while still under the guidance of the faculty can be as important as an approach that presents him with currently useful facts, theories, and principles.

The *third* objective of gaming concerns the type of experience that the participant receives. Gaming may be used not only to give students vicarious experience in anticipation of their real-world responsibilities, it may also be used to give them experience that they may never receive in the real world. Specifically, a game may be used to give students experience at a higher level of management than they may be expected to attain in the real world. For example, a participant in a business game may play the part of a corporation president, even though it is unlikely that he will become president of a real corporation. Similarly, a participant in a military game may play the part of an Army commander, and a participant in an urban game may play the part of a mayor, even though both are unlikely to assume such positions in real life. Even if they do assume such positions, it will usually be long after they have completed their formal education.

There is a valid purpose in requiring a student to play such a part. By experiencing the problems of being in the "hot seat" at the top of an organization, he is better able to appreciate the problems of the people for whom he will be working. Such an appreciation is especially valuable for students of urban management. Most of these students will start as policy analysts and will eventually become department managers with civil service status. Few will become political appointees or run for public office. By participating at the top levels of a simulated city, such students can begin to appreciate the political, financial, and moral pressures that continually impinge on elected officials. Thus, they may begin to appreciate the occasional necessity to compromise economic, technical, and operational feasibility with political feasibility.

The *fourth* objective of gaming is that it allows participants to establish their own performance standards under the general supervision of an educational staff. This is far more realistic than an approach in which an instructor sets the standards, for such standards are usually subject to negotiation in the real world. For example, the performance standards of business managers are established in part by boards of directors and those of senior city managers by the electorate. By negotiating these standards (either with a computer or with other game participants) the participant can learn not only how to meet given objectives but also how to determine a realistic set of objectives.

ISSUES IN URBAN GAME DESIGN

Before outlining a proposed urban game, we will examine two principal issues in the design of such a game. The first is the degree to which decisions not under the direct control of the urban manager will be included in the play of the game and the way in which this will be accomplished. There are five ways in which these decisions may be incorporated into the game.

First, some of the decisions might be omitted from the game. For example, political decision making may be omitted by appointing the mayor and the city council at the start of the game and possibly appointing other participants to these positions as the game progresses. Similarly, certain socially dysfunctional decisions (riots, strikes) might be outlawed (or not even mentioned) in the game manuals. Although it would not be wise to omit all such decisions, a selective omission may serve to focus the attention of the participants on key issues.

A *second* approach is to program the decisions as a part of the simulation. The decisions would be explicitly considered in the game, but the participants would not be allowed to make them. Thus, the participants would be made aware of the importance of the programmed decisions, but they could concentrate their energies on other, presumably more important, decisions. For example, residential location decisions might be programmed and calculated by the game model.

A *third* approach is to allow some of the game participants to make the decisions. For example, some participants might buy and sell land and determine the use of the land. This approach is more realistic than programming the decisions, for it requires the participants playing the urban managers to negotiate with people rather than to anticipate the response of a preprogrammed calculation. But it also requires that some of the participants play parts other than urban managers for at least a part of the play of the game. This would be an advantage if the purpose of the game were to give the players an appreciation of the variety of decisions affecting the quality of life in a city, but it also detracts from the vicarious experience that the participants can obtain in managing a city government.

A *fourth* method of treating decisions not under the control of the urban manager is for the game administrators to make the decisions. For example, the game administrators might play the part of state and federal officials. The advantage of this approach is that the game administrators can control the interactions between the game participants and the uncontrolled decisions. However, it requires that the game administrators lose some of their objectivity as they become game players.

The *fifth* approach is to include real-world decision makers in the game and to ask them to make some of the decisions not under the control of the urban managers. The game participants would negotiate with the real-world participants in an attempt to influence their decisions. This approach, even if limited to a few decisions, can add substantial realism to the game. Our experience with management games suggests that it is difficult for players to obtain realistic vicarious experience if they interact only with other players and a computerized model. Although such models may realistically represent certain physical and aggregate behavioral phenomena, they do not adequately represent the personal interactions and institutional complexities that must be mastered by a successful manager. The incorporation of a few real-world decision makers would allow the game participants to obtain far more realistic experience.

The second issue in the design of an urban game is the specification of the temporal and spatial dimensions of the game. The temporal dimension is especially important, for it is difficult to bring about significant changes in the economic, social, and (to a lesser extent) political state of an urban system in a few years. This suggests that each play of the game should represent one or a few years, so that the participants can observe the evolution (or decay) of the city over a period of 20 or 30 years. This would also allow the participants to observe the feedback process that cause urban decay to feed on itself and that cause attempted solutions to an urban problem to aggravate the same or other problems. (Forrester[7] examines these processes in detail.) On the other hand, such a game would not allow the participants to experience the "crisis management" atmosphere that exists at the top of most government organizations. This atmosphere can be simulated most realistically when the time dimension is of the order of a few weeks or months.

The specification of the spacial dimension is more straightforward. An urban game must reflect the locational nature of urban decision making. That is, the game participants should have to determine not only levels of various urban activities (e.g., number and capacity of schools, police stations, public housing projects), but also the locations at which the activities are to take place. The easiest and probably the best solution is to use a Cartesian street map to partition the city into square (or rectangular) blocks. The map would then be used in the input of decisions and the calculation and communication of the economic and social state of the city. The political aspects of the game (voting districts) could also be based on the map. The game "City Model" developed by the (federal) Environmental Protection Agency uses a Cartesian map to describe a variety of social, economic, and political variables. For a description and illustration, see Laska[10].)

A PROPOSED URBAN GAME

Having investigated the central issues in the design of an urban game, we now outline a proposed game. The perspective of the game is that of the senior decision makers in a city government, specifically, the major, his staff, the senior appointed officials, and the city council. The purpose of the game is to provide vicarious management experience to graduate and advanced undergraduate students interested in the management of public organizations and to members of city, state, and national government agencies attending executive development programs or advanced professional certificate programs. The latter participants may be policy analysts, who may be familiar with analytical techniques but often not with the political and bureaucratic difficulties of implementing policies, and existing bureaucrats and politicians, who are usually in the opposite position.

The game participants (or players) would be partitioned into three teams. Two teams would play the part of the city administrations (one in office and one out of office) as diagrammed in Fig. 1. This other would be the city legislature. The administration in office would make a sequence of decisions similar to those made by urban executives (concerning taxes, housing, transportation. etc.), probably on a weekly basis. Each week of elapsed time would represent six months to one year of game time, and the total game time would be approximately eight years. This will allow the game to span three successive administrations of the city government.

The decisions would be coded and entered into a computerized model of the city and of its environment, the consequences of these decisions would be calculated (by a computer and in part by an Urban Game Committee), and the players would receive summaries of these consequences. In addition, players would interact with representatives of the real world, as discussed below.

The legislative team (city council) would review the decisions of the city administration and have final control over all major decisions. However, the game would be sufficiently complex (in terms of the number of decisions, the interactions between them, and the uncertainties about

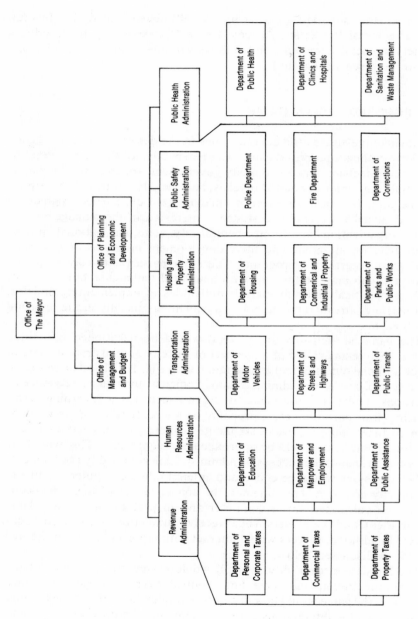

Fig. 1 The city government.

their consequences) that the legislative team could exert only a general or aggregate control. The administration would present its proposed decisions to the legislative teams in the form of a proposed yearly budget. The content and format of the budget, the extent to which it is a program budget (i.e., the amount and type of performance measures), and the amount and type of planning information (e.g., a five-year financial plan) would be determined by the administration with the approval of the legislature.

The administration and the city council would also interact with an electorate, who could turn them out of office. There would be one model, one legislature, one electorate, and two administrations competing for public office. Every two or three weeks of elapsed time the administration in office would report to the electorate. On alternate weeks each member of the city council would report to selected members of the electorate, and members of the team not in office may complete for council membership. The electorate would consist of representatives of various social, economic, and racial groups, and each would be assigned sectors of the city in which he or she lives, works, shops, seeks recreation and entertainment, etc. He would receive a summary of the state of the city (calculated by the computer model) as it pertains to his social, economic, and geographical group. Both administrations, the one seeking election and the one seeking reelection, would communicate with the electorate, who would determine which administration would govern the city until the following election.

The determination would be both direct and indirect. Each member of the electorate would be asked to vote for one of the teams and would also be questioned about the relative importance of various urban issues. The response would be entered into the political component of the game model—a model of the electoral process. The model would transform the votes and opinions of the external participants into the simulated votes of an economically, sociologically, and locationally more diverse group, and would make possible a movement of simulated residents from and to the city during the game without changing the number of external participants. It would also give the Urban Game Committee some control over the characteristics of the (simulated) electorate. For example, it might allow incumbents to be easily voted out of office after several consecutive terms, so that the other team might have a greater chance. The term of office should be 2–3 simulated years, so that there would be at least three elections during the course of the game. In addition, it would allow the players to perform more sophisticated opinion sampling (political polls) than would otherwise be possible.

The political model would be similar to those often used to analyze real-world electoral behavior—for example, the simulation developed by the Simulatics corporation to analyze national voting processes (see Pool *et al.* [15]). However, it might contain some of the nonlinearities and interdependencies characteristic of "microanalytic" simulations of marketing processes (see Amstutz[1]).

A suggested geography for the cities is illustrated in Fig. 2. The city will be partitioned into four districts: a Residential District containing middle class residents; a Disadvantaged District (or ghetto) containing working and non-working poor; a Business District in which most commercial transactions take place; and an Industrial District that provides most of the "blue-collar" jobs in the city. A Cartesian map containing these districts will be used to define the location of residents, facilities, and activities.

The interactions between the districts are also defined in Fig. 2. There will be three major interactions. First, the public and private organiza-

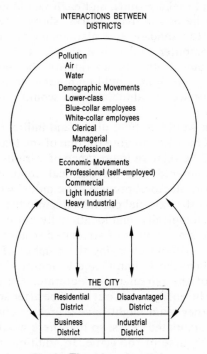

Fig. 2   The urban geography.

tions in each district may influence the levels of air and water pollution in the others. Second, residents may move from one district to another, primarily in response to job opportunities and improvements in social services and the quality of life. Finally, economic organizations may move some of their activities from one district to another, thus changing the number of jobs available in each.

The external participants in the game are illustrated in Fig. 3. The Federal and State governments would provide categorial and noncategorial grants to the city. They would also exert judicial control over the constitutionality of city laws. The city unions would negotiate wages and working conditions of city employees. The financial community would determine the interest rate for municipal bonds. The electorate would vote for the mayor and the council.

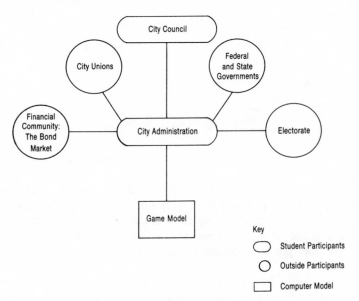

Fig. 3 Participants in the urban game.

The simulation would consist of two major modules, as diagrammed in Fig. 4 (see Blumberg[4] for a more complete discussion of the system of models needed to describe a city and of the executive program through which the models would communicate). The first, a Policy Implementation Model, would calculate the costs and benefits of the player decisions.

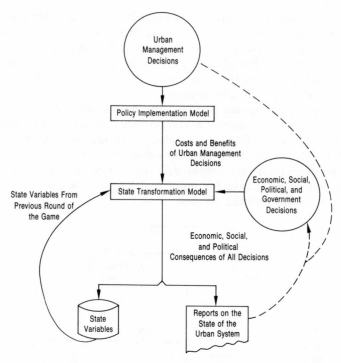

Fig. 4   Information and decisions in the urban game.

The second, a State Transformation Model, would calculate the economic, social, and political state of the urban system. The latter model would modify the state of the system as calculated during the previous play of the game and would receive as its inputs both the costs and benefits of the player decisions and the decisions of any external participants.

The participants begin the game by reviewing the history of the previous administration. These histories will be the line item budgets for the previous two years and summary quarterly departmental reports for the previous two years. The purpose of the histories is to enable the game participants to begin playing the game and to provide a data base for policy analysis.

All participants would receive selected reports on the consequences of their decisions. These would consist of quarterly accounting and performance reports for each department (illustrated in Fig. 1) and a description of any short range events (crises) precipitated by the model or by the external participants (e.g., a strike by some city employees).

A game of this type appears most useful as a part of a one semester course on urban management, as a part of an intensive executive development program, or as a substitute for the senior thesis requirement or the M.B.A. or M.P.A. thesis requirement in a degree program. The relationship of the game to the remainder of the (academic or nondegree) program would depend on the purposes of the program, the education and experience of the students, and the time available for the game. However, we feel that there is one essential relationship between the game and the remainder of the program: there must be a comprehensive review and critique at the conclusion of the game that attempts to relate the experience acquired during the game with the lessons taught elsewhere. Where possible, the review should include statistical analyses of game data and tests of any hypotheses presented in the other parts of the program. Even if the review consists only of a narrative discussion of the evolution of the simulated city, it is during this discussion that much of the learning will take place.

CONCLUSION

The purpose of this paper is to examine the differences between the use of gaming in training urban decision makers and the more traditional uses of gaming. We have seen that the principal difference reflects an important distinction between urgan management and the management of other organizations—the relative lack of control by the urban manager over the consequences of his decisions. A major purpose of an urban game should be to teach the student to cope with the problems of making decisions in such an environment.

This position is not universally accepted. Our observation has been that the greatest skepticism is found in schools of business administration that are beginning to implement programs in urban studies. The skeptical response is that "management is management"—that is, that there are general principles of management that transcend the type of organization in which the principles are to be applied. This response then leads to the conclusion that an educational program on urban management may confortably be fitted into the existing framework of management education with only marginal modification. Our observation, experience, and intuition suggests to us that this is not the case. We feel that if such general principles exist, they are so general as to be of little use. It is not true that a successful business manager is also likely to be successful in the management of public organizations, nor that an educational program in public management should be similar to a program in business management. In this paper we have attempted to uncover the most significant differences between these two types of education and to suggest how these differences must be considered in the design of an urban game.

REFERENCES

1. Amstutz, Arnold, *Computer Simulation of Competitive Market Response*, Cambridge: The MIT Press, 1967.
2. Baker, John H. *Urban Politics in America*, New York: Scribner's, 1971.
3. Banfield, Edward C. and Wilson, James Q. *City Politics*, New York: Vintage Books, 1966.
4. Blumberg, Donald F. The city as a system, *Simulation*, Vol. 17, No. 4 (October 1971), pp. 155–167.
5. Braybrooke, David, and Lindbloom, Charles E. *A Strategy of Decision: Policy Evaluation as a Social Process*, New York: Macmillan, 1963.
6. Dobriner, William M. *Social Structures and Systems: A Sociological Overview*, Pacific Palisades, Calif.: Goodyear Publ. Co., 1969.
7. Forrester, Jay W. *Urban Dynamics*, Cambridge: The MIT Press, 1969.
8. Galbraith, John Kenneth, *The New Industrial State*, Boston: Houghton Mifflin, 1967.
9. Kibbee, Joel M., Craft, Clifford J., and Nanus, Burt, *Management Games*, New York: Reinhold, 1961.
10. Laska, Richard M. City models challenge urban managers, *Computer Decisions*, (February 1972), pp. 6–10.
11. Lewin, Arie Y. and Seidler, Lee J. Introducing the real world to a complex management game, *Proceedings Eight Symposium National Gaming Council*, Booz Allen Applied Research Inc, New Shrewsbery, N.J., June 1969.
12. Linsay, John V. *The City*, New York: W. W. Norton, 1969.
13. Netzer, Dick, *Economics and Urban Problems*, New York: Basic Books, 1970.
14. Perloff, Harvey S. and Wingo, Lowdon, (eds.), *Issues in Urban Economics*, Baltimore: John Hopkins, 1968.
15. Pool, Ithiel de Solla, Abelson, Robert P., and Popkin, Samuel, *Candidates Issues and Strategies—A Computer Simulation of the 1960 and 1964 Presidential Elections*, Cambridge: The MIT Press, 1964.
16. Rowland, Kendrith M. and Gardner, David M. The uses of business gaming in education and laboratory research, *Faculty Working Paper No. 10*, University of Illinois, Urbana: College of Commerce and Business Administration, April 27, 1971.
17. Schultz, Charles L. *The Politics and Economics of Public Spending*, Washington: The Brookings Institution, 1968.
18. Wilson, Andrew, *War Gaming*, Middlesex: Penguin Books, 1970.
19. Wilson, James Q., (ed.) *The Metropolitan Enigma*, Garden City, N.Y.: Doubleday, 1970.

Implications and Questions

Executives must learn how to make use of computers if their beneficial impacts are to be fully utilized. And, education is the key for equipping executives with the capability to integrate modern information technology into management processes. Three criteria for measuring educational effectiveness are provided by Mr. Auerbach:

1. Educational needs.
2. Techniques.
3. Objectives for computerization.

Educational needs

The executive's need for education in computers and electronic data processing is defined by two dimensions: (1) developing the right attitudes instead of just gaining a large number of facts, and (2) a detailed emphasis on *what* the computer can do rather than *how* it actually does it. Traditional approaches to executive training include in-service seminars, night session programs, or short courses at local universities. In accordance with the Auerbach recommendations, it is proposed that comprehensive regional electronic data processing seminars for public managers be established to meet the educational need which cut across the jurisdictional lines of national and local governments. In the United States, for example, the Civil Service Commission could be responsible for this seminar. By means of a steering committee constituted of agencies participating, the program could be effectively coordinated for different management levels in the various governmental jurisdictions. Constituting student bodies from the various jurisdictional levels of government would have the further benefit of intellectual cross-fertilization, leading to greater understanding of each other's administrative and service problems as well as their resolution.

Techniques

For improving the techniques of education, Professors Blanning, Lewin, and Uretsky suggest the utilization of the simulation game. Although their proposal is aimed at training urban administrators, the simulation game format may be considered a general training tool that is already being used in educating private executives and may be considered part of a larger educational program for executives' on-going education.

The specific utilities of the simulation game are:

1. To provide the participant with the opportunity to see how newly learned knowledge may be used.
2. To give training instructors an opportunity to evaluate how well the student has integrated the material taught and what use he may be expected to make of this knowledge in back-on-the-job conditions.
3. To allow for the formulation of performance standards based on performance in the simulation.

Objectives for Computerization

The last criterion for measuring educational effectiveness involves setting the objectives for computerization. For education to be effective here, it is essential to consider the respective organizational environments of the student. Whereas, some of these environments may be authoritarian and others free, most fall between the two which always complicates matters. These organizational environments must be carefully evaluated before the actual education program commences because different environments will respond in different ways to personnel with increased working knowledge of computers. This is where the resistance to computers generally sets in and where organization ruptures result. The scenario is as follows: one staff member in a higher managerial capacity attends a short course and returns all fired up about how computers can help the agency. This is looked upon by associates and subordinates as threatening and any attempts to improve management, performance, or efficiency through the computer are contested. In order to circumvent this problem it is proposed that in constituting training programs the various participating agencies provide students representative of the respective departments that constitute the agency. This would tend to disseminate the knowledge fairly broadly and would tend to minimize hostile environments.

Both the student and the educator must bear in mind that educating for computer utilization is a complicated task that must be carefully planned, cautiously implemented, and regularly monitored. There are no panaceas in the business of education, particularly when adults are involved. Ineffective education in this context may be more harmful than no education at all, confirming the old aphorism that a "little knowledge may be dangerous."

In the final chapter we broaden our sights and turn to an area of discussion about the impact of the computer on society. Emphasis is on what the computer has already accomplished in public agencies, and what should be done or what is being ignored.

Selected Bibliography

ARTICLES

Ameiss, Albert P. EDP education in the 1970's, *National Public Accountant*, Vol. 15 (June 1970), pp. 22–24.

Back, Kenneth, The value of ADP in property tax administration, *Assessors Journal*, Vol. 1, No. 3 (October 1966), 1–7.

Boulden, James B. and Buffa, Elwood S. Corporate models: On-line, real-time systems, *Harvard Business Review*, Vol. 48 (July–August 1970), pp. 65–83.

Brenman, Edwin, Analyzing work performance with a budget, *Administrative Management*, Vol. 30, No. 3 (March 1969), 20–21.

Cadman, Theodore W. and Munno, Frank J. Fundamentals of analog computation, *Water and Wastes Engineering*, Vol. 5, No. 1 (January 1968), 50–54. Part II: (March 1968), 42–50.

Computer simulation: Management puts it to work, *Savings and Loan News*, Vol. 91 (August 1970), pp. 30–35.

Danziger, Erwin and Hobgood, Sandy, The impact of computers on education, *Journal of Data Management*, Vol. 6, No. 4 (April 1968), 22–26.

Diebold, John, Bad decisions on computer use, *Harvard Business Review*, Vol. 47, No. 1 (January–February 1969), 14–28.

Gorry, G. Anthony and Morton, Michael S. S. Management decision systems; A framework for management information systems, *MIT Sloan School of Management*, Cambridge, Mass., Fall 1971, 55–70.

Kiriat, Philip, J. Digital computer simulation modeling concepts, Santa Monica, Calif.: *Rand Corporation*, 1967.

Kurtzman, David, H. Problems involved in executive utilization of information technology, *Proceedings of the Conference on EDP Systems for State and Local Governments*, New York University, Graduate School of Public Administration and System Development Corporation, (September 30–October 2, 1964), pp. 118 and 120.

Miller, Irvin M. Computer graphics for decision making, *Harvard Business Review*, Vol. 47 (November–December 1969), pp. 121–132.

Salton, Gerard, Information science in a Ph.D. computer science program, *Communications of the A.C.M.* (Association for Computing Machinery), Vol. 12, No. 2 (February 1969), 111–117.

Schick, Charles W. and Perrill, Vickie J. Using the computer as an auditing tool, *New York Certified Public Accountant*, Vol. 39, No. 1 (January 1969), 57–60.

Stitelman, Leonard, Computers and the problems of urban cooperation, *Urban Affairs Quarterly*, (December 1967), pp. 69–78.
Wolfe, Harry B. ADP in public utilities commissions, an "Output" article in *Public Automation*, Vol. 3, No. 9 (September 1967), insert.

BOOKS

Committee on Information Systems, *Guidelines for Automated Data Processing Education and Training in State Government*. Lexington, Ky.: Council of State Governments, 1967.
Gardner, James B. and Purdy, Gerry J. *Computerized Training Programs*, New York, N.Y.: Hafner, 1970.
Information Systems Current Developments and Future Expansion, Montvale, N.J.: American Federation of Information Processing Systems, 1971.
Tomeski, Edward A. *Computer Revolution: The Executive and the New Information Technology*, New York, N.Y.: Macmillan, 1969.
Wirtz, Willard, *Professionalism in the Computer Field: Report of a Roundtable Meeting*, sponsored by AFIPS, Montvale, N.J.: American Federation of Information Processing Systems, 1973.

MONOGRAPHS

Greenwood, Frank and Danziger, Erwin M. *Computer Systems Analyst: Problems of Selection, Education, and Training*, Management Bulletin 90, New York: American Management Association, 1967.
Schwartz, H. A. and Haskell, R. J., Jr. IBM Corporation, Poughkeepsie, A study of computer-assisted instruction in industrial training, *Journal of Applied Psychology*, Vol. 50, No. 5 (1966), 360–363.

CHAPTER V

Conclusion: The State of the Art

In retrospect, the first 25 years of the computer age can be viewed as a parochial era during which computer usage was expensive but justified for a fairly narrow though common class of numerical and clerical tasks. The computer appeared remote from daily life because it was separately housed, tended only by technicians, and only occasionally, improved day-to-day operations.

In comparison, the next 25 years may become a universal era for computers. They will become more economical to use and more widely utilized in tasks that now seem impossible.

In the three articles in this concluding chapter we appraise: (1) computer systems and applications in the public sector to date, and (2) the remaining tasks for computers improving public administration. These are juxtaposed to show that, although the accomplishments of computer utilization to date are significant in terms of government improving the delivery of social services, there still remain many problem areas where computers could significantly improve governmental performance and thereby quality of life.

Mr Gottlieb in this regard charges public administration with the responsibility for directing computer applications to improve the living conditions of all segments of our society. The accomplishments to date, Mr. Gottlieb argues, primarily benefit the more affluent segments of our society: for example, computer airline reservation systems, computerized car rentals, etc. The concerns of the poorer segments, however, to a large degree are not profitable enough to harness the computer's power for significantly improved quality-of-life of these people.

Professor Weizenbaum continues in a similar vein. He questions the utility of this new "mega-machine" (to borrow Minniford's famous phrase). The technology by itself, he argues, is a nightmare. The systems derived from it are primarily used by large organizations such as governments and corporations. We must make sure that these uses are for man's benefit rather than to his detriment. It is the responsibility of those in charge of computer systems to prevent dehumanization. It is on this level that the job still remains to be done.

21

Computer Applications in State and Local Government: a Survey of Accomplishments

SAMUEL J. BERNSTEIN

Baruch College, City University of New York

I. INTRODUCTION

Computers, it may be said, have become an indispensible element in all internal and external aspects of government operations. As such it is reasonable to anticipate a continuing growth rate of computer installations, applications, and systems in the next decade particularly at the state or province and local government levels. This projection may be confirmed in part by the facts, that: since 1965, the *Muncipal Yearbook* devotes a separate section to reporting the uses of data-processing equipment by cities; over 3000 computers of various types and sizes are already in use by state and local government in the U.S.A.

A survey of computer accomplishments to date in state and local governments is provided for two purposes: to define the present state of the art in order to indicate gaps where greater computer utilization may lead to improved performance in the public sector; and to show a development path for the fourth generation computers which will drastically increase information processing capacity of governments. The expected benefit of increased utilization is improved governmental performance—the scope of which is also to increase in the next decade. Derivatively, the quality of life of the citizenry should be significantly enhanced.

427

II. MANAGERIAL ADMINISTRATIVE AREA

Management Information Systems

Although growing lip service is paid to the importance of information systems in improving state and local governments' performance, the accomplishments to date are far less than expected. For even where federal aid is made available for the development of comprehensive management information systems, these systems do not achieve full utilization as planned due to the financial inability of state, municipal, and local governments to shoulder the ongoing cost of gathering, maintaining, and processing the information necessary for the system to be valuable for administration and decision purposes. The state of Louisiana stands out as an example to be emulated in this regard. It effectively operates an automated management system based on federal aid programs to the state and its political subdivisions (parishes).

The system coordinates, on annual bases, applications for federal aid by the parishes or the state operating agencies; moniters spending on all federal grants; and manages the budgets of governmental units. To ease the burdens of development and maintenance of information systems for municipalities and local governments, we propose the establishment of central/cooperative data-processing centers at either state or intercounty levels. The model for such development ought to be central municipal and local governmental processing centers of Holland and Israel. Some sample planning and management data services to be provided by such an agency may include: population and industry registers on subareal bases, social services information, property tax files, land use profiles, budget management, salary payment, and financial status reports. The aim is to enable better integration and coordination of governmental information files in order to attain governmental efficiency and effectiveness. This would then result in more effective sharing of information with a commensurate reduction in the cost of public service delivery.

Two pioneering efforts of this sort are underway in the United States today: California, through the Intergovernmental Board on EDP and the Pennsylvania Interagency Municipal Information Systems Advisory Committee.

Personnel Administration

A state government's most valuable resource is its personnel. How a government treats its employees can greatly affect their productivity. In one state, employees are frequently hired to fill vacant positions prior to civil service qualification. Due to reliance upon an incredibly inept data handling system, 18 months may go by from the time an individual is hired to fill a position to the time a civil service examination is given for that position. Once hired, an employee may wait six to twelve weeks in New York City before receiving a paycheck. Employees that are paid monthly or bimonthly commonly take weekly advances—a cumbersome "make-work" procedure that satisfies neither the employer not the employee. Computer failure is the common excuse given for the occasional late payroll.

Needless to say, well designed automated personnel payroll systems are in operation in most state, county, and even municipal governments. However, the utilization is primarily, if not exclusively, devoted to check printing and issuance. The role of the computer has to be increased in this area by providing more and up-to-date information to personnel officers for effective personnel administration. The parameters of personnel information may include coded employee history files, absentee and overtime files, manpower utilization, need projections, and salary planning. An ongoing system in this regard is shown in Chapter III, Article 10.

Financial Administration

The general rise in local and state government expenditures and the corresponding steep increases in property, sales, state and even municipal taxes, demands the implementation of *automated revenue management* and *accounting/budgetary control systems* which interface with an overall management information system.

Revenue management systems should provide the information in the first case to effectively administer new taxes as well as to process tax returns. An efficient use of teleprocessing for revenue management is in operation in Nebraska. A terminal input and inquiry system enables that state to process an individual income tax refund within seven work days of receipt of the tax return, even though over 75% of the returns filed result in a refund.

Accounting and budget control systems should provide the information necessary to make decisions regarding the allocation of available funds and to monitor the efficient utilization of funds already allocated. Ohio's State fiscal management reporting system demonstrates this capability.

1. An accounting control checks the accuracy and validity of each transaction prior to acceptance is provided.

2. Potential fiscal problems may be pinpointed before they become critical by the provision of daily reports giving the status of all accounts.
3. Monthly and annual reports are given on the first day following the close of the previous work period allowing payments to vendors to be made no later than the date they are due.

As a side benefit cash control and investment procedures are improved resulting in a threefold increase in income to the state. Improved financial knowledge of this sort stands in contrast to the classic example of the agency head seeking authorization for a new program toward the end of a fiscal year: "Funds to cover this cost, I believe, are not available."

Three of the problems of poor fiscal management which may be avoided by the computer are:

1. Vendors may stop dealing with state and municipal governments because they could no longer afford to carry the outstanding balances due to them; or in the alternative, vendors build in higher carrying charges in their pricing to local government purchasing.
2. Poor fiscal management weakens the borrowing capacity of governments as witnessed by New York City.
3. Over-centralized fiscal control dampens management initiative.

An example of this latter point follows. In operating agencies the chief may be required to obtain Finance Department approval each time his agency wants to move in a new direction or develop a new capital project in a portfolio of ongoing projects. While such a control may help to prevent misuse of funds it tends:

1. To force organizational inertia which is presently characteristic of public management.
2. To inhibit intelligent resource allocation decisions.
3. To fail in the prevention of other forms of mismanagement.

An automated fiscal administration system, however, would go a long way toward relaxing tight central management in favor of responsible decentralized operations. By computer-based planning, accounting, budgetary controls and evaluation, effective monitering of operations could be maintained as well as management initiative. Further, given, the "on-line" inquiry and retrieval capabilities of third and fourth generation computers, the appropriate legislative and executive bodies could easily gather the data necessary for analyzing program effectiveness and efficiency to determine the wisdom of requested budgetary allocations.

III. FUNCTIONAL ADMINISTRATIVE AREAS

Community Planning and Development

In view of the complexity inherent in the formulation of economic plans, it is exceedingly difficult, if not impossible, to prepare regional and statewide plans without the assistance of a computer. Wisconsin's Bureau of State Planning has begun the implementation of a comprehensive planning information system that produces the planning data required for the preparation of plans by various state agencies. The computer-based outputs are in the form of a real profiles indicating population projections, utilities availability, and summaries of socio-economic activities. This data profile is generated from a data base, which is regularly updated in accordance with changes that have occurred over specific time intervals. In this regard Alabama State may be cited for the development of an industrial site location system which matches a company's requirements with a particular area or subarea according to the available labor pool, transportation facilities, utilities availability, and industrial sites. Such a computer system is of considerable value for aiding a states', countys', or citys' industrial development goals.

Public Safety

Criminal Identification

A number of statewide computer telecommunications network systems have been implemented which aid police intelligence in tracking down crime. A policeman can radio the license number of a vehicle under surveillance to his dispatcher and in a matter of seconds know whether the vehicle may have been reported stolen or used as a getaway car in a serious crime. In addition to FBI, state, and local police data on vehicles, these systems contain information on stolen parts and equipment, boats, firearms, license plates, stocks, bonds or other securities, and wanted or missing persons. In New York State, police officers may obtain information on any registered vehicle and licensed driver in the state. For example, the Motor Vehicle Department may respond to special requests of police by rapidly providing a list of light green two-door sedans with the last digit of the state license plate a five. Similarly, many states quickly post court convictions for traffic violations to the driver's license file by computer.

The computer is increasingly being used as a police laboratory tool providing detailed information on such diverse items as fingerprints, fibers, firearms, blood, hair, minerals, vegetables, paper, paint, stains, and tools. In New York, 41 facsimile installations across the state are used to transmit fingerprints to the New York State Identification and Intelligence System. Upon receiving and classifying a set of fingerprints, an automated search is conducted to determine if there is a prior criminal history on file for the individual. If there is, a computer printed summary of the individual's criminal history is transmitted to the law enforcement agency that requested the fingerprint search.

While dealing with criminal history and suspected criminal activity information systems, careful attention must be paid to the maintenance of data security and privileged information. No doubt such consideration is not limited to public safety applications alone, however, the issue is formally raised here because of the required sensitivity for a person's constitutional rights as mandated by the Courts and Congress.

The need for data security should be evident to every state agency. Unfortunately, in some states computer room doors are left unlocked. In one instance, a Welfare Department's computer was still accessible to any passerby several months after it had been taken over by a group of protestors. Within the context of state governmental data handling, the computer properly used can serve as a powerful protector of individual rights. Often the data to be computerized already exists in manual files—sometimes it lies around on desk tops or in unlocked file cabinets open to view by any staff member or casual visitor irrespective of his need to know. One state maintains a file of individual court appearances on an estimated 5 million index cards. In some states, arrest histories and court records have been illegally sold to credit bureaus, banks, and brokerage houses.

Computers properly programmed and with source data properly coded could aid in guaranteeing the security of privileged information such that any information obtained by tapping a data file would be undeciperable. In addition to keeping track of persons having a right to access certain information by maintaining a log on who accessed the information, and when, there are other validity checking and data purging procedures which could be instituted. For example, the legitimacy of a user may be determined by means of fingerprint and/or voice print comparisons.

Criminal Justice Administration

The United States Court of Appeals in the second circuit (1971) recently held that criminal indictments not tried within six months must be dismissed; if not tried within three months, the defendant must be admitted to bail. Such a normative prescription stands in stark contrast to the staggering backlog of both criminal and civil cases in state courts throughout the country. For example, in Pennsylvania there remains over 18,000 untried criminal indictments or complaints (including more than 100 pending capital cases) and over 65,000 untried and pending civil cases. In New York City, a 40-month wait for trial is not uncommon. Computer systems and applications clearly cannot substitute for the badly needed additional judges and other court personnel, but they can help reduce the amount of time lost due to inadequate communications, information handling, and inefficient case scheduling. On the one hand, the criminal intelligence systems described in the previous section have expanded the capabilities of the police, however, the weakly administered court system more than offsets the potential benefits of the former. This condition is further aggrevated by the inefficiencies of court related services, relating to youth, corrections and parole agencies.

It is proposed that integrated or compatible public safety computer services be developed to encompass all aspects of the administration of justice. These are to be sponsored either by the municipal and/or county governments, which are directly related with the provision of this service to the citizenry. The development and the management of the system should be by an interagency committee with its own director. This would provide the necessary organizational representation in conjunction with a unity of purpose to significantly improve the individual case work load and agency resource allocation which are directly related to more effective criminal rehabilitation.

Education

Educational computer systems and applications focus on two areas: instruction and administration. Hitherto, the trend has been to separate the two at every level—primary, secondary, and even higher education. A computer-based educational information processing system is presently being implemented in Oregon and is expected to combine both tasks without sacrificing the instructional applications. Similarly, the twin cities of Minneapolis and St. Paul are cooperating with their respective school boards and with each other to develop joint administrative and computer aided instruction (CAI) systems. This system is to include administrative components involving information for pupil and staff processing, curriculum planning and management, scheduling of centralized school programs, complex simulations for planning, remote terminal entry for

CAI and resource requirements for educational facilities management. In regard to resource and facilities management the Triangle Universities Computation Center in North Carolina is of particular significance. A computer-based model utilizing student enrollment as basic components is used for processing students for college admissions, and then, for planning models to estimate and manage resources and facilities.

Any discussion of education and computers would be incomplete without consideration of Library applications. At the present, little has been accomplished in the way of developing statewide automated library systems. These would be needed to improve reference and information retrieval services for both educational and professional purposes as well as library ordering, processing, cataloguing, and shelving operations. The "Medlar" tapes system for medical libraries may provide the model in this regard for future library information reference systems.

Transportation

Highway planning has been traditionally confused with transportation planning although the latter has a much broader scope at present. State highway departments, therefore, with the encouragement of the oil lobbyists emphasize highway planning in their work. The most prevalent computer use in this regard is automated network models which convert origin/destination travel data into highway link densities. The Michigan Highway Department, for example, uses such a model both for evaluating proposed changes in interurban highway links and for forecasting future traffic loads.

Indiana's State Highway Commission uses a computer assisted route location system to generate alternative corridors for highway locations. The parameters considered in the model include earthwork characteristics, pavement construction, right-of-way acquisition costs, trip distributions, and the relationship to existing road network. The system uses minimum path analysis to produce a series of ranked alternatives between any desired points.

The automated creation of maps from aerial photographs is another area of computer applications that has drastically reduced the amount of field surveying work done by the Texas Highway Department. In a similar vein, New York City has digitized street and block mapping and thereby improved development planning in the city. Overall, it may be said that, the state of the art of computer applications in highway planning is fairly advanced to the degree where many packaged civil engineering systems are available. One such outstanding package is the MIT civil engineering system.

While, to date, the states use computers for highway design, they make little use of the computer for the more pressing problems of urban transportation planning, traffic management, and facilities management. Applications toward this end should come in developing and operating mass transit operations, port development, and management as well as urban traffic management. The cities of Baltimore, New York, and Los Angeles have experimented in this realm by computerizing traffic lights on major thoroughfares. Further, the articles by Cantilli, and Dial and Bunyan in Chapter III indicate the fertility of computer applications in the related areas of traffic management and transportation planning.

Construction of Public Buildings and Housing

Design and appropriation of construction funds have become backlogged such that they now require more than a year longer to disburse than they did a decade ago. Furthermore, when projects move into construction phases they suffer from seemingly needless cost overruns. Reducing delays in design, approval, and construction of public and private capital projects thus is essential for improving the public administration of capital project development. Various proposals have been advanced in this direction but few have come to fruition. A computer-based construction management system is proposed which would have the following components: accurate control of construction accounts; a related file of project records; estimated construction costs of projects prior to appropriation; scheduled phasing of work completion; and monitering of progress. From this system, performance evaluation on various designs and contractors could be derived, which could be very helpful in assigning future projects. To date, however, there are few operating systems of this type. Dodson in Chapter III outlines such a system for the construction and management of low-cost housing.

Welfare

Welfare has been aptly described as the growth industry within government. A spot survey by the New York Department of Social Services revealed that approximately 25% of the state's medical assistance recipients and nearly 30% of the people on relief rolls were ineligible. Since it is difficult to determine how many people continue to receive welfare benefits after becoming ineligible, there is an obvious need for implementing a computerized case control system to moniter welfare eligibility and eliminate duplicate, excessive, and possibly even fraudulent payments. These computer-assisted case control systems offer the best and probably the only hope of improving the administration of the welfare system and service to be provided to the citizentry by the welfare system.

The generally debilitated structure of the welfare system is further aggravated by the Medicaid programs which in some states account for nearly 65% of the welfare caseload and almost 45% of all the welfare dollars spent. For the state that does not have an automated Medicaid payments system (e.g., California) payments have fallen so far behind that some pharmacists claim they have had to borrow money to stay in business because of outstanding bills owed to them by the state. Some physicians report that reimbursements lag two to three years behind, and, the largest hospital in the state has sought a court order to require the immediate payment of interest for overdue bills which may reach 10 million dollars.

In contrast is the state of Florida, which uses an on-line Medicaid payments system that checks recipient eligibility prior to the receipt of medical services. "A computer printed provider's statement" is issued within ten days of patient treatment. After verification by the provider as to type and cost of treatment, the statement is returned to the Florida Department of Health and Rehabilitative Services from where it is paid within 30 days. The system can also provide Medicaid utilization reports by type of service for the previous day, week, and month date and year to date.

In addition to the help provided in effectively maintaining Medicaid programs, computers could further aid in planning for improved performance. For example, given the data on utilization data of health services, realistic bases for the assignment of fees could be developed. Fee schedules might be formulated encouraging office visits rather than hospitalization. This in turn could help to control rising hospital costs and provide for better allocation of available health research.

Environment and Pollution

The environment and its pollution has already shown itself to be a fertile area for computer applications. These have included content of fish catches, game kill estimates, cost calculations on forest fires, agricultural and fisheries marketing analyses. In contrast to these specific applications, Kentucky, with the assistance of the United States Department of

Agriculture, is formulating a computerized outdoor recreation management information system to aid in the preparation of comprehensive recreation plans for serving local and regional needs. The system will operate within the framework of an overall statewide resource control plan and should enhance the capability of Department of Parks personnel to perform analytical studies of recreation need, project feasibility, and community impact. Kentucky is also developing a water management information system to assist in water resource planning. On the basis of water resource data and economic and demographic data, the system projects water demand and supplies for municipal and industrial needs, recreation, power navigation, and irrigation. When fully implemented, the system will help identify problem areas and compute the effects of proposed solutions.

A pollution control system to provide for the automatic monitoring of air and water conditions is being implemented by New York. Twelve water and 11 air-monitoring stations have been placed in critical locations across the state. A computer automatically polls each air station once every 15 minutes and each water station once an hour. Air and pollution status information are compared to preset criteria, and if acceptable environmental limits are not met, the computer generates a warning message. Monitoring stations recording the unusual readings can also initiate warning messages. The system presently records data for ten water and 18 air characteristics.

Eventually some 60 water and 50 air stations monitoring an even wider range of characteristics are expected to play a major role in New York's air and water pollution control activities. Computer programs are presently being written to simulate air or water pollution levels under varying environmental conditions. An example of one such program calculates the potential pollution damage attributable to industrial smokestack emissions. A significant review of the computers role in managing the environment is provided by Koenig, Haynes and Fisher in Chapter III.

IV. OTHER RECENT DEVELOPMENTS

Manpower Planning

Under the direction of the U.S. Department of Labor, statewide job bank programs are being established throughout the country. Missouri's Division of Employment Security provides computer output microfilm listings of job openings to its local offices in the St. Louis metropolitan area. Utah has a computerized job matching system that permits on-line

S. J. BERNSTEIN

comparisons of applicant qualifications with listed job requirements on the basis of specified criteria. Up to 36 job selection factors including as many as three "must" factors may be used in an inquiry. Job opportunities or applicants most closely matching the selection criteria are displayed for possible referral. The Utah computer system also monitors the quality of service being provided to job applicants. The system prints out and sends to the local office a full copy of the application of any individual in the active file who was not serviced during the preceding 15 days, has been selected five times but never referred for a job, or referred three times but never hired. The system also reminds local office personnel of any selections, call-ins, or referrals that have been pending for three days. Should an applicant who is receiving unemployment insurance or welfare benefits be placed on a job, fail to apply for or refuse to accept a suitable job, the system immediately notifies the local unemployment insurance claims office of the Department of Public Welfare.

Public Health Services

Two potential applications areas may be considered in public health: one dealing with medical provisions and the other with mental health provisions. Of the two the greater efforts for computerization have been expended on the former which are seemingly more pressing in their need. State Health Departments routinely use computers to support infant immunization, tuberculosis evaluation, and cancer research programs. They are also used as an aid to comprehensive health planning through the retrieval and analysis of vital statistics. In South Carolina, a computerized system for reporting the activities of nurses provides information about public health nursing services and community health problems. Similarly, the Massachusetts Public Health Council recently (January 1971) adopted new rules designed to improve the delivery and quality of health services provided by the state's nursing and convalescent homes. This change in nursing home regulations—the first major revision in 17 years—came about as a result of computer assisted studies which indicated that a majority of Massachusetts' long-term facilities were not providing services appropriate to the needs of most patients and that the charges for services were largely unrelated to patient care.

The mobile chest X-ray unit is a common reminder that disease detection and prevention are among the most pressing of all public health tasks. Computer-based screening systems capable of detecting the danger signals of a number of chronic diseases and reporting the presence of certain others have been developed. Data generated by a medical history questionnaire and a series of laboratory procedures including blood tests, urine analysis, electrocardiogram, and chest X-rays are compared with normal ranges and indications of the possible presence of disease are reported. Computer assisted health check-ups are relatively inexpensive (the above battery of tests might be more than five times as expensive if performed by a hospital laboratory). Moreover, the computer-assisted analyses can be performed in mobile units by nurses or paramedical workers. In view of the low percentage of Americans presently getting periodic health check-ups, we may say that we are nowhere near the full utilization of presently available computer capability in public health.

An example of a comprehensive utilization of computers in the mental health area is in the Missouri system. Symptoms exhibited by a patient entering a state mental institution along with demographic and medical history data taken from a psychiatric diagnosis, are coded, automatically stored, and analyzed. A resultant summary computer print-out shows an assessment of the patient's diseases, the disposition for self-harm, and the need for long or short-term care. Not only is the diagnostic role for computers significant in the treatment of illness, it is as well an aid for more effective management of mental health resources and facilities.

The workload of Mental Rehabilitation Commissions has greatly increased due to the increased rehabilitation problems associated with increased drug abuse. A sample review of budgeting requests reveal an increase in spending by a factor of four or five by Rehabilitation Commissions in the last decades. The work of these agencies opens whole areas for improved performance stemming from computer applications. The state of New Jersey has pioneered in developing new approaches here. It's Rehabilitation Commission has an automated system for analyzing a rehabilitation client's emotional and physical capacities and incapacities. This system provides a functional profile of the client, mentally or physically in consistent terms, which can be used as an aid in planning vocational rehabilitation.

22

The Computer and the Job Undone*

ABE GOTTLIEB

Research Planner,
Pennsylvania State Planning Board, Harrisburg, Pennsylvania

Abstract. The computer and its technology is continuing to make major inroads into all aspects of American life. Many of its applications are destructive and when computer capabilities are applied to urban problems, their focus is on the physical inventories of streets, traffic, land use, police records, tax statements, etc. A large-scale and sustained effort should be made to utilize this technology to aid the ill, the poor, and other disadvantaged segments of the population. Such a redirection would require computer applications at three levels: data management and organization; problem solving; and process control. However, urban specialists and the military-aerospace systems analysts who are frequently called in as consultants are decidedly lukewarm to computer applications for the analysis and delivery of socially oriented services.

If the computer can be considered a machine, we are right in asking why is it not being used or used more effectively in the struggle for a better social environment? The machine and the factory did, after all, transform most of our societies in the 19th century and, for better or for worse, revolutionized every aspect of human thought and conduct. Can we and should we control the computer more skillfully, more purposefully, than our ancestors controlled their factories, mills, and machinery of production?

It might be argued that our industrial and postindustrial societies are a fortuitous by-product of non-control, sobered or addled (depending on your point of view) by ad hoc incursions of government into the social

---

*Reprinted from the *Proceedings of the Urban Symposium*, of the Association of Computing Machinery, October 1971, pp. 1–9.

and economic affairs of man. But beyond the theorizing around this subject, present day advocates of major social changes in our cities are demanding, in a cumulative more insistent manner, that all resources (human, money, and technological) be harnessed for tangible improvements in housing, health, quality of air, and water, education, and economic opportunities. This should begin to define the computer and its uses as an important agent of social change.

We may be too locked into our time frame to see it but it is probable that the computer is the same kind of transforming agent that the mill and its machinery was in the early 1800s in England and later on in the rest of the Western world. Direct analogies cannot be spun out too finely because a century and a half of social, economic, intellectual, and institutional changes separates the primitive machines then from the newly fashioned computers now. Nevertheless, the parallels are real and provoking.

The computer today occupies a central position in American life and makes strong claims to even greater centrality in the coming decades. We now have about 90,000 machines installed or working for business, government, science, making war, reporting fires, catching criminals, and expediting gambling ventures. These represent an approximate investment of $10 billion not counting the currently elitist work force that tend them and the direct spinoff congeries that are closely dependent on their constant operations.

Even if we continue to squander this burdgeoning resource on useless and dangerous operations, its impact on individual, corporate, and intellectual life in the United States will be enormous. Unlike the machines of the early 1800s, no "dark satanic mills" have sprung up to feed its insatiable demands; a few glimpses inside our research installations prove quite contrary. Nor will computer technology organize and set into motion the warring economic classes that accompanied the industrial revolution. Clearly, it is not that kind of revolutionary agent.

It, nevertheless, presages fundamental changes and adjustments. For one thing, its data munipulation and problem solving capabilities have already and will continue to induce far reaching adjustments in management structure and policy at almost all levels in government, industry, and university life. Its range, depth, flexibility, and (hopefully) ability to explore and clarify program options will probably call into being new bureaucracies staffed by people with new and generally powerful ties to the decision makers. The "deciders" themselves might be somewhat transformed in the process and, if they cannot make other accommodations would conceivably drop themselves out.

Computer technology is also inevitably reshaping the less esoteric patterns of our lives and the structures that fashion them. Without indulging in the "gee whiz" technology that inaccurately and foolishly talks about microseconds of output, it is possible to see what lies ahead. For example, the individual's daily, monthly, and yearly accounts with local and national governments and with the retail and personal services he utilizes, is undergoing significant shifts. As a consumer, his accounts with everyone who has a claim on them is moving into a new pattern. In the process, our money economy may, at least, partially disappear or become unrecognizably changed. We may also expect a vastly different kind of educational process to surface as television is linked to home computers in a form of "network" instruction especially for younger children. In these and other areas of human interaction, the computer and its applications will induce far reaching changes in American life and will probably do so with a minimum of institutional intervention.

For a nation that has rediscovered its vulnerable poor, aged, ill, and unprotected people, these kinds of present and contemplated uses are not enough. However, to move the capabilities of the computer squarely into the urban social arena, all kinds of "interventions" will be necessary, first and foremost of which is a fundamental reappraisal of our international policies and priorities. This would be a transformation of the first magnitude and one should not minimize the political, military, and bureaucratic obdurancy that must be overcome for this shift to take place. With or without Vietnam, the cart cannot come before the horse and it would be idle to expect a significant mobilization of research and technology into these fields without major reordering of national and world-wide programs and priorities.

It is, indeed, regrettable that, during the past two decades, the most sophisticated machines we possess have been, for a while, working almost exclusively and incessantly on hundreds, perhaps thousands of military applications, ranging from simple weapons inventory to the games that men play around the national survival possibilities in the event of a nuclear holocaust. More lately, computer applications to space technology and communications have begun to preempt these funds and resources. Even when the Federal government began to open a trickle of research funds to the urban areas in the early and mid 1950s, the programs to enlist the greatest computer support were for origin and destination studies and traffic computations. These transportation and related land use explorations still buy a very substantial portion of all machine use in our states, cities, and metropolitan areas.

The gap between what the computer might contribute towards altering our social environment and what it actually has been doing is a very deep one indeed. This does not mean that our Federal agencies are blind to its possibilities. The computerized censuses of 1960 and 1970, the Social Security System, the Internal Revenue Service, and a number of other formidable inventories are now locked into the computer and ready for use. But nothing approching the imaginative interplay between man and machine that has been possible in military and space research has begun to unfold in the areas of social and urban concern. Slowly, and at a pace that suggests forever, our machine technology has barely been considered for the evaluation and choice of social programs or for the coordination and delivery of health and welfare services.

But even if our sense of priorities were to shift appreciably, we would nevertheless be faced with important obstacles. A very pervasive lack of data that measures or characterizes the conditions of the ill, aged, low income, and other deprived groups seriously inhibit the initiation of machine use towards programs in these areas. Furthermore, the traditional orientation of cities and municipalities around extremely narrow housekeeping functions has accumulated for them the kind of data inventories that describe buildings, structures, land parcels, tax records, police and fire records, and other information, all basically object rather than people focused. Computer applications, even in the largest cities, are more at home with these inventories and what little success has been achieved in metropolitan problem solving and policy or program research has been with these "hard" data and subject areas. The generally uncertain or weak state of the art seems to be reinforcing the desire of urban management specialists to avoid the human resources complexities of their cities and ghettos. Unfortunately, new HUD aid programs for computerized municipal information systems are not likely to encourage experimentation in anything but the "safe" areas.

We should reaffirm, at this point, that the computer will remain, for some time to come, a device used by mortals to aid in problem solving and process control. It would be patent nonsense to assume that its use and application could lead to push button solutions to the social tinder boxes that have so explosively disrupted our urban lives in the past decade. We need merely to examine the elaborate and finely tooled economic defense mechanisms that have been incorporated into our economy in the 1930s, almost entirely without computer aid, to understand this fact. For that matter, the entire social, financial, and economic reformation of the New Deal in that decade unfolded without "computer support." Clearly, the alchemy of social change (progress?) needs more than merely the blessings of IBM.

Nevertheless, when we look back we are somewhat amazed that is happened the way it did. Are we likely to duplicate this bravura performance in the coming decades? Is our structure too complicated to move ahead without the computer? The only thing we can be sure of is that the major style with which we approach complex social issues in the 1970s will be different from the preceding decades. We have, it seems, amply demonstrated our increasing attachment to the unique capabilities of the computer even though its performance in both the "hard" and "soft" areas of urban policy and program research has been very lean indeed. So be it then. If we must live with the device, let us define the preconditions that will allow it to perform for the weakest groups in our midst.

By now, we ought to expect substantial computer assistance in three levels of penetration, namely: data management and organization; problem solving; and process control. Stated in the context of a substantive social objective such as the need for vastly improved health services, we may translate these terms as follows:

1. Data management and organization: A body of knowledge identifying the health status and characteristics of the population.
2. Problem solving: The anticipation of health needs and facilities for the future; the impact of current and proposed programs on the client population and on related social welfare programs; the measurement of effectiveness of existing and proposed health programs; the choice of "best" or maximum benefit programs.
3. Process control and delivery of services: Systems for the delivery of preventative, diagnostic, and treatment assistance to all segments of the population; formulation of community health information and referral systems; data networks among hospitals, laboratories, and other intake centers.

It need not be difficult to define these levels of computer application to other than health problems and solutions. For example, public assistance and all the interrelated aspects of crime (detection, detention, community-police relations, and possibly prevention) could be susceptible to this tripartite approach. As a matter of fact, progress in each of the stages would add measurably to our ability to probe the area of concern and then deliver the program or service associated with it. While research with computers may be and frequently is undertaken separately at each level indicated above, this need not be the only scheme. Indeed, for many problems that are more than logistic in nature, it would seem that all three stages are conceptually and in many instances sequentially related.

Let us assume that we want to run our machines full tilt ahead, that is, we will enlist the maximum support of the computer in the social arena and seek to exploit its full potentialities in data management and organization, problem solving, and process control. Yet, by some continuing myopic tropism, we have shut ourselves off from the inventory and intelligence that makes much of this possible. In "Towards a Social Report" of the Department of Health, Education and Welfare, we are made painfully aware of the fact that "the nation has no comprehensive set of statistics reflecting social progress or retrogression. There is no government procedure for stock taking of the social social health of the nation." Yet, if the machine can do nothing else, it is uniquely qualified to accept, storage, organize, and manipulate information.*

Our knowledge vacuum is truly an anomalous situation. For it is with us despite the fact (and sometimes even because of the fact) that the federal, state, and local governments have amassed and computerized a vast body of statistical knowledge. Paradoxically, while we are inundated in a sea of paper, ink, and printouts, we cannot measure the human toll of illness, the pollution of the environment, the quality of our education, and the nature of the alienation expressed in burning and looting in the ghetto, strife on the campus, and crime in the city streets. This paradox suggests that a general expansion of statistical efforts is not enough but that we need to define new ideas about what kinds of data and information ought to be collected.

This point was graphically made in recent testimony before the Senate Labor Committee by Joseph A. Califano, formerly President Johnson's chief advisor for domestic affairs. He commented on the fact that it took the Administration nearly two years merely to find out who were the 7 million people then receiving about 4 billion dollars annually in welfare payments. No real study of welfare recipients, at least nationally, had ever been made. Similarly, after the eruption at Watts in 1965, a federal team of investigators could not develop a coherent picture of life and its

---

*We might turn this socio-technological lag to our benefit by playing the game called "How to Use the Machine by Not Using It." I am suggesting that we ought to keep accumulating machine capacity, not use it for a period of time, let our deep fear of "unused capacity" take hold and then proceed to generate the finest set of social indicators we are capable of assembling. This would not displease the computer manufacturers and may hasten a socially desirable goal.

conditions there based on the data available on the community and its people.

At the national and local levels, the socially based information necessary for understanding, evaluation, and decision is lacking and this gap all too often paralyzes action or prevents the most useful and appropriate programs from being defined. As stated by Mr. Califano:

> The disturbing truth is that the basis of recommendations by an American Cabinet officer on whether to begin, eliminate or expand vast social programs more nearly resembles the intuitive judgment of a benevolent tribal chief in remote Africa than the elaborate, sophisticated data with which the Secretary of Defense supports a major new weapons system.

Programs to generate social statistics or indicators have been and continue to be endemic in Washington but no serious assessment of their success, partial success, or failure is ever made. For example, a tentative first step towards the organization of a network of State Centers for Health Statistics was initiated about a year and a half ago. At that time, the National Center for Health Statistics of the Department of Health, Education, and Welfare, proposed a very substantial intensification of efforts to obtain coordinated and reliable information on health conditions, services, and resources in each state. Recognizing the fact that the planning, evaluation, and delivery of programs and services require a major qualitative and quantitative addition to our present meager intelligence, the National Center drew up a blue print (the more acceptable term is guide) for the organization, data coverage, and administration of the proposed State Centers. Like many other forays that sought to extend our grasp of social data, this may be a mere pious wish if the states are not geared financially, ideologically, and operationally to undertake the task.

A similar program, but with much more administrative underpinning is now proceeding in another segment of the far-flung Department of Health, Education, and Welfare. This demonstration program, funded by the federal and state governments, seeks to develop a computer-based system that will integrate the often conflicting and even contradictory public assistance programs and data efforts of all the states. Again, if this program moves in the direction of a nationwide expansion of basic information about the environment of poverty (and this seems likely), it would represent a significant advance in the use of computers to manage and prepare a basic national inventory.

When we consider the prospects of machine use for problem solving, we move into a somewhat different realm. In an operational sense, data organization can be achieved with relatively little human intervention, that is, the computer needs somewhat simple instructions to organize, process, and "deliver" large and complex inventories. This is generally not true when we expect it to aid in problem solving such as projections, cost effectiveness studies, and other kinds of program evaluations. For this purpose, the man and machine relationships must be closer and the "instructions" are of a quite higher order. Consequently, a shift in emphasis away from the computer and towards the state of the art (the ability of the researcher to formulate the problems and derive the solutions) becomes important. At the level of problem solving, we have to assess the responsibility somewhat differently than we have done heretofore and inquire into the limits and possibilities of man-machine effectiveness rather than the role of the computer alone.

In a recent article in the New York Times, Daniel Moynihan wrote that: "The attempted solution of a (political) problem leads to the creation of a knowledge problem .... but the linkage of knowledge with policy is an extraordinarily complex process central to modern society."

This linkage has been even more baffling and elusive in the areas of health, education, crime, and welfare than in the harder disciplines of economics and transportation. The avenues of research and computer applications during the past several years have veered towards the planning, programming, and budgeting process and centers around the need to understand the impact of existing social programs on the populations they profess to serve and on the ability to measure the comparative effectiveness of these programs. Yet the ability to first conceptualize and then quantify program costs and benefits so that policy options become available above the level of a mere hunch lies at the core of the man-machine interplay required at the problem solving level.

Very little has been attempted thus far either in data organization for the broad study of social characteristics or in the more focused schemes for program evaluations. It is, therefore, of some value to look at what might be considered the more significant recent explorations at the state and national levels and then assess the degree to which these attempts have yielded satisfactory results or even hold promise of doing so.

New York State has approached what it calls a central social environment study very gingerly. It nevertheless hopes, during the next few years, to mount a computer-based research program that will make it possible to develop an adequate social data base for the state and its communities. From this vantage point, it looks forward to delineating the social characteristics of its cities, the changes in the conditions of its population and then surfacing such information about the "subgroups" that will portray their interactions with each other and with the institutions that affect them. Much of the thrust of this program is towards the development of a body of social indicators that will identify the health, housing, education, training, and welfare status of the population. Together with its objective to measure and monitor critical shifts in social composition, the state's efforts might yield a significant addition to the management, organization, and analysis of social information. If it were to accomplish this, it would fill some of the major data gaps that obscure and inhibit subsequent action for the programming and delivery of social services.

But the New York study proposes to move somewhat beyond that point and will address itself specifically to tracing and measuring the effects of government programs on separate and distinct groups such as the unskilled; the educational progress of children from poor families; welfare recipients and delinquent youth. These explorations should encounter the rough terrain that Mr. Moynihan has termed the linking of policy and knowledge. Much depends on the direction in which the impact analysis moves. If the state is willing to relate the effects of current and proposed programs to some definable standards or quality of health, independence, and well-being, it will be treading new ground albeit conceptually firm enough. However, if the emphasis is on seeking the most effective patterns of state resource allocations among health, welfare, housing, and training functions, it will quickly come face to face with the severe limitations that have begun to surface in the planning, programming, budgeting process.

For what seems eminently feasible in the application of computer technology to the management of social data and the analysis of the urban environment with that information, becomes beset with major pitfalls when men and machines are asked to solve problems of program effectiveness for the purpose of choosing among the most useful course of action in and among health, welfare, education, and similar programs.

Almost five years have passed since President Johnson directed that the program evaluation that had shown promising results in the Defense Department be instituted in all other executive agencies. The Department of Health, Education, and Welfare responded with a modest but concentrated attempt to evaluate the costs and benefits of achieving defined social objectives. It soon became apparent and has since percolated down to all levels of government that operations researchers, with or without computers, are not about to take over the decision-making functions or replace the political processes and value judgments that constitute the fabric within which they are made. Nevertheless, some significant conclusions about the consequences of choices emerged from these studies.

Health, Education, and Welfare examined four program areas to test impacts and evaluations. These included selected health programs, that is, cancer, arthritis, syphilis, tuberculosis, and auto injury prevention; human investment programs such as vocational rehabilitation, adult education, and Title I of the Elementary and Secondary Education Act; programs for improving maternal and child health care; and options for income maintenance such as increasing Social Security, expanding welfare programs or a negative income tax.

Perhaps because health data were more available and usable or because the researchers were willing to move further along with it in this area than in the others, it was possible to ultimately measure the effectiveness of 22 program alternatives in the major health areas mentioned above. For each of the alternatives, the following estimates were made:

1. Total program costs.
2. Estimated program savings, that is, dollars that would have been spent on all forms of medical care plus earnings saved because the patient did not die or was not incapacitated due to illness or injury.
3. The ratio of costs to savings (benefit-cost ratio).
4. Number of deaths averted.
5. Cost per death averted.

As one would expect, the lack of relevant data in all four areas (health, human investment, child care, and income maintenance) was monumental. We quote from a principal participant* in these studies:

> Those who picture Washington as one mass of files and computers containing more information than they would like will be comforted by the experiences of program-planners in attempting to evaluate on-going programs. Whatever the files and computers do contain, there is precious little in them about how many and whom the programs are reaching, and whether they are doing what they are supposed to do. If the purpose of an adult basic education program is to teach people how to read and write, the Office of Education might reasonably be expected to know how many people thereby actually learned how to read and write but it does not . . . . The Public Health Service might be expected to know whether its various health services are in fact making people healthier but it does not. The study of disease control was to have encompassed more diseases, but so little was known about the effective treatment of alcoholism and heart disease that these components had to be dropped. Those working on the income maintenance study found that the Welfare Administration could not tell them very much about the public assistance case load—who was on welfare, where did they come from, why were they on it, what they needed in order to get off.

*Drew, Elizabeth B. HEW grapples with PPBS, *The Public Interest*, Summer 1967.

But lack of data was just one impediment. How to define and measure benefits posed conceptual problems that were not easily resolved then and are major stumbling blocks today. For example, which of the following benefits should be measured to evaluate the effectiveness of a single educational program: increased reading comprehension, growth in confidence, decline in school dropouts, increased movement on to college, or higher earnings? And if measurements within a single program were not sufficiently opaque, what then of the possibilities of comparing benefits among two or more different programs where improvements accrue to different individuals or groups in the population? How does one assign "weights" to improvements that have varying impacts on the lives of the recipients? Especially in the social programs, the promise of PPB falters because of the short distance it can go to identify, measure, and weigh the costs and benefits.

Thus far, the assistance of the computer has not significantly improved the program planners ability to make choices among health, education, and welfare programs. Such "big" choices are not yet possible even though the Health, Education, and Welfare studies did indicate that existing or proposed programs with common objectives within a single area such as health or income maintenance could be compared with each other in a systematic and measurable fashion. Even these narrower choices are exceedingly difficult to derive and PPB remains, at this time, a frontier field that has done little more than focus attention on the objectives of government programs and the range of choices in an explicit way.

The third level of computer application deals with the control of systems or processes. Both in private and public enterprises, inventory control, and payroll disbursement were among the first kind of processes to be handled by the computer but new applications became more appropriate in the light of the increasing complexity of the urban structure, the size of the population, and the immense number of transactions and interactions between people and institutions. A few of the larger cities and even some of the middle sized ones are now beginning to direct their computer capabilities to the control of urban processes and to the improvement and rationalization of the services they perform. While none of the "global" strategies necessary for program evaluations are needed here, it is at this level of machine application that something directly and immediately affecting the lives of people could be achieved.

Unfortunately, the use of computer technology is not likely to be oriented around the urban systems for delivering health, legal, welfare, and similar aid to the people who need them most. As we have indicated earlier, the accumulated data inventories of cities but, even more importantly, their basic frame of reference is geared towards the most efficient use of buildings, streets, fire fighting equipment, and traffic movements. More recently, there has been added an intense preoccupation with the instantaneous reporting of criminal and driving violations so that every arm of the law becomes part of a network of intelligence from the Governor of the State down to the local dog-catcher.

This strong partiality for the physical life and operations of the city was reflected in the subject matter that occupied several days of the 1969 Annual Symposium on the Application of Computers to Urban Society. On this occasion, some of the major current programs in New York and elsewhere were discussed and it was revealing to learn that they dealt with:

An Application of Incidence Analysis to the Deployment of Fire Companies in New York City

Commuterized Community Shelter Plan for New York City

Computers and Public Transportation—MIT

Creation of a Geographic Information System—New York City

Determining Air Pollution Emissions from Transportation Systems

A Dynamic Land Use Allocation Model

An Information System for Solid Waste Operations—Wichita Falls, Texas

Los Angeles Police Department Operations Simulation

Systems Analysis of New York City's Primary Water Distribution Network

Relevance, like much else, is in the eyes of the beholder, but it is evident that computer applications to urban life is defined very strangely indeed. It does suggest that the hardware and software fraternity and the public administrators who not only bless these operations but buy and install them as well, really want above all else, a set of smoothly and efficiently run municipal operations. Perhaps we ought not to look a gift horse in the mouth. Perhaps, well placed fire stations, effective police forces, and computerized air raid shelters are what we have all been breathlessly waiting for in the past decade, especially since Watts, Newark, Washington, D.C., and others. If not, we should feel troubled by this turn of events since much of the logic and thrust of these kinds of applications is emanating from the former aerospace and military software specialists, many of whom are now "between jobs" and are rapidly becoming "partners" with the urban specialists in defining how the computers will be used for the control and delivery of urban services.

The City of Los Angeles recently hired the Technical Services Corporation, described by its president as a "hybrid of the Institute for Defense Analysis and the Aerospace Corporation."* In 1968, the TSC analyzed the city's need for an effective command-control system to permit unified direction and control during major civil disasters such as floods, earthquakes, or enemy attacks. With all cities, including Los Angeles, under great pressure to double their police manpower, the Corporation prepared estimates showing that it would be much cheaper to invest $100 million for the development and installation of a computer driven police control system. Urban renewal came to be known as "negro removal," and we wonder what this will be called if it ever becomes visible.

It, therefore, looks as though this kind of bias is going to be built into the way we use and apply the computer to the control and delivery of "urban systems." A number of federal agencies have recently combined to initiate and fund a series of demonstration projects in six cities with populations under half a million. The purpose of the projects is to computerize all or the major segments of their operating records thereby allowing for much more interchangeability and flexibility of use among these records. In two of the six pilot cities, the data of all municipal functions will be mechanized while in the other four, electronic processing of data will be undertaken in one of the following areas: public safety; municipal financial records; physical and economic development; and human resources. As one commentator from General Electric's Re-Entry System, Missile and Space Division said: "We are going to computerize the hell out of all this data." Certainly a laudable objective if something more than efficiency or even dollar savings in the management of city processes result. To any sentient person who has lived and observed the past ten years, smoothly operating data flows within and among city departments of housing, police, revenue, traffic, and taxation cannot occupy a high priority in the amalgam that continues to make a shambles of our urban fabric.

With the possible exception of the area of human resources, this national demonstration program will strongly encourage the manipulation of the existing urban inventories. But if municipal officers would dare

---

*Selected Papers from the ASPO National Planning Conference, Cincinnati, April 19–24, 1969.

look forward to using the computer for processes or systems that can deliver community or diagnostic health services to the ill, or public assistance to the poor, or legal counseling and referral service for those unable to pay, new avenues might be opened to improving modes of urban livability. Yet, at the level of process control, the computer can be directed to work in man's favor if the arid combination of urban specialists and corporate systems analysts are not allowed to dominate the disposition of computer capabilities.

Let us look at some specific applications in the delivery of health services that would illustrate the direction in which we could move. For example, why not establish and expand a continuous monitoring of critical hospital patients to spot potentially serious conditions? Or the use of computers by physicians to relate symptoms to diagnoses? Beyond that, a host of community health services might be fashioned and strengthened if computer applications were approached imaginatively. We certainly possess the technological capability to establish community health information and referral centers especially in the high density areas of our major cities. Moreover, is it too utopian to consider a centralized file of patient illnesses reported from all sources and the structuring of this file on a city and regional basis via computer networks?

Moreover, law enforcement and criminal justice need not be supported solely by a mechanized super-sleuth system especially if we are concerned with prevention and rehabilitation as well as the efficient detection of crime and criminals. Could we use the computer in another form of communication network, that is, tying together the information flows among police records, courts, prisons, and parole systems? Probably so, and very possibly for the benefit of those enmeshed in its webs. It seems quite likely that when the underlying violence-prone situations are examined outside the context of quick and efficient arrest possibilities, many extensions of the computer are possible. In that kind of approach, the research that is now slowly being directed towards understanding the tension-building features in cities, neighborhoods, and even blocks will suggest legitimate and nonpunitive roles for the use of the computer. We would, indeed, be bankrupt of wit, intelligence, and compassion if the command-control networks emerge as the sole or principal expression of the relationship between the police and the community.

We, therefore, conclude with a number of observations surrounded by qualifying phrases. At the level of data organization and management, the computer would perform admirably in the areas of health, public assistance, and other social services if knowledge about our status, conditions, and characteristics, nationally and locally, were available for use and application. Program evaluations and other studies that would clarify policy options for administrators need both the basic operations data and the yet unraveled ability to compare and quantify the results or impacts of these programs. And to put the computer actively to work for the control and delivery of services for the disadvantaged requires an outlook that stretches beyond the needs for efficient municipal operations.

23

On the Impact of the Computer on Society*

How does one insult a machine?

JOSEPH WEIZENBAUM†

Center for Advanced Study in Behavioral Sciences, Stanford, California

The structure of the typical essay on "The impact of computers on society" is as follows: First, there is an "on the one hand" statement. It tells all the good things computers have already done for society and often even attempts to argue that the social order would already have collapsed were it not for the "computer revolution." This is usually followed by an "on the other hand" caution which tells of certain problems the introduction of computers brings in its wake. The threat posed to individual privacy by large data banks and the danger of large-scale unemployment induced by industrial automation are usually mentioned. Finally, the glorious present and prospective achievements of the computer are applauded, while the dangers alluded to in the second part are shown to be capable of being alleviated by sophisticated technological fixes. The closing paragraph consists of a plea for generous societal support for more and more large-scale computer research and development. This is usually coupled to the more or less subtle assertion that only computer science, hence only the computer scientist, can guard the world against the admittedly hazardous fallout of applied computer technology.

In fact, the computer has had very considerably less societal impact than the mass media would lead us to believe. Certainly, there are enterprises like space travel that could not have been undertaken without

---

*Reprinted from *Science*, Vol. 176 (May 12, 1972), pp. 609–614.

†The author is also professor of computer science, Massachusetts Institute of Technology, 545 Technology Square, Cambridge 02139.

computers. Certainly, the computer industry, and with it the computer education industry, has grown to enormous proportions. But much of the industry is self-serving. It is rather like an island economy in which the natives make a living by taking in each other's laundry. The part that is not self-serving is largely supported by government agencies and other gigantic enterprises that know the value of everything but the price of nothing, that is, that know the short-range utility of computer systems but have no idea of their ultimate social cost. In any case, airline reservation systems and computerized hospitals serve only a tiny, largely the most affluent, fraction of society. Such things cannot be said to have an impact on society generally.

SIDE EFFECTS OF TECHNOLOGY

The more important reason that I dismiss the argument which I have caricatured is that the direct societal effects of any pervasive new technology are as nothing compared to its much more subtle and ultimately much more important side effects. In that sense, the societal impact of the computer has not yet been felt.

To help firmly fix the idea of the importance of subtle, indirect effects of technology, consider the impact on society of the invention of the microscope. When it was invented in the middle of the 17th century, the dominant commonsense theory of disease was fundamentally that disease was a punishment visited upon an individual by God. The sinner's body was thought to be inhabited by various so-called humors brought into disequilibrium in accordance with divine justice. The cure for disease was therefore to be found first in penance and second in the balancing of humors as, for example, by bleeding. Bleeding was, after all, both painful, hence punishment and penance, and potentially balancing in that it actually removed substance from the body. The microscope enabled man to see microorganisms and thus paved the way for the germ theory of disease. The enormously surprising discovery of extremely small living organisms also induced the idea of a continuous chain of life which, in turn, was a necessary intellectual precondition for the emergence of Darwinism. Both the germ theory of disease and the theory of evolution profoundly altered man's conception of his contract with God and consequently his self-image. Politically, these ideas served to help diminish the power of the Church and, more generally, to legitimize the questioning of the basis of hitherto unchallenged authority. I do not say that the microscope alone was responsible for the enormous social changes that followed its invention. Only that it made possible the kind of paradigm shift, even on the commonsense level, without which these changes might have been impossible.

Is it reasonable to ask whether the computer will induce similar changes in man's image of himself and whether that influence will prove to be its most important effect on society? I think so, although I hasten to add that I don't believe the computer has yet told us much about man and his nature. To come to grips with the question, we must first ask in what way the computer is different from man's many other machines. Man has built two fundamentally different kinds of machines, nonautonomous and autonomous. An autonomous machine is one that operates for long periods of time, not on the basis of inputs from the real world, for example, from sensors or from human drivers, but on the basis of internalized models on some aspect of the real world. Clocks are examples of autonomous machines in that they operate on the basis of an internalized model of the planetary system. The computer is, of course, the example par excellence. It is able to internalize models of essentially unlimited complexity and of a fidelity limited only by the genius of man.

It is the autonomy of the computer we value. When, for example, we speak of the power of computers as increasing with each new hardware and software development, we mean that, because of their increasing speed and storage capacity, and possibly thanks to new programming tricks, the new computers can internalize ever more complex and ever more faithful models of ever larger slices of reality. It seems strange then that, just when we exhibit virtually an idolatry of autonomy with respect to machines, serious thinkers in respected academies (I have in mind B. F. Skinner of Harvard University [1]) can rise to question autonomy as a fact for man. I do not think that the appearance of this paradox at this time is accidental. To understand it, we must realize that man's commitment to science has always had a masochistic component.

Time after time science has led us to insights that, at least when seen superficially, diminish man. Thus, Galileo removed man from the center of the universe, Darwin removed him from his place separate from the animals, and Freud showed his rationality to be an illusion. Yet man pushes his inquiries further and deeper. I cannot help but think that there is an analogy between man's pursuit of scientific knowledge and an individual's commitment to psychoanalytic therapy. Both are undertaken in the full realization that what the inquirer may find may well damage his self-esteem. Both may reflect his determination to find meaning in his existence through struggle in truth, however painful that may be, rather than to live without meaning in a world of ill-disguised illusion. However, I am also aware that sometimes people enter psychoanalysis unwilling to put their illusions at risk, not searching for a deeper reality but in order to convert the insights they hope to gain to personal power. The analogy to man's pursuit of science does not break down with that observation.

Each time a scientific discovery shatters a hitherto fundamental corner-stone of the edifice on which man's self-esteem is built, there is an enormous reaction, just as is the case under similar circumstances in psychoanalytic therapy. Powerful defense mechanisms, beginning with denial and usually terminating in rationalization, are brought to bear. Indeed, the psychoanalyst suspects that, when a patient appears to accept a soul-shattering insight without resistance, his very casualness may well mask his refusal to allow that insight truly operational status in his self-image. But what is the psychoanalyst to think about the patient who positively embraces tentatively proffered, profoundly humiliating self-knowledge, when he embraces it and instantly converts it to a new foundation of his life? Surely such an event is symptomatic of a major crisis in the mental life of the patient.

I believe we are now at the beginning of just such a crisis in the mental life of our civilization. The microscope, I have argued, brought in its train a revision of man's image of himself. But no one in the mid-17th century could have foreseen that. The possibility that the computer will, one way or another, demonstrate that, in the inimitable phrase of one of my esteemed colleagues, "the brain is merely a meat machine" is one that engages academicians, industrialists, and journalists in the here and now. How has the computer contributed to bringing about this very sad state of affairs? It must be said right away that the computer alone is not the chief causative agent. It is merely an extreme extrapolation of technology. When seen as an inducer of philosophical dogma, it is merely the reductio ad absurdum of a technological ideology. But how does it come to be regarded as a source of philosophic dogma?

THEORY VERSUS PERFORMANCE

We must be clear about the fact that a computer is nothing without a program. A program is fundamentally a transformation of one computer into another that has autonomy and that, in a very real sense, behaves. Programming languages describe dynamic processes. And, most importantly, the processes they describe can be actually carried out. Thus, we can build models of any aspect of the real world that interests us and that we understand. And we can make our models work. But we must be careful to remember that a computer model is a description that works. Ordinarily, when we speak of *A* being a model of *B*, we mean that a theory about some aspects of the behavior of *B* is also a theory of the same aspects of the behavior of A. It follows that when, for example, we consider a computer model of paranoia, like that published by Colby *et al.*[2], we must not be persuaded that it tells us anything about paranoia on the grounds that it, in some sense, mirrors the behavior of a paranoiac. After all, a plain typewriter in some sense mirrors the behavior of an autistic child (one types a question and gets no response whatever), but it does not help us to understand autism. A model must be made to stand or fall on the basis of its theory. Thus, while programming languages may have put a new power in the hands of social scientists in that this new notation may have freed them from the vagueness of discursive descriptions, their obligation to build defensible theories is in no way diminished. Even errors can be pronounced with utmost formality and eloquence. But they are not thereby transmuted to truth.

The failure to make distinctions between descriptions, even those that "work," and theories accounts in large part for the fact that those who refuse to accept the view of man as machine have been put on the defensive. Recent advances in computer understanding of natural language offer an excellent case in point. Chomsky and Halle, to mention only the two with whom I am most familiar, have long labored on a theory of language which any model of language behavior must satisfy[3]. Their aim is like that of the physicist who writes a set of differential equations that anyone riding a bicycle must satisfy. No physicist claims that a person need know, let alone be able to solve, such differential equations in order to become a competent cyclist. Neither do Chomsky and Halle claim that humans know or knowingly obey the rules they believe to govern language behavior. Chomsky and Halle also strive, as do physical theorists, to identify the constants and parameters of their theories with components of reality. They hypothesize that their rules constitute a kind of projective description of certain aspects of the structure of the human mind. Their problem is thus not merely to discover economical rules to account for language behavior, but also to infer economic mechanisms which determine that precisely those rules are to be preferred over all others. Since they are in this way forced to attend to the human mind, not only that of speakers of English, they must necessarily be concerned

with all human language behavior—not just that related to the understanding of English.

The enormous scope of their task is illustrated by their observation that
in all human languages declarative sentences are often transformed into
questions by a permutation of two of their words. (John is here → Is John
here?) It is one thing to describe rules that transform declarative
sentences into questions—a simple permutation rule is clearly
insufficient—but another thing to describe a "machine" that necessitates
those rules when others would, all else being equal, be simpler. Why, for
example, is it not so that declarative sentences read backward transform
those sentences into questions? The answer must be that other constraints on the "machine" combine against this local simplicity in favor of
a more nearly global economy. Such examples illustrate the depth of the
level of explanation that Chomsky and Halle are trying to achieve. No
wonder that they stand in awe of their subject matter.

Workers in computer comprehension of natural language operate in
what is usually called performance mode. It is as if they are building
machines that can ride bicycles by following heuristics like "if you feel a
displacement to the left, move your weight to the left." There can be, and
often is, a strong interaction between the development of theory and the
empirical task of engineering systems whose theory is not yet thoroughly
understood. Witness the synergistic cooperation between aerodynamics
and aircraft design in the first quarter of the present century. Still, what
counts in performance mode is not the elaboration of theory but the
performance of systems. And the systems being hammered together by
the new crop of computer semanticists are beginning (just beginning) to
perform.

Since computer scientists have recognized the importance of the
interplay of syntax, semantics, and pragmatics, and with it the importance
of computer-manipulable knowledge, they have made progress. Perhaps
by the end of the present decade, computer systems will exist with which
specialists, such as physicians and chemists and mathematicians, will
converse in natural language. And surely some part of such achievements
will have been based on other successes in, for example, computer
simulation of cognitive processes. It is understandable that any success in
this area, even if won empirically and without accompanying enrichments
of theory, can easily lead to certain delusions being planted. Is it, after all,
not terribly tempting to believe that a computer than understands natural
language at all, however narrow the context, has captured something of

the essence of man? Descartes himself might have believed it. Indeed, by way of this very understandable seduction, the computer comes to be a source of philosophical dogma.

I am tempted to recite how performance programs are composed and how things that do not work quite correctly are made to work via all sorts of strategems which do not even pretend to have any theoretical foundation. But the very asking of the question, "Has the computer captured the essence of man?" is a diversion and, in that sense, a trap. For the real question "Does man understand the essence of man?" cannot be answered by technology and hence certainly not by any technological instrument.

THE TECHNOLOGICAL METAPHOR

I asked earlier what the psychoanalyst is to think when a patient grasps a tentatively proffered deeply humiliating interpretation and attempts to convert it immediately to a new foundation of his life. I now think I phrased that question too weakly. What if the psychoanalyst merely coughed and the cough entrained the consequences of which I speak? That is our situation today. Computer science, particularly its artificial intelligence branch, has coughed. Perhaps the press has unduly amplified that cough—but it is only a cough nevertheless. I cannot help but think that the eagerness to believe that man's whole nature has suddenly been exposed by that cough, and that it has been shown to be a clockwork, is a symptom of something terribly wrong.

What is wrong, I think, is that we have permitted technological metaphors, what Mumford[4] calls the "Myth of the Machine," and technique itself to so thoroughly pervade our thought processes that we have finally abdicated to technology the very duty to formulate questions. Thus, sensible men correctly perceive that large data banks and enormous networks of computers threaten man. But they leave it to technology to formulate the corresponding question. Where a simple man might ask: "Do we need these things?," technology asks "what electronic wizardry will make them safe?" Where a simple man will ask "is it good?," technology asks "will it work?" Thus science, even wisdom, becomes what technology and most of all computers can handle. Lest this be thought to be an exaggeration, I quote from the work of H. A. Simon, one of the most senior of American computer scientists[5]:

> As we succeed in broadening and deepening our knowledge—theoretical and empirical—about computers, we shall discover that in large part their behavior is governed by simple general laws, that what appeared as complexity in the computer program was, to a considerable extent, complexity of the environment to which the program was seeking to adapt its behavior.
>
> To the extent that this prospect can be realized, it opens up an exceedingly important role for computer simulation as a tool for achieving a deeper understanding of human behavior. For if it is the organization of components, and not their physical properties, that largely determines behavior, and if computers are organized somewhat in the image of man, then the computer becomes an obvious device for exploring the consequences of alternative organizational assumptions for human behavior.

and

> A man, viewed as a behaving system, is quite simple. The apparent complexity of his behavior over time is largely a reflection of the complexity of the environment in which he finds himself.
>
> ...I believe that this hypothesis holds even for the whole man.

We already know that those aspects of the behavior of computers which cannot be attributed to the complexity of their programs is governed by simple general laws—ultimately, by the laws of Boolean algebra. And, of course, the physical properties of the computer's components are nearly irrelevant to its behavior. Mechanical relays are logically equivalent to tubes and to transistors and to artificial neurons. And, of course, the complexity of computer programs is due to the complexity of the environments, including the computing environments themselves, with which they were designed to deal. To what else could it possibly be due? So, what Simon sees as prospective is already realized. But does this collection of obvious and simple facts lead to the conclusion that man is as simple as are computers? When Simon leaps to that conclusion and then formulates the issue as he has done here, that is, when he suggests that the behavior of *the whole man* may be understood in terms of the behavior of computers as governed by simple general laws, then the very possibility of understanding man as an autonomous being, as an individual with deeply internalized values, that very possibility is excluded. How does one insult a machine?

The question "Is the brain merely a meat machine?," which Simon puts in a so much more sophisticated form, is typical of the kind of question formulated by, indeed formulatable only by, a technological mentality. Once it is accepted as legitimate, arguments as to what a computer can or cannot do "in principle" begin to rage and themselves become legitimate. But the legitimacy of the technological question—for example, is human behavior to be understood either in terms of the organization or of the physical properties of "components"—need not be admitted in the first instance. A human question can be asked instead. Indeed, we might begin by asking what has already become of "the whole man" when he can conceive of computers organized in his own image.

The success of technique and of some technological explanations has, as I have suggested, tricked us into permitting technology to formulate important questions for us—questions whose very forms severely diminish the number of degrees of freedom in our range of decision making. Whoever dictates the questions in large part determines the answers. In that sense, technology, and especially computer technology, has become a self-fulfilling nightmare reminiscent of that of the lady who dreams of being raped and begs her attacker to be kind to her. He answers "it's your dream, lady." We must come to see that technology is our dream and that we must ultimately decide how it is to end.

I have suggested that the computer revolution need not and ought not to call man's dignity and autonomy into question, that it is a kind of pathology that moves men to wring from it unwarranted, enormously damaging interpretations. Is then the computer less threatening that we might have thought? Once we realize that our visions, possibly nightmarish visions, determine the effect of our own creations on us and on our society, their threat to us is surely diminished. But that is not to say that this realization alone will wipe out all danger. For example, apart from the erosive effect of a technological mentality on man's self-image, there are practical attacks on the freedom and dignity of man in which computer technology plays a critical role.

I mentioned earlier that computer science has come to recognize the importance of building knowledge into machines. We already have a machine—Dendral—[6] that commands more chemistry than do many Ph.D. chemists, and another—Mathlab—[7] that commands more applied mathematics than do many applied mathematicians. Both Dendral and Mathlab contain knowledge that can be evaluated in terms of the explicit theories from which it was derived. If the user believes that a result Mathlab delivers is wrong, then, apart from possible program errors, he must be in disagreement, not with the machine or its programmer, but with a specific mathematical theory. But what about the many programs on which management, most particularly, the government and the military, rely, programs which can in no sense be said to rest on explicable theories but are instead enormous patchworks of programming techniques strung together to make them work?

INCOMPREHENSIBLE SYSTEMS

In our eagerness to exploit every advance in technique we quickly incorporate the lessons learned from machine manipulation of knowledge in theory-based systems into such patchworks. They then "work" better. I have in mind systems like target selection systems used in Vietnam and war games used in the Pentagon, and so on. These often gigantic systems are put together by teams of programmers, often working over a time span of many years. But by the time the systems come into use, most of the original programmers have left or turned their attention to other pursuits. It is precisely when gigantic systems begin to be used that their inner workings can no longer be understood by any single person or by a small team of individuals. Norbert Wiener, the father of cybernetics, foretold this phenomenon in a remarkably prescient article[8] published more than a decade ago. He said there:

> It may well be that in principle we cannot make any machine the elements of whose behavior we cannot comprehend sooner or later. This does not mean in any way that we shall be able to comprehend these elements in substantially less time than the time required for operation of the machine, or even within any given number of years or generations.
> An intelligent understanding of [machines'] mode of performance may be delayed until long after the task which they have been set has been completed. This means that though machines are theoretically subject to human criticism, such criticism may be ineffective until long after it is relevant.

This situation, which is now upon us, has two consequences: first, that decisions are made on the basis of rules and criteria no one knows explicitly, and second, that the system of rules and criteria becomes immune to change. This is so because, in the absence of detailed understanding of the inner workings of a system, any substantial modification is very likely to render the system altogether inoperable. The threshold of complexity beyond which this phenomenon occurs has already been crossed by many existing systems, including some compiling and computer operating systems. For example, no one likes the operating systems for certain large computers, but they cannot be substantially changed nor can they be done away with. Too many people have become dependent on them.

An awkward operating system is inconvenient. That is not too bad. But the growing reliance on supersystems that were perhaps designed to help people make analyses and decisions, but which have since surpassed the understanding of their users while at the same time becoming indispensable to them, is another matter. In modern war it is common for the soldier, say the bomber pilot, to operate at an enormous psychological distance from his victims. He is not responsible for burned children because he never sees their village, his bombs, and certainly not the flaming children themselves. Modern technological rationalizations of war, diplomacy, politics, and commerce such as computer games have an even more insidious effect on the making of policy. Not only have policy makers abdicated their decision-making responsibility to a technology they do not understand, all the while maintaining the illusion that they, the policy makers, are formulating policy questions and answering them, but responsibility has altogether evaporated. No human is any longer responsible for "what the machine says." Thus, there can be neither right nor wrong, no question of justice, no theory with which one can agree or disagree, and finally no basis on which one can challenge "what the machine says." My father used to invoke the ultimate authority by saying to me, "it is written." But then I could read what was written, imagine a human author, infer his values, and finally agree or disagree. The systems in the Pentagon, and their counterparts elsewhere in our culture, have in a very real sense no authors. They therefore do not admit of exercises of imagination that may ultimately lead to human judgment. No wonder that men who live day in and out with such machines and become dependent on them begin to believe that men are merely machines. They are reflecting what they themselves have become.

The potentially tragic impact on society that may ensue from the use of systems such as I have just discussed is greater than might at first be imagined. Again it is side effects, not direct effects, that matter most. First, of course, there is the psychological impact on individuals living in a society in which anonymous, hence irresponsible, forces formulate the large questions of the day and circumscribe the range of possible answers. It cannot be surprising that large numbers of perceptive individuals living in such a society experience a kind of impotence and fall victim to the mindless rage that often accompanies such experiences. But even worse, since computer-based knowledge systems become essentially unmodifiable except in that they can grow, and since they induce dependence and cannot, after a certain threshold is crossed, be abandoned, there is an enormous risk that they will be passed from one generation to another, always growing. Man too passes knowledge from one generation to another. But because man is mortal, his transmission of knowledge over the generations is at once a process of filtering and accrual. Man does not merely pass knowledge, he rather regenerates it continuously. Much as we may mourn the crumbling of ancient civilizations, we know nevertheless that the glory of man resides as much in the evolution of his cultures as in that of his brain. The unwise use of ever larger and ever more complex computer systems may well bring this process to a halt. It could well replace the ebb and flow of culture with a world without values, a world in which what counts for a fact has long ago been determined and forever fixed.

POSITIVE EFFECTS

I have spoken of some potentially dangerous effects of present computing trends. Is there nothing positive to be said? Yes, but it must be said with caution. Again, side effects are more important than direct effects. In particular, the idea of computation and of programming languages is beginning to become an important metaphor which, in the long run, may well prove to be responsible for paradigm shifts in many fields. Most of the commonsense paradigms in terms of which much of mankind interprets the phenomena of the everyday world, both physical and social, are still deeply rooted in fundamentally mechanistic metaphors. Marx's dynamics as well as those of Freud are, for example, basically equilibrium systems. Any hydrodynamicist could come to understand them without leaving the jargon of his field. Languages capable of describing ongoing processes, particularly in terms of modular subprocesses, have already had an enormous effect on the way computer people think of every aspect of their worlds, not merely those directly related to their work. The information processing view of the world so engendered qualifies as a genuine metaphor. This is attested to by the fact that it (1) constitutes an intellectual framework that permits new questions to be asked about a wide-ranging set of phenomena, and (2) that it itself provides criteria for the adequacy of proffered answers. A new metaphor is important not in that it may be better than existing ones, but rather in that it may enlarge man's vision by giving him yet another perspective on his world. Indeed, the very effectiveness of a new metaphor may seduce lazy minds to adopt it as a basis for universal explanations and as a source of panaceas. Computer simulation of social processes has already been advanced by single-minded generalists as leading to general solutions of all of mankind's problems.

The metaphors given us by religion, the poets, and by thinkers like Darwin, Newton, Freud, and Einstein have rather quickly penetrated to the language of ordinary people. These metaphors have thus been instrumental in shaping our entire civilization's imaginative reconstruction of our world. The computing metaphor is as yet available to only an extremely small set of people. Its acquisition and internalization, hopefully as only one of many ways to see the world, seems to require experience in program composition, a kind of computing literacy. Perhaps such literacy will become very widespread in the advanced societal sectors of the advanced countries. But, should it become a dominant mode of thinking and be restricted to certain social classes, it will prove not merely repressive in the ordinary sense, but an enormously divisive societal force. For then classes which do and do not have access to the metaphor will, in an important sense, lose their ability to communicate with one another. We know already how difficult it is for the poor and the oppressed to communicate with the rest of the society in which they are embedded. We know how difficult it is for the world of science to communicate with that of the arts and of the humanities. In both instances the communication difficulties, which have grave consequences, are very largely due to the fact that the respective communities have unsharable experiences out of which unsharable metaphors have grown.

RESPONSIBILITY

Given these dismal possibilities, what is the responsibility of the computer scientist? First, I should say that most of the harm computers can potentially entrain is much more a function of properties people attribute to computers than of what a computer can or cannot actually be made to do. The nonprofessional has little choice but to make his attributions of properties to computers on the basis of the propaganda emanating from the computer community and amplified by the press. The computer professional therefore has an enormously important responsibility to be modest in his claims. This advice would not even have to be voiced if computer science had a tradition of scholarship and of self-criticism such as that which characterizes the established sciences. The mature scientist stands in awe before the depth of his subject matter. His very humility is the wellspring of his strength. I regard the instilling of just this kind of humility, chiefly by the example set by teachers, to be one of the most important missions of every university department of computer science.

The computer scientist must be aware constantly that his instruments are capable of having gigantic direct and indirect amplifying effects. An error in a program, for example, could have grievous direct results, including most certainly the loss of much human life. On September 11, 1971, to cite just one example, a computer programming error caused the simultaneous destruction of 117 high-altitude weather balloons whose instruments were being monitored by an earth satellite[9]. A similar error in a military command and control system could launch a fleet of nuclear tipped missiles. Only censorship prevents us from knowing how many such events involving non-nuclear weapons have already occurred. Clearly then, the computer scientist has a heavy responsibility to make the fallibility and limitations of the systems he is capable of designing brilliantly clear. The very power of his systems should serve to inhibit the advice he is ready to give and to constrain the range of work he is willing to undertake.

Of course, the computer scientist, like everyone else, is responsible for his actions and their consequences. Sometimes that responsibility is hard to accept because the corresponding authority to decide what is and what is not to be done appears to rest with distant and anonymous forces. That technology itself determines what is to be done by a process of extrapolation and that individuals are powerless to intervene in that determination is precisely the kind of self-fulfilling dream from which we must awaken.

Consider gigantic computer systems. They are, of course, natural extrapolations of the large systems we already have. Computer networks are another point on the same curve extrapolated once more. One may ask whether such systems can be used by anybody except by governments and very large corporations and whether such organizations will not use them mainly for antihuman purposes. Or consider speech recognition systems. Will they not be used primarily to spy on private communications? To answer such questions by saying that big computer systems, computer networks, and speech recognition systems are inevitable is to surrender one's humanity. For such an answer must be based either on one's profound conviction that society has already lost control over its technology or on the thoroughly immoral position that "if I don't do it, someone else will."

I do not say that systems such as I have mentioned are necessarily evil—only that they may be and, what is most important, that their inevitability cannot be accepted by individuals claiming autonomy, freedom, and dignity. The individual computer scientist can and must decide. The determination of what the impact of computers on society is to be is, at least in part, in his hands.

Finally, the fundamental question the computer scientist must ask himself is the one that every scientist, indeed every human, must ask. It is not "what shall I do?" but rather "what shall I be?" I cannot answer that for anyone save myself. But I will say again that if technology is a nightmare that appears to have its own inevitable logic, it is our nightmare. It is possible, given courage and insight, for man to deny technology the prerogative to formulate man's questions. It is possible to ask human questions and to find humane answers.

REFERENCES AND NOTES

1. Skinner, B. F. *Beyond Freedom and Dignity*, New York: Knopf, 1971.
2. Colby, K. M., Weber, S., and Hilf, F. D. *Artif. Intell.* Vol. 1, No. 1 (1971).
3. Chomsky, N. *Aspects of the Theory of Syntax*, Cambridge, Mass.: MIT Press, 1965; —— and Halle, M. *The Sound Pattern of English*, New York: Harper & Row, 1968.
4. Mumford, L. *The Pentagon of Power*, New York: Harcourt, Brace, Jovanovich, 1970.
5. Simon, H. A. *The Sciences of the Artificial*, Cambridge, Mass.: MIT Press, 1969, pp. 22–25.
6. Buchanan, B., Sutherland, G., and Feigenbaum, E. A. in *Machine Intelligence*, B. Meltzer, ed., New York: American Elsevier, 1969.
7. Martin, W. A. and Fateman, R. J. The Macsyma system, in *Proceedings of the 2nd Symposium on Symbolic and Algebraic Manipulation*, New York: Association for Computer Machines, 1971; Moses, J. *Commun. Assoc. Computer Mach.* Vol. 14, No. 8, (1971) 548.
8. Wiener, N. *Science*, Vol. 131 (1960) 1355.
9. Gillette, R. ibid. Vol. 174 (1971), 477.

Conclusion

The preceding discussion has attempted to survey the scope of computer systems and applications in the public sector. The review is far from exhaustive but is indicative of present utilization patterns. Much, however, remains to be accomplished in computer systems and applications before full potential of the computer is harnessed for improving governments and quasi-institutions providing services to their citizen clients.

Given present accomplishments and the indication of untapped potential for continued improved public services based on computer systems and applications, however, leads many of the uninitiated in computers to think that service improvements in the public sector will flow automatically from installation of new systems. There is an inherent fallacy in this mode of thought to date as shown. What is essential first is a comprehensive re-thinking of the role of computers in the public service. This will enable the setting of new directions and guidelines for more effective and efficient utilization of computers in the delivery of socially oriented government services. That is, computers should be considered not only as a way to reduce data handling costs but also as a means to further the basic goals of society through government.

Selected Bibliography

ARTICLES

Annual data processing progress report for New York City Fiscal Year 1969–1970, *Office of the Mayor*, New York, N.Y.

Cheetham, Terry, Progress with computers, *Municipal and Public Services*, May 21, 1971.

Club of Rome; Computerizing the world, *Business Week*, April 10, 1971, p. 42.

Downs, Anthony, A realistic look at the final payoffs from urban data systems, *Public Administration Review*, Vol. 27, No. 3 (September 1967), 204–210.

Improving the flow of government information, *Public Automation*, Vol. 4, No. 8 (August 1968), 1,4.

Office equipment and computers in Asia, *Far Eastern Economic Review*, (Annual Supplement), January 1970.

Petrie, J. M. The use and value of computers in highway planning and design, *Journal of the Institute of Municipal Engineers*, Vol. 94 (November 1967), 381–391.

Rowan, Charles, Information systems technology in state government, *State Government*, Spring 1971.

Russo, John A., Jr. and Weiner, Myron E. An inter-municipal information handling service for Connecticut municipal governments and school systems; research and development of generalized fiscal and public safety computer applications, *Institute of Public Service of the University of Connecticut*, Storrs, Connecticut, 1970.

Weiser, Alan L. Testimony for the defense—A case for computers, *Socio-Economic Planning Sciences*, Vol. 4 (December 1970).

World city of the future, *Public Automation*, Vol. 5, No. 1 (January 1969), 1–4.

BOOKS

Bemer, R. W. ed. *Computers and Crisis: How Computers are Shaping our Future*, Philadelphia, Pa.: Auerbach, 1972.

Chartrand, L. L. *Computers in the Service of Society*, London and New York, Pergamon Press, 1972.

Computer and Invasion of Privacy, U.S. Government Hearings on the Proposed National Data Center, New York: Aino Press Reproduction, 1966.

Computerization of government files: What impact on the individual, *UCLA Law Review*, 1969.

George, F. H. *Computers, Science and Society*, Prometheus Books, Buffalo, N.Y., 1972.

Greenberger, Martin, ed. *Computers and the World of the Future*, Cambridge, Mass.: The MIT Press, 1962.

Hargreaves, John, *Computers and the Changing World: A Theme for the Automation Age*, London, England: Hutchinson, 1967.

Miller, A. R. Employment application tests: Excerpt from The Assault on Privacy, *Saturday Review*, Vol. 54, No. 30 (April 17, 1971).

Parkhill, Douglas F. *The Challenge of the Computer Utility*, Reading, Mass.: Addison-Wesley Publ. Co., 1966.

Pool, Ithiel de Sola, Behavioral technology, *Toward the Year 2018*, Edited by Foreign Policy Association, New York: Cowles Education Corporation, 1968, 87–96.

Sachman, Harold, *Computers, Systems Science and Envolving Society*, New York, N.Y.: John Wiley and Sons, 1967.

Yavitz, Boris and Stanback, Thomas M., Jr. *Electronic Data Processing in New York City—Lessons for Metropolitan Economics*. New York: Columbia University Press, 1967.

Subject Index

Author Index

477